D0961095

Opponents of War, 1917–1918

OPPONENTS OF WAR

1917–1918

H. C. Peterson and Gilbert C. Fite

THE UNIVERSITY OF WISCONSIN PRESS

Madison, 1957

Published by The University of Wisconsin Press,
430 Sterling Court, Madison 6, Wisconsin

Copyright © 1957 by the Regents of the
University of Wisconsin

Copyright, Canada, 1957. Distributed in
Canada by Burns and MacEachern, Toronto

Printed in the United States of America
by Vail-Ballou Press, Inc., Binghamton, N.Y.

Library of Congress Catalog Card No. 57-5239

TO

HARRIET

viii   Foreword

FOREWORD

This is the story of a conflict between prowar and antiwar people. It is a story which abounds with violent words, violent deeds, violent laws, and violent individuals. This book deals with nonconformists, with extremists—anarchists, I.W.W.'s, Socialists—acting as one might expect them to act. It is also concerned with conservative people who displayed an intemperance that would do credit to the wildest of radicals. The story involves mostly Americans, although at times many of them talked and acted as if they were inhabitants of the Balkans. Much of this book is not a pretty tale. Basically, it involves disagreement over the right to disagree. It deals with the old problem of the meaning of freedom.

No pretense is made at having exhausted the subject under consideration. Some of the matters which space has permitted giving only brief treatment deserve more extensive study. An attempt has been made to bring together a substantial amount of material on those people and organizations which, for one reason or another, opposed World War I. The aim has been to present a synthesis which will, within one book, show the reader what individuals or groups opposed the war, why they acted as they did, and what happened to them. It has been necessary, of course, to give considerable attention to the prowar elements and their attitudes and actions toward opponents of war.

This book does not purport to be a full study of public opinion during World War I, although it deals with aspects of this important subject. Generally, the treatment has been more descriptive than analytical, although a considerable amount of analysis has been included. The major objective has been to present an extensive picture of intolerance and the demand for conformity and to show how these demands manifested themselves. A fuller interpretation of American intolerance and hysteria as a part of the American character has been left for another book. On these problems not only history, but psychology and social psychology have much to say. It is hoped that this book will provide some of the materials for such a study.

Strictly speaking, some of the people dealt with here were not opponents of war. Yet they were accused of disloyalty and of opposition to the country's war objectives. In this connection, the power of patriotism is seen as a factor in maintaining a national "consensus." As Sigmund Diamond has written, not only does patriotism "direct loyalty and allegiance toward the objects it sanctifies, but under certain circumstances it transforms criticism directed against the function of a part of society into a threat to the whole of society." * This principle was well illustrated in the demands for reform by the Socialists, Nonpartisan Leaguers, and I.W.W.'s, who were then attacked on the basis that they were disloyal and unpatriotic—a threat to the entire nation.

Many have assisted in the preparation of this study. The beginning of the research was made possible by a grant from the Social Science Research Council. Manuscript collections were made available by the American Civil Liberties Union, the Library of Congress, the National Archives, the Oklahoma State Historical Society, and the Minnesota State Historical Society. Newspapers, magazines, and books were consulted in municipal libraries in New York City, Chicago, Seattle, Los Angeles, Salt Lake City, and Minneapolis, and in the Libraries of the University of California, the University of Southern California, the University of Washington, the University of Minnesota, the University of Wisconsin, the University of Oklahoma, and the Claremont Colleges. Records of law cases were obtained from the College of Law of the University of Oklahoma, the Bar Association of the City of New York, and the Supreme Court of the United States. Various clerks of federal district and appellate courts throughout the United States assisted in finding material on specific law cases.

For reading the manuscript in part or in whole, and for suggestions, thanks are due to Dr. Oma Stanley, Dr. W. H. Cooke, Mr. Norman Thomas, Mr. Roger Baldwin, and Mr. Arthur Garfield Hays. In the final revision of the manuscript, very valuable suggestions were made by Professor Cedric C. Cummins of the University of South Dakota. Miss Opal Carr, Reference Librarian at the University of Oklahoma, was of special help. Greatest assistance in the preparation of this book, however, was given by Mrs. H. C. Peterson. The errors, omissions, and opinions are exclusively those of the authors.

For several years prior to his untimely death in 1952, Professor Peterson had been working on this book. He viewed it as something of a com-

* Sigmund Diamond, *The Reputation of the American Businessman* (Cambridge, Mass., 1955), p. 182.

panion study to his *Propaganda for War* (University of Oklahoma Press, 1939). At the time of his death, Professor Peterson had several manuscript versions completed. None of these, however, was entirely suitable for publication. At the request of Mrs. Peterson, I undertook to check, revise, and rewrite the best of the accounts which her husband had left. The present book follows roughly the organization adopted by Professor Peterson, but it is a somewhat new and different presentation. My work has involved a recheck of the sources, rewriting, some additional research, as well as adding important changes in emphasis and interpretation. In the final analysis the book stands as a collaborative effort, except that I alone have made the final decisions, some of which Professor Peterson would undoubtedly disapprove.

Gilbert C. Fite

September 1, 1956

CONTENTS

CONTENTS

LIST OF ILLUSTRATIONS

Opponents of War, 1917–1918

▲▼

Chapter I

INTO THE ABYSS

February through April, 1917

With the breaking off of diplomatic relations between the United
States and Germany in February, 1917, pacifists sprang into action. To
prevent the rupture from ending in war the American Union Against
Militarism published a national appeal on behalf of peace.[1] Emergency
Peace Federations appeared everywhere. Their members tried to influence Congress and the press, and police chased some of them from
the steps of the Capitol.[2] Petitions against war flooded Congress. The
Seattle Union-Record of April 7, 1917, stated that labor organizations in
Seattle, Spokane, and Chicago opposed a declaration of war. On the
same day, the *Sacramento Bee* reported that most of the mail addressed
to California congressmen was against war. President Wilson, it was said,
received thousands of telegrams reminding him that he had been elected
to keep the country out of war.[3]

On March 23 there was a meeting at Carnegie Hall in New York
City to celebrate the Russian Revolution. At this gathering Mayor John
P. Mitchel remarked that the country was on the verge of war with Germany. Shouts from the gallery of "No!" "No!" greeted the annoyed mayor.
The following day the *New York Times* said that Socialists had been
responsible for the denunciations of the mayor who had left the meeting
in a huff.

The kindly and idealistic president of Stanford University, David
Starr Jordan, spoke against war in Boston, New Haven, New York, Philadelphia, and Princeton, although President John G. Hibben had refused

to permit a peace meeting at Princeton University.[4] Jordan campaigned for peace in the very home of the war advocates. He was among the speakers at a huge meeting in Madison Square Garden. The gathering was peaceful. In fact, there was even some unexpected support. Urban radicals, people quite alien to Jordan, cheered him on. The puzzled college man noticed that they seemed to oppose this war only because "Wall Street" and "The System" favored it. A unanimous boo welled up from the crowd, Jordan recalled, "when the names of Root and Roosevelt were incidentally mentioned as recipients of the Nobel Peace Prize." [5]

In Baltimore, however, the prowar group struck back. The scene was the great hall of the Academy of Music where Jordan was scheduled to speak. It was packed with an audience estimated at 5,000. Just as Jordan began his plea for peace a mob of war enthusiasts laid siege to the building, demanding that the meeting be stopped. The Los Angeles *Times* of April 2 reported that nearly a thousand men were "howling, hissing, and shaking their fists" at the police who blocked their way. Fights broke out; twenty people were injured and one man was beaten so badly that he had to be hospitalized. After the excited building manager asked the pacifists to leave, the meeting was adjourned. Jordan walked out the front door while the mob paraded around chanting that "we'll hang Dave Jordan to a sour apple tree." [6] Thus the tone was set for the events of the next twenty months.

William Jennings Bryan spoke against war day and night. His reception was not dissimilar to that of Jordan. The same Baltimore crowd that opposed Jordan also sang, "We'll hang Bill Bryan to a sour apple tree." But Bryan would not be silent. According to Merle Curti's account of Bryan's efforts, "on March 28, when all seemed lost, he made a final impassioned plea to Congress, mustering all his forces to make his words both moving and convincing. Ridiculed and abused, taunted with being a traitor, threatened with assassination, Bryan did not haul down the flag until the very last." [7]

On the night of April 2, 1917, Woodrow Wilson asked for a declaration of war against Germany. Among other things, he said that "the world must be made safe for democracy." The conservative, nationalistic groups represented by men like Theodore Roosevelt and Henry C. Lodge could look with amusement and with an "I told you so!" attitude on the President who had been "too proud to fight." The editor of the Los Angeles *Times* wrote on April 6, 1917, "The American people now freely forgive Woodrow Wilson for his inconsiderate, unconsidered, and sometimes dangerous actions and utterances in the past." But though the American people could forgive, the editor inferred that they could not forget that "President Wilson . . . unthoughtfully, and unwisely, and unpatriotically put life into the sleeping treason that would avoid the righteous sacrifices of war."

The opponents of war in Congress such as Robert M. La Follette, George W. Norris, and James K. Vardaman were glum, realizing that they had lost completely and absolutely. Yet they could not become reconciled to the President's request for war. They might not stem the tide, but they would at least express their antiwar convictions before the fatal step was taken.

On April 4, as the Senate debated the war resolution, Senator Norris warned that "we are going into war upon the command of gold." He argued that munitions makers and bankers were instrumental in taking the country toward war. "I would like to say to this war god," he exclaimed, "You shall not coin into gold the lifeblood of my brethren." Then he told his colleagues, "I feel that we are about to put the dollar sign upon the American flag." But despite these bitter words, Norris made it clear that, once war was declared, "all of my energy and all of my power will be behind our flag in carrying it on to victory." [8]

La Follette of Wisconsin maintained that the crisis with Germany was of the Administration's own making, a natural result of its unneutral co-operation with the British. "From early in the war," he declared, "[we] threw our neutrality to the winds by permitting England to make a mockery of it to her advantage against her chief enemy. Then we expect to say to that enemy, 'You have got to respect my rights as a neutral.' What is the answer? I say Germany has been patient with us." [9]

La Follette also warned against committing the United States to an unknown future. He pointed out that terms of any agreements among the Allies were not then known. "We do not know what they are," he said. "We do not know what is in the minds of those who have made the compact, but we are to subscribe to it. We are irrevocably, by our votes here, to marry ourselves to a nondivorceable proposition veiled from us now. Once enlisted, once in the copartnership, we will be carried through with the purposes, whatever they may be, of which we now know nothing." [10] The Senator, too, opposed the idea of making the Germans throw out their government. He reminded his colleagues that England was an hereditary monarchy and was hardly promoting democracy in Ireland, Egypt, or India. Even Senator Warren G. Harding objected to the idea of overthrowing the German Government. He wanted it understood that he was not "voting for war in the name of democracy . . . . It

is my deliberate judgment that it is none of our business what type of
government any nation on this earth may choose to have. . . ." [11] Congressman Ernest Lundeen expressed the thought that it was impossible
to "thrust democracy with loving bayonets down the throats of unwilling
peoples." [12]

Norris and La Follette, as well as others who were bold enough to
speak against war, were bitterly denounced both in and out of Congress.
Senator Reed of Missouri said that Norris' utterances would certainly
bring comfort to "the heart of a Hapsburg or a Hohenzollern." If the
speech was not treason, he continued, it was so near treason that it
would give aid and consolation to the enemy.[13] La Follette's address,
said Senator John Sharp Williams, was "pro-German, pretty nearly pro-
Goth, and pro-Vandal." The Wisconsin Senator's speech was "absolutely
worthy of Bethmann-Hollweg in the Reichstag," he observed.[14] The Los
Angeles *Times* on April 6 ran a cartoon showing the Kaiser pinning an
iron cross on La Follette.

President Wilson's statement that the German Government had declared war without the "previous knowledge or approval" of the German
people set off an argument which was to last for months. War opponents
insisted that, before Americans criticized German autocracy and Prus-
sianism, there should be a war referendum in the United States. Jane
Addams appeared before a congressional committee and asked that the
approval of the American people be obtained before any war declaration
was made.[15] In his answer to Wilson's war speech, Senator Vardaman
commented:

> The President . . . suggested that if the people who are now engaged
> in this war in Europe had been consulted there would have been no
> war. If I may be permitted to indulge in a little speculation I will say,
> Mr. President, that if the people of the United States—I mean the
> plain, honest people, the masses who are to bear the burden of taxation
> and fight the Nation's battles, were consulted—the United States
> would not make a declaration of war against Germany to-day.

> .   .   .   .

> If it is wrong for a king to plunge his subjects into the vortex of
> war without their consent, it can not be less reprehensible for the
> President of the United States and the Congress to involve their con-
> stituents in a war without their consent.[16]

Other opponents of war argued in a similar vein. La Follette challenged the "President and the supporters of this war bill" to submit it "to a vote of the people before the declaration of war goes into effect." La Follette declared that if the people had a chance to vote they would

FOR SERVICES RENDERED.
—*Los Angeles Daily Times*, April 6, 1917.

register their opposition ten to one. Proof that war was not popular, La Follette argued, could be seen in "the espionage bills, the conscription bills, and other forcible military measures which we understand are being ground out of the war machine in this country . . . ." [17] Senator A. J. Gronna of North Dakota admitted that he did not know if a majority wanted war. No man knew that, he said. However, he strongly urged that the people be given the right to vote on the question of war or peace.[18] But the die was cast. War would come and there would be no popular referendum. On April 4 the Senate passed the war resolution 82 to 6. Two days later the House adopted it 373 to 50.[19]

On April 7, the day after war was declared, an emergency meeting of Socialist leaders was held in St. Louis. Out of this gathering came a series of resolutions on the war which were supported by the more radical element in the party. As months passed, enthusiastic supporters of the war came to look on these resolutions as outstanding examples of disloyalty. Prowar newspaper editors denounced them viciously and they received considerable attention in Congress. Since these resolutions were to be cited so often during the war to prove disloyalty by Socialists, lengthy quotations follow.

> The Socialist Party of the United States in the present grave crisis solemnly reaffirms its allegiance to the principle of internationalism and working-class solidarity the world over and proclaims its unalterable opposition to the war just declared by the Government of the United States.
>
> Modern wars as a rule have been caused by the commercial and financial rivalry and intrigues of the capitalist interests in the different countries. Whether they have been frankly waged as wars of aggression or have been hypocritically represented as wars of "defense," they have always been made by the classes and fought by the masses. War brings wealth and power to the ruling classes and suffering, death, and demoralization to the workers.
>
> They breed a sinister spirit of passion, unreason, race hatred, and false patriotism. They obscure the struggles of the workers for life, liberty, and social justice. They tend to sever the vital bonds of solidarity between them and their brothers in other countries, to destroy their organizations, and to curtail their civil and political rights and liberties.
>
> The Socialist Party of the United States is unalterably opposed to the system of exploitation and class rule which is upheld and strengthened by military power and sham national patriotism. We, therefore, call upon the workers of all countries to refuse to support their governments in their wars. The wars of the contending national groups of capitalists are not the concern of the workers. The only struggle which would justify the workers in taking up arms is the great struggle of the working class of the world to free itself from economic exploitation

and political oppression. As against the false doctrine of national patriotism we uphold the ideal of international working-class solidarity . . . .

The mad orgy of death and destruction which is now convulsing unfortunate Europe was caused by the conflict of capitalist interests in the European countries.

.   .   .   .

Our entrance into the European war was instigated by the predatory capitalists in the United States who boast of the enormous profit of $7,000,000,000 from the manufacture and sale of munitions and war supplies and from the exportation of American foodstuffs and other necessaries. They are also deeply interested in the continuance of war and the success of the allied arms through their huge loans to the Governments of the allied powers . . . .

Ruthless as the unrestricted submarine war policy of the German Government was and is, it is not an invasion of the rights of American people as such, but only an interference with the opportunity of certain groups of American capitalists to coin cold profits out of the blood and sufferings of our fellow men in the warring countries of Europe.

It is not a war against the militarist régime of the central powers. Militarism can never be abolished by militarism.

It is not a war to advance the cause of democracy in Europe. Democracy can never be imposed upon any country by a foreign power by force of arms.

It is cant and hypocrisy to say that the war is not directed against the German people . . . .

.   .   .   .

The American people did not and do not want this war. They have not been consulted about the war and have had no part in declaring war. They have been plunged into this war by the trickery and treachery of the ruling class of the country through its representatives in the national administration and National Congress, its demagogic agitators, its subsidized press, and other servile instruments of public expression.

The resolutions were followed by a pledge of "continuous, active, and public opposition to the war." [20] The signatures included those of Kate Richards O'Hare, Victor L. Berger, C. E. Ruthenberg, and others who were to come into open combat with the Government. The issuance of this antiwar document split the Socialist party wide open because many of its members refused to oppose the war. Such prominent Socialists as John Spargo, A. M. Simons, and Charles Edward Russell became war patriots.

The doctrinaire interpretation of the United States' entry into the war propounded by the Socialists will satisfy few students of that event. However, the interpretation of the interventionists also lacked substance and conviction. It is not surprising that the debate widened into conflict.

Despite the overwhelming vote in Congress for war, many war opponents claimed that 90 per cent of the voters of the country would have opposed war if they had had an opportunity to vote on it in 1917.[21] This is assuredly incorrect, and the 90 per cent figure was used loosely and carelessly by those who fought American entry into the war.

Studies in public opinion in Indiana and Missouri show widespread approval of Wilson's call for war. Cedric C. Cummins found that Indiana citizens hoped that war would not come, but if it did, they were resigned to accept it.[22] The Columbia (Indiana) *Evening Republican* editorialized on April 2, 1917, that midwesterners would not meet "a declaration of war joyously and with a smile on their lips. Rather will they meet it with a deep feeling of responsibility, a feeling that if the test has come they must meet it and be men." [23] The situation was similar in Missouri. There the President received almost unanimous press support for war.[24] John C. Crighton declared that "Missourians with a high degree of unanimity concluded that the maintenance of American rights and the preservation of a world balance of power favorable to the United States were more important than the safeguarding of peace." [25] Most North Dakota citizens, on the other hand, were opposed to going to war in 1917.

The American people certainly did not want war, but a vast majority was willing to accept it as something that had to be fought and won. A popular referendum might have seen a sizable vote against war in some areas, and any such reaction would have embarrassed and weakened the Administration.[26]

Regardless of what the exact situation may have been before April 6, 1917, afterwards it was entirely different. Thousands who had opposed war now felt it was their duty to support it. Representatives and Senators who had spoken and voted against war now voted for bill after bill to carry on the war. Bryan offered his services to Wilson. Later, in his editorials, he approved limiting freedom of speech and criticized conscientious objectors and resistance to the draft.[27] David Starr Jordan gave prowar speeches. Using arguments originally devised by the interventionists, he appeared awkward and labored. However, Jordan probably expressed the opinion of many antiwar Americans when he later wrote that it was "neither wise nor reasonable to oppose in any way the established policy of the nation." [28] Some Socialists left their party and "became more patriotic than the patriots." [29]

As time passed, more and more people became increasingly intolerant and partisan in their views. To a growing degree they approved the nationalists' attitude toward the opponents of the war. By 1918 the nationalist hysteria was reflected by the citizenry at large. One explanation may be found in the remarks of a literary critic of that time who said, "You cannot expect to incite people to the emotional level at which they willingly give their lives or the lives of their sons, and at the same time have them view with cool magnanimity the indifference or obstructiveness of their neighbors." [30] Indeed, the statement that "personal freedom is the first casualty in any war" was soon to be substantiated. And President Wilson had clearly foreseen what might happen. "Once lead this people into war," he had prophetically told Frank I. Cobb on April 2, "and they'll forget there ever was such a thing as tolerance. To fight you must be brutal and ruthless and the spirit of ruthless brutality will enter into the very fibre of our national life, infecting Congress, the courts, the policeman on the beat, the man in the street." [31] Probably even the President did not imagine the worst results of intolerance.

THE IMPLEMENTS
OF REPRESSION

The declaration of war by the United States on April 6, 1917, left many Americans angry and bitter. Some, such as the Socialists, said openly that participation in the war was a crime. Many diverse elements in the country hated conscription and were not reluctant to express that hatred. Still others condemned governmental policies which tended to repress and restrict those who opposed the prosecution of the war. And there were, of course, those who expressed suspicion of the ultimate aims of the majority committed to the conflict.

This continuing opposition was now met by a progressive demand that critics be silenced. Some suggested that physical violence should be used to quiet pacifists. Others were to suggest that opponents of governmental policies be jailed.

One group—a small but effective minority—was typified by Theodore Roosevelt and his militant followers. This faction strongly favored smothering criticism of national war policies. These leaders were united, as some had been during the Spanish-American War, by an interest in international politics. They now longed to use American wealth and power in competition with other nations. Some of their interest developed from their belief in this particular war; some of it from a peculiar psychosis which would have made war palatable almost any time; part of it from a simple enjoyment of violence. In this particular conflict, there were special claims upon their enthusiasm. Here was an opportunity to fight alongside and against the leading nations of the world. For the first time, their country would be participating in what European statesmen identified as *la grande politique*. This idea alone was attractive to some, and for them it carried the obligation to silence opposition.

Joined with the proponents of international adventuring, and including some of the same people, were "moral fundamentalists," people whose tendency was to interpret all life as a struggle between God and the devil. For them, the American nationalist cause evoked by war assumed an almost religious character; and per contra, German militarism represented the forces of deepest evil. As in the history of religion, where ecclesiastical and doctrinal differences left no room for charity, there was no place for differences of opinion. The opponents of war were at once subjected to an unrelenting attack by believers in the moral righteousness of a conflict which they considered a holy war.

A strong third element, much larger than either of the others, which supported a policy of repression was made up of super-patriots who, either knowingly or unwittingly, tended to place their nation above the laws of morality or reason. To them the state could do no wrong.[1] The attitude of "my country, right or wrong" controlled those minds which could not justify American prosecution of the war, even though they could not condone the cause of Germany and her allies.

There were also those whose demand for repression stemmed from economic motives. In the name of patriotism and loyalty conservatives were able to attack economic and political radicals, labor union members, and others who were demanding some kind of change or reform. This theme will be amply illustrated later.

In addition to these groups there were many people who simply had no concern about opposing repression. Some had sons or husbands in the armed forces and felt that hostility to the war was hostility to members of their family. Others, now that the die was cast, felt that nothing should be allowed to interfere. These moderates felt that clear and sudden danger overrode all questions of civil liberty. Moreover, the high idealism of war propaganda, particularly of Wilson's speeches, made them feel that participating in this war gave meaning and even a sense of nobility to their individual lives. Here was something worth while. The extremism of people who rejected freedom of thought and expression usually was disguised or hidden behind high-sounding phrases. To themselves as well as to others, their intolerances appeared as righteousness, their bigotry as idealism, and their hatreds as loyalty.

War advocates may have been moved by patriotism, by nationalism, by moralism, or perhaps by economic factors. But whatever the motivation, extreme supporters of the war very soon lashed out at all who stood in their way. And moderates, by their silence, gave them encouragement. Vituperation, epithet, ridicule, and abuse were heaped upon "pacifists." The swear word "isolationist" was applied to those who opposed war— and many sincere pacifists puzzled over its logic. Jane Addams wrote, "We were constantly accused of wishing to isolate the United States . . . . We were, of course, urging a policy exactly the reverse." [2]

Very soon the verbal attacks were to be accompanied by implication or suggestion that pacifists should be silenced, jailed, or even killed. As early as April 10, 1917, the *New York Times* quoted Elihu Root as saying that "we must have no criticism now." Root told a cheering crowd at the Union League Club on August 15 that "there are men walking about the streets of this city tonight who ought to be taken out at sunrise tomorrow and shot for treason." [3] Speaking before the Harvard Club the same evening, Theodore Roosevelt referred to those who wanted peace as pacifists, Socialists, I.W.W.'s, and "a whole raft of sexless creatures." [4] Two days later, as reported by the *New York Times* of August 18, he was urging "vigorous police action against orators preaching veiled treason on street corners and elsewhere." Earlier, on July 4, according to the *New York Herald* of July 5, 1917, he had berated "half-hidden traitors" and had demanded "one allegiance, one flag, one language." Even high government officials fell into this pattern. In November Attorney General Gregory added to the attacks on war opponents with his remark, "May God have mercy on them, for they need expect none from an outraged people and an avenging Government." [5] The President himself remarked in his Flag Day address, June 14, 1917, "Woe to the man or group of men that seeks to stand in our way in this day of high resolution . . . ." [6]

Throughout April and May some individuals who attacked American entrance into the war were arrested. In such cases pacifists were usually charged with "disorderly conduct" or "unlawful assembly," and the result might be jail sentences of up to three months and occasionally a small fine.[7] But there began to develop a desire on the part of war supporters to give stiffer sentences to anyone and everyone who spoke out against the war.

Even before the declaration of war on April 6 the Department of Justice had sought legal power to punish espionage. As early as February 8 the Attorney General had recommended legislation concerning "publication of information which might be useful to an enemy of the United States." [8] After the declaration of war, Senator George E. Chamberlain of Oregon introduced a bill making the entire United States "a part of the zone of operations conducted by the enemy." This bill would have classified as a spy every person who published anything "endangering the success of the military forces" and would have made him subject to the death sentence by court-martial. However, the bill was defeated as a result of opposition by President Wilson.[9]

During this period Congress evolved what was to become the Espionage Act. The bill, introduced on April 2, was an amalgamation of seventeen

DON'T WAIT TOO LONG, UNCLE!
—Darling in the New York *Tribune* as reproduced in *Literary Digest*, LV (Sept. 1, 1917), 11.

bills prepared in the Attorney General's office.[10] Some of the original drafts were much more drastic than the one that came out of committee. There is reason to believe that supporters of the measure did not realize the power it had or how it could be used to strike down opponents of the war. The name indicates that it was intended to outlaw spies, and debate in Congress turned time and again to blueprints and photographs of military installations which spies might acquire. Congressman Edwin Y. Webb, who guided it through the lower house, stressed the fact that it was an attempt to "safeguard and protect our national defense secrets." [11]

Senator Borah was suspicious. On April 19, 1917, when the bill to punish espionage was being discussed, he described it as "omnipotently comprehensive . . . though nebulous in its terms." "No man can foresee," he said, "what it might be in its consequences . . . ." [12] Thomas E. Watson, editor of the Thomson, Georgia, *Jeffersonian,* attacked it in his newspaper with intense earnestness. It would establish, he said, "the same kind of autocracy in this country that the *lese majestie [sic]* laws create in Germany . . . . Must we begin our war upon European autocracy *by creating one,* here at home? . . . *Don't abuse me*—ANSWER ME!" [13]

The principal opposition turned upon a section which gave the President the right to censor the press. Newspapers throughout the country objected. The American Newspaper Publishers petitioned Congress to delete this section.[14] The Los Angeles *Times* of May 3, 1917, called it un-American. In reply the bill's sponsors in Congress emphasized time and time again that the bill "gives you the right to criticize all you please." [15] They quoted the provision which said that "nothing in this section shall be construed to limit or restrict . . . any discussion, comment, or criticism of the acts or policies of the Government or its representatives, or the publication of the same." [16] But Senator Hiram Johnson of California was dubious. He asked Senator Overman, "Would you have me think, sir, that you have written one provision and then nullified it by the next?" The purpose of this proposed statute, he said, was "to render impossible legitimate criticism . . . of those who may lead during this war, and lead in incompetence and in inefficiency." [17] President Wilson also entered the fight. He wrote a letter to Congressman Webb which appeared in the *New York Times* on May 23, saying that the Administration must have authority to censor the press. This was "absolutely necessary to the public safety," he wrote.

The censorship provision was defeated, and after its elimination a majority of the national lawmakers apparently believed that the bill could not be used to suppress critical opinion.[18] Actually, however, the aim of curbing recalcitrant newspapers could be achieved under Title XII of the Espionage Bill. Part of this section prohibited sending through the mails any materials "advocating or urging treason, insurrection, or forcible resistance to any law of the United States." In effect, this was to give the Postmaster General the right to determine mailable matter.[19] And it might be added that the elimination of the much quoted sentence which gave citizens the right to criticize "the acts or policies of the Government or its representatives" was about as much of a victory for repression as the original censorship provision would have been.

The real teeth of the Espionage Bill were to be found in the paragraph which stated that whenever anyone shall wilfully make or convey false reports or false statements with intent to interfere with the operation or success of the military or naval forces . . . [or] shall wilfully cause or attempt to cause insubordination, disloyalty, mutiny, or refusal of duty in the military or naval forces of the United States, or shall wilfully obstruct the recruiting or enlistment service of the United States . . . [he] shall be punished by a fine of not more than $10,000 or imprisonment for not more than twenty years or both.

On the surface this appeared to be innocuous. There apparently was no threat to freedom of speech. In the debate in Congress this provision received relatively little consideration. Congressman Harold Knutson asked what would happen if someone revealed bad conditions in some army camp similar to those which had existed during the Spanish-American War. "Would that lay the writer open to a criminal prosecution?" Congressman Webb hastened to reply, "Certainly not . . . . Conditions, policies of the Government, and acts of its officers would always be open to criticism." He then stressed the fact that there could be prosecutions only when statements were "willfully false." Other questions were answered in about the same way.[20]

On June 15, 1917, the Espionage Bill became law. Eventually, in *Schenck* v. *United States,* Mr. Justice Holmes wrote the majority decision which upheld the law. In this decision was propounded the theory of "clear and present danger." [21] But this rather liberal interpretation quite apparently was not the guiding principle of American courts. Instead, courts often relied on the "bad tendency" doctrine. Zechariah Chafee stated that the Espionage Act, as interpreted by the courts, "renders civilians severely punishable during a war for questioning its justifiability or the methods of conducting it." [22] Many court cases bearing out this judgment will be discussed later. Undoubtedly, one of the main purposes of the law was to minimize domestic opposition to the war. But regardless of the exact intent of Congress, when the law began to be interpreted by judges and juries it became clear that opponents of war could and would be suppressed. For example, on August 16 a press notice announced that the Espionage Act might be used to provide punishment for anyone opposing the draft.[23]

States and municipalities also joined in the move to quiet opposition against the war. The laws of some western states where the I.W.W. and the Nonpartisan League were strong were especially severe. For example, in Minnesota it was illegal to say "that men should not enlist in the military

or naval forces of the United States or the state of Minnesota . . . ."
Nine states passed laws making it a crime to use language opposing
various aspects of the war effort. Several states passed some kind of
sedition laws, and fifteen states enacted criminal syndicalism statutes.[24]
On the local level, an Indianapolis ordinance made it illegal "to incite,
urge or advise strikes." [25] The Maryland compulsory work law seems even
more antilabor.[26]

Many organizations co-operated to make local, state, and national
laws successful. There already existed city, county, state, and national
police and detective forces. These were expanded and new units were
formed. In addition, numerous semiofficial and private organizations for
the purpose of suppressing opposition to the war were set up throughout
the country. Among these were the American Defense Society, the National Security League, the American Protective League, the Home Defense League, the Liberty League, the Knights of Liberty, the American
Rights League, the All-Allied Anti-German League, the Anti-Yellow Dog
League, the American Anti-Anarchy Association, the Boy Spies of
America, the Sedition Slammers, and the Terrible Threateners.

The American Defense Society was extremely active. The *New York
Herald* of August 18, 1917, reported, "More than one hundred men enrolled yesterday in the American Vigilante Patrol at the offices of the
American Defense Society . . . . The Patrol was formed to put an end
to seditious street oratory." On the twenty-second the organization's first
capture was announced. An individual by the name of Bedford was
accused of saying in front of a crowd at 37th and Broadway that he did
not approve of sending U.S. troops to France to fight England's battles.
The *New York Tribune* of August 22 reported that the Vigilantes had
Bedford arrested and charged with disorderly conduct. In a letter to
George Creel, H. D. Craig, secretary of this Society, recommended that
stringent action be taken against all alien enemies and "enemy sympathizers whose conduct imperils or impedes the conduct of the war." [27] In
March, 1918, the Society attempted to get official sanction of the Council
of National Defense "for the specific purpose of suppressing sedition." [28]
The honorary president of the group was Theodore Roosevelt, and
honorary vice-presidents included Robert Bacon, Perry Belmont, Charles
J. Bonaparte, and John G. Hibben.

The National Security League displayed much the same point of
view. George Creel has stated that the League and the American Defense
Society "were easily the most active and obnoxious [of chauvinist or-
ganizations]. At all times their patriotism was a thing of screams, violence,
and extremes, and their savage intolerances had the burn of acid." [29]

The state and municipal Councils of Defense were also active in hitting at opponents of the war. In each state, however, the situation varied. In some places these organizations led the war on pacifists. In others they participated feebly if at all. The parent body in Washington gave out the following instructions: "If you will continue to have your local councils, under your supervision, investigate and report upon cases of disloyalty and seditious utterances, communicating with the Department of Justice whenever it would appear to be advisable, we think you will be carrying out the policy of the Council of National Defense and fulfilling your obligation to your own legislature." [30]

The most omnipresent of the repressive organizations was the American Protective League, sponsored by the Department of Justice. By June, 1917, it had units in some 600 cities and towns with a membership of nearly 100,000. In 1918 the membership had increased to around 250,000.[31] The members of this League, one observer declared, were "the leading men in their communities. They were bankers, they were railroad men, they were hotel men, they were the choice of the citizens in their particular locality." [32] A biographer of the League, Emerson Hough, wrote in 1919, "The mails are supposed to be sacred . . . . But let us call the A. P. L. sometimes almost clairvoyant as to letters done by suspects . . . . It is supposed that breaking and entering a man's home or office place without warrant is burglary. Granted. But the League has done that thousands of times and has never been detected!" [33] Hough estimated that the League "brought to judgment three million cases of disloyalty." [34]

Secretary of the Treasury McAdoo was disturbed. He objected to the fact that a person, for seventy-five cents or a dollar, could obtain membership in the American Protective League and have the authority "with the approval of the Department of Justice, to make investigations under the title of 'Secret Service.' " [35] President Wilson wrote to Gregory, "It seems to me that it would be very dangerous to have such an organization operating in the United States, and I wonder if there is any way in which we could stop it." [36] The Attorney General refused to withdraw his support, and Wilson did not press the matter.

An example of the more active state organized groups was the Minnesota Commission of Public Safety. This Commission, created by state law, was formed on April 23, 1917. It was headed by the Governor and was backed by a body of Home Guards. It closed saloons and moving picture theaters, directed a census of alien land ownership, established a policy of "work or fight," boosted the sale of Liberty bonds, examined and tested people for loyalty and pro-Germanism, and took other actions to bring conformity and all-out support of the war.[37] On August 8, 1917, the *Minneapolis Journal* carried an appeal issued by this Commission "for all patriots to join in the suppression of anti-draft and seditious acts and sentiment." The official report of the Commission published in 1919 stated: "Misinterpreting the Constitutional guarantee of freedom of speech and of the press, these leaders of radical groups thought or pretended to think, that even in war times they could properly oppose the Government's policies in speech and writing." [38] The Commission was referring to groups like the Nonpartisan League. The *St. Paul Daily News* on June 29, 1918, reported, "The Commission thinks that as a matter of law it cannot be restrained in the performance of its public functions by any Minnesota court."

As soon as these nationalistic societies were formed and the desired laws were passed, official and unofficial spokesmen of the groups urged people to become informers. The *New York Times*, June 6, 1917, editorialized, "It is the duty of every good citizen to communicate to the proper authorities any evidence of sedition that comes to his notice." The *Literary Digest* requested its readers to watch for sedition and "to clip and send to us any editorial utterances they encounter which seem to them seditious or treasonable." [39] Attorney General Gregory announced that "complaints of even the most informal or confidential nature are always welcome." [40] The Committee on Public Information issued advertisements urging readers to "report the man who spreads pessimistic stories. Report him to the Department of Justice." [41] Even George Creel himself was known to have written, "I think this man might be watched with profit." [42] Apparently Creel had in mind magazine and newspaper articles which he wanted to make the basis for legal prosecution. [43]

President Wilson was also concerned with this problem. He wrote on one occasion, "Any item, great or small [dealing with pro-German activity], with which you would be kind enough to furnish us would be taken up and acted on with promptness . . . ." [44] In August, 1917, Wilson asked the Attorney General what could be done about an individual opposing an expeditionary force. [45] About a month later he asked if certain writings could not be made the basis for a treason trial. Gregory replied that this would not be possible, but that the writer might be silenced under the Espionage Act. [46]

By 1918 the Attorney General was able to declare, "It is safe to say that never in its history has this country been so thoroughly policed." [47] Many opponents of war had found this to be true through personal experience.

"It is in no sense a conscription of the unwilling."

THE OPENING FIGHT
AGAINST CONSCRIPTION

In the decades before 1917, thousands of people had fled to the United States to escape the miseries of Europe. Intolerance, persecution, and poverty had impelled many of them to come. But high on the list of the evils they had sought to escape was conscription. Immigrant women had explained their desire to become Americans by saying they wanted their children to grow up where there was no military domination, no conscription. From all over Europe such people had come, bringing with them their hopes of living in a country dedicated to peace instead of to war. Once in America, they had found their hopes daily reflected by writers and speakers.

But now conscription was to come to the New World. Even before the declaration of the war there had been indications that the volunteer system was to be abandoned, and on April 5 the Army Bill revealed the formal request for enforced service in the army. Protests were immediate. Idealists and liberals were indignant. Radicals were frightened and angered. Congressman William P. Borland of Missouri said he thought that conscription was the "fairest, safest, and most democratic method of national defense," but he admitted that "the very suggestion of universal liability to military service as applied to our own country seems to have caused a shock to the minds of many gentlemen in this House." [1]

Again there were protests before congressional committees; there were protests from the floor of Congress; there were attempts to get a popular referendum. Champ Clark, Speaker of the House, strongly favored trying the volunteer system. "I protest with all my heart and mind and soul against having the slur of being a conscript placed upon the men of Missouri," he said. "In the estimation of Missourians there is precious little difference between a conscript and a convict." [2] Congressman George Huddleston of Alabama called conscription un-American and charged that its chief proponents were representatives of big business and high finance. These interests, he said, wanted big armies and navies for conquest and exploitation abroad and for the throttling of critics at home. According to Huddleston, these business groups claimed that "we have too much discontent, too many Socialists, too many I.W.W.'s, too many strikes, too much industrial disorder, too much freedom of speech, too many ranting demagogues and labor agitators." Huddleston believed that "they would suppress all this with the iron hand of the military." [3]

And then, of course, Senator La Follette attacked conscription. He reminded the Senate that "the power once granted will attach to the office [of the President], and will be exercised so long as this Nation shall last, by every successive incumbent, no matter how ambitious or bloody-minded he may be." La Follette not only opposed the principle of conscription, but he resented the speed with which the bill was being pushed through Congress. "Never in all my years of experience in the House and in the Senate," he declared, "have I heard so much democracy preached and so little practiced as during the last few months." [4]

Widespread opposition to conscription was also found outside the halls of Congress. Socialists, Anarchists, I.W.W.'s, and other radicals vigorously propagandized against selective service or any law which required a man to fight. The American Union Against Militarism, a Socialist organization, was especially active. Hulet M. Wells, a prominent Seattle Socialist, and Sam Sadler issued a circular entitled *No Conscription, No Involuntary Servitude, No Slavery*. It stated that

> the President and Congress have no authority to set it [the Thirteenth Amendment] aside. That can only be done by a majority vote of the legislatures of three-fourths of the separate states. For the President and Congress to do it is to usurp the powers of autocrats and if unresisted means the abandonment of democracy and the destruction of the Republic . . . . Resist! Refuse! . . . Thou shalt not Prussianize America!

It was impossible to silence these men for opposing a bill under consideration by Congress. However, they were shortly sentenced to serve

two years in the federal penitentiary for conspiring to prevent the execution of the joint resolution of Congress declaring war.[5]

For a while friends of the bill were alarmed over its possible defeat.
A report from the *New York Tribune*'s Washington Bureau published on
April 10 said, "If a vote were taken today and every man in the House
were to vote the way he is talking, the majority against the President's
conscription plan would be tremendous." President Wilson wrote to
Charles W. Eliot of Harvard, "If you were here, I think I could make
you realize very vividly the elements I am dealing with and the impossibility which exists at present of bringing the Congress to the adoption
of any sort of permanent system." [6]

But supporters both in and out of Congress put on the pressure.
Wilson issued a statement saying he believed the safety of the nation
depended upon it. The *New York Times* of April 10 carried headlines
proclaiming, "Billy Sunday Holds a Council of War" and "Major General
Wood and Colonel Roosevelt With Him at Rockefeller Home." Other
conservative elements rushed into the fray. Most of the press and many
pulpits resounded in favor of conscription. For example, Cummins found
that in Indiana most newspapers favored conscription even before the
declaration of war.[7] Within a few days the conscription bill passed both
houses by large majorities. The draft bill became law on May 18, 1917.
This result, however, was not so much a matter of nationalistic advocates
of war winning out over ardent opponents of war and conscription. The
vast majority of people had simply accepted conscription in rather calm
resignation as the best and fairest way to provide the necessary armed
forces. It must be remembered that England had tried the volunteer
system and abandoned it before the United States entered the war.

On the same day President Wilson urged support of the measure on
the grounds "that each man shall be classified for service in the place to
which it shall best serve the general good to call him." "It is in no sense
a conscription of the unwilling," he argued, but a manner of "selection
from a nation which has volunteered in mass." [8]

Sporadic outbursts of opposition greeted the passage of the Selective
Service Act in many parts of the country. On the evening of May 18 a
large anticonscription meeting was held at the Harlem River Casino
where the Government was denounced as a dupe of the capitalist classes.
"No Conscription" circulars were distributed. The *New York Times* said
the crowd was made up mostly of I.W.W.'s, Anarchists, and Socialists.[9]
No arrests were made, but police reporters were present. However, the
Government quickly showed its determination to let nothing interfere
with the successful execution of the draft law. Within a few days reports

from all sections of the country told of people being arrested for allegedly interfering with the draft. Seven men were arrested at Snyder, Texas, on May 22 and held on charges of seditious conspiracy "in planning to resist conscription by force." They were supposedly members of the Farmers' and Laborers' Protective Association. At about the same time, an Abilene, Texas, man said to have once been connected with the I.W.W. was also arrested for purported anticonscription activities. From Michigan, Illinois, Washington, Virginia, and other states came similar stories. The Attorney General said that these arrests should be recognized by the country as a warning against interfering with the draft act.[10]

Most of those arrested in late May were Socialists, I.W.W.'s, Anarchists, and others who held unpopular political and economic ideas. It is not easy to tell whether the arrests were actually made to maintain federal authority or whether opposition to conscription was used as an excuse to quiet dissident groups. The latter was probably true in some instances. The *New York Times* editorialized on June 10, 1917, "The Selective Draft Act gives a long and sorely needed means of disciplining a certain insolent foreign element in this nation."

Arrest and conviction of people who opposed the Selective Service Act continued without abatement as the country approached the registration date of June 5. Vicente Carrillo, a Mexican in Los Angeles, was caught on May 27 and charged with making a speech against registration. Later he was sentenced to a year in jail for refusing to register.[11] On May 27 in Detroit the *Michigan Socialist* appeared with a violent anticonscription edition in which the declaration of war was denounced and a pledge made not to enroll on registration day. The men involved were jailed. The principal defendant, Maurice Sugar, was fined five hundred dollars. Later he was sentenced to a year in prison for failing to register.[12]

At the same time in Cleveland, Socialists attempted to hold an anticonscription meeting, but it was broken up by the police. Charles E. Ruthenberg and some others were arrested for disorderly conduct. Later they were found guilty of having persuaded one individual to refuse to register. The sentence was one year in jail.[13] In another part of Ohio some men were arrested for circulating a pamphlet entitled *Down with Conscription*. It urged men not to register for conscription and those involved were later sent to the penitentiary.[14]

Two men in Kansas City attempted to obtain an injunction to prevent the governor, the mayor, and other officials from enforcing registration for the draft. The court refused the request and the two men were arrested.[15] An attempt to block the draft legally also failed in California.

Antidraft literature was seized in Ohio, New York, and Minnesota.[16]

On May 31, 1917, Louis Kramer, Morris Becker, and others were arrested in front of Madison Square Garden while distributing announcements of an antidraft meeting to be held June 4. They were accused of suggesting that young men should not register. The defense intimated that the entire affair was a frame-up. There seems to be evidence that the presiding judge was impatient and abrupt. He sentenced Kramer to two years in Atlanta and fined him ten thousand dollars. Becker was given twenty months in Atlanta.[17]

On June 4 people began to assemble inside and outside of Hunt's Point Palace in the Bronx in New York City. Two hours before the meeting started, according to the Providence *Daily Journal*, June 5, 1917, people "were packed in solid phalanxes for a distance of four blocks from the hall." The doors were locked by order of the fire department and, to judge by the newspaper accounts, the speakers gave their addresses "amid riotous scenes." One of the speakers, Leonard D. Abbott, was quoted by the *New York Herald* of June 5 as saying,

> Conscription is immoral, unAmerican, and unconstitutional. Why in the name of humanity drag us into a war which we disapprove . . . . Conscription is the thin entering wedge of military despotism . . . . Go to Europe and fight Germany if you want to, but do not try to drag us with you . . . . The Government must have a guilty conscience when it arrests college boys and girls and tries to break up meetings that are opposed to its conscription.[18]

The *Herald* report of the meeting noted that there were two hundred police, two hundred detectives, and twelve armed soldiers in the hall, sent by the Department of Justice. It also reported that scores of people were injured.

The two principal speakers were to have been Anarchists Emma Goldman and Alexander Berkman. After Berkman got well into his speech there were threats of disorder. Goldman rushed to the center of the stage and gained the attention of the audience. "Friends, friends —wait, wait! . . . The soldiers and sailors have been sent here to cause trouble, and the police are in league with them. If we lose our heads there will be bloodshed, and it will be our blood they will shed! . . . We must refuse to be provoked to it . . . . Therefore I declare the meeting closed." [19]

Nothing happened to Goldman and Berkman until two weeks later when they denounced Judge Julius M. Mayer for the sentences imposed upon Kramer and Becker. The following day, Anarchist party headquarters were raided, and Goldman and Berkman were arrested and charged with being "principals in a nationwide conspiracy against the Government." They were tried before the same Judge Mayer they had previously attacked. Goldman was accused of saying, "We will support all those who refuse to be conscripted." [20] The result was a foregone conclusion, and Goldman and Berkman were given the maximum sentence permitted at that time, two years in the penitentiary and a ten-thousand-dollar fine.[21] Berkman stated, "We have been convicted because we are anarchists, and the proceeding has been very unjust." Goldman asked for several minor personal considerations at this time, all of which were denied. She finally called back the judge as he was leaving the court. "One more word! I want to thank you for your leniency and kindness in refusing us a stay of two days, a stay you would have accorded the most heinous criminal. I thank you once more." According to Miss Goldman in her book *Living My Life,* the judge was white with anger. "He moved his lips as if to speak, then abruptly turned and left the bench." [22]

Many enthusiastic proponents of the war were puzzled and angered by the opposition to registration. Some Administration leaders were nervous, fearing a repetition of the Civil War draft riots. Secretary Baker wrote the President that he hoped registration could be conducted in such a manner that "a strong patriotic feeling" would be created.[23] But if patriotism did not silence opposition to conscription, there would be other means to achieve the Government's objectives.

The Los Angeles *Times* of May 25, 1917, carried the headlines, "Antiwar Agitators Liable to Prosecution for Attacking Conscription" and "Death For Treason Awaits Anti-Draft Plotters." On May 27 Attorney General Gregory said his attention had been called to literature designed to discourage registration. He promised that the Government would deal vigorously with such cases.[24] President Wilson was cited by the Los Angeles *Times* on May 31, 1917, as the source of the news story which carried the headline, "Anti-Draft Agitators To Be Treated With No Leniency." On June 2, the *New York Times* headline read, "Government Watches All Ports So That None May Flee to Avoid Registration." President Wilson was reported to have warned young men against going abroad to evade service. In Minneapolis, the *Journal* of June 4 reported that five hundred special deputies were ready to guard registration places. In Los Angeles the *Times* announced on June 5, "One thousand men will police Los Angeles City and County today to prevent possible rioting."

On June 5 most young Americans registered for the draft. It was a remarkably peaceful day. In some places bands played; in other places there was no fanfare. The large element in favor of war seemed enthusiastic. Another large element, opposed to the war but feeling an

FINE CHANCE HE HAS OF STOPPING THE DRAFT!
—Ireland in the Columbus *Dispatch* as reproduced in *Literary Digest*, LIV (June 16, 1917), 1832.

obligation to support it, displayed no antagonism. And probably the rigorous action taken by the Government against opponents of conscription before June 5 reduced disturbances that might otherwise have occurred. In any event, the National Security League was so impressed with the success of registration that it sent a letter to congressmen stating that the results proved "that permanent universal military training is popular." The President and his advisers were encouraged.[25] The Chicago *Herald* declared editorially, "In spite of objections, oppositions, agitations, plots, it is clear that the vast majority of the people in America believe in this summons to arms." [26]

There were, however, many people who still bitterly opposed both the war and conscription. Among these were some foreigners whom Jane Addams knew well. Of them she wrote in *Peace and Bread*, "I knew many of them had come to this country seeking freedom from military service quite as much as they sought freedom of other sorts, and here they were about to be securely caught once more." Conscription and war, she continued, were "something which belonged to the unhappy Europe they had left behind. It was as if their last throw had been lost." [27]

On July 3, 1917, the Los Angeles *Times* reflected one defense of conscription when it said that if these people "are opposed in principle to military service they should be living now in a state where military service is not required . . . . [They] received no guarantee that military duty would not be exacted of them."

Despite the general success of registration, ugly incidents developed in various parts of the country. The *Minneapolis Journal* of June 5 and the *New York Herald* of June 6 reported that a man in Mineral Wells, Texas, was shot and killed on registration day. He was a member of the Farmers' and Laborers' Protective Association and was accused of having tried to avoid conscription. The newspaper reports claimed that he opened fire first and that he was a wife-beater! The Los Angeles *Times* of June 13 reported that another man in Virginia, Minnesota, an I.W.W., was shot in the back while running away from arrest on a charge of being a slacker. The *New York Times* of June 6 reported that "six hundred paraders with a twelve foot red flag at their head inscribed 'Down With War!' " began a demonstration against registration at Butte, Montana. An Irish organization, the Pearce-Connolly Club, apparently organized this parade. The procession had gone only four blocks when it was attacked by "patriotic citizens, reinforced by the police." The *Times* also stated that "several shots were fired and a score of persons were arrested." The city was placed under martial law. The *New York Herald* of June 6 in its account of the Butte incident claimed that the state militia "with fixed bayonets proceeded to disperse the mob." These are only some of the examples of demonstrations against registration.

In Rockford, Illinois, about 150 I.W.W.'s and Socialists submitted voluntarily to the authorities for evading the Registration Act. Bill Haywood wrote of the trial before the judge, Kenesaw Mountain Landis, as follows:

As was expected, the "Honorable" (save the mark) judge, simply "kangarooed" the boys, giving all but a few the limit, and in order to make their sentence harder, sentenced them to the Bridewell in Chicago, where, as he said, "The work is much harder than in the Federal Prison." He also took advantage of their helplessness to deliver an insulting speech to them in which he called them cowards and "whining, belly-aching puppies" because they would not register to fight for Morgan and his loans.[28]

In this Rockford case an attorney asked for a change of venue for three of the accused. Landis commented, "These affidavits do not state my position at all . . . . They say that I have openly committed myself to a prior conviction, without a hearing, and that I am in no position to judge a free and unenslaved people." Landis granted the request, but he seemed highly irritated and let the lawyer know it.[29]

Some opponents of conscription had refused to register in order to test the law in court. Several cases were grouped together and eventually —in 1918—came before the Supreme Court in what was known as the *Arver* case. The two principal defendants, Joseph F. Arver and Otto H. Wangerin, claimed that conscription was unconstitutional, but the Court ruled that Article I, Section 8, of the Constitution—which gives Congress the right to declare war and to raise and support armies—was authority for conscription. The decision of the court was unanimous.[30] On January 9, 1918, the editor of the *Chicago Daily News* wrote that the language of the chief justice shows "with how little respect or even patience the so-called arguments that were made against selective conscription were received." Arver had been sentenced to a year in the St. Cloud Reformatory by the trial court. Wangerin received a similar sentence. After his release Wangerin was called by the draft, refused to serve, was court-martialed and sent to Leavenworth.[31]

President Wilson wrote to his private secretary that "anybody is entitled to make a campaign against the draft law provided they don't stand in the way of the administration of it by any overt acts or improper influences." [32] However, already it had become clear that this would not be the case. The pressure of public opinion and the attitude of the courts showed that opposition to the draft act would be dealt with severely. The tragedy of this situation was not conscription itself. Rather, it was that the majority which favored conscription refused the right of opponents to criticize the policy. The real tragedy then was the suppression of debate and inquiry so important to the democratic process.

▄▄▄

"CONSCRIPTION IS UPON US"

June–September, 1917

During the summer of 1917, the fight over conscription became even more heated. The numerous arrests prior to registration day on June 5 did not silence the opponents of conscription. Generally, the same people who had opposed United States entry into the war also fought against compulsory military service. There was no organized effort on a national scale which was aimed solely against the draft act. But from one end of the country to the other attacks were made on the practice; from one end of the country to the other the attackers were arrested and jailed. The incidents which developed over opposition to conscription were to raise some basic questions of freedom of speech and press in wartime.[1]

Anticonscription speeches were common in many areas and literature opposing the draft was distributed on a fairly wide basis. For example, Edwin Firth, state secretary of the Socialist party of West Virginia, circulated a pamphlet entitled *Are We Facing a Militarized America?* It contained the statement that "conscription has been thrust on an unwilling people without a referendum" and suggested that Americans "demand the repeal of the Conscription Act."[2] He was given six months in jail.

An anticonscription meeting in New York City on June 15 occasioned a near riot. After the meeting started, word was spread that soldiers and sailors had surrounded the hall and were going to question all those in attendance. At this point the audience started to leave. According to an account in the *New York Times*, June 16, 1917, "the fifty or more soldiers tried in vain to stem the tide. But they couldn't stop the 2,000 persons inside who hit the soldiers at the door in flying wedges, and threw themselves outside, where 10,000 persons were gathered, hissing and cursing the soldiers."

The next day a disturbance occurred at the City Hall. Women from the East Side had come with a petition asking for the repeal of the state's military census law. After scuffling with the police, three of them were arrested.[3] On July 4, a man in New York City circulated copies of the Declaration of Independence with the appended query, "Does your Government live up to these principles?" The local magistrate sentenced him to ninety days in the workhouse, although he later gained his freedom on a writ of habeas corpus.[4]

In nominating Morris Hillquit for mayor early in July, the New York Socialists adopted a strong anticonscription platform. The resolution declared: "We most emphatically protest at this manner of forcing love of country upon the people and of compelling them to fight against their wills . . . ."[5]

There was also strong opposition to conscription in Philadelphia. Joseph Stilson published and circulated a pamphlet entitled *Let Us Not Go to the Army*. In this pamphlet conscription was vigorously denounced and men were urged to go to prison rather than be drafted. Stilson was also editor of a Lithuanian newspaper, *Kova*. On October 19, 1917, his paper carried a sarcastic editorial which stated: "Postmaster General Burleson says that the Government will not destroy all Socialist newspapers; only those will be destroyed that point out that American capitalists have drawn this country into war . . . those who shall criticize [the imperialist] policies of America and her allies; those who interfere with the compulsory military conscription . . . ." For these writings Stilson was sentenced to three years in the penitentiary. His assistant, Joseph Sukys, received a three-month sentence.[6]

In some cases local citizens took the law into their own hands. Early in July several Philadelphia Socialists were distributing antiwar circulars which demanded the repeal of the draft law and criticized the President. People in the neighborhood began to beat and kick them. Before the police could arrive to protect them the mob had torn off their clothing and divided it for souvenirs.[7]

Other disturbances arose in Philadelphia over the distribution of a pamphlet entitled *Long Live the Constitution of the United States*. This document argued that a conscript was little more than a convict, deprived of liberty and the right to think and act as a free man. It urged the election of officials who were opposed to conscription and asked people to sign a petition demanding that Congress repeal the Selective Service Act. Conscription laws, the pamphlet said, belonged to a bygone age and had no place in a democratic country.[8] On July 13 several young Socialists were arrested for distributing this pamphlet, and in August others were arrested. This time, according to the Philadelphia *Public Ledger*, August 8, 1917, they "were saved from physical injury only by the interference of a group of twenty [national] guardsmen . . . who turned the six over to the police." They were charged with treason.

In August a group of sailors and marines broke up an anticonscription meeting at the Arch Street Theatre even before people could assemble. The *Public Ledger* account of August 26 stated, "As they repeatedly charged the throngs they jeered and yelled, striking terror among the several hundred young women who had come to hear a plea against conscription." Police arrested some of the individuals distributing literature. The next day the Director of Public Safety stated, according to the same account, that he would permit no seditious meetings. He said that the order preventing "Socialist gatherings where protests against the United States Government's war policy are voiced will be rigidly enforced."

On August 28 the Socialist bookstore and office were raided. Charles T. Schenck, the general secretary of the party, and several other persons were arrested. They were accused of circulating material in an attempt to cause insubordination and disloyalty in the military and naval forces and of obstructing recruitment and enlistment for service.[9] Among the literature found in Schenck's possession was *Long Live the Constitution of the United States*. Schenck was sentenced to six months in jail while the others were dealt with more leniently.[10]

In upholding the decision in the Schenck case the Supreme Court affirmed the constitutionality of the Espionage Act. Justice Holmes wrote:

> The question in every case is whether the words are used in such circumstances and are of such a nature as to create a clear and present danger that they will bring about the substantive evils that Congress has a right to prevent. It is a question of proximity and degree. When a nation is at war many things that may be said in time of peace are such a hindrance to its efforts that their utterance will not be endured so long as men fight and that no Court could regard them as protected by a constitutional right.[11]

In other words, the Supreme Court held that war limits the right of freedom of speech; in wartime the first amendment of the Constitution does not strictly hold; courts, including the Supreme Court, would not protect individuals who openly opposed war or conscription.

An organization in California known as the American Patriots Association issued a document early in August entitled *Legal Opinion and Advice on the Conscription Law to American Patriots*. The leader of the group was a lawyer, Daniel O'Connell. On August 8, 1917, he was in San Francisco participating in a meeting of the People's Council. The police entered the meeting and forcibly took him from the hall. This action so enraged former Senator Works that, according to the *Sacramento Bee*, August 9, he arose and denounced the "sad spectacle." Then he added, "A peaceable assembly of American citizens discussing one of the greatest problems that has confronted this country in all its history, attempting to express honest convictions upon that great problem, has been interrupted by an officer of the law seeking to arrest one of their number, evidently for the purpose of intimidation." "Are we in free America?" he asked. "Is this a democracy or is this an autocracy?" At his trial O'Connell was accused of attempting to persuade men not to enlist in the army. He was found guilty and sentenced to a federal penitentiary for five years; the sentence was later commuted to two years.[12]

E. R. Hoffman, who was also involved in this affair, was sentenced to three years at McNeil Island. The Attorney General reported that Hoffman had collected money from draft opponents and had circulated anticonscription propaganda written by O'Connell. He had also stated that soldiers should not be sent overseas and that if the Government should "attempt to do so, an injunction would be served to prevent the embarkation of the troops." The attitude of the Attorney General, as well as that of many lawyers, judges, and juries, was revealed in the statement that Hoffman was "unregenerate and unrepentant." [13]

Much American propaganda emphasized the bloody sacrifices being made by the enemy, but supporters of the war would not tolerate similar statements concerning potential American losses. One pamphlet which described such possibilities in lurid tones was *The Price We Pay*, by Irwin St. John Tucker. A high-water mark in the anticonscription literature, it caused widespread indignation. In the words of the Attorney General, it "overstated the horrors of war." [14] Tucker wrote:

> Conscription is upon us; the draft law is a fact. Into your homes the recruiting officers are coming. They will take your sons of military age and impress them into the army . . . . They will be

shipped through the submarine zone by the hundreds of thousands to the bloody quagmire of Europe. Into that seething, heaving swamp of torn flesh and floating entrails they will be plunged, in regiments, divisions, and armies, screaming as they go. Agonies of torture will rend their flesh from their sinews, will crack their bones and dissolve their lungs; and every pang will be multiplied in its passage to you. Black death will be a guest at every American fireside; mothers and fathers and sisters, wives, and sweethearts will know the weight of that awful vacancy left by the bullet which finds its mark. And still the recruiting officers will come; seizing age after age, mounting up to the older ones and taking the younger ones as they grow to soldier size; and still the toll of death will grow . . . .[15]

On July 11, 1917, two men, Romanus E. Baker and Jacob M. Wilhide, were indicted for circulating this pamphlet. These Marylanders were accused of "attempting to induce those subject to the Selective Draft Act to disobey it." Judge Rose directed a verdict of not guilty. He stated, "There is a very lurid description of the horrors of war in that circular —some of it well-written, some of it not so well-written. But, after all, there is no difference of opinion that war is a terrible catastrophe, and involves many terrible things." Insofar as the Draft Act was concerned, the judge said, "Any man may do anything, in itself legal, to secure the repeal of any law in force." But, he continued, "as long as the law is the law, it is the duty of every man to obey it." According to Judge Rose, the question was: "Can the Government show, always beyond a reasonable doubt, that these men were trying to persuade people to disobey the law?" The defendants should be acquitted, he told the jury, unless it was satisfied beyond a reasonable doubt that they intended "to prevent men within the military age from obeying the law . . . ." But Judge Rose believed that *The Price We Pay* was aimed principally at getting people to join the Socialist party. Then he added the significant statement, "I do not think that we ought to attempt to prosecute people for that kind of thing." [16]

Judge Rose's point of view—so completely unsatisfactory to the fervent supporters of the war—was soon to be overruled. Following the release of Baker and Wilhide, Socialists in Albany distributed copies of this same pamphlet. As the situation developed, Clinton H. Pierce, a Socialist, was in an Albany saloon where John J. Scully spoke out heatedly against the draft. Scully was an agent of the American Protective League and was apparently acting as an *agent provocateur*. Because of his remarks Pierce gave him a copy of *The Price We Pay*. Pierce was then arrested, brought into court, and accused of making false reports to discourage enlistments and obstruct recruiting. According to the indictment, the pamphlet impugned, misrepresented, and falsified the motives of Congress and the President. The indictment carried quotations from the pamphlet which stated, among other things, that the United States went to war to protect J. P. Morgan's loans. It declared that "all of [these] statements and reports were and are wholly false and untrue . . . ." In his charge to the jury the judge said, "Does this pamphlet, gentlemen, . . . represent the ideas, the beliefs, and the principles of the Socialist Party? If so, is it opposed to the war, its prosecution, the selective draft act, and the recruiting of the Army to carry on the war?" [17]

The broad interpretation so desired by enthusiastic nationalists was now adopted by the court. "Obstruct" came to have an all-inclusive meaning. In order to be guilty of obstructing the war effort it was not necessary to prove that, as a result of certain statements or actions, any particular individual had refused military service. A man was liable for prosecution even if he only wrote or spoke against conscription or the war. Justices Holmes and Brandeis dissented when this principle was upheld by the Supreme Court. They maintained that "to hold that a jury may make punishable statements of conclusions or of opinion . . . by declaring them to be statements of facts and to be false would practically deny members of small political parties freedom of criticism and of discussion in times when feelings run high . . . ." [18] That was essentially what was to happen.

Kate Richards O'Hare had been national secretary of the Socialist party. She was a leading figure in the antiwar wing of the party and had helped to promote the passage of the antiwar resolutions at St. Louis. On July 17, 1917, Mrs. O'Hare made a speech in Bowman, North Dakota, before a small crowd. In denouncing conscription, she was reported to have said in substance "that the women of the United States were nothing more nor less than brood sows, to raise children to get into the army and be made into fertilizer." Mrs. O'Hare also declared that the purpose of the war was not to make democracy safe but to enrich bankers and munitions makers.[19] The Attorney General stated that "aside from her distorted and erroneous views on socialistic subjects [she] was undoubtedly a sincere, earnest, and worthy woman." Yet she had helped to promote the antiwar resolutions in St. Louis.[20] That alone was enough to damn her in the minds of strong war proponents. And now that she was fighting conscription, extreme nationalists insisted that she be silenced.

She was sentenced to five years in the Missouri State Penitentiary, although she served only a little more than a year. According to one critic, Judge Martin Wade of Iowa who sentenced Mrs. O'Hare was a "Bourbon, anti-Bryan Democrat . . . and has recently developed a sort of mania for denouncing 'traitors' on all possible occasions." [21]

An example of perhaps one of the most extreme cases of injustice was that of Walter Matthey of Iowa. One evening he attended a meeting where the speaker, Daniel H. Wallace, strongly attacked conscription. Matthey was not prosecuted for any comments or organizational activities, but for his *appearance* at the meeting. The United States Attorney General later reported that "petitioner's offense of which convicted consisted in his attending a meeting, listening to an address in which disloyal utterances were made, applauding some of the statements màde by the speaker claimed to be disloyal, their exact nature not being known, and contributing 25¢. Petitioner left the hall when the address was about half over." [22] Yet Matthey was sentenced to a year in jail.

In South Dakota a group of twenty-seven Socialist farmers of German extraction led by Emanuel Baltzer sent a petition to Governor Peter Norbeck expressing their opposition to the draft and saying that an unduly high quota was being exacted from their county. They asked for a new quota arrangement, for a referendum on the war, for payment of war expenses from taxation, and for a repudiation of war debts. They threatened to defeat Norbeck and other officials at the polls if they did not comply.[23] The defendants were sentenced to from one to two years in the penitentiary, although their conviction was later reversed.

Walter Heynacher, an elderly South Dakotan, argued with a young man about enlistment. The man testified that Heynacher had urged him not to enlist, "that the present war was all foolishness and . . . that my talk of enlisting was all nonsense; that the war was for the big bugs in Wall Street; that it was all foolishness to send our boys over there to get killed by the thousands, all for the sake of Wall Street; that he should not go to war until he had to." Heynacher's sentence was five years at Leavenworth Penitentiary.[24]

Late in June, 1917, William J. Head circulated a petition in South Dakota to repeal the Draft Act. He stated to a prospective signer of the petition that "the draft law was unconstitutional and they could not make anyone go to war if they did not want to go." He also said that "the war was caused by the money interests in the East and Morgan was one of the men mentioned and the Government had no right to send out young men to France to fight," and that "we were all damn fools" for supporting the war. Head was sentenced to three years in Leavenworth and fined five hundred dollars, although this judgment was later reversed on confession of error.[25]

In the small town of Philip, South Dakota, on August 17, 1917, a farmer named Fred Fairchild was engaged in a heated conversation concerning the war. Fairchild was a Socialist. In 1916 he had been the party's nominee for governor. As a result of the St. Louis antiwar platform he had withdrawn from the party, but he apparently still maintained his dislike of conscription. He was accused of having said at this time, "If I were of conscription age and had no dependants and were drafted, I would refuse to serve. They could shoot me, but they could not make me fight." For making these statements he was charged with attempting to cause disloyalty and insubordination in the military forces of the United States. He was fined five hundred dollars and sentenced to a year and a day in Leavenworth Penitentiary.[26]

In Sibley County, Minnesota, Abraham L. Sugarman, state secretary of the Socialist party, was accused of "denouncing the Selective Service Act and suggesting that if they [apparently meaning young men] all held together the act could not be enforced, as there were not jails enough to hold all the people." According to the testimony of a secret service representative who was present, Sugarman stated that it was a capitalist war and that the Government had no right to send men to France. Speaking outside the hall where a Socialist meeting was being held, Sugarman was reported to have said, "This is supposed to be a free country. Like Hell it is." Then he remarked that the Selective Draft Act was unconstitutional and there was no obligation to abide by it. A petition for its repeal was circulated in the crowd. Sugarman was charged with wilfully attempting "to cause insubordination, disloyalty, mutiny, and refusal of duty in the military forces of the United States." That no "military forces" were present at the meeting made no difference. The court held that this phrase included all who had registered under the Selective Service Act, thus widening governmental power under the Act. Sugarman was sentenced to three years in Leavenworth Penitentiary.[27]

At New Ulm, Minnesota, a large crowd of between five and ten thousand people gathered to discuss the draft and related matters. The mayor of the town and the president of a local college presided. Most of the speeches were discreet. Some, however, were not. Apparently many people thought that men should not be sent out of the country without their permission, and a petition to this effect was circulated and signed. This meeting aroused the wrath of conservative elements throughout the state. The Governor stepped in and had the Mayor ousted. This was approved by the *Minneapolis Journal* which remarked on August 23, 1917, "He [the Mayor] knew that no minority in New Ulm or anywhere else in the Union had the right to question the decisions of Congress." Previously, on August 14, the editor had commented, "In some way seditious utterances in this nation will have to be suppressed." The Governor of Minnesota heartily agreed. He was quoted by the *Journal* of August 17 as saying:

> If anti-American meetings cannot be stopped by local officials, every resource at our command will be used to punish the offenders and prevent such meetings from being held. If, by means of this action on our part, bloodshed and loss of life will result, the responsibility therefore will rest on those who are back of and support, by their presence, these un-American demonstrators.

On July 31, 1917, a preacher by the name of William Madison Hicks, president of the World Peace League, gave a speech against the draft act in Ellis County, Oklahoma. He was alleged to have said, "The men who are at the head of this war are nothing but a bunch of grafters and robbers. I would not register and I would not answer a call to the colors and I do not believe anyone has to . . . . Boys, what can they do to you for refusing to go?" [28] Indirectly his question was answered the following year when he was tarred and feathered at Elk City, Oklahoma. On October 2, 1918, he was sentenced to twenty years in Leavenworth Penitentiary and fined ten thousand dollars.[29] Later his sentence was reduced to five years.

In this same district a Socialist candidate for Congress, Orville E. Enfield, also got into difficulty. On March 31, 1917, he signed a protest against entering the war. Early in April he wrote an article entitled *Weep Not for Me* in which he stated that the workers' sons would be the ones to die in defense of rich men's profits. On the night of July 29 Enfield attended a meeting in which the subject of arming to oppose the draft was said to have been considered. At another meeting on August 5 there was a discussion of burning bridges and cutting telegraph lines to keep the "boys" home. Enfield was sentenced to twenty years in Leavenworth and fined five hundred dollars, although this verdict was subsequently reversed by a higher court.[30]

During August, twenty-four men were arrested in Rains County, Texas, and accused of organizing forcible resistance to the draft. One man was convicted and sentenced to three years in Atlanta. Another supposed conspiracy was uncovered in West Texas among members of the Farmers' and Laborers' Protective Association, an organization formed to support co-operative marketing and to oppose war. At some meetings of this group there was talk of buying rifles and opposing the draft. Fifty-five people eventually went on trial in this case and three were convicted.[31]

The activities of the opponents of conscription were intensified during August when men began to be called. The *New York Herald,* August 1, 1917, reported that in New York City ninety out of the first hundred draftees claimed exemption. In Minnesota, the *Minneapolis Journal* of August 6 and 7 carried headlines as follows: "Draft Opposition Fast Spreading In State"; "Conscripts Give False Addresses"; "U. S. To Publish Names To Check Exemption Claims." The *Journal* had stated on August 1, "Registrants for the draft army who fail to respond to the summons of the exemption boards will be apprehended and punished as deserters from the army if they do not appear within ten days." On August 7 the *Journal* noted that there was "no diminishing in the percentage of drafted men claiming exemption" and that there was increasing "evidence of bitterness against the draft process creeping out." According to the *Journal* the attitude of some drafted men shocked members of the draft boards.

Two Negro farm hands in Florida mutilated themselves to avoid being called. Taking a shotgun and heading into the woods, one of the men blew off four fingers on one hand while the other shot off his arm below the elbow.[32] In some areas men committed crimes in order to be jailed so that they would not have to report for military service. A New York judge said, "I am of the opinion that many of them have made themselves felons to avoid the draft." [33]

One of the best known and most vigorous fighters against conscription, especially its constitutionality, was the former Populist, Tom Watson of Georgia. He appealed for contributions to contest the Selective Service Act in the courts and reportedly collected $100,000. He also scheduled a huge antidraft convention to be held at Macon to consider "the recent unconstitutional and revolutionary acts of Congress." Local authorities declared that the meeting would not be allowed. Violence was threatened. Because of this attitude Watson called off the meeting and said, "The world must be made safe for democracy, even though none is left in these United States." [34] Senator Thomas W. Hardwick of Georgia later declared that in his state "there was undoubtedly general and widespread opposition on the part of many thousands of . . . people to the enactment of the draft law. Numerous and largely attended mass meetings held in every part of the State protested against it, and in many instances challenged its constitutionality." [35]

By early August reports from several sections of the country were reaching Washington, telling of resistance to the draft law. The most colorful attempt to oppose conscription by force, however, occurred in Oklahoma in what is known as the Green Corn Rebellion.[36] Among some of the state's poor tenants and sharecroppers there was much ignorance, religious superstition, and discontent. Slaves of misery, their economic condition was essentially devoid of hope. They knew nothing about the war in Europe and had no desire to give their lives to perpetuate the conditions in which they lived. Previous to 1917 many of them had joined the radical movements known as the Working Class Union and the "Jones Family." The first of these organizations was connected indirectly with the Industrial Workers of the World.

Late in July, 1917, there were reports of disturbances in various Oklahoma localities. Several arrests occurred. The danger of radical action by debt-ridden sharecroppers in the east-south-central part of the state particularly aroused bankers and businessmen at Wewoka. On August 2 the sheriff of Seminole County set out to investigate the area south of Seminole. He and his deputy were surprised by a party of Negroes, and the deputy was shot. Excitement increased as rumors circulated that about three hundred men were going to resist the draft by force.

Meanwhile, the Working Class Union held a mass meeting on a sandbar in the South Canadian River bed. The plans included destroying a railroad bridge and cutting telegraph wires in order to block military enlistments. The principal objective, however, was to organize members of the W.C.U. for a march on Washington in an attempt to force the Government to stop the war. They hoped to be joined en route by thousands of other draft objectors throughout the country. The name Green Corn Rebellion was derived from the fact that the marchers intended to eat green corn and an occasional barbecued steer on their way to Washington.

On the morning of August 3, members of the W.C.U. were scheduled to gather at "old man" Spears' farm. To meet this threat posses were assembled throughout the area, and on that Friday morning they moved against Spears' Bluff. When the forces of law and order appeared, the misguided tenant farmers fled. Throughout the week end, members of the Working Class Union, the "Jones Family," and other agrarian radical organizations were rounded up and placed under arrest.

By August 16 approximately 450 individuals accused of participating in this Green Corn Rebellion were held in the state penitentiary at Mc-Alester, Oklahoma. Even there the rebels were threatened by highly patriotic convicts. This hostility may have been partly encouraged by the attitude of the local newspapers. Luther Harrison, editor of the *Wewoka Capital-Democrat,* advocated, on August 9, the scaffold or life imprisonment for everyone involved in the draft resistance. Federal officials seemed to be of the same mind and deliberately set bail at prohibitive figures. Poverty-stricken sharecroppers, who had probably never seen a hundred dollars at one time, found their bail set at from five hundred to ten thousand dollars. It was announced that the captives would be charged with treason and that the death penalty would be asked.

Many of the people originally arrested were released, but the leaders of the revolt were given from three to ten years in the penitentiary. Minor offenders received terms of sixty days to two years. The trials were characterized by bitterness and intolerance. No Socialists were permitted to serve on the jury, and the presiding judges seemed over-severe when one considers the nature of the "crimes."

These sharecroppers had never known anything but poverty and want. Their economic complaints were great and they did not understand the war. When they saw the comfortable commercial classes in their districts become leaders of the patriotic movements, they came to hate patriotism. If those whom they regarded as their oppressors were in favor of it, it must be wrong. But the success of local authorities in crushing the Green Corn Rebellion not only helped to enforce the draft law; it went a long way to defeat the radical elements in the state.

The instances in which men and women were convicted and sentenced for opposing the draft could be multiplied at will. Enough has been related, however, to show that a strong minority bitterly resented the war and conscription. It is clear also that the action of the courts in dealing with anticonscription cases went beyond what was needed to enforce the law and thereby endangered freedom of speech and press. Local magistrates, judges, and juries, supported by super-patriots of the community, were often the most intolerant, the most harsh, and least likely to be concerned about the preservation of fundamental rights. In some cases the defendants were finally vindicated by higher courts, but the chance of getting into legal trouble if one spoke out against the draft, coupled with a hostile public opinion, deterred most of those who opposed conscription. Many people who might have signed antiwar or antidraft petitions, or who might have publicly opposed the Selective Service Act, probably did not do so because of the risk of being jailed or having to undergo an expensive lawsuit.

The Attorney General declared in 1918 that early in the war there had been "systematic disloyal propaganda" aimed especially at the "adoption and operation of the Selective Service Act." But, he said, that "propaganda was almost immediately suppressed and destroyed." [37] A look at the history of the period largely confirms this contemporary opinion. In September, 1917, Senator Thomas Hardwick of Georgia, who bitterly opposed the draft law, declared that he was saddened by the "spirit of intolerance, the spirit of suppression, the spirit of oppression, if you please, that seems to me to lurk in these times." [38] But for those who opposed the war, the worst was yet to come.

Chapter v

THE WAR ON SOCIALISTS
AND I.W.W.'S
April–July, 1917

The struggle over the principle of freedom of thought and action during World War I inevitably raised fundamental questions regarding the American economic system. Many people who opposed the war, such as the Socialists, either openly condemned the prevailing capitalistic economy or held serious doubts about its soundness and desirability. Probably at no time in American history up to that time did the capitalistic system come under so much attack as during the second decade of the twentieth century. Some people opposed the war because they believed it was a capitalistic plot.

Yet the economic system known as capitalism was probably the most workable arrangement yet devised for man. His freedom to carry on economic activities allowed him to make the most of his own decisions, to go his own way, and to achieve whatever he personally was able to achieve. Within the rules, the strong desire for personal ownership was unfettered. No co-operative scheme could so completely satisfy human aspirations as did this crude, somewhat anarchistic system. Under it were produced the culture, the advances, the comforts of Western civilization. It was indeed modern civilization itself.

But it was inevitable that so much freedom and power in economic matters resulted in abuses. These, in turn, caused the appearance of reformers—liberal and radical—demanding changes in the system. These critics, during the early twentieth century in particular, became especially disturbed because among the injustices arising out of capitalism were many which were by-products of capitalistic influences in government.

From one end of the country to the other, previous to April, 1917, reformers denounced government for the benefit of the wealthy. They demanded that the activities of the "trusts," of "big business," of "malefactors of great wealth" be curtailed. From William Jennings Bryan to Big Bill Haywood, that is, from the mildest to the wildest, reformers condemned the subjection of government to the interests of the upper economic and propertied classes.

For some fifty years the reformers had waged war on "capitalists," on "big business." There had been the Greenback movement, the Grange, the Farmers' Alliances, the Populists, the Free Silverites, Theodore Roosevelt and the Progressives, and Woodrow Wilson and the New Freedom. Neither reformers nor radicals would be silenced.

The war between the left and the right had resulted periodically in bloodshed. There were the strikes at Cripple Creek, Colorado, and at Lawrence, Massachusetts; the dynamiting of a former governor of Idaho and of the Los Angeles Times building; the wild struggles of the I.W.W. to gain the right of free speech at San Diego and Seattle; and the preparedness day explosion and the Mooney case at San Francisco. All these left anger and bitterness in their wake.

While condemning these outbreaks the moderate person must remember that extremists of the left and of the right make valuable contributions to society. Radicals are usually a compound of utter insanity and remarkably clear thinking. They distort their causes beyond all reason. Nevertheless the noise they make inevitably attracts attention to that which is right in their program. The radicals of the left play the part of shock troops, or to use another figure, pioneers in the wilderness of social welfare. Their presence out in front makes it possible for reformers with moderate solutions to gain a hearing. The radicals take the abuse, and, in so doing, they protect the more temperate liberals. The radicals of the right—the reactionaries—shriek at the dangers in programs propounded by the left. Their attacks slow down the liberals and prevent them from introducing cures which are worse than the ills being attacked. If extremists of the left or of the right gain power, they are apt to wreak havoc. And yet, if either group is suppressed, the other tends to get power. Few things are more important for a democratic society than the defeat—and the protection—of such people.

The conflict between reformers and conservatives which had been going on for at least a half-century gained new life with the outbreak of hostilities in Europe. To a large extent the reformers remained "isolationists" and the capitalists became "interventionists." Even the head of the Administration's propaganda program could say, "Before we got into [the war] . . . our entrance had its chief impulsion from our most reactionary and least democratic elements. Consequently, nearly all our most progressive and liberal leaders had marked themselves as opposed to it." [1] Or, to quote Socialist Victor Berger, "If democracy were the object of the war, it would have a different set of enthusiasts." [2]

Whether accidentally or as a result of cold calculation, it is a fact that almost immediately after the beginning of World War I people of the political right used the war as an excuse to attack people of the left. They did so by accusing leftists of being disloyal. Inherent in their thinking was the idea that radicals should abandon their warfare against businessmen and the capitalist system and co-operate with them instead. In every community businessmen were among the leading "patriots." They were often in charge of the Red Cross, the Y.M.C.A., state Councils of Defense, war charities in general, and draft boards. But to Socialists, I.W.W.'s, Anarchists, and other leftists, businessmen and capitalists were still authentic villains. Their fight was a sacred cause which gave meaning to their lives. To stay with it many radicals had sacrificed money, jobs, respectability, and sometimes even their lives. They brought a burning faith and complete devotion to their cause which an international war could not change. And they quite naturally opposed a conflict which had such fervent support from their traditional enemies. Because the leftists would not change their views, the rightists were given an unparalleled opportunity to attack and crush them. The situation was ideal—for conservatives.

The mob actions and legal moves already mentioned in the fight against declaring war and conscription were often directed against leftists because it was these who most openly opposed the war. Kramer, Berkman, and Goldman, for instance, were all radicals of the extreme left. As previously indicated, some Socialists came to support the war, but generally members of the party refused to do so willingly.

On Sunday, July 1, 1917, members of several radical organizations in Boston staged a parade protesting against the war. They carried flags and banners with such inscriptions as these: Democratize Germany? A Six-Hour Day in Socialist Russia, Why Not Here? Is This a Popular War, Why Conscription? Who Stole Panama? Who Crushed Haiti? Liberty Bonds Are First Mortgages on Labor. We Demand Peace! The

New York Call of July 2 reported that there were about 8,000 paraders including "4,000 members of the Central Labor Union, 2,000 members of the Lettish Socialist organizations, 1,500 Lithuanians, Jewish members of cloak trades, and other branches of the party."

As the paraders formed lines they were attacked by soldiers and sailors. There were indications that the attack was not spontaneous, that it had been carefully planned. The *Boston Evening Record* of July 2 stated that the "enlisted men attacked in regular formation when an officer had given a command. After the attack was over a non-commissioned officer addressed the men from an automobile. He congratulated them on the thoroughness of their work, and advised them to disperse without further disturbance."

The Socialist *New York Call* described the affair on the following day in these words:

> Hundreds of Socialists were beaten and forced to kiss the flag on their knees. The headquarters of the Socialists was raided and wrecked. Furniture and pamphlets were thrown into the street and burned. Red flags were taken from paraders and torn to bits . . . . For three hours the rioting raged on the Common and in and about the Square, near the offices of the Socialist Party of Massachusetts. The crowd engaged numbered around 10,000. Police were powerless or passive, seeming to sympathize with the enlisted men and the hundreds of rowdy volunteers who assisted them.

The *Boston Journal* dared to criticize. On July 2 it referred to the attack as "a deep disgrace to Boston and a sorry stain to the American uniform . . . . And this in Boston, U. S. A.,—and in a year when the nation has been urged to give its blood to 'make the world safe for democracy!' . . . Incidentally, no single misfortune in all the country in these troublous times has done as much as this will do to harden the hearts of the already numerous skeptics against our war for democracy." Victor Berger claimed in the *Milwaukee Leader*, July 9, 1917, that a Boston banker identified with the preparedness and interventionist movements had inspired this particular mob action. In any event, ten of those attacked were arraigned in the Boston municipal court. The *Boston Evening Record* of July 2 reported that "five were charged with assault and battery and five with 'participating in an affray in Tremont Street near Boston Common.'"

Another early Socialist case involved Frederick Krafft. Krafft's parents were "forty-eighters," antimilitarist and antiautocratic Germans who fled to this country after the abortive revolutions of 1848. Krafft joined the Socialist party and eventually became a candidate for governor in New Jersey on the Socialist ticket. Early in August, 1917, he was speaking on a street corner in Newark. He was reported to have said, "I can't see how the Government can compel troops to go to France. If it was up to me, I'd tell them to go to hell. It's a damn shame. I can't see why the Socialists here have not the same rights as in Germany." [3] He was also supposed to have said that Thomas Paine was a much greater man than George Washington. At this point some soldiers in the crowd began to cause a disturbance. Krafft appealed to the police, but instead of receiving protection he was arrested and charged with having wilfully attempted to cause insubordination and disloyalty in the armed forces. He was sentenced to five years at Atlanta and fined one thousand dollars. [4]

Even before the *Krafft* case, Post Office officials had started their attacks upon Socialist newspapers which had opposed American entry into the war and had attacked conscription and other governmental policies. When the *American Socialist* was barred from the mails, its editor, J. Louis Engdahl, was reported by the *Milwaukee Leader*, July 2, 1917, to have said, "This looks like the beginning of a campaign of terror to wipe out every Socialist and every radical publication in the country." He was about right. Almost immediately some sixty Socialist newspapers were deprived of their second-class mailing rights, which virtually amounted to suppressing them.

Among those who disapproved the action of the Post Office Department was Clarence S. Darrow. In reply to his letter of protest, President Wilson wrote on August 9 that he would "try to work out with the Postmaster General some course with regard to the circulation of the Socialistic papers that will be in conformity with law and good sense." [5] However, this was not done.

One of the most important Socialist publications was the *Milwaukee Leader*. In September, 1917, it lost its mailing privilege and consequently many of its fifteen thousand subscribers. President Wilson wrote to Burleson expressing grave doubts about the justice of suppressing the *Milwaukee Leader*. He declared, "I am afraid you will be shocked, but I must say that I do not find this hearing very convincing. Some of the things quoted probably cross the line and I have very little doubt that they were all intended to have sinister results, but I must frankly say that I do not think that most of what is quoted ought to be regarded as unmailable." Wilson said there was "a wide margin of judgment here and I think that doubt ought always to be resolved in favor of the utmost freedom of speech. It does not appear from the hearing what was done. Was the paper . . . given another chance?" [6] It was not. The court ruled that the Postmaster General had been justified in his action because the paper had violated the Espionage Act by interfering with the success of United States military forces.[7]

Restrictive actions by the Post Office Department were not confined to newspapers. Editor Victor Berger, a former member of the House of Representatives, stated later that the *Leader* and its editors were not permitted to receive business letters through the mails, or even the *New York Times* or the *Chicago Tribune*.[8] Rulings and actions by the Postmaster General had caused the Socialist *New York Call* to write on August 14: "No Pope during the Inquisition, no absolute monarch at any stage of the world's history, ever displayed more high-handed tyranny in his actions toward a subject than the mediocre monarch now mismanaging the post office displays in mistreating the mail of a citizen . . . . To denounce him is to dignify him. In very truth he is beneath contempt." Burleson, however, had the last word. On November 13, 1917, he deprived the *Call* of its mailing privilege.[9]

Socialist meetings protesting against the war were called in many parts of the country, but these gatherings were frequently broken up by the "patriots." In Michigan, according to one writer, the American Protective League "put all of these meetings out of business. . . ." [10] Since Minnesota Socialists were particularly outspoken against the war, they were given especially rough treatment. For instance, a Socialist meeting in Brunswick, Minnesota, was dispersed by a mob. One young woman was accused of tearing off an American flag which had been pinned on her by a "loyalist." [11] In Minneapolis eight Socialists were arrested and put in jail for making antiwar statements. Then while still in jail they were inducted into service. Apparently they were political conscientious objectors. Upon their continued refusal to do military service, seven were sentenced to twenty-five years and the eighth, A. S. Broms, to twenty years in the penitentiary. Broms and W. H. Tressler were native Americans. The others were born in Sweden.[12]

The radical group which came in for the most prolonged attack in these months was the Industrial Workers of the World—the I.W.W. This industrial union represented the extreme left in the country's labor organizations. Since they favored direct action, it was said that members burned threshing machines, put spikes in logs in lumber mills, threw migrant workers off moving trains when they would not join the organization, used the slow-down and any other sabotage tactics that would advance their cause. Wherever there was a bitter labor struggle the I.W.W. tried to participate, showing fellow workers that they were willing to meet violence with violence. Without question they were tough and lawless in any tough and lawless situation. The boom brought on by the war starting in 1914 gave them new opportunities. They fought for higher wages in mills, mines, and fields to meet higher living costs. Sometimes enraged employers had to give in. The success of the I.W.W. in the free speech fights in California and in the state of Washington, and the moderate success in the Lawrence strike had brought the organization some popularity among the workers. By early 1917 there were about 60,000 paid up members, although some 300,000 membership cards had been issued since the organization was founded in 1905.[13]

As an organization the I.W.W. constituted a serious threat to businessmen. The violent talk of class warfare and overthrow of the capitalistic system frightened conservative groups. The organization of unskilled workers, migrant workers—the poor, the underprivileged, the uneducated, the people without a stake in society—posed a threat to all the contented people who owned—and ran—the world. The philosophy of the union was expressed in the preamble of the I.W.W. constitution which came to be quoted in court cases, newspapers, and elsewhere by those who feared the organization and wanted to prosecute it. In part the preamble stated:

> The working class and the employing class have nothing in common. There can be no peace so long as hunger and want are found among millions of working people and the few, who make up the employing class, have all the good things of life. Between these two classes a struggle must go on until the workers of the world organize as a class, take possession of the earth and machinery of production, and abolish the wage system.[14]

As might be expected, I.W.W. leadership was bad. The bitterness, the beatings, the jailings, the long life of failure which had gone before made these men recalcitrant and combative. They were mostly uneducated and had little conception of the political needs of their positions. Their talk and writings were threatening and abusive. They expounded the economic bigotry of the class struggle and employers' uselessness. They advocated the abolition of the wage system and the taking over of factories by the workers. They talked of the general strike and of "revolution." Finally, they put their own war against employers above the common national campaign. Thus they gave their enemies the chance to say that they were not patriotic. In this connection it must be stated that it was not really hatred of war that motivated members of the I.W.W. They simply had no interest in this particular war. They preferred to devote all their effort to the private war being carried on against employers. Class warfare came first.

One I.W.W. gave the following classic answer to Carleton Parker when Parker queried him about the I.W.W. attitude toward the war:

> You ask me why the I.W.W. is not patriotic to the United States. If you were a bum without a blanket; if you had left your wife and kids when you went west for a job, and had never located them since; if your job had never kept you long enough in a place to qualify you to vote; if you slept in a lousy, sour bunkhouse, and ate food just as rotten as they could give you and get by with it; if deputy sheriffs shot your cooking cans full of holes and spilled your grub on the ground; if your wages were lowered on you when the bosses thought they had you down; if there was one law for Ford, Suhr and Mooney, and another for Harry Thaw; if every person who represented law and order and the nation beat you up, railroaded you to jail, and the good Christian people cheered and told them to go to it, how in hell do you expect a man to be patriotic? This war is a business man's war and we don't see why we should go out and get shot in order to save the lovely state of affairs that we now enjoy.[15]

Not only did the I.W.W. hate the war, but it also came to oppose the Government bitterly because of what was considered an alliance between the Government and the capitalist class. The rumor that the federal Government was in a conspiracy with employers' associations to destroy labor unions under cover of war in Europe accorded with the beliefs of most I.W.W. members. Lincoln Steffens wrote that "labor thinks . . . this is a class war . . . and I heard groups of workers and one group of businessmen declaring that the Administration was in the 'plot' to 'fix' organized labor now for good and all." [16] Business leaders retaliated fiercely.

The war created boom conditions in many industries. Profits jumped as the prices of lumber, minerals, and manufactured goods rose rapidly. But wages went up more slowly and then sometimes only under the pressure of strikes. Eventually organized labor was to get higher wages—eventually, but not immediately. Meanwhile the I.W.W. and some other labor groups hoped to capitalize on the needs of war. Why should war profiteers get all the gain, they asked. Thus workers began to exert pressure on employers for higher wages, better working conditions, and improved labor relations machinery.

But now in wartime the bellicose, revolutionary remarks of the wrathy I.W.W. leaders and their open advocacy of physical force in strikes were viewed as a grave threat to the nation. Conservative, anti-labor forces not only used the traditional tactics in fighting unions, but added the charge that striking workers were unpatriotic. It was often said that the insistence upon higher wages by the I.W.W. was only a pretext to cover up the organization's real program which was the destruction of capitalism and the wage system. Secretary of Labor Wilson wrote on this point:

> One of the annoying features of the situation [labor trouble in Arizona], and one that I know would lead to a great deal of friction among the workmen if it became generally known, is that whenever any disposition is shown by the workers to demand an increase of wages commensurate with the increased cost of living, the employers immediately assume that the action is inspired by traitors or spies and is therefore treasonable.[17]

Representative Albert Johnson of Washington warned his colleagues that the I.W.W. preached treason and bred sedition.[18] Senator Henry L. Myers of Montana claimed that the organization had "made many well-meaning and honest workmen dissatisfied with their condition." [19] Newspapers, especially in the western states where the I.W.W. was strongest, tended to blame most labor disputes on that organization and pictured it as extremely dangerous to the war effort and to the country's security. Before long hysteria dominated most thinking about the group.

As mentioned earlier, immediately after the American declaration of war, several states passed criminal syndicalism laws which were aimed directly at the I.W.W. Passage of such laws was generally supported most vigorously by the business interests and industrialists who had had trouble, or who were anticipating it, with the I.W.W.[20] On April 23 the *Sacramento Bee* ran the headline, "Anti-I.W.W. Bill Goes to Senate." Ten days earlier Minnesota passed a criminal syndicalism law. But law or no law, local citizens saw to it that I.W.W. meetings were suppressed or controlled.[21] The *Minneapolis Journal,* April 26, 1917, reported that saloons "in that portion of down town Minneapolis infested by I.W.W. sowers of sedition" were closed. On June 24, the *Journal* reported that in Duluth people carrying I.W.W. cards were arrested on vagrancy charges.

There was militant opposition to the I.W.W. all over the West, but the best known and most vigorous direct attacks on the organization occurred in Arizona in July, 1917, and in Montana the following month. For some time there had been labor trouble in Arizona. As early as 1906 the I.W.W. had tried to organize the miners. In January, 1917, they organized a local of the Metal Mine Workers Industrial Union No. 800 at Phoenix, and dissatisfied miners joined rapidly. There was a strong demand throughout the area for better working conditions and higher wages, not only by the I.W.W., but by other labor groups. According to Delaney and Rice in *The Bloodstained Trail,* "the mines are veritable hell's in the bowels of the earth and above ground the conditions surrounding the existence of the miners is not one whit better." [22] The copper companies apparently had gunmen in their employ to keep down agitation and also had the support of some of the local police forces.

In March, 1917, the I.W.W. workers arranged a dance in Miami, Arizona, to raise funds for striking miners and their families. The police broke up the party. In the trial of I.W.W. members in Chicago the Miami chief of police was asked:

Q.—Did you have a warrant to raid the hall?
A.—No.
Q.—Was there trouble at the hall that caused you to make the raid?
A.—No, but I knew that money would be collected for the I.W.W. who are known to be enemies of the United States Government.

The witness testified that he was a member of the Loyalty League, whose members comprised the conservative element including businessmen and even some ministers.[23]

On June 26, 1917, a strike was called in the copper district. The questions of hours and wages were involved. Support was widespread, and it looked as if the miners might win their demands. To the mine owners and their supporters it seemed like time for action. The New York *Evening Post,* July 3, 1917, reported that a conservative union leader had accused the I.W.W. of plotting to close the copper mines, which would severely handicap the war effort. There were charges that the strikers had German financial backing. Now the conservative, antilabor press had a field day. On July 7 a front-page Los Angeles *Times* headline read, "Globe [Arizona] Citizens Demand Stockade for I.W.W." The next day its headlines were "I.W.W. Plot to Ruin Oregon Industries is Charged" and "Beware of Anarchists, Warning of Governor." On July 9 the *Times* carried a news story of cavalry being used to prevent the striking miners in Arizona from holding a meeting. The headline was "Troops Rout I.W.W.'s: Arizona Strike Fiasco." The *Sacramento Bee* followed somewhat the same line. On July 6 it ran a story under the headline, "I.W.W. to Burn Crops in South Dakota." Other papers carried vague stories of this nature based on no evidence, but certain to create hysteria and cause animosity toward the I.W.W. On July 7 a *Sacramento Bee* headline read, "I.W.W. Leaders in Arizona Are to be Arrested."

The situation in Arizona seemed ideal for those who wanted not only to crush the strike, but also to discredit and eliminate I.W.W. troublemakers. The I.W.W., it was said, was thwarting the war effort by closing down the copper mines. This was sabotage—sabotage financed by German money. The enemies of the I.W.W. decided that legal processes were too slow and ineffective. Could they not use the tactics of direct action and then justify the proceedings in the name of patriotism? On July 10, citizens armed with guns and clubs rounded up some 67 strikers in the town of Jerome, herded them into cattle cars, and sent them across the border into California. According to the *Sacramento Bee,* July 11, 1917, there "a force of [California] citizens armed with sawed-off shotguns . . . replaced the ten armed guards who accompanied the men from Jerome." The strikers were held in jail for three weeks and then shipped back into Arizona. No action was ever taken against the individuals or officials responsible.

The success of the Jerome deportation may have encouraged the antilabor leaders in Bisbee, Arizona, to carry out a similar maneuver. Although the strike there had been going on for over two weeks, Bisbee was perfectly quiet. The hysterical attitude of the press was in strange contrast to the calmness at the mines. On the evening of July 11 a meeting of the local Citizens Protective League was called. Prominent among those in attendance were officials of the Copper Queen and Consolidated Mining Company [Phelps-Dodge Corporation] and of the Calumet and Arizona Mining Company. Plans were made to round up and deport the strikers and their sympathizers. Those who engineered the deportation justified their projected extralegal action on the basis that "violence was *contemplated* by the strikers and sympathizers with the strikers." [24] The charge that radicals were "contemplating violence" appeared many times in the moves against them by conservative forces.

At 6:30 A.M. the next morning, the vigilantes struck under the leadership of Sheriff Harry E. Wheeler of Cochise County. The watchword of the vigilantes was "Until every I.W.W. is run out." A *New York Times* report of July 13 declared that five bands of armed citizens suddenly appeared from alleys, storerooms, and business buildings. At gun point men were dragged from their homes or taken off the streets as the vigilantes swept through the workers' district. Not only were I.W.W.'s captured and held, but also sympathizers and people who could not satisfactorily explain their presence in Bisbee. Among those rounded up was William B. Cleary, a prominent attorney, who had been heard to express sympathy with the I.W.W. During the fracas two men were killed, a member of the Citizens Protective League and James Brew, a striker.

Before long 1,186 workers had been collected and were held at a baseball park. They were then herded into cattle and freight cars, and the train was started toward Columbus, New Mexico. Many of the men were without food or water. However, the citizens of Columbus would not permit the train to discharge its human cargo, so the men were unloaded at the little desert station of Hermanas, New Mexico. Here they were abandoned by their guards and left to shift for themselves. Shortly, the army came to the aid of the deportees and temporarily provided them with food and other necessities. [25]

When news of this disgraceful and extralegal event reached Washington, Joseph Tumulty suggested that President Wilson issue a statement saying that he looked with grave apprehension on such illegal actions. [26] Incensed at the obvious violation of justice, Wilson did wire Governor Campbell of Arizona, warning against the danger of people taking the law into their own hands. [27] He also appointed a mediation commission to investigate the labor situation in Arizona. Later Wilson remarked privately that the affair was "very discreditable" and "grossly illegal." However, the President's actions did not satisfy many labor groups. The Arizona State Federation of Labor wired to Washington asking if the President intended to "act in restoring law and order in Cochise County, Arizona, and return to their homes the deported men of Bisbee. Are we to assume that Phelps Dodge interests are superior to the principles of democracy?" Wilson told Samuel Gompers that he considered the letter an "unjust and offensive" intimation. [28]

Criminal suit was instituted against the leader of the mob, but to no avail. The defendant was acquitted. In commenting on the situation later, the *Seattle Union-Record* remarked, "This little item will be additional evidence that there is one law for the rich and another for the poor in America." [29]

An attempt had been made at Bisbee to prevent news of these actions from going out over the telegraph wires, but this was only temporarily successful.[30] Fred Moore, attorney for the I.W.W. who went to Arizona under express and written authorization from Governor Campbell, was deported by the sheriff and the Loyalty League. According to the *New York Herald,* August 9, 1917, a committee of the Arizona Federation of Labor also attempted to investigate but was turned back. Even in faraway Michigan, the police in Detroit prevented a meeting called to protest the deportation.[31]

The vigilantes remained in control at Bisbee and on July 21, nine days after the deportations, the sheriff rounded up and arrested men for vagrancy unless they had local "clearance" cards permitting them to get work.[32] In Gallup, New Mexico, thirty-two alleged I.W.W.'s were deported, and in Miami, Arizona, something in the nature of a deportation was tried but failed.[33]

About the same time, July 23, G. J. Bourg, branch secretary of the Agricultural Workers Industrial Union, was jailed in Aberdeen, South Dakota. At two o'clock in the morning he was taken from jail, driven to the outskirts of town, and turned over to a mob of businessmen. According to one witness, he was knocked to the ground, held with his face downward, and beaten with heavy clubs.[34]

The traditional American sense of justice and fair play seemed submerged in the passions of war. Anyone who expected widespread and popular condemnation of the illegal proceedings in Arizona or elsewhere was to be disappointed. Western newspapers especially cheered the actions of the vigilantes at Jerome and Bisbee. The Los Angeles *Times,* July 15, 1917, editorialized, "The citizens of Cochise County, Arizona, have written a lesson that the whole of America would do well to copy." The *Sacramento Bee* of July 14 attacked President Wilson for his appointment of a conciliator to adjust matters between the I.W.W. and the citizens in Arizona. The *Bee* called the appointment "very foolish" and said that it was an entirely unjustifiable recognition of that "hellish organization." The *Bee* also stated that the "idiocy, if not the infamy, of it is that President Wilson . . . saw fit to appoint anybody . . . to confer with them." No man with sound sense, the *Bee* argued, appoints a committee "to confer with a mad dog. He shoots the dog." On July 16 this paper scoffed at the Fresno *Republican* for advocating only legal steps against the I.W.W. "When a mad dog attacks a man's child . . . he simply shoots." And the *Sacramento Bee* noted that "when this gang of cutthroats was in Sacramento they were clubbed and hosed out of the community."

From the other side of the continent, the *New York Times* of July 14 chimed in: "It is intolerable that these itinerants of anarchy should infest great regions of the West, stir up internal discord in time of war, reduce the production of copper, shut up lumber camps, stir up strikes, threaten the destruction of crops . . . . The sheriff of Bisbee was on the right track when he instructed his deputies to arrest the I.W.W. men on charges of vagrancy." The editor admitted, however, that "a sheriff who makes his own law is on dangerous and indefensible ground; and in-humanity is worse than the I.W.W." Yet he made no protest. As might be expected, Theodore Roosevelt applauded the direct-action methods of Arizona citizens. He wrote that "no human being in his senses doubts that the men deported from Bisbee were bent on destruction and murder." [35]

It should be said, however, that there were those who stood up against the hysteria and who recognized some of the basic issues in the Arizona copper mining region. One such man was Felix Frankfurter, who served as counsel for President Wilson's Mediation Commission. Frankfurter pointed out that there was "total want of justification on the part of those who participated in the deportations." It was, he said, the long and persistent fight by operators in the area against "social justice" which had caused the strikes. Then Frankfurter added signifi-cantly, "It is easy to disregard economic abuses, to insist on the exercise of autocratic power by raising the false cry of 'disloyalty.' " [36] Robert W. Bruere, a writer who accompanied the President's Mediation Commission part of the time, wrote that surely men would not act as they did at Bisbee unless some dread conspiracy was at hand. But, he said, the more he investigated, the more he was unable to find any "treasonable conspiracy" or any "traces of German gold." His conclusion was that the leaders, the "patriots," had been inspired not by "extraordinary considerations of patriotism" but by "ordinary strike-breaking motives." The mine owners had only operated behind the screen of patriotism in their lawlessness.[37] The President's Mediation Commission concluded that "the deportation was wholly illegal and without authority in law, either State or Federal." [38]

Other than the Bisbee deportations, the most notable attempt to destroy or intimidate the I.W.W. in the summer of 1917 was at Butte, Montana. The background to the violence was the bitter antiunion position of the Anaconda Copper Company and then a fire in one of Butte's principal mines on June 8. About 160 miners were burned to death in the Speculator Mine. It was said that the company had violated the state mining law in building solid concrete bulkheads and not providing a manhole in them. These bulkheads were the cause of the high death toll. One witness testified that he "viewed several of the charred corpses at the morgue in Butte, and that their fingers were worn to the second joint, showing a protruding bone, the result of the men having clawed at the granite doors which were locked." [39] A few days after this disaster the miners began preparing for a strike. On June 12 a general strike of fifteen thousand men in all the Butte mines was called by the United Metal Mine Workers, an independent union. Among other things, they demanded higher wages and better safety standards.[40]

At this point an I.W.W. organizer by the name of Frank Little entered the picture. He was a member of the General Executive Board of the I.W.W. According to Bill Haywood, Little was "an energetic worker, part Cherokee Indian, black-eyed, hot-blooded, and reliable." [41] He was a small, crippled fellow with only one eye, who had had a stormy career as a leader in the I.W.W. Delaney and Rice wrote of Little, "Wherever the workers had been driven beyond the point of endurance this fellow would always show up and had an ever ready and willing hand to offer to the miners. He had been in jails, many of them, had been beaten up and had gone through about as much persecution as it was possible for a human to stand, yet he was always on the job and ready to help." [42] Just before going to Montana early in July he had written to Governor Campbell a bitter letter of protest concerning the Bisbee deportation, which brought a reply telling him to mind his own business.

On July 19 he made a typical I.W.W. speech attacking the capitalist class. He was particularly bitter about the use of troops in putting down strikes. Union men understood only too well what he meant by the phrases, scabs in uniform, Pershing's yellow legs, and Government thugs. But the conservative elements in Butte resented such remarks.[43]

About three o'clock in the morning of August 1, several men in an automobile drove through the darkened streets of Butte until they arrived at Little's boardinghouse near the I.W.W. headquarters. The housekeeper, a Finnish woman, answered their knock and asked who they were. They stated they were officers and wanted Frank Little. Breaking into Little's room, the vigilantes grabbed the crippled I.W.W. and dragged him to the waiting car in the street.[44] Little was eventually tied behind the car and dragged through the streets until his kneecaps were scraped off.[45] Finally arriving at the railroad trestle outside of town, he was hanged. The sign "Others take notice. First and last warning. 3–7–77," the insignia of frontier vigilantes, was left pinned to his clothes. So died Frank Little. When he was buried in a little cemetery on a hill outside of town, more than three thousand miners walked the five miles to attend the service. Bloody Butte seemed an appropriate name.

MONTANA'S SHORT CUT TO LAW AND ORDER. —Cesare in the New York *Evening Post* as reproduced in *Literary Digest*, LV (Aug. 18, 1917), 13.

When the Montana Governor was asked if he contemplated any action in relation to the lynching, he would not express an opinion. The news accounts which came from Butte certainly expressed no sympathy for Little or the strikers.

A. W. Walliser of the Butte *Evening Post* was questioned at the trial of I.W.W. members in Chicago:

Q.—What is the attitude of your paper on the labor issue in Butte? Did it support the strikers during the recent strike?
A.—Oh, no, sir, no.
Q.—Who reported the fire in the Speculator Mine?

A.—There were three or four of us. I was up there.

Q.—Did you report in your paper that there were concrete bulkheads in that mine with no manholes and it trapped the men and were responsible for their deaths, to the number of about two hundred?

A.—No, sir.

Q.—You did not?

A.—No, I did not.

Q.—Were you there when the bodies of those miners were brought out?

A.—I was there part of the time.

Q.—You never colored anything you wrote to fit what you understood to be the policy of the paper?

A.—I might have colored things. I might have toned down things, and I did repeatedly.

. . . .

Q.—Now, you were in Butte on the First of August.

A.—Yes, sir.

Q.—The day Frank Little was hanged?

A.—Yes, sir.

Q.—Do you know who committed the lynching?

A.—No, sir.

. . . .

Q.—Did you ever try to find out who the occupants of that car were [the car in which Little was taken to his death]?

A.—No, sir.

Q.—If I give you the names will you publish them?

A.—No, sir.

Q.—You won't?

A.—No, sir.

Q.—If I give you the name of the boy that drove that car, will you publish it in your paper? . . .

A.—No! [46]

Nor was there a demand to end mob action. One Helena newsman heard "substantial citizens" saying in regard to any projected legal action against those responsible for the Little hanging, "Better start with a coroner's jury and have it reach a verdict of suicide." [47] The *New York*

Times stated on August 4, 1917, that the lynching was "deplorable and detestable," but "the I.W.W. agitators are in effect, and perhaps in fact, agents of Germany. The Federal Authorities should make short work of these treasonable conspirators against the United States." Congressman Johnson of Washington implied in the House of Representatives that Little hardly deserved protection and asked if he did not belong "to an organization which declares that it owes allegiance to no government?" [48]

The *Literary Digest* summed up the opinion of numerous editors throughout the country who, "though deploring the manner of his taking off, inclined to the belief that Little received his just deserts, and that his sudden end may prove a salutary warning." Again, as was true in the Bisbee situation, the strongest support for direct action against the I.W.W. came from the West where the organization was strongest. Many editors in the Midwest, East, and South reacted differently and made a strong plea to respect the processes of law. The Newark *News*, Chicago *Herald*, St. Louis *Globe-Democrat*, Springfield *Republican*, and Macon *Telegraph* were among those protesting against vigilante activities in Butte. The *Globe-Democrat* said that "the lynchers have done a more lasting hurt to society than Little and all his followers."

The editor of the Macon *Telegraph* commented, "We suspect that outraged patriotism had mighty little to do with the lynching of Frank Little out in Butte but we do suspect that certain influences very much opposed to strikes in general and strikes for higher wages in particular might have had a fairly efficient left-handed part in it." [49] The Macon editor came close to the heart of the controversy between local businessmen and their supporters, and the I.W.W. Employers, however, were not only opposed to strikes for higher wages; they were also fighting to maintain the "open shop." By successfully identifying the I.W.W. in the public mind with sabotage, pro-Germanism, radicalism, and disloyalty, the summer campaign against the I.W.W. had gone a long way to weaken and destroy the organization. And there was more to come.

WIDENING

CLASS WARFARE

June–November, 1917

The general absence of public criticism against intolerance probably encouraged American war advocates. At any rate, their demands for repression became more insistent than ever. Under these circumstances, it even became increasingly unpopular to say anything in defense of people being attacked, and moderation was looked upon as unpatriotic.

On August 11, 1917, Senators Myers of Montana, King of Utah, Poindexter of Washington, and Hollis of New Hampshire joined in a senate discussion about the dangers of the I.W.W. Senator King said he had received numerous communications about the "pernicious activities, the crimes, and violence of the Industrial Workers of the World." His colleague Poindexter added that the best way to curb the I.W.W. was to have a force of militia, home guards, or troops in areas where the organization might cause trouble.[1] The *Milwaukee Leader,* August 23, 1917, quoted the extreme attack on the I.W.W. by the Kokomo, Indiana, *Dispatch*: "The time has come when the nation should crush with relentless hand the traitorous organization styling itself the I.W.W. . . . Every man of them is a traitor to the country and ought to be dealt with as such." The Tulsa *Daily World* on August 18 ran a story about the I.W.W. which said, "In Washington the officials are in favor of giving them the limit of the law if the occasion arises, and we suspect that a few hangings or other sudden deaths of agitators will be about the remedy needed to restore peace and loyalty."

Steps to implement these ideas quite naturally followed. In Bingham, Utah, an "admitted" I.W.W. was accused of having cursed the Government and damned the U.S. flag. The Tulsa *Daily World* of August 4, 1917, reported that this man was resting in jail "with a deep bayonet wound in his back, received when he resisted national guardsmen who arrested him." At Franklin, New Jersey, on August 29 an I.W.W. by the name of John Avila was taken in broad daylight by the chief of police and an auto load of businessmen to nearby woods and there hanged to a tree. But, according to Harrison George, "on second thought they cut him down before death came and, unconscious and bleeding, they returned him to town where . . . [he was sentenced] to three months at hard labor." [2]

Now the Administration joined in the attack. For some time there had been demands for the United States Department of Justice to take vigorous action against the I.W.W. For example, the Minnesota Public Safety Commission sent a representative to Washington in July appealing to the Attorney General to curb I.W.W. activity.[3] Big Bill Haywood claimed that Samuel Gompers inspired the move.[4] Regardless of what prompted Administration action, by August government officials had agreed to smash the I.W.W. The Council of National Defense, the Attorney General, the Secretary of Labor, and President Wilson seemed to agree to the plan.[5] The Department of Justice and the Post Office Department worked together on the matter. The American Protective League entered into the attack with enthusiasm. The League's official historian, Emerson Hough, wrote, "With this great case, the American Protective League had been connected practically all the time from the date of its own inception. It had men shadowing the suspects, men intercepting their mail, men ingratiating themselves into their good graces, men watching all their comings and goings . . . ."[6] I.W.W. leaders were fully aware that they were being constantly shadowed, but that did not deter them in their fight.[7]

The Government's attack on the I.W.W. was planned along military lines. On September 5, the day set for the first raid, federal agents swarmed down upon I.W.W. headquarters in thirty-three different cities. They made eight simultaneous raids in Chicago alone. Private homes were also searched, and in at least one case old love letters were confiscated![8] In the weeks that followed, other raids were carried out. Agents of the Department of Justice "continued to raid the general and local headquarters of the I.W.W. both with and without search warrants, in order, they stated, to secure additional evidence."[9] The men and the evidence were all shipped to Chicago in preparation for a great mass trial in that city.

On September 28, 1917, indictments were issued for 166 officers, organizers, and secretaries of the I.W.W. Of these, only 113 were arraigned. The trial was set for the spring of 1918, but before it could begin, the prosecution had to search through five tons of materials which had been taken from the accused. It was a gigantic fishing expedition to find justification for the indictments. There were letters, account books, minute books, and a varied assortment of bulletins, pamphlets, newspapers, and other publications.[10] Most of the material had been written before the passage of the laws which the prisoners were accused of violating.

Meanwhile the press continued its attack on the I.W.W. The *Minneapolis Journal,* September 8, 1917, suggested that the "slow-moving processes of civil justice [are] becoming irksome to the loyal public." On October 1 the *Journal* carried a news story about the I.W.W. with the headline, "I.W.W. Alleged to Have Planned to Pollute Water at Sheridan Post." On the same day the *Sacramento Bee* ran a cartoon showing Uncle Sam gripping the neck of a figure labeled I.W.W. The title of the cartoon was "Throttle Him!" Most of the criticism centered around the ideas that the I.W.W. was lawless, disloyal, pro-German, revolutionary, and that strikes were disloyal because they interfered with the war effort.[11]

The government arrests and the newspaper attacks naturally fomented additional acts of violence against the organization. The offices of the union in Duluth and Los Angeles were raided. An account of the raid on the Los Angeles offices stated that a crowd of soldiers "variously estimated from 200 to 400, wrecked the headquarters of the I.W.W. here late today. Typewriters and furniture were broken, windows smashed and all movables demolished. There were no reported casualties and no arrests."[12] Still other raids followed. In Kansas City the I.W.W. hall "was raided many times and members were first beaten by militiamen and then arrested by police."[13]

Four union organizers in Arkansas, said to be I.W.W.'s, made the mistake of attempting to solicit memberships among Negroes working in the rice fields. They urged the Negroes to demand a five-dollar-a-day minimum wage. The union-hating, race-conscious proprietors quickly resorted to direct action. On Tuesday, September 26, 1917, the union men were arrested and jailed for disturbing the peace. Then, late one night, 150 armed men took the prisoners to a place north of Stuttgart where they were given a severe whipping. "By that time," according to one writer, "the tar had been melted and the hot liquid was liberally applied to the naked bodies of the four men. The coat of feathers came next." The "Wobblies" were then told to leave the county and warned that failure to heed such advice would mean a "necktie party." [14]

The campaign against the I.W.W. in the late summer of 1917 was only one aspect of the conservatives' drive against radicals. Both small and large nonconformist groups were to encounter similar attacks whenever they failed to appear as enthusiastic supporters of the war. The *Minneapolis Journal,* September 29, indicated what was planned when it referred to the arrest of the Chicago I.W.W.'s: "Extermination of antiwar propaganda will be carried into every suspicious organization in the country."

One group that had already gained the enmity and suspicion of conservative classes was the Nonpartisan League. Beginning in North Dakota and spreading into neighboring states, this organization grew out of a decade of hard times in the Northwest and the feeling that state governments in that region were controlled by big business. It is true that the states were in the hands of the traditional parties which were quite acceptable to most business people. Consciously or not, the dominant state politicians did not often irritate bankers, industrialists, newspaper owners, railroad stockholders, or those who owned and managed the milling industry. Farmers, however, had many complaints which were regularly ignored by the local politicians. They paid high interest rates on their mortgages. Railroad and elevator rates were considered unreasonable. Furthermore, farmers believed that elevator operators down-graded their grain, thus cheating them out of several cents on every bushel.

In both 1912 and 1914 the people of North Dakota voted to establish state-owned elevators as a means of solving some of their marketing problems. Despite farm pressure, the lower house of the legislature defeated the measure in February, 1915. A leading opponent of the state elevator was reported to have told farmers to "go home and slop the hogs." This remark may never have been made, but it probably reflected accurately the attitude of North Dakota businessmen toward a state-ownership program, and it made debt-ridden farmers bitterly angry.

In February, 1915, Arthur C. Townley, a bankrupt farmer and former Socialist, began organizing the Nonpartisan League. Within a few months Townley and other organizers had enrolled thousands of farmers in the new organization. By 1916 the Leaguers had a full slate of candidates in state races who campaigned on a platform calling for a state bank, state-owned terminal elevators, flour mills and packing plants, a rural credits system operated at cost, and state hail insurance on farm crops. The crude attacks on "Big Biz" seemed partially Populist and partially Socialist. In any event, the organization was a political success. To the surprise of some and the distress of others, the League won a sweeping victory in the 1916 elections. In January, 1917, the League set up national headquarters in St. Paul.

Conservative elements were fully aware of what this agrarian revolution meant. They were aghast at the thought of farmers using the state government for their own benefit, instead of its being used for the benefit of businessmen, bankers, and industrialists. Thus, from the beginning of its existence, the League was assailed in a most extreme manner. Nonpartisan Leaguers, especially the leaders, were attacked as being, among other things, revolutionaries, "red Socialists," free lovers, traitors, agitators, anarchists, and atheists.[15]

One of the earliest and most consistent lines of attack was to call the League socialistic. After April of 1917, however, the idea of charging it with disloyalty became popular. Many League members did oppose the war and now conservatives contended that such opposition was seditious or unpatriotic. League organizers had spoken out against American participation, and after the country actually declared war, they and many of their followers had not changed their ideas. When farmers saw the war effort being organized around their traditional enemies—farm produce dealers, bankers, and other businessmen—they wondered if the "patriots" were not for war because it increased their chances for profiteering. It is no wonder that farmers became cynical when, as one writer put it, "a grain buyer suspected of using a short scale, declares that this is a war for universal participation in the world's good things." [16] Yet farmers in North Dakota heavily oversubscribed the liberty loan allotments for their state, despite drouth and crop failure.[17]

Representatives of the League spoke out boldly against the war and against conscription, and, like other opponents of war, they suffered the consequences of their position. On July 3, 1917, H. J. Trelease, a League organizer, made a speech at Strawberry Lake, North Dakota, in which he was reported to have said that "the war with Germany was a rich man's war; that they were sending your boy and mine to fight to protect the moneyed interests and Wall Street; that the Draft Act was an injustice, unconstitutional, and wrong; . . . that, if the United States had loaned money to Germany, we would be fighting on their side . . . ." He was quoted as having told one young man who had enlisted in the navy that "you are a damn fool to enlist in the navy to fight in the interest of the rich." Trelease was sentenced under the Espionage Act to two years in Leavenworth Penitentiary for making these remarks.[18]

Trelease expressed sentiments similar to those of other Nonpartisan League members, and, under the circumstances, provided fuel for the conservative forces which hoped to destroy the organization. Earlier, on June 9, 1917, the *Minneapolis Journal* stated, "Governor Theodore Wold of the Minneapolis Federal Reserve Bank said officially . . . that the bank had received what appeared to be substantial evidence that the Nonpartisan League is working to defeat the success of the Liberty Loan campaign in the northwest." [19] Actually, there was no truth in this propaganda and League members bought generously of that bond issue.

On the evening of August 18, 1917, a local meeting of the Nonpartisan League was held in Kenyon, Minnesota. One of the speakers was Joseph Gilbert. His comments were in many ways similar to those of Trelease. According to testimony given at his trial in 1918, he was accused of having said:

> We are going over to Europe to make the world safe for democracy, but I tell you we had better make America safe for democracy first. You say, what is the matter with our democracy? I tell you what is the matter with it: have you had anything to say as to who should be President? Have you had anything to say as to who should be Governor of this state? Have you had anything to say as to whether we should go into this war? You know you have not. If this is such a great democracy, for Heaven's sake why should we not vote on conscription of men. We were stampeded into this war by newspaper rot to pull England's chestnuts out of the fire for her. I tell you, if they conscripted wealth like they have conscripted men, this war would not last over 48 hours.[20]

Gilbert was fined five hundred dollars and sentenced to a year in jail. His appeal, as will be seen later, was unsuccessful. Louis W. Martin, who took part in arranging this meeting and who later stated that he considered Gilbert's statements true, was convicted at the same time. The Court said, "We fail to see why a person who heard these statements does not teach the same doctrine when he asserts to another person who heard them that he knows them to be true and accepts and approves them as his standard of patriotism." [21] Martin was later granted a new trial.

As an organization, the League became suspect by super-patriots when Townley and other leaders demanded that the Government take over and operate the main war industries and that all war profiteering be stopped. The League was also among those farm organizations which were bitter at the Administration for setting the minimum—in fact, the maximum—price of wheat at $2.20 a bushel in the early fall of 1917. Townley argued that farmers should receive at least $3.00 for wheat, and he expressed the widely held belief among farmers that it was unfair to regulate the price of wheat while other industries were subject to no such controls. In order to discuss the problems of producers and consumers in the war, the League called a convention to meet in St. Paul September 20.[22] One of the main speakers was to be Senator La Follette.

The invitation to La Follette was questioned by some members of the League because of the Senator's leadership in the fight to keep the country out of the war. They feared that La Follette's presence might add to the unpopular loyalty record which the League was already developing. Members of the war party from one end of the country to the other were violently attacking congressmen who had voted for the Gore-McLemore Resolutions, who had opposed the bill to arm merchant ships, and who had voted against war. La Follette was "wrong" on all these measures, and the conservative "patriots" were viciously attacking him. But worst of all in the eyes of the nationalists was his refusal to recant and go along with the Administration's program. He had opposed conscription, he had fought the Espionage Act, and he had criticized the Administration's tax program as being too favorable to wartime profiteers. On August 11, 1917, he introduced a resolution asking that Congress refuse to aid any belligerent which was prolonging the war in order to annex territory and that the allies restate their peace terms.[23] Two weeks before, on July 28, the *New York Times* had condemned Borah for making the same suggestion. On August 13 the *Times* announced that the "La Follette Move Will Be Squelched." At the end of the month La Follette introduced a bill which attempted to place "the strain of financing the conflict upon big incomes and profits derived from the war." This would have resulted in taxes of 50 per cent upon incomes over a million dollars. The bill was bitterly opposed and defeated.[24] All of this was fresh in people's minds when it was announced that La Follette would appear.

One of the preliminary speeches in the convention was made by former Congressman Charles A. Lindbergh, Sr. A typical Populist attack on the moneyed interests, it aroused thunderous applause. He was followed by a Liberty Bond speaker who gave a conventional prowar talk. The fervently nationalist *Minneapolis Journal* reported on September 20,

1917, "Where five minutes before the audience had yelled hoarsely and stamped their feet in enthusiasm when C. A. Lindbergh said America did not offer equal opportunity to all, they applauded stiffly and spasmodically at the appeal of Judge Torrance." The next day, September 21, Townley presided. Some speakers sharply criticized the press and attacked Big Business. Townley pointed to the press table and, according to the *Minneapolis Journal,* September 21, said, "At this moment is being carried over the wires absolute misrepresentations of what is being said. There are right here some of these prostitutes who lie, lie!" He constantly referred to the "kept press."

When La Follette began to speak, the *Minneapolis Journal* noted that "the crowd, which had come near turning into a disorderly mob when A. C. Townley, president of the Nonpartisan League, denounced the newspapermen present as 'liars' burst into a frenzy of enthusiasm at every La Follette attack on the justice of the war." La Follette apparently forgot his promise to Townley that he would not refer to the war, for he very soon turned to that subject. As he proceeded, the *Journal* commented, "his blood grew hotter and he tossed aside the manuscript uncorking his suppressed antiwar oratory and pacing the floor in a sort of frenzy." The substance of his speech was as follows:

Now, fellow citizens, we are in the midst of a war. For my own part I was not in favor of beginning the war. I don't mean to say that we hadn't suffered grievances; we had at the hands of Germany, serious grievances! We had cause for complaint. They had interfered with the right of American citizens to travel upon the high seas— on ships loaded with munitions for Great Britain. I say this, that the comparatively small privilege of the right of an American citizen to ride on a munition-loaded ship, flying a foreign flag is too small to involve this Government in the loss of millions and millions of lives! Four days before the *Lusitania* sailed President Wilson was warned in person by Secretary of State Bryan that the *Lusitania* had 6,000,000 rounds of ammunition on board, besides explosives; and that the passengers who proposed to sail on that vessel were sailing in violation of a statute of this country; that no passenger shall sail or travel upon a railroad train or upon a vessel which carries dangerous explosives . . . .

In these days of 1917, with the flags all about us commemorating liberty—constitutional liberty—we are inhibited from even discussing this war, from even suggesting that there might be some way with honor and credit to our Government to terminate and stop the awful slaughter and the awful expense. Let me say, in a word, if Abraham Lincoln was a patriot, if Daniel Webster was a patriot, if Clay and Webster and Lincoln and all the men of that time understood the Constitution and the rights of the people, you, the humblest one of you, have the right to discuss freely the question of whether this war might not be terminated with honor to the Government and the awful slaughter discontinued.[25]

The local newspapers and a few others gave the speech in the foregoing form. Over the Associated Press wire, however, a version went out which said, "We had no grievances" instead of "We had at the hands of Germany, serious grievances." [26] State Councils of Defense, G.A.R. posts, Governor Burnquist of Minnesota, and many other organizations and individuals bombarded Washington with demands that La Follette be removed from office. Governor Burnquist said that an investigation was being made to determine just what La Follette had said. If the Senator's statements were found to be disloyal and seditious, the Governor declared that, as head of the Minnesota Public Safety Commission, he would ask for La Follette's arrest.[27]

Even before the St. Paul speech La Follette had been subjected to vicious editorial treatment because of his antiwar stand. The *Providence Daily Journal* had called the Senator "a conscious co-partner of *Kultur*." The Dallas *News* wished to convict him of treason, and the Los Angeles *Times* wanted to expel him from the Senate.[28] But now the editorial blasts became even harsher. The St. Paul *Pioneer Press* thought that Senator La Follette should not be treated differently from "the soap-box orators who are being arrested in so many cities." The *Minneapolis Tribune* said the speech was "more disloyal, more treasonable, than the utterances that have landed lesser pro-Germans in prison and sent them into internment." [29]

Theodore Roosevelt, of course, also wanted La Follette ousted from the Senate. Speaking at a luncheon in Kansas City, the former President said that if he were in the Senate he would be ashamed to keep his seat until some way had been found to remove the Wisconsin Senator. La Follette, Roosevelt said, was "loyally and efficiently serving one country —Germany." [30] The *Minneapolis Journal* of September 28, 1917, told of Nicholas Murray Butler speaking before the American Bankers Association convention. The headline stated, "Bankers Cheer Plea to Oust La Follette." The *New York Times,* October 3, 1917, in an editorial called

"Deserved Punishment" referred to the expulsion move against La Follette and reported that a demand existed to remove other opponents of the war from the Senate, including Stone, Gronna, Hardwick, Reed, and Vardaman. Many people believed that these men were "obstructing essential war legislation." The Wisconsin State Council of Defense drew up resolutions condemning La Follette and sent them to President Wilson, who passed them on to Tumulty with the following remarks: "I doubt if it would be wise for me to return a personal acknowledgement of these resolutions because they so directly reflect upon the character of a Senator of the United States. Do you not think it would be well for me to delegate to you the acknowledgement along with an expression of my warm appreciation of the patriotic feeling and purpose embodied." [31]

The *Free Press* in Milwaukee, although it attacked the St. Paul speech, did maintain that the newspapers had been unjust to La Follette. It said:

> Whatever policy a newspaper may entertain about the war-attitude of Senator La Follette, it owes its readers a truthful account of the meetings he addresses, a true report of the enthusiasm with which he is being received . . . . The general failure of American newspapers to give an honest report of La Follette's speeches, their contrary avidity to distort and suppress the facts, is a most decisive reflection upon their own Americanism, their ethics as well as their patriotism. It completely bears out the claim that a large part of the press can not be depended upon for truthful disinterested statement. [32]

La Follette was not unaccustomed to a critical press. But now the newspaper attacks seemed unusually severe even for him. Part of the cause was the garbled misstatement which had him saying that the United States had no grievances against Germany. Equally important, however, was his discussion of the *Lusitania* incident. The sinking of this ship was fast becoming one of the basic tenets in the war party's "party line." It was coming to represent part of the great moral justification for entrance into the war; to some it was becoming *the* grievance. The impact of the story had grown until it aroused the strongest emotions in people. Many years later it remained a symbol in American thinking, and the general public seemed to accept it as at least a contributing cause for American entrance into the first World War. The fact that the war declaration did not occur until almost two years after the sinking seemed

to be forgotten. In his speech Senator La Follette had made it appear to
be a highly questionable cause for sending an American army overseas.
The *Lusitania* incident, however, had become a "sacred cow" in the
thoughts of the supporters of the war, and La Follette had questioned its
sacredness. This was heresy and the "believers" were enraged; their
hatred of La Follette knew no bounds.

It is unnecessary to recount in detail the events which followed.
They have been described by Fola La Follette in Volume II of *Robert M.
La Follette*. Suffice it to say that as a result of the flood of complaints,
and particularly as a result of a resolution by the Minnesota Public
Safety Commission, the Senate began an investigation of La Follette.
A special committee was formed headed by Senator Pomerene of Ohio,
and various versions of the St. Paul speech were laid before it. Opponents
of the Senator demanded that the committee act promptly, but the members of that body hesitated. They seemed uncertain as to just what should
be done.

However, on September 16 the Senator appeared before the committee, handed Pomerene a letter, and then walked out. The letter, quoted
in the *New York Times*, October 17, 1917, stated:

> You say the committee has challenged the accuracy of no statement
> in the speech. Then I must be entitled to be advised who has chal-
> lenged the accuracy of any statement in the speech before another
> step is taken in this proceeding . . . . Every Senator and every man
> is entitled to have the statements made by him accepted as accurate,
> at least until someone appears and questions their accuracy. To
> deny that right to any man is an insult.

La Follette insisted that he should have a chance to meet his accusers
face to face and, if necessary, to cross-examine them.

La Follette's action, as the *New York Times* said, put the committee
"in a hole." [33] The *Seattle Union-Record* said on November 3, 1917, that
the "Senate committee gets the wrong sow by the ear and casts around
for an easy way out." The committee used the old expedient of delay
and finally did nothing until the war was over. On January 16, 1919, the
Senate voted favorably on a resolution dismissing the charges against
La Follette. Perhaps the real motive behind the fight against him was
found in the statement of one Senator who was reported to have said,
"Damn him anyway he ought to be thrown out of the Senate he is always
against money." [34]

Late in May of 1918 the Associated Press apologized for misquoting La Follette. In this connection the *New York Tribune* editorialized that "whether this was done maliciously or accidentally will probably never be known, but the fact remains that irreparable injury was done to the Senator." [35] Not only had La Follette been injured personally, but his effectiveness as an opponent of war had been reduced by the St. Paul incident. Almost anything he said about the war after that was likely to be discounted, as he was considered irresponsible, unpatriotic, and pro-German.

The La Follette speech had other repercussions, too. Since the St. Paul meeting had been sponsored by the Nonpartisan League, attacks on the League were now stepped up and an increasing number of its leaders were threatened and arrested for disloyalty. There is no doubt that this was eventually damaging to the League and its program. [36] Furthermore, La Follette's speech stimulated the prowar groups to even more vigorous action against the dissidents. For example, after the meeting in St. Paul the Minnesota Public Safety Commission maintained constant surveillance on public gatherings in an effort to ferret out disloyalty and crush the opponents of war. [37] In Georgia a strong protest arose when it was learned that Senator Hardwick had been invited to address a Five County Fair. The Grand Jury of Burke County passed a resolution condemning Hardwick as a man "who by his treasonable utterances and persistent antagonism to the war policy of our Great President" had discredited himself throughout the United States. [38] And so intolerance grew.

^^

"Wartime is no time to quibble about constitutional
rights and guarantees."

THE WAR

ON SOME MINOR GROUPS

August–November, 1917

The cloak of patriotism served as an ideal camouflage for the conservative economic and political interests which sought to crush radical
labor and farmer movements. Although economic motivation was clearly
present in the campaigns against the Socialists, the I.W.W., and the
Nonpartisan League, there were other opponents of war who could
hardly be classified as radicals. Warfare against some of the lesser groups
shows the nationalistic motivation much more clearly.

For instance, all during August of 1917 a group calling itself the
Friends of Irish Freedom sought to gain a hearing in this country, especially around New York and Boston. The loose talk of liberty and
freedom as wartime objectives prompted these individuals to try to exploit the situation for the benefit of Ireland. Their sincerity seems beyond question. But, of course, they sought freedom from England, not
Germany. Opponents of Irish independence, including the nationalists
and Anglophiles in the United States, were thoroughly disturbed by such
activities. These Irish sympathizers even questioned English motives, and
with the acceptance of much English propaganda by the American press
and government, such questioning seemed pro-German.

A man named Walter Austin wrote to President Wilson, complaining about the "false and malicious statements" being made by the Irish
sympathizers in meetings around Boston. He wanted such activities
stopped. Tumulty wrote to Wilson, "I think there is dynamite in this,

and that, if it must be acknowledged it will be sufficient for me to make a simple acknowledgement, stating that the matter will be brought to your attention." To this suggestion Wilson wrote "Okeh." [1]

There were several pro-Irish meetings in New York City. On August 23 the *New York Times* reported a meeting in which La Follette was praised and attacks were made upon vigilantes and the "vocal Volcano of Oyster Bay." The reporter noticed that "every reference to peace brought prolonged cheers." However, the pressure of the nationalists became too strong, and the city government in New York agreed to suppress such meetings. On August 28, the *Times* reported that "the Board of City Magistrates . . . took a forward step in the campaign . . . to prevent the preaching of sedition on street corners . . . . The Magistrates find that the statute defining disorderly conduct is broad enough to cover the preaching of sedition." Carrying out this decision, the police and soldiers raided a meeting on August 29. The *Times* stated on August 30, "In one of the wildest scenes that Broadway ever witnessed the police, assisted by soldiers, last night broke up the largest meeting held by the Friends of Irish Freedom." Police arrested several people for "obstructing traffic" and prevented the howling Irishers from conducting any discussions. According to the *Times*, "the police were pushed about, cursed, and abused." After this the Espionage Act was used, as well as local ordinances, and the pro-Irish activities were stopped. "Free speech, in a reasonable sense, will not be interfered with," editorialized the *Times* on August 25, but the expression of treason, sedition, or incitement to violence could not be tolerated.

The supporters of the war were also disturbed for a time by a loose organization of opponents of the war which went under the name of the People's Council of America for Peace and Democracy. By the fall of 1917 it was the most important organization fighting for a quick peace. The People's Council had been formed by Louis P. Lochner, a pacifist who had been a member of Henry Ford's ill-fated peace expedition of December, 1915. There was about every shade of political opinion among members of this group—except prowar opinion. One of the original leaders was ex-Senator John D. Works of California whom Theodore Roosevelt characterized as being "perfectly unreasonable about peace." [2] David Starr Jordan's name was sometimes connected with the organization, but he had little to do with it. Under the hammer blows of the fervent nationalists, the more conservative elements gradually dropped out and the People's Council fell into the hands of radicals. By September, 1917, Scott Nearing, James M. Maurer, and Morris Hillquit were members of the executive committee. Nearing became chairman of the executive committee and Lochner was executive secretary.

At times the People's Council demanded the repeal of the draft act. At times it worked for the repeal of laws restricting freedom of speech. However, its principal objective late in 1917 was a public statement of peace aims and, if possible, a negotiated peace. It adopted the slogan, "Peace By Negotiation—Now."

Even before the People's Council had been completely organized, meetings had been held to oppose the draft. The antidraft meeting of June 15, 1917, in New York City had been called by this group. A meeting in New York on July 1 was one of the Council's most successful gatherings. In Chicago, on July 8, another well-attended meeting was held. There, a man named Wentworth was quoted as saying, "We are in an unjust war. There is no reason for it. The cry of democracy is a blind." [3] The Reverend Irwin St. John Tucker was quoted by the *New York Herald,* July 8, 1917, as saying, "We must first make it plain to Germany that we believe in democracy before we can claim that we're fighting for it . . . . President Wilson and Congress are guilty of black treason against democracy by concealing the reasons we went to war." At this meeting Wentworth also assailed American newspapers. A few weeks later, on August 13, Senator Works was quoted by the Tulsa *Daily World* as saying that the country's newspapers, as well as the Associated Press, were virtually "under the domination of the capitalist interests and dare not speak [their] sentiments or tell the news truthfully."

Early in August a meeting was held in Washington, where representatives of the People's Council sharply criticized the draft law and overseas expeditions to France. Unless the Selective Service Act was repealed, they said, the current Congress should be turned out.[4] At a meeting held in San Francisco on August 8 Daniel O'Connell was put under arrest. Later in August, meetings in Philadelphia and Wilmington, Delaware, were broken up. At the Wilmington meeting a near riot began after one speaker was reported to have "denounced conscription, President Wilson and a lot of other persons and things. He said the President was suppressing newspapers by keeping them from going through the mails." [5] Upton Sinclair wrote to President Wilson concerning a local gathering in Pasadena, California:

Here in my home city the People's Council, which favors . . . a constitutional petition [to repeal the draft law], have been forbidden to hold meetings *in a private home.* I know this particular group, and can testify that they are sincere and devoted people and true democrats. I think they are mistaken about the war; I think I can answer their arguments, and for this very reason I resent the intrusion of violence into the controversy.[6]

Instead of its receiving the toleration suggested by Sinclair, attacks against the group increased. Some of the hostility toward it came from the fact that it took up a slogan coming from leftist sources in Europe— "No annexations and no indemnities." Radical groups in Russia, the Socialists in Germany, and various groups in other countries were urging this as a basis of peace. Since this principle was advocated by radicals, it became anathema to conservative elements everywhere. Insofar as Western Europe was concerned, it also went contrary to national ambitions. Late in August, 1917, Louis P. Lochner stated that the principles of the People's Council were: "To demand an early peace in harmony with the program of New Russia—no annexations, no punitive indemnities; to induce the United States to state the terms upon which it will end the war; to urge international organization for the prevention of future wars; to work for the repeal of the conscription law; to safeguard labor standards, and to preserve and extend liberty and democracy in America."[7] Some American newspapers, however, adopted the attitude that discussion of peace on any basis except complete defeat of Germany was a pro-German plot. The Council was a "Bolshevik" organization according to some editors.

By the end of August there was growing pressure to silence the People's Council. George Creel, head of the Committee on Public Information, wrote to an individual in Minneapolis that the People's Council is "made up of traitors and fools, and we are fighting it to the death . . . . Have patriotic societies and civic organizations pass resolutions condemning the People's Council as pro-German and disloyal . . . . Get a good committee together to go around and see all the newspapers and see to it that they get the point of view and action that I am giving you now." Then Creel added, "Tear this letter up."[8]

The People's Council had been under attack from many quarters, and when it attempted to hold a national convention, patriotic societies, civic organizations, and newspapers let out a torrent of abuse. The meeting was scheduled for September 1 in Minneapolis. However, Governor Burnquist of Minnesota announced on August 28 that the meeting could not be held there because it would give aid and comfort to enemies of the

United States.[9] Then there was talk of going to Fargo, North Dakota, but the city officials quickly squelched that move. Leaders of the People's Council who were en route west from New York faced a difficult situation. After hurried conferences it was decided to meet in Chicago.

On September 1 the People's Council met as scheduled. Proceedings continued for about three hours when the police appeared and brought

STOP GREASING THE RAILS.
—Chapin in the St. Louis *Republic* as reproduced in *Literary Digest*, LVI (Mar. 30, 1918), 14.

the gathering to a sudden halt. This action aroused Mayor Thompson who said, "Pacifists are law-abiding citizens. I shall not have it spread broadcast that Chicago denies free speech to anybody." [10] He promised protection to the People's Council if it wanted to hold a meeting the next day. Mayor Thompson, however, was out of step with the militant advocates of war. When Governor Lowden heard about the Mayor's action, he sent four companies of troops to Chicago on September 2 to keep the People's Council from meeting. He did this after the Chicago Chamber of Commerce warned the Governor that such a meeting would be "antagonistic to our national purposes in the present world crisis." [11]

But before the troops arrived, the People's Council had approved a platform calling for "progressive disarmament of all nations, repeal of the Selective Draft Law by the United States Congress, a concrete statement by the Administration of its war aims, and peace without conquest, annexation, or indemnities." Rabbi Judah L. Magnes of New York City was the principal speaker, but Senator Works and Congressman

William B. Mason of Illinois also appeared. All three spoke heatedly of the treatment which friends and members of the People's Council were receiving.

THE VENTRILOQUIST.

—Brown in the Chicago *Daily News* as reproduced in *Literary Digest,* LV (Sept. 15, 1917), 17.

Rabbi Magnes was reported to have said, "Is it worthy of a democracy that citizens holding divergent views be driven from place to place to find opportunity for discussion? That they be threatened with imprisonment, that they be spied upon and maligned because . . . they speak and labor and struggle for democracy." Congressman Mason contended that "no worse thing ever happened in the history of the United States than is happening now when people like you are branded as criminals and denied the right of free assembly." He also declared that the only people who welcomed the war were bankers and editors.[12] The *New York Herald,* September 3, carried Works' comment, "I wonder if democracy in this free republic is dead."

The campaign against the Council continued unabated. It was under constant attack by Samuel Gompers, who denied that the Council in any way represented labor. The National Security League announced that it would follow the People's Council wherever meetings were held and do everything possible to counteract the peace propaganda. About the time of the Chicago meeting, the Washington, D.C., police department announced that it would not permit the People's Council to meet on Washington streets.[13] On October 6 a People's Council meeting was broken up in Cincinnati.

In some instances these opponents of war were given rough treatment, similar to that received by I.W.W.'s. For example, Herbert S. Bigelow, a preacher, pacifist, and speaker for the People's Council, was seized on October 29 as he was entering a hall to make a speech in Newport, Kentucky. He was gagged, handcuffed, and thrust into a waiting automobile. Upon reaching a dense forest some twenty miles from the city, the mob stripped him to the waist and read these words: "In the name of the poor women and children of Belgium this man should be whipped." According to the *New York Times* account of October 30, "at a signal a man clad from head to foot in white stepped out of a huge circle that had been formed, produced a long blacksnake whip, and delivered numerous lashes upon the back of Bigelow. The ropes were then cut. Bigelow was warned to stay away from Cincinnati, and was released, while the members of the party made their way back to their waiting automobiles and disappeared."

As was true in other cases of direct-action punishment of opponents of war, many editors refused to get alarmed about the threats to personal rights and freedoms. The *Green Bay Press-Gazette* editorialized on October 30, 1917, that, although whipping was deplorable, "there comes a time when public patience is exhausted by the antics of mouthy disloyalists." The New York *Middleton Times-Press* stated on November 1:

> The *Times-Press*, of course, does not uphold such lawlessness. However, unless the country deals with such traitors as they should be dealt with, either by locking them up or by shipping them over to Germany, it invites such proceedings . . . . It is not likely the Government will capture the men who whipped Bigelow. Somehow we have a sort of notion that it will not try very hard.

This latter observation of the editor was quite correct. Assistant Attorney General John Lord O'Brian insisted that no statement against the abductors would be given consideration unless it was by a "responsible citizen." This clearly meant someone who favored the war. Certainly the Government would not give any credence to testimony by a member of the People's Council.

For a "responsible citizen," William R. Vance, Dean of the University of Minnesota Law School, went about as far as anyone in denouncing opponents of war. At a luncheon where he bitterly attacked the People's Council, he said in effect that "wartime was no time to quibble about constitutional rights and guarantees." [14]

Thus the noose of intolerance gradually tightened around those who opposed the war or who demanded that an earnest effort be made to seek peace. The vast majority of people who favored the Great Crusade were determined that its rightness and righteousness should not be challenged. The *Minneapolis Journal* said that the "peace-at-any-price" speakers were being used by Germany to show that the United States was not united in prosecuting the war. It made no difference, the editor wrote, whether they were "mistaken zealots or German agents"; the result was the same. However, the New York *Evening Post* took a different view. It editorialized that it was not so important whether the pacifists were "mischievous, misguided, or merely misunderstood" as it was whether "legitimate law-abiding free speech as guaranteed by the Constitution of the United States is or is not dead in America." [15] By the end of 1917 the People's Council found that free speech had become drastically circumscribed and the organization was, for all practical purposes, driven out of existence.

"I ask of you, Sir, please look into this case for me and give me my freedom."

ALIENS AND NEGROES UNDER ATTACK

Hatred of the enemy is a thing striven for in wartime. It is also often accompanied by a hatred of all foreign people, of all who are alien in any way. The differences—the loyalties to strange nations, to strange gods —are ignored when men are at peace; but with war comes a passionate denial of the right of anyone to have any other loyalty, any other god.

The United States is a land of many races, many nationalities, many religions. It is only natural that a world war would bring about friction among these elements. The first and most obvious clash came in the realm of nationality. Theodore Roosevelt spoke for nationalists everywhere when he dealt with this issue on a number of occasions in 1917: "The Hun within our gates masquerades in many disguises; he is our dangerous enemy; and he should be hunted down without mercy." [1] "Every man," he wrote in 1918, "ought to love his country . . . . [But] he is only entitled to one country. If he claims loyalty to two countries, he is necessarily a traitor to at least one country." [2] "Weak-kneed apologists for infamy say that it is 'natural' for American citizens of German origin to favor Germany," Roosevelt wrote at another time; "this is nonsense, and criminal nonsense to boot." Then he added, "We can have no 'fifty-fifty' allegiance in this country." [3]

Roosevelt notwithstanding, a man's love of his homeland is something deep and abiding that cannot be entirely changed by emigration or by naturalization papers. However much a man might wish to lose interest in the land of his birth, it is not easy to do so. An American might become a naturalized Briton, German, or Frenchman, but he would still—in spite of everything—retain something within himself that would be forever American and forever alien to his adopted country. He may not "favor" America, but he could not lose all his affection for her.

The same was true of people of foreign birth and background in the United States in 1917. Those who came from the Allied nations, and particularly from England, could be passionately devoted to the land of their birth and still pass as patriotic Americans. Those from Germany and Austria could not do this. To them, as Jane Addams has said, "a war between the United States and the fatherland meant exquisite torture." [4]

In 1917 there were hundreds of thousands of Germans and Austro-Hungarians, or people of German and Austrian ancestry, living in the United States. There were also large numbers of foreign groups, such as Poles, Finns, and Russians, who felt indifferent toward the war or unsympathetic with the Allies. Many of these people were not yet citizens of the United States. Recognizing that residents of foreign background would have major problems of adjustment under circumstances of war, there were those in the United States who recommended tolerance and kind treatment for enemy aliens. A certain sympathy continued for a few months after war began, but by the end of the summer of 1917 the public's attitude had changed noticeably. Perhaps it would be better to say that the attitude of a section of the public had changed. The bitter opposition to conscription irritated nationalists, and they looked with especial suspicion upon any critic of this practice who was of enemy birth. Then there was the wild drive against radicals. Here again, when a man was a radical and also an alien no sympathy could be expected for him. Many newspaper stories dealing with aliens began to carry an overtone of dislike merely because of their foreignness. The Governor of Arizona in one of his early justifications for the Bisbee deportation accused the I.W.W.'s of being foreigners. [5]

Nonetheless, thousands upon thousands of Germans and Austrians served in the Army of the United States, and other thousands gave their American-born sons to serve in the war against Germany and Austria. They usually said little or nothing, apparently suppressing any feelings they may have had. Yet there were those who felt that they could not actively engage in war against the country of their birth or a nation where they had relatives and friends. For example, Captain D. A. Henkes tried to resign as an army officer because his father had been born in Germany and his family still had many relatives and friends there. "I cannot force myself to the conviction that I am capable of making war on my kindred upon their soil in a manner that would become my duty and station," he wrote the Secretary of War. "I earnestly request that I may not be required to undergo this ordeal . . . . As an only alternative, if my services will not be dispensed with, I would suggest duty in another field." [6] But Captain Henkes was sent to Europe. He carried out his duties as required, but he still felt that he should not participate in a war against Germany. On October 10 he wrote another letter pleading for the acceptance of his resignation. He was finally placed under arrest, tried and convicted by a general court-martial, and dismissed from the service. His sentence was twenty-five years at hard labor at Leavenworth Penitentiary.[7]

The *New York Call* of September 21, 1917, carried the story of Joseph Kirrin, a draftee from Connecticut, who resisted conscription. Kirrin said, "My father and my brothers, my whole family, is in the Austrian army. I will not become a soldier here to fight my own family and the country where I was born. They can shoot me if they want to, but I will not go." Kirrin refused to march to the railroad station. He was arrested and taken to the police station where officers handcuffed him and physically carried him to a cell.

A similar case was that of Tony Petroshki. He related his situation to the American Civil Liberties Union in a letter of February 2, 1919:

I am 26 years old, born in Russia and came to America when I was 20 years of age. My home is in Connecticut. In 1917 I was called for military service. I registered as an alien. I could not read nor write the English language. I did not go for physical examination because I did not understand I was to go, thinking I did not have to be a soldier. An officer came and took me to Camp Devens, Mass. I was told to put on the uniform and I said, I am a Russian. I do not want to be a soldier. On November 20, 1917, I was tried before a court-martial. I could not understand what was said and do not know what was sworn against me. I was sent to the United States Penitentiary and have been at this prison since November, 1917, or thereabouts. Recently I learned that my term of sentence is for 20 years. I do not see why I should be sent for such a long time, when I have harmed no one. Will you please help me? [8]

On July 14, 1917, almost simultaneously with the deportation of strikers from Bisbee, Arizona, some foreign miners in Flat River, Missouri, were rounded up and driven out of town by "patriotic" elements. A local citizen justified this treatment by claiming that foreigners were taking jobs away from Americans.[9] On July 16 a *New York Herald* dispatch from Flat River stated: "Today weary mothers carrying babes, with older children trudging along in the dust, lined almost every road out of town. They were going to join their husbands, who were driven out yesterday or the day before, but many of them did not know just where to go . . . . Reports of pillage continue to be made."

Aliens whose affection for their native land was of the strident, nationalistic variety caused the most trouble. These individuals who, supposedly, were authentic pro-Germans made a great deal of difficulty for other people of alien birth who were trying to be loyal Americans. On April 2, 1917, an unidentified man in Wyoming—probably a German —was reported to have exclaimed "Hoch der Kaiser." He was hanged and saved from death only by the arrival of the town marshal. According to the *Minneapolis Journal* of April 3, when he revived he was forced to kneel and kiss the American flag.

In Iowa a Lutheran pastor by the name of Wilhelm Schumann, a native of Germany, was arrested for a sermon in which he attacked the draft in the presence of men of military age. He also was supposed to have said that it was a war for the capitalist class and that buying Liberty bonds was "a great big humbug," that the United States entered the war to help England, and that Germany was actually right. Furthermore, he refused to take up a collection for the Red Cross, stating that the money should be used to help Germans and that "it was a money war and men were making money out of it; that he did not believe in the YMCA at all; that it is gotten up by the Methodists . . . . Our boys should not go over to shed their blood to help England." Schumann was sentenced to five years in Leavenworth Penitentiary, although his sentence was commuted after two years.[10]

In North Dakota a minister by the name of Fontana ran afoul of the law. Born in Germany, he had come to this country when he was sixteen years old. At the time he was arrested he had a wife and five children. The Sunday after the United States entered the war he preached a sermon in which he said, "We are now at war with the old Fatherland. This is our country. We adopted this country when we became citizens of the United States, and we promised and swore to the constitution that we would stand by this country. Now is the time to prove and show it that we are willing to do our duty . . . ." At other times, however, he was reported to have prayed for the success of the German armies and to have said that he was proud of the noble fight the Germans were making. He was greatly in debt and refused to subscribe to the Liberty

Loans. He was sentenced to three years in the penitentiary.[11] On appeal, however, judgment in this case was reversed.

When the presiding judge, C. F. Amidon, sentenced Fontana he declared that even Germans who had been residents of the United States for many years still had "Made in Germany" written on their faces. "I do not blame you and these men alone," he said. "I blame myself. I blame my country. We urged you [Germans] to come; we welcomed you; we gave you opportunity; we gave you land; we conferred upon you the diadem of American citizenship—and then we left you. We paid no attention to what you have been doing." [12]

Judge Amidon was correct in his analysis, but he was wrong if he thought his remarks applied only to Germans. The Irish seldom lose their love for Ireland; the English, generations away from England, are often violently pro-British; the Germans are not different from other nationalities in that respect. The crucial question in all these cases was how to understand the patriotism and the nationalism of men from countries other than their adopted land.

Puerto Ricans were somewhat like the Irish. They objected to being conscripted into what they regarded as an alien army. The Espionage Act, however, was used to force them into line. Florencio M. Romero was accused of saying that Puerto Ricans owed no military obligations to the United States and should not be subject to military duty because they were not citizens of the United States. He was accused also of having counseled and advised Puerto Ricans to resist the draft, and of having tried to form an antimilitarist organization.[13] Monserrate Sanchez echoed this sentiment. He was indicted for damning the American Government and saying that he was more German than the Kaiser. Both men were sentenced to four years in Atlanta Penitentiary.[14]

Vicente Balbas, a Puerto Rican, was one of a small group who had declined to take American citizenship. He was editor of an anti-American newspaper called the *Heraldo de las Antillas* and was strongly opposed to the conscription of Puerto Ricans by the United States. On October 27, 1917, he published an editorial against recruiting, and on November 10 he wrote his objections to the ruling of the United States Provost Marshal that Puerto Ricans who were not American citizens must enter the army. He editorialized that the Provost Marshal pressed upon the defenseless and the weak, that he compelled by might a man to fight for a flag that was not his own. "Can all this be done in a nation where the rights of freedom exist?" Balbas asked. It could be and was, at least temporarily. Balbas was convicted, sentenced to eight years in the penitentiary, and fined four thousand dollars.[15] The Court of Appeals, however, later reversed this decision.

Of the millions of aliens in the United States only about 6,300 were arrested. Of the 2,300 aliens who were interned by the military authorities, some were later freed or paroled. The method of handling many of these cases, however, was often shameful. Suspects were arrested and held without trial. In some instances the courts offered only scant protection, if any at all.[16] Vigorous application of both legal and extralegal methods against aliens, however, went a long way to suppress alien elements who opposed the war. According to the Attorney General, alien enemies were sometimes held "for a limited period to produce a disciplinary effect." This policy seemed successful, because he reported that detention and internment "has acted throughout the country as a powerful deterrent against alien-enemy activity." [17]

The action taken against aliens underlined significantly what had come to be looked upon as normal, accepted human intolerance. During a war, mob hysteria spreads even to those who, in more settled times, pride themselves on their sufferance and liberality. The demand for conformity and uniformity becomes pandemic. The results are so effective that the schoolboy mistranslation of Terence—"nothing foreign is human to me" —emerges with deadly irony as an accurate verbal map of the public state of mind.

Under the exigency of this universal demand that everything be alike and on one level, the public cannot see that widely differing elements in society strengthen it economically, intellectually, and culturally. And so, when the United States entered the war in 1917, prejudice burgeoned; its tentacles reached everywhere. Extremists attacked not only the Germans, but all alien elements. And this assault naturally included that permanent alien element in America, the Negro. To be sure, race prejudice was no new phenomenon in American life, but the emotionalism and intolerance generated by the war served to intensify mob violence against Negroes.

As a result of the war boom, a shortage of labor in northern industries developed. Many employers turned to the South and actively recruited workers. Negroes went north in great numbers, beginning a migration which was to change the population make-up of several northern cities. At the same time, the point of view of many northerners was also changed. Factory and mining towns were flooded with colored workers only recently occupants of cotton patches.

As these men and women came into the North some of them thought they would be escaping from the race antagonism that had plagued them in the South. After all, was it not the North that had carried on the war to free the Negro from slavery? Would not the North give the Negro equality? And then there was another thing. The country was flooded with talk of this war being a libertarian war, a war for democracy, a war which would result in the suppression of autocratic people. Would it not result in less autocracy among the American whites?

Of this there were some doubts. The greatest preacher of this cause of liberty and democracy was President Woodrow Wilson, and the Negroes knew Wilson as a southerner. In April, 1917, a Negro minister wrote that "while the colored people were loyal citizens, few of them were enthusiastic in their support of the President and his Administration." To this Wilson replied, "Your letter was the first notice I had that many of the members of the colored race were not enthusiastic in their support of the Government in this crisis." [18] But Wilson had misunderstood. It was not the Government but the southern individual who was at the head of the Government who failed to arouse their enthusiasm.

Before long the Negro became aware that there was not much difference between the northern white man and the southern white man. In May, 1917, the newspapers carried the story of a Negro who was burned to death by a white mob in Tennessee. The man was accused of killing a girl. A week later, the *New York Times* of May 27 reported a small race riot in New York City. One Negro was killed and seven others were wounded. But the first major outbreak after this population movement began occurred in East St. Louis, Illinois.

During 1917 some 10,000 to 12,000 Negroes migrated to East St. Louis, many of them lured there by exaggerated advertisements of businessmen promising high wages. Others were imported as strikebreakers. Bitter racial feeling was aroused as scores of minor conflicts developed between Negroes and whites. A corrupt local political machine added further instability to the situation which began to explode in late May of 1917.

The height of this disgraceful race riot was reached on July 2. The previous evening one or two carloads of white men drove through the Negro section of the city shooting promiscuously into many homes. Although no one was hurt or killed, angry Negroes now armed themselves and set out to avenge the unprovoked attacks on their homes. Shortly, they encountered several police officers in a car. Thinking it was the car from which shots had been fired into their homes, the Negroes fired upon it, killing one policeman and mortally wounding another.

The next day, July 2, one of the worst race riots in American history erupted in East St. Louis. Negroes were killed indiscriminately as police and soldiers stood idly by or, in some instances, even participated in the fray. The instances of inhuman brutality to innocent people are too numerous to relate here. Besides, they have been fully recorded by a congressional committee. One or two instances are enough to indicate the actions of the emotion-maddened mobs. One Negro who was trying to escape from thirty or forty whites was "knocked down, kicked in the face, beaten into insensibility; and then a man stood over him and shot him five times as he lay helpless in the street." [19] And the savage brutality was not confined to Negroes who were residents of East St. Louis. A Negro man with his wife and son were passing through that city when a mob grabbed them at Collinsville and Illinois avenues, beat the man to death, shot the 14-year-old boy, and scalped the woman. The mob, said the House Committee which investigated the affair, "spared neither age nor sex in their blind lust for blood." [20] The attacks on individuals were aggravated by the burning of over 300 Negro homes. The exact number of people killed is not known, but at least eight whites and 38 Negroes lost their lives and hundreds were wounded and maimed. One estimate gave 110 as having been killed. Some convictions were finally obtained and various punishments were meted out. Eleven Negroes and eight white men were sent to the State Penitentiary. But no jail sentences or other punishment of guilty parties could undo the damage of those awful days. [21] It was increasingly difficult for the Negro to accept the war as a war for freedom and democracy. "Race-riots in East St. Louis," said the *Literary Digest,* "afford a lurid background to our efforts to carry justice and idealism to Europe." [22]

Other areas experienced riots during July, although they were minor compared to that in East St. Louis. On the third there was trouble in the San Juan Hill section of New York City when policemen had trouble with a colored guardsman. On July 25 riots occurred in Chester, Pennsylvania, where four Negroes were shot and sixty arrested. The next day three Negroes were killed and many were wounded. The rioting continued through July 28 when two more Negroes were killed. [23]

These and other race riots aroused general public condemnation. Some newspapers attempted to blame the East St. Louis riot on organized labor while politicians occasionally hinted that German agents must have been behind the racial difficulties. But most editorial writers deplored the mob action. Theodore Roosevelt denounced the rioters and gained some praise. President Wilson received many protests and demands for remedial action. One writer said the riot was "worse than anything the Germans did in Belgium." [24] After reading one complaint Wilson wrote that the particular individual "cannot feel more distressed than I do at the terrible things which have recently been happening." [25] He said that he wanted to make a statement "if it can be made naturally and with the likelihood that it will be effective." [26] Nevertheless, Negroes believed that the President did not take vigorous enough action to guard against future race disturbances.

Negroes held a protest parade in New York City and in many other ways attempted to arouse public opposition to such attacks. From Los Angeles a Negro group sent a telegram to President Wilson stating:

> In view of the fact that our country is asking of us to give up our very lives for civilization against barbarism and to establish world democracy . . . we feel, as human beings, we could ask for nothing less . . . for back of all loyalty there must be love of country, but if the country will not protect us in the time of need, we feel that it is not humanly possible to nourish our hearts to loyalty by memory of cold neglect from [the] general government.[27]

Wilson asked his secretary to acknowledge the telegram, saying that the matter was "having my gravest and most anxious consideration." [28]

When a group of Negro leaders in Maryland sought an interview with the President to discuss the East St. Louis riot, Wilson said he was too busy to grant the request. This prompted Professor Kelly Miller of Howard University to write the President, "The Negro feels that he is not regarded as a constituent part of American democracy. This is our fundamental grievance." Miller added that there was no use trying to spread democracy abroad while Negro citizens in East St. Louis, Memphis, Waco, and other places were being mobbed and killed. Finally, he accused Wilson of maintaining a "lukewarm aloofness from the tangled issues of this problem." [29] On August 15 Wilson did issue a statement condemning acts of violence against Negroes.

Nonetheless, violence against Negroes continued. The next most serious riot occurred in Houston. With colored troops stationed near Houston, more or less continuous trouble had developed over the enforcement of the Jim Crow laws. There were instances in which the Houston police had mistreated Negro soldiers. The riot was set off on August 23 when police officers raided a dice game in the colored section. Some of the Negro soldiers fled and sought refuge in the house of a woman. When officers tried to arrest the woman, a Negro soldier attempted to interfere. He was handled roughly and arrested. Later in the day this same police officer had trouble with a Negro member of the military police who was shot at and arrested. News of this reached the army camp, and colored soldiers, seeking revenge on the Houston police, "left the camp armed, approached the town, and committed various murders, assaults, and acts of terrorization." Fifteen persons were killed.[30] The military authorities moved quickly to restore order. Forty-one Negroes were given life sentences at Leavenworth Penitentiary, and thirteen were hanged in an arroyo about two miles east of Camp Travis.[31] Secretary Baker later wrote Wilson that because of the "speed with which the death sentences . . . were executed, some feeling was aroused in the country." Baker recommended that in the future death sentences should be reviewed in Washington.[32]

After the execution of the thirteen soldiers a Negro newspaper, the San Antonio *Inquirer,* carried an article signed by C. L. Threadgill-Dennis which said: "We would rather see you shot by the highest tribunal of the United States Army because you dared protect a Negro woman from the insult of a southern brute in the form of a policeman, than to have you forced to go to Europe to fight for a liberty you cannot enjoy . . . ."[33] Although the editor, G. W. Bouldin, claimed he was out of the city at the time and knew nothing of the article, he was indicted for attempting "to cause insubordination, disloyalty, mutiny, and refusal of duty." Bouldin was sentenced to two years in Leavenworth Penitentiary.

A pathetic case involving a Negro preacher, J. H. Ellis, occurred in Arkansas in November, 1917. Ellis seems to have expressed sympathy for Negro field workers. On November 30 Pastor Ellis wrote to President Wilson from his cell in the Newport, Arkansas, jail explaining that he had been "arrested on the strength of the complaint of a Negro who is an enemy of mine and charged with TREASON. But, Honorable Sir, to tell you the truth, the things that man swore never entered my brain or heart." He then related that his enemy had charged him with saying the war was a white man's war and the flag a white man's flag; that the South was no place for Negroes. But Ellis denied ever having uttered such statements. The only thing he had done was to preach "the gospel of the Lowly Nazarene," Ellis wrote.[34] In any event, he was "carried one cold night in an automobile forty miles away to Batesville, Arkansas. I was not allowed to see any one. I did not know until the day of my trial was called who would appear against me nor from what place the complaint came.

I had no one to assist me. I love the stars and stripes and this our Country and have never said one thing against it." Then Ellis continued:

I am a poor Baptist preacher without money. I am not able to employ high priced lawyers to fight well-versed lawyers against the state and nation. I am not able to put up the money to have witnesses brought here and I have been told by the prosecuting attorney . . . that if I get them I will have to pay for it. I would like to have bond. I ask of you, Sir, please look into this case for me and give me my freedom.[35]

Ellis' letter probably never reached the President, but the Civil Liberties Bureau heard of the case and gave him assistance. In the middle of February, 1918, he gained his release. Afterward Ellis wrote to Roger Baldwin:

I was in jail ninety-six days. The sheriff sent word to the jailer last night to turn me out. As I came out of the door about three dozen men composed of the high sheriff, the prosecuting attorney, the postmaster, and others pounced upon me and began beating me right there in the jail yard with clubs and beat me down and put me in an automobile and carried me about a mile out in the woods and there they beat me man after man until they became tired trying to make me say that I knew something about the I.W.W. And trying to make me say that the National Civil Liberties Bureau was an I.W.W. organization. They wanted to know from me how did your organization learn about my case. The men who beat me up are the leading white citizens of this town and I know the names of six of them.[36]

PURGING THE MOVIES
AND THE PRESS

Much has been written about the problem of freedom of the press during World War I.[1] For this reason no detailed account of this important matter will be given here. However, in any discussion of the opponents of war one must give the problem some consideration. Clamps tightened on the press, and to some degree on movie producers, were an important part of the over-all pattern of repression aimed at those who lacked enthusiasm for the war. The nationalism of the movies and of the press had to be unquestioned.

As soon as war was declared the Government asked that films be withheld which had a pacifist slant or which might discourage enlistment or reflect on the United States or its allies. The motion picture industry itself recognized that it must get in line with government policy. One of the industry's trade journals stated that producers should not make films that might create "an influence prejudicial to the government's prosecution of the present war." If this advice was not heeded, the editor said, "federal authorities will suppress such pictures without hesitation." [2] Within a short time this prediction was proved true. The ban fell on such pictures as *War Brides, Civilization,* and *The Battle Cry of Peace.*

The most important example of disciplining the motion picture industry occurred in connection with a film called *The Spirit of '76.* This picture had been made sometime before April, 1917, by Robert Goldstein. It portrayed some details of the American Revolution, including scenes of the Wyoming Valley massacre. According to one account, a British soldier was shown "impaling on a bayonet a baby lying in its cradle and then swirling it around his head so impaled. Other unspeakable atrocities committed by British soldiers, including the shooting of harmless women, the dragging off, sometimes by the hair of the head, of young American girls," were exhibited.[3] The picture was released during the summer of 1917 and in November it was shown in Los Angeles. At that point the courts intervened. The district attorney of Los Angeles seized the film after obtaining a writ and a search warrant. Goldstein was prosecuted for violating the Espionage Act, sentenced to the penitentiary for ten years, and fined five thousand dollars. Judge Bledsoe said that "history is history, and fact is fact," but he added that the United States must unite in the common cause of war and that no one should be permitted to detract from the war effort. The film, said the judge, tended to arouse people's passions and "to question the good faith of our ally, Great Britain." As was true of the principle established for freedom of speech, that which might be shown in ordinary times could not be shown in time of war.[4]

For all practical purposes, the movie makers quietly followed the war-party line after Goldstein's experiences. *The Curse of Iku* was released early in 1918 and ran for a short time, but, after insistence by government officials, the film was revised on a voluntary basis so as not to arouse race prejudice against the Japanese. On the other hand, the moving picture industry played an important part in building up mob feeling in the country. Pictures such as *Hearts of Humanity, The Beast of Berlin, Face to Face with Kaiserism, Hearts of the World,* and many others helped to inflame hatred toward Germany. The moving picture industry was one of the greatest instruments for propaganda in the war. It must be given some responsibility for the hysteria and repressive activities of 1917 and 1918.

It was hardly necessary to discipline American newspapers and magazines during the first World War. Most of the big, influential publications were commercial undertakings, conservative in outlook and thoroughly attuned to the war. They usually reflected the sympathies and interests of the wealthy, of the conventional, and of those in power. Unpopular causes, no matter how righteous, earned no money and received scant attention. In order to get economic support, editors were likely to emphasize popular issues and gave only meager consideration to dissenting views and ideas, except possibly to criticize them. The financial losses of Oswald Villard's New York *Evening Post* illustrate the difficulties of a newspaper which refused to follow the line of the super-patriots. As the war had the general support of conservative elements, it was only natural that the commercial press would back it enthusiastically. It would, of course, be unfair to say that publishers were motivated only by economic interests. Probably most newspaper owners and editors honestly believed in the righteousness of the American and Allied cause, a belief partly generated by their own and the Government's propaganda.

The major papers and magazines came in for an occasional scare during these months of tumult, but since most of them took a strong nationalistic stand there was no drive against them. They peddled the views handed out by the Committee on Public Information and escaped trouble. George Creel wrote to Wilson in November, 1917, "I have been surprised and gratified at the results I have been able to achieve. Our matter goes into the papers by thousands of columns, and aside from the personal attacks of a few New York papers, like the *World,* feeling has grown very friendly." [5] Furthermore, there was the fact that officials did not want to come into conflict with an adversary they might not easily defeat. There was, for example, bitter criticism of the Hearst papers for opposing aspects of the war, but the Government did not invoke the Espionage Act against them. As one contemporary declared, "Obscure papers have been interfered with, while the Hearst journals, powerful but insidiously disloyal, have been countenanced without question." [6] Hearst could criticize President Wilson, he could say that the war was an economic struggle, that Ireland ought to be free, and that England could do no right—he could say these things and not be prosecuted. There was a great difference between trying to censor a powerful voice like that of Hearst and the relatively weak *Milwaukee Leader.* But even Hearst waved "the flag in unison with the news columns" after the spring of 1918. [7]

Popular magazines such as the *Independent* and the *Literary Digest* had an almost shocking lack of serious discussion of the war and its meaning, although they carried many axe-grinding articles. [8] The same is true of most of the big city papers. Newspapers such as the *New York Times,* the Los Angeles *Times,* the *Minneapolis Journal,* and the *Atlanta Constitution* displayed a remarkable similarity in the material they published. There were, of course, exceptions even among the big papers. The New York *World,* the New York *Evening Post,* the *Detroit Free Press,* and the St. Louis *Post-Dispatch* usually gave more evidence of independent thought.

There was no lack of means by which the federal Government could control the press. As mentioned earlier, section 12 of the Espionage Act permitted a high degree of censorship, and a Censorship Board was established. Furthermore, the C.P.I. could direct newspapers not only by the type of releases but also by limiting the material distributed. The Government also had control of cables and wireless. Censorship by government officials varied from recommendations to absolute prohibitions. In May, 1917, Creel asked the press to omit any speculation about possible peace or about differences of opinion among the Allies or with neutrals.[9] Editors, when in doubt, consulted Creel's office.[10] At one time Creel was reported to have informed a State Department official "that he wanted nothing whatever published in regard to cable or mail censorship . . . , the less said about any sort of censorship the better. That it is desirable that no one should know just where the censorship is working."[11] The federal Government was also successful in obtaining a fair degree of voluntary censorship. This started as soon as the country entered the war. There were also cases of local censorship, especially of the foreign-language press.

The censorship exercised by the Postmaster General, Albert Sidney Burleson, was perhaps more effective than that of all the other individuals and organizations combined.[12] His authority to withhold mailing privileges from publications violating the Espionage Act gave him tremendous power. To criticize American entry into the war, to question American or Allied motives, to discourage enlistments, or to discredit the military forces were among the things considered violations of the Espionage Act. And Burleson took his job seriously. Opponents of war need not expect any quarter from him. After the passage of the Espionage Act he declared that newspapers could criticize the Government and government officials all they pleased, but, he added, "there is a limit." The limit was reached when a newspaper "begins to say that this Government got in the war wrong, that it is in it for wrong purposes, or anything that will impugn the motives of the Government for going into the war. They can not say that this Government is the tool of Wall Street or the munitions-makers . . . . There can be no campaign against conscription and the Draft Law."[13]

It was the little newspapers, the reform or radical publications, along with the foreign-language press, which were suppressed by the Government. Opposing the war on both economic and idealistic grounds, these papers naturally clashed with the ideas held by the war party. Socialist publications were the special objects of attack. By the fall of 1918, some 75 newspapers had been interfered with in one way or another and, according to one writer, about 45 of these were Socialist.[14] Postmaster

General Burleson said no Socialist publication would be molested unless it contained treasonable or seditious matter. But then he was reported to have said, "Most Socialist papers do contain this matter." [15] As already mentioned, the *Milwaukee Leader* and the *New York Call,* both major Socialist publications, were suppressed by November, 1917.

One of the first antiwar publications attacked was the lively radical sheet known as the *Masses.* In the issue of June, 1917, Max Eastman wrote:

> It is not a war for democracy. It did not originate in a dispute about democracy, and it is unlikely to terminate in a democratic settlement. There is a bare possibility that a victory of the Allies will hasten the fall of the autocracies in central Europe but there is a practical certainty that in trimming for such a victory the Allies will throw out most of the essence of their own democracy. We will Prussianize ourselves and will probably not democratize Prussia . . . .
>
> It is ungracious to harp upon these things just at a time when the nation is united in a ceremonial emotion of self-esteem. There is something so strident about this kind of bad manners that they seem almost treasonable, and men have already been sent to jail since April sixth upon the theory that it is treason to tell an unpleasant truth about one's country.

Eastman urged Socialists to "resist the war-fever" and save themselves for the "real struggle for liberty" which would come after the war.[16] This publication also carried numerous cartoons which irritated the prowar patriots. For instance, Billy Sunday was pictured leading Jesus, and Uncle Sam, "all ready to fight for liberty," was "wearing the handcuffs of censorship and the ball and chain of conscription." Capitalism and big business were attacked in a cartoon showing a group of big businessmen around a table looking at war plans. Congress says, "Excuse me, gentlemen, where do I come in?" Big business replies, "Run along now; we got through with you when you declared war for us." [17]

With the appearance of the August, 1917, issue Burleson ordered the postmaster in New York City not to accept the magazine for mailing. The publishers then went into court and asked for a restraining order. Although it was clear that Judge Learned Hand did not agree with the views expressed in the *Masses,* he nevertheless issued a temporary restraining order.[18] But despite the court ruling, Burleson still kept the publication out of the mails. He refused to admit the September or later issues to the second-class mailing privilege "even if absolutely free from any objectionable passages, on the ground that since the magazine had skipped a number . . . it was no longer a periodical." [19] This same reasoning was used later in denying other publications the use of the mail. In the case of the *Masses,* however, Burleson soon got court support for his actions. In November the temporary restraining order was reversed by the Circuit Court of Appeals. The court held that "liberty of circulating may be essential to freedom of the press, but liberty of circulating through the mails is not, so long as its transportation in any other way as merchandise is not forbidden." [20] The decision in *Masses Pub. Co.* v. *Patten* was a major victory for repression. As Chafee has written, the effect of this decision "was to establish the old-time doctrine of remote bad tendency in the minds of district judges throughout the country." [21]

Oswald Garrison Villard complained to Tumulty about the suppression of newspapers and magazines. But Wilson replied that "he [Villard] is entirely mistaken about certain papers having been 'suppressed.' Nothing of the kind occurred. Certain copies of certain newspapers were excluded from the mails because they contained matter explicitly forbidden by law." [22] Nonetheless, as a result of numerous complaints, Wilson appealed to the Postmaster General, saying, "Now Burleson, these are well-intentioned people. Let them blow off steam!" Burleson said that he replied, "I am willing to let them blow off steam, providing they don't violate the Espionage Act. If you don't want the Espionage Act enforced I can resign. Congress has passed the law and has said that I am to enforce it. We are going into war, and these men are discouraging enlistments." According to Burleson, Wilson laughed and said, "Well, go ahead and do your duty." [23] The trouble with Burleson, declared the New York *Evening Post,* was that he did not know the difference between "well-intentioned criticism and willful obstruction." [24]

It was almost inevitable that the foreign-language press should be attacked unless it outdid the super-nationalists in its patriotic outbursts. The very psychology of the situation made criticism of the war or of American policies written in German seem even more dastardly and disloyal than the same thing presented in English. Theodore Roosevelt was reported to have said on September 20, 1917, "We are convinced that today our most dangerous foe is the foreign-language press." [25] To meet this problem stiff restrictions on foreign-language newspapers and magazines were incorporated in the Trading with the Enemy Act of October, 1917. Editors of these papers were required to file with the proper officials translations of material dealing with government policy and aspects of the war, or to secure permits exempting them from this burden.

The German-language papers, the most important element of the foreign-language press, had generally opposed American entry into the war. Thus when war was declared a change of attitude was necessary for self-preservation. Throughout the summer of 1917 there was a rapid shift in editorial policy by most German-language newspapers. As Carl Wittke has written: "Position after position was abandoned, until before the end of the summer of 1917, practically all German-language papers, with the exception of a few small Socialist papers which clung tenaciously to the traditional principles of the party, became intensely loyal, not to say blatantly patriotic, in their public professions of devotion to their country's cause." [26]

A major move by the Government against the foreign-language press occurred in connection with the prosecution of the editor and other officials of the *Philadelphia Tageblatt*. After being acquitted of treason, members of the *Tageblatt* staff were indicted under the Espionage Act for the same written statements. The main charge against the *Tageblatt* was that it reprinted material and changed the meaning by making omissions. It was not a matter of the truth or falsity of the articles, but "merely that they differed from the originals, and had been altered or mistranslated so as to bear a changed meaning which was depressing or detrimental to patriotic ardor." [27]

One of the deletions to which the Government took exception dealt with the fall of Riga to the Germans. The sentence omitted was as follows: "From this it can be concluded that the fall of Riga has united the opposing political factions in Russia." To judge by the events which were soon to follow, the *Tageblatt* editors were more correct than were the writers of the original story. In addition to this and similar cases, the *Tageblatt* carried an article in the issue of July 4, 1917, which was strongly anti-British, antiwar, and anti-Wilson. The case dragged out until 1919 when three of the five officials of the paper were sentenced to the penitentiary for terms of from two to five years. Justice Brandeis was not impressed with the majority decision. He commented in his dissenting opinion:

> To hold that such harmless additions to or omissions from news items, and such impotent expressions of editorial opinion, as were shown here, can afford the basis even of a prosecution, will doubtless discourage criticism of the policies of the Government. To hold

that such publications can be suppressed as false reports, subjects to new perils the constitutional liberty of the press . . . .[28]

Pressure from government officials, substantially aided by state Councils of Defense and other local super-patriots, was too much for scores of foreign-language papers. "The German-language press lost ground steadily after 1917," said Wittke. "Many papers suspended publication, either for all time, or for the period of the war, sometimes voluntarily, sometimes by order of state councils of defense, or in response to a public pressure which became unbearable." [29]

The Government moved steadily against newspapers which did not conform in their attitude toward the war. The *Jeffersonian,* a weekly newspaper published in Thomson, Georgia, by the former Populist leader Tom Watson, was denied the use of the mails in August because it was said to have advocated treason and disloyalty. The following quotations from the *Jeffersonian* were given in court as the basis for the decision: "Men conscripted to go to Europe are virtually condemned to death and everybody knows it," and "Why is your boy condemned to die in Europe?" Watson also wrote, "Does he, the President, not know that the Conscription Act, forcing citizens out of the Union to die in Belgium and France, is every bit as lawless as the action of the Phelps-Dodge Copper Company in forcing these one thousand one hundred miners out of Arizona? What are 1,100 miners to six hundred and eighty-five thousand (685,000) conscripts whom our Caesar has condemned to death in 'foreign fields of blood?' " "What about a carload of German soap made out of our boys," asked Watson. After his mailing privilege had been denied, Watson sought an injunction against the post office official who had withheld his paper from the mail. However, he was unsuccessful and the *Jeffersonian* soon suspended publication. The courts were reluctant to reverse decisions made by Burleson. In the *Jeffersonian* case the judges actually praised the Postmaster General. The court said, "Had the Postmaster General longer permitted the use of the great postal system which he controls for the dissemination of such poison, it would have been to forgo the opportunity to serve his country afforded by his lofty station." [30]

Backed by the courts, Burleson effectively censored newspapers and magazines which criticized the conduct of the war. Many radical publications were summarily put out of business by the withdrawal of their second-class mailing privileges. Burleson suppressed one issue of the *Public* when it advocated raising more of the wartime budget by taxation and less by loans. The *Freeman's Journal and Catholic Register* was censored for printing a statement by Thomas Jefferson that Ireland ought to be free. The *Irish World* aroused Burleson's displeasure when it declared that the French were materialistic and that Palestine would probably not become a free Jewish state, but rather an English protectorate.[31] Burleson told the editor of *Pearson's Magazine* that "the Administration would not tolerate discourteous treatment of our Allies." In 1918 this magazine was twice barred from the mails.[32] In the spring of 1918 the Intercollegiate Socialist Society distributed several hundred copies of a pamphlet, *Why Freedom Matters,* by Norman Angell. The pamphlet contained nothing critical of the war, but it did carry a strong argument against censorship. The main trouble with this pamphlet, said William Hard, "was purely the fault of proving that free speech is a good thing." The Post Office Department detained the copies of the pamphlet and ultimately destroyed them.[33]

One of the most notable cases of censorship took place against the *Nation.* The issue of September 14, 1918, was barred from the mails because of an article entitled "The One Thing Needful" which criticized the Administration's labor policy and Samuel Gompers. "No journal of the standing of the *Nation,*" said Oswald Villard, the editor, "had been molested before." In any event, the ban was lifted four days later because of direct presidential intervention. In recounting his experiences, Villard said that Burleson had misconceived his job of preventing treason and sedition and was attempting to control public opinion.[34] Senator Borah of Idaho was indeed right when he later declared that there was scarcely any more effective way of controlling the press than by giving the Postmaster General the power to keep matter out of the mails.[35]

Naturally, there was vigorous criticism of Burleson's policies in some quarters. Upton Sinclair, who had left the Socialist party on the war issue, asked Wilson on October 22 to answer the Socialist carping with reason, rather than bar publications from the mails. He said he could no longer withhold his protest after seeing the Postmaster General "going from one extreme to the other." Procedure in the *Masses* case, he said, "can only be described as disgraceful." Banning one issue from the mails and then taking away its mailing privilege for not publishing regularly was like a policeman's knocking a man down and then when he cried with pain arresting him for disturbing the peace, Sinclair wrote. Then he added, "It is hard to draw the line, Mr. President, as to the amount of ignorance permitted to a government official; but Mr. Burleson is assuredly on the wrong side of any line that could be drawn by anyone." [36]

Wilson recognized that the Government was dealing with a delicate and difficult problem. "The matter of censorship is growing daily more difficult and more important," he wrote to Louis Wiley on July 23, "because there are certain hostile and disloyal elements in the press of the country which are taking advantage of the present situation and doing the most dangerous and hurtful things." [37] On October 27, 1917, he wrote to Creel, "This is a thorny business we are handling in the matter of these disloyal newspapers, but I am keeping in close touch with the Postmaster General and I believe the thing is being worked out with some degree of equity and success." [38] When John Spargo protested to Wilson over the suppression of Socialist papers, the President wrote the following note to Tumulty:

I don't like to answer this letter myself but I would be very much obliged if you would answer it in the kindest spirit . . . . Please tell him that he is mistaken in supposing that this matter is being handled entirely by the Postmaster General and his subordinates, that I am trying to keep in constant touch with it, and that he will find in the long run that the ban is applied to very few papers indeed, only to those indeed whose offenses against the law are manifest and flagrant. [39]

And along the same line, Wilson wrote to Max Eastman:

I think that a time of war must be regarded as wholly exceptional and that it is legitimate to regard things which would in ordinary circumstances be innocent as very dangerous to the public welfare, but the line is manifestly exceedingly hard to draw and I cannot say that I have any confidence that I know how to draw it. I can only say that a line must be drawn and that we are trying, it may be clumsily but genuinely, to draw it without fear or favor or prejudice. [40]

Wilson's analysis was undoubtedly correct. But unfortunately his subordinates drew the lines with prejudice—prejudice against the opponents of war. Many of Wilson's old friends were bitterly disappointed that he did not take a vigorous and active part in trying to maintain freedom of the press.

Chapter x

A LESSON

FOR THE TEACHERS

During the period 1917–18, individuals in the field of education were usually mild and noncombative. Accustomed to being pressured by school boards, trustees, parents, and local clubs, they often frightened easily. The nationalists had an extensive, though not difficult, job in disciplining some members of this group. After the United States entered the war, schools became seminaries of patriotism. Teachers usually did what they were told to do, and there was little fighting back. Many conformed because they believed in the war, some because they were used to conforming, others because they were frightened into it. After all, most teachers were, and still are, so financially dependent that economic necessity compelled them not to arouse the ire of their administrative superiors.

College presidents and professors, principals and teachers, had talked strongly against war before 1914. Indeed, their opposition to war was rather traditional and many of them had been active in peace movements. Now they either supported the war enthusiastically or kept quiet. Members of the war party saw to it that they knuckled under. According to Howard Beale, "not only teachers who openly opposed the War or had formerly been known as 'pacifists,' but all who were suspected of not giving vigorous support to it, were subjected to local pressures, investigated, and made to give positive proof of their 'loyalty' to the war system." [1] However, in the academic profession there were notable examples of opponents of war.

The New York *Evening Post* reported as early as April 6, 1917, that a political economist had been dismissed from the University of Pennsylvania. The University stated that he was retired because of his age; he was sixty-five. The professor was of the opinion that he had been dismissed because he was a pacifist. In the same month the Socialist professor, Scott Nearing, "resigned" from Toledo University. Actually, as Trachtenberg has pointed out, "authorities were able, in many instances, to take advantage of the war psychology to discharge certain radicals whose presence had proved embarrassing, but for whose dismissal it would have been difficult to find a satisfactory public explanation." [2]

Some of the most highly publicized cases of silencing antiwar students or professors occurred at Columbia University. On April 2, 1917, the *New York Herald* told of the expelling of a student editor of the campus comic magazine for calling the University's president, Nicholas Murray Butler, a czar and for saying that others on the campus were jingoistic. It should be remarked that Butler, prominent in the organization known as the Carnegie Endowment for International Peace, had long been an articulate exponent of peace and freedom of opinion. Now he climbed on the bandwagon of the war party with great agility. After the war started, Butler denounced those who questioned the wisdom of American participation. [3]

Sometime later other students were to incur the wrath of the authorities. But much more important cases involved faculty dismissals. Early in October of 1917 two of Columbia's outstanding professors were ousted. Henry W. L. Dana of the English department was dismissed because of his association with the People's Council and other pacifist groups. Professor James M. Cattell, a distinguished psychologist, was fired at the same time because he had publicly opposed sending conscripts to Europe and had opposed measures which he considered militaristic. The formal statement of the University trustees declared that Dana and Cattell "had done grave injury to the University by their public agitation against the conduct of the war." [4] The *New York Times* editorialized on October 3 that the trustees had "done their duty to the University . . . by expelling two members of the faculty who . . . fomented disloyalty."

Yet some members of Columbia's faculty were not cowed by University officials or editorial writers. Charles A. Beard, John Dewey, and James Harvey Robinson strongly objected to the dismissals. Professor Beard, outstanding historian and political scientist, had stated earlier in the year, "If we have to suppress everything we don't like to hear, this country is resting on a pretty wobbly basis. This country was founded on disrespect and the denial of authority, and it is no time to stop free discussions." [5] Shortly after Dana and Cattell were dismissed, Beard resigned in protest. He wrote to President Butler that the University was controlled by trustees who had no "standing in the world of education, who are reactionary and visionless in politics, narrow and mediaeval in religion." Turning to the question of Germany and the war, he said: "I was among the first to urge a declaration of war by the United States, and I believe that we should now press forward with all our might to a just conclusion. But thousands of my countrymen do not share this view. Their opinions cannot be changed by curses or bludgeons. Argument addressed to their reason and understanding are our best hope . . . ." [6]

Beard declared that he had resigned after concluding that a small group of trustees planned "to take advantage of the state of war to drive out or humiliate or terrorize every man who held progressive, liberal, or unconventional views on political matters in no way connected with the war." [7]

James Harvey Robinson, who also objected to the treatment of Dana and Cattell, had one of his books criticized by some members of the war party. The critic wrote to George Creel, apparently hoping that the Government would do something about supposedly objectionable passages. However, Creel replied that the book was being revised with the assistance of another historian, James Shotwell, "whose anti-German feelings are beyond question." [8]

Early in December Henry Raymond Mussey, a professor of economics, tendered his resignation to Dr. Butler. Late in April, 1918, a professor of international law, Dr. Ellery C. Stowell, handed in his resignation. The *New York Call*, May 2, 1918, said of Stowell, "A staunch supporter of the present war, Dr. Stowell has nevertheless denounced time and again, the attempts to nullify academic freedom in college life."

But the campaign against nonconformists was not confined to Columbia. In July, 1917, the State Council of Defense of Nebraska charged that certain professors at the State University were pro-German. The professors fought back. One of them, Clark E. Persinger of the history department, said he would continue to wage "a vigorous fight against autocratic and aristocratic elements whether it cost him his position or not." Another professor declared there were good and bad qualities in Germans, Englishmen, and Austrians, and said, "If that is unpatriotic let them make the most of it." When these statements were brought to the attention of the Chancellor, he was "very much surprised." [9] On July 12 the *Sacramento Bee* quoted this official as follows: "There are, however, in every faculty a few who have indulged in day dreams of internationalism, world justice, and universal peace to such an extent that they find it difficult to reconcile themselves to the thought of the use of force even in the most just cause." Over this comment the newspaper ran the headline, "Nebraska Chancellor Admits Disloyalty of University Professors."

On June 19, 1918, the *New York Tribune* reported that the regents of the University demanded the resignations of Professors Persinger and Luckey because their public utterances had been "indiscreet and of such a nature as to involve themselves and the University in public criticism." They also demanded the resignation of Professor E. B. Hopf because he held "conscientious scruples against personally helping in the belligerent activities of the Government."

Occasionally storms aroused over the opinions of professors would pass without serious consequences. For instance, a distinguished history professor at the University of California had discussed the economic motives back of the American Revolution. The *Sacramento Bee,* March 23, 1918, lashed out furiously, demanding that "disloyalty" be rooted out. In this case apparently nothing happened to the professor.

Alvin Goodnow Whitney was an instructor in Syracuse University. He was held for the Grand Jury in August, 1917, "for claiming exemption on his New York State military census blank upon the ground that he had conscientious scruples against serving under the national or state governments 'in their present dishonorable war.'" [10] However, no indictment was returned.

In Ashland, Wisconsin, Professor E. A. Schimmel, who taught modern languages, was kidnapped, tarred, and feathered by a local Knights of Liberty mob. Evidently a little odd, Schimmel was reported to have attempted to make people believe he was a spy. After the mob action an inquiry was staged, and Schimmel was completely exonerated. Nothing was done to the members of the mob.[11]

Throughout 1917–18, newspapers continued to report dismissals of professors for disloyalty. In Maine the dean of the University Law School was removed by the board of trustees. The St. Louis *Globe-Democrat,* March 11, 1918, stated that his lectures were tinged with pro-Germanism. The *New York Call,* May 13, 1918, reported that the Board of Regents of the University of Michigan had dismissed several members of the faculty. At that time agents of the Department of Justice were reported to be in Ann Arbor. According to the Seattle *Union-Record,* April 27, 1918, because some members of the University of Washington had been accused of making "half-loyal" statements, the Regents gave the University president the "full power of dismissal over the members of the faculty." The *Ithaca Journal,* October 30, 1918, reported that Henry W. Edgerton, a young professor of law at Cornell University, was granted "an indefinite leave of absence." Professor Edgerton had registered as a conscientious objector. After the war hysteria had died down, however, he returned.

Accusations of disloyalty were made against five faculty members of the University of Illinois in December, 1917. A subcommittee of the Board of Trustees reported that they were not disloyal but that they had been discourteous to an agent of the Department of Justice who was investigating their opinions. The professors had probably not yet adjusted themselves to the new situation in the United States. In reporting the story, the *Evening Call,* December 12, noted that the Board of Trustees had issued a warning to faculty members to be discreet and guard their utterances. One of the five individuals accused at Illinois was Carl Hassler, who was to be one of the most famous conscientious objectors in the first World War.

Professor W. A. Schaper, professor of political science at the University of Minnesota, was dismissed because of his strong antiwar views. After the war declaration, however, he had recommended co-operation with the Government in its activities. He had not, however, gone out "boosting the war." The regents asked him if he was "the kaiser's man" and what he thought of Belgium. A member of the board at Minnesota, Pierce Butler of St. Paul, was quoted by the *Minneapolis Journal,* September 14, 1917, as saying, "Professor Schaper's removal is in harmony with the present tendency to silence disloyal communities, institutions, publications, officials, and individuals." Governor Burnquist and the Public Safety Commission strongly supported the dismissal. Schaper had to give up his profession for some time.

Leon R. Whipple, a professor of journalism at the University of Virginia, made a speech entitled "The Meaning of Pacifism" before the Current Events Club at Sweet Briar College on November 20, 1917. He declared that to make the world safe for democracy and to insure our own democracy everyone should work for peace. He also stated that he was a pacifist "because war does not remove the menace of autocracy, make the world safe for democracy, or protect our own democracy, and we should be busy trying new, noble, even visionary, methods of securing peace." [12] The next day the president of the University received the following telegram from Senator Carter Glass: "As a citizen and taxpayer of Virginia, I protest against the retention at the University of

Leon R. Whipple. Every hour that he remains is a profanation of the history, the traditions, and the aspirations of the institution. He should be dismissed without ceremony for his atrocious utterances at Sweet Briar." [13] The trustees agreed and Professor Whipple was discharged.

President Wilson intervened personally in one case. A teacher at Goucher College came to be a victim of the general hysteria and was on the point of being dismissed. Wilson wrote to President Guth that he was surprised to learn that the trustees intended to dismiss Professor Hans Froelicher because of alleged disloyalty. "I have known so much of Doctor Froelicher through my daughters, and have formed so favorable an impression of him by direct contact with him," Wilson said, "that I am sure that if any such impression on the part of the Trustees exists, it must be based upon some cruel misunderstanding." [14] Froelicher was retained.

But only a very few teachers had friends of such great influence. There was no activity on the part of the Government to protect the unknown. An instructor of German at Vassar College, Miss Agatha Richrath, was arrested on charges that she justified the German invasion of Belgium and the sinking of the *Lusitania*. She was reported to have remarked that "if a person knew that a murder was being committed in a house two doors away he would be justified in going through a building that did not belong to him to prevent it." As for the *Lusitania*, she was alleged to have said that "the ship was carrying bullets for the murder of German fathers." [15]

At the University of Wisconsin an incident occurred involving students and an outside patriotic speaker. Robert McNutt McElroy, a Princeton professor and a speaker for the National Security League, had been invited to give an address at a loyalty meeting being conducted by the citizens of Madison. The University cadets were asked to participate. These cadets had no more than started to march to the hall where the meeting was to be held than a cold, disagreeable rain began. During McElroy's speech the drenched students were forced to sit in the unheated and drafty pit. The meeting lasted for about three hours. Most of the audience got impatient and went home. The cadets were forced to remain and, perhaps naturally, became restive and inattentive.[16] McElroy lost his temper. He stated later:

> Finally, I couldn't stand it any longer. I determined to find out whether it was my fault or whether it was the American point of view that these men object to. So I leaned forward and I deliberately

insulted them. "Do you know what I think of you from your conduct tonight?" I said. "I think you're a bunch of damned traitors!" Well, what do you think happened? A loud cry of protest? A stampede to pull me down on the platform? A demand that I retract that affront to their University? No sir: not any of those things. What happened was absolutely nothing—not a murmur, not a sound, except that toward the back of the room a few men snickered . . . . I was not only thunderstruck; I was appalled. If a speaker said that to a group of men at my University, Princeton, I should hate to have to answer for the consequences.[17]

One might question the actuality of such a childish performance, but people of this type were connected with the National Security League and other super-patriotic organizations. If McElroy did make these statements—and some questioned his version of what happened—little attention was paid to them. In reply to McElroy's published accusations the University issued an effective rebuttal, and the affair was dropped. The incident in itself was unimportant. It does, however, present a rather clear picture of the conceit, the foggy mentality, and the hysteria of so many of the self-styled patriots. George Creel wrote to William E. Dodd, "Few instances have struck me as more disgraceful than the McElroy affair . . . . The National Security League seems to put press notices above patriotism." [18]

In addition to the foregoing incidents, the *New York Times* of March 4, 1918, reported that the resignation of one faculty member had been "accepted" at the University of Missouri, that one faculty member had been dismissed at the University of Indiana and one at the University of Cincinnati. Two or three were being "watched" at Temple University, it was said, and at Notre Dame officials were on a "sharp lookout." Actually, however, these cases tell only a small part of the story. There were many other places where the professors were silenced or disciplined without the matter being reported in the press. Undoubtedly, a number of professors were suspended or dismissed to "prove" an institution's loyalty. Trustees were likely to get nervous if they heard news reports of alleged disloyalty at their college or university. It seemed to require the cleansing procedure of firing someone to show the community and the nation that their institution was properly nationalistic.

Not every professor who came under fire for disloyalty was dismissed. There were some courageous administrators and boards of trustees who refused to be stampeded into hasty action and who resisted the prevalent hysteria. Sometimes faculties voted support to, or sympathy for, a dismissed colleague, but not often did they do much more.

The American Association of University Professors, formed in 1915, was unable, and to a large extent unwilling, to try to protect college teachers who were attacked on charges of disloyalty. The A.A.U.P. condemned the action in Cattell's case and called it a "grave abuse of the power of dismissal." But it went no further. However, even this mild censure was attacked by the nationalist press. The New York *Telegram* of February 13, 1918, suggested the disbandment of the committee and the devotion of its energies to making poison gas. The committee issued a statement later essentially approving the dismissal of other college teachers who did not have conventional views of the war. Concerning this report the *New York Times* editorialized: "Is it not a little singular that the ablest, the most scholarly, the most useful professors are not the ones who are the centers of academic teapot-tempests? It is the shallower and noisier sort that gets into trouble. Why should the judicious and thoughtful professors bother their heads about the denial to the other kind of the academic freedom to put on the fools cap?" [19]

As might be expected, pressure upon teachers in high schools and grammar schools was very strong. On November 16, 1917, the *New York Times* reported that some officials in the New York City school system were watching for teachers who held views "which were subversive of discipline in the schools and which undermined good citizenship." The superintendent told the principals to submit to him the names of teachers whose patriotism was doubtful. The *Times* approved driving out those guilty of pacifism or opposition to the war. It was not a matter of teachers being "actively disloyal." They must be actively loyal. The American Defense Society joined in the clamor. Early in 1918, it also backed a teachers' oath drive. Among the most notable cases of dismissal which occurred in the New York City school system were those of Thomas Mufson, who was charged with maintaining a neutral attitude while discussing anarchism in a classroom; Henry Schneer, who stated that patriotism should not be discussed in classes and that persons in military uniform should not be permitted to address a student body; and Samuel D. Schmalhausen, who was accused of permitting one of his pupils to write an antiwar letter to President Wilson. Schmalhausen was also accused of saying that he did not consider it his duty "to develop in the students under his control instinctive respect for the President of the United States as such, for the Governor of the State of New York as such, and other Federal, state, and municipal officers as such." [20] According to the *New York Herald,* January 21, 1918, Mufson thought anti-Semitism was back of the dismissals. He claimed that all three dismissed teachers and four of six others who were transferred to other schools were Jewish. Supporters of the teachers said it was their independence and lack of subservience which got them fired. In any event, the so-called disloyal teachers received little or no solace from local writers. The *New York Tribune* editorialized, "This action of the Board of Education is a wholesome precedent. There is every reason to believe that among the teachers there is not only tacit disloyalty, but active sympathy for the enemies of the United States." The editor added that the United States did not want to Prussianize itself, but that stern repressive measures must be taken against "half-baked theorizing," "anarchist tendencies," and a "Bolshevik attitude toward the government." [21]

In December, 1917, a Brooklyn teacher, Miss Fannie Ross, was suspended for six months. The *Flushing Evening Journal,* December 27, 1917, reported that "she had been found guilty of opposing the draft and of having used her influence against military enlistment." Another teacher, Mary S. McDowell, was discharged because she was a Quaker and opposed war on religious grounds. She expressed her views only privately, not in class.[22] In the same school a German-born teacher, Gertrude Pignol, was dismissed. She was said to have questioned the accuracy of stories about German atrocities and to have encouraged a German woman not to return to Germany because all available food was needed by the Germans. The slaughter and hardship of war had greatly moved Miss Pignol. Yet, according to Pierce, "the possession of a locket, engraved by her father and carrying the picture of the Kaiser's grandfather on one side and the cornflower on the other, was put in evidence as additional proof of her hostility to the cause of the United States." She said that she loved this country but that she loved Germany also and did not want her native land crushed. For this Miss Pignol was considered an unfit teacher.[23]

In Poughkeepsie, New York, a teacher named B. Hiram Mattingly was dismissed because he was supposed to have said at a Socialist meeting that the Espionage Law was a despotic measure, that the government should be restored to the people, and that the first step should be the election of a Socialist administration in New York.[24] A teacher in Chicago issued a pamphlet stating that the purpose of the war was to restore England's supremacy on the sea and that "if we continue this war the people will pay the bill and the financiers will reap the profit." He was discharged.[25]

In Peoria, Illinois, Charles H. Kammann, a German-born history teacher who was also principal of the school, discussed the war in one of his history classes. He was accused in court of having stated that "it is all nonsense, to talk about getting the Kaiser; we might just as well talk about getting the President." It was also reported that he said the Kaiser did not start the war and that Germany could not be defeated unless she was starved out. The trial court permitted evidence to be brought in to show that Kammann had opposed loans to belligerents during the neutrality years before April, 1917. He was sentenced to three years in Leavenworth Penitentiary and fined five thousand dollars. The most important part of this case, however, was the action of the Circuit Court of Appeals which reversed the decision. The court spoke bluntly when it declared that Kammann's statements had been taken out of context and that there was no evidence to show they had interfered with the war effort in any way.[26]

Examples of pressure and punishment can be found almost everywhere, and the numbers could be multiplied many times. After carrying on a class discussion of the causes of the war, one English teacher was told by her superintendent that she should confine her teaching to English. The superintendent then warned all history and English teachers "to limit themselves to what was 'in the book.'"[27] The Board of Education in Los Angeles even went so far as to forbid teachers to permit intramural debates on such subjects as the program of the League to Enforce Peace.[28]

Even before the declaration of war, the Los Angeles *Times*, April 3, 1917, reported that a resolution was passed forbidding "criticism of the President of the United States or Congress by teachers in the Los Angeles public schools." And after the United States entered the war, a New Jersey teacher was ordered out of town for making unfriendly utterances about the United States and President Wilson.[29] Leon Battig, a teacher in Albia, Iowa, "on suspicion of disloyalty, was dragged out by a mob, stripped to the waist, painted yellow, and marched in this condition around the public square carrying a flag."[30] Another teacher in Maine was dismissed for the simple act of taking driving lessons from an unnaturalized German.[31]

Early in November, 1917, there was a Liberty Loan parade in Sacramento, California. Because some teachers did not march, the *Sacra-*

mento Bee became its usual excited and intolerant self. On November 12, 1917, the *Bee* published an article under the headline, "All Disloyal or Apathetic School Teachers Should Be Expelled." It strongly objected to one teacher who said that she did not know if the United States was right in the war. In this same issue, the *Bee* declared:

> It is time for her to be put out of the public schools and to be put out forever . . . . And when another declares she doesn't believe the Board of Education has the right to interfere with her religion and her conscience . . . then it is high time a drastic lesson be taught her . . . to the effect that the religion of Liberty and the conscience of the United States are above her creed and her opinion, and that she will have to obey!

Afterwards it developed that there was some question as to whether teachers had been ordered to parade in the Liberty Loan celebration. The *Sacramento Bee* insisted on November 14, 1917, that "if orders were given [to teachers] by the Board of Education . . . those among them who did not march and were not sick should be expelled. Discipline in these matters must be maintained." In the same issue of the *Bee* Will C. Wood, Commissioner of Secondary Education, was quoted as "flaying" teachers who were disloyal. He was also quoted as saying that "the public school system was founded upon the principle of supporting the state." In December, 1917, when the fight with teachers in New York City was at its height, the *Sacramento Bee* ran a cartoon on disloyal teachers with the caption, "Wipe 'Em Out!"

The records show that many teachers were controlled through militant school boards. In many places, however, no records were left, because there was no trial and no one to defend a teacher accused of disloyalty. But, as Beale has said, "the worst and most general sort of repression . . . occurred in the thousands of cases where public opinion or fear of disciplinary measures silenced teachers so completely that they ceased, for the duration of the War, to have views of their own." [32]

DISCIPLINING
THE CLERGY

The record of church support of wars is a long one. Sometimes this support has come because of the religious aspect of a war. At other times it has been given merely because of the close connection between the church and state. More often than not, however, the churches have preached war primarily because their members wanted and expected them to do so. Churches are composed of men and it is only natural that they should reflect men's whims and desires. During 1917 and 1918 most clergymen vigorously backed the war. The American cause became God's cause, the war against Germany a "holy war." [1]

Two of the most strident jingoists in the country, Newell Dwight Hillis and William A. (Billy) Sunday, were ministers. Hillis, pastor of the Plymouth Congregational Church of Brooklyn, toured the country repeating the most gory atrocity stories.[2] George Creel complained to Professor Robert McElroy of the National Security League, "We are hearing some very disturbing reports as to the speeches that are being made by Dr. Hillis. In every community he seems to arouse bitterness, and such speeches as we have been able to see are somewhat reckless as to facts. The matter has been brought to the attention of the President repeatedly." [3]

Sunday, a sensational gymnastic type of missionary evangelist, had romped through American headlines for years. His antics and turgid emotionalism provided pleasing copy for journalists, and even the most conservative newspapers treated him with respect. Blatantly anti-German,

Sunday, who held revival meetings in many large cities during the war, declared that "if you turn hell upside down you will find 'Made in Germany' stamped on the bottom." [4] On one occasion he got into a fist fight over differing attitudes toward the Germans. During a sermon in Atlanta, Georgia, in December, 1917, Sunday digressed from his main theme to attack the Germans and assure his audience that the United States would win the war with God's help and blessing. It could not be, Sunday said, that God would be on the side of "a dirty bunch that would stand aside and allow a Turk to outrage a woman." [5] At this point a member of the audience stepped forward to challenge Sunday's statement. Several of the evangelist's aids attempted to keep the man from reaching the platform but without success. Before the crowd tore the disrupter away several blows were exchanged—an exchange which the *New York Times* reporter said was about even. [6] Members of the crowd then knocked the man from the platform and beat him. All of the facts of this incident are not clear, but it indicates that one of the nation's leading clergymen was willing to engage in fisticuffs, if necessary, to enforce his strong anti-German views.

Not only did most ministers give strong support to the war, but the Government could count on the backing of churches and organizations of churches. For example, the Federal Council of Churches of Christ in America co-operated closely with the Government. Its main war influence was to help people to bridge the mental and spiritual gap between peace and war. The Federal Council did much to show how the war would defend Christianity and promote the will of God. [7]

Despite the situation just described, there was a sizable number of churchmen who opposed not only this war, but all wars. Indeed, some of the most important opponents of war came from the ranks of the clergy. Taking Jesus at his word, these ministers argued that the teachings of the Prince of Peace forbade engaging in war; that the true Christian could not resort to violence. Being true to their consciences, some ministers preached against war from their pulpits. If opposition to war by any groups or classes was to be tolerated, one might expect that it would be opposition by ministers of the gospel. However, these men of God received no more tolerance or respect from the super-patriots than those who opposed war for secular reasons. During 1917 and 1918, the press frequently carried accounts of ministers being fired or resigning —usually under pressure—for loyalty reasons. A detailed cataloguing of these events would serve no useful purpose, but some examples will show how the clerical opponents of war fared under popular hysteria.

As early as June 15, 1917, the Los Angeles *Times* reported that in Long Beach, California, a Unitarian minister was accused of disloyalty because he disapproved of a remark attributed to Attorney General Gregory that people should "keep their mouths shut and obey the law." The New York *Evening Call* reported on December 24, 1917, that in Utah an Episcopalian bishop with the good American name of Paul Jones was forced to resign because of his pacifistic utterances. At about the same time, E. P. Ryland, superintendent of the Los Angeles district of the Methodist Church, was forced to resign because he refused to join the bishop in a series of patriotic addresses.[8] In Astoria, New York, a pacifistic Episcopalian rector, Leigh R. Urban, removed an American flag from his church contrary to the wishes of his congregation. He was shortly requested to leave. The Reverend Urban argued that after prayer and meditation he had concluded that Jesus would not have His followers overcome evil with war.[9] Although Urban was a mild-mannered, gentle pacifist, the *New York Times* editorialized that his position was "sedition thinly disguised" and that he had in every way "except by open avowal put himself in the ranks of the nation's enemy."[10] Here was a case where the congregation, as well as the editorial writer, seemed to agree with Theodore Roosevelt when he said that "the clergyman who does not put the flag above the church had better close his church and keep it closed."[11]

The congregation of the Union church of Palisades, New Jersey, became aroused because of the sermons of its "pacifist" preacher, Marion J. Bradshaw. The minister had declared that the Christian church had failed to use its influence to avoid war. Members of the church said that Bradshaw's sermons, outside of those on war, were very helpful.[12] Nonetheless, Bradshaw had to go. At Newton, Massachusetts, the Reverend Abraham J. Muste resigned under pressure because he opposed the war.[13]

In some cases ministerial opponents of war were handled roughly or even jailed. Reverend Samuel Siebert of Carmel, Illinois, was jailed in December, 1917, because he said in a sermon that he opposed war. In Audubon, Iowa, two men, one of them a minister, were seized by a crowd who put ropes around their necks and dragged them toward the public square. After one of them signed a check for a thousand-dollar Liberty bond he was released. The minister was released because of the intervention of his wife. The *Sacramento Bee*, December 27, 1917, headlined the report, "Near Lynchings Give Pro-Germans Needed Lesson."

In California several ministers organized a group called the Christian Pacifists. Members of fourteen different religious denominations took part.

The preliminary meeting was called by the Reverend Floyd Hardin, minister of the Methodist Episcopal church of Atwater, California, on July 27, 1917, and was held in the First Baptist church of Los Gatos with the co-operation of its minister, the Reverend Robert Whitaker. As a result of this meeting, a conference of the group was called to protest against the militaristic attitude of the Christian church.

The conference was scheduled to meet in Long Beach, but superpatriots prevented its being held there. When the group tried to meet in Los Angeles, members were not permitted to enter Flower Auditorium. Incited partly by leading clergymen, nationalists raised a terrific cry against the Christian Pacifists. It was reported that Billy Sunday, who was then trying to win Los Angeles for the Lord, declared that "the Christian Pacifists ought to be treated as Frank Little was at Butte and then let the coroner do the rest." The Reverend George Davidson of the St. John's Episcopal church told the local loyalty league that "the name pacifist is just a veneer to shield a traitor. We must fight fire with fire and stamp out all pacifism in Los Angeles." [14]

In spite of this kind of opposition, the pacifist ministers met in the Douglas Building in Los Angeles on October 1, 1917. At this point the police staged a raid, and three ministers, Robert Whitaker, Floyd Hardin, and Harold Storey, were arrested and jailed, although they were shortly released on bail. The charge against the men was most odd. They were accused of "discussing, arguing and preaching certain thoughts and theories in opposition to the orderly conduct of the affairs of the United States of America, and which said thoughts and theories were calculated to cause any American citizen then and there present to assault and batter the persons so uttering the same." [15] Seven additional sessions of the conference were held in private homes under police surveillance before the last meeting was broken up by the South Pasadena Home Guards. Storey, a Quaker, was taken in a car, then turned loose to a mob which beat him. According to one account, a "man who copied the number of the auto which carried Storey off was thrown down, beaten and relieved of the book in which he had made the memorandum." [16]

The trial of Hardin, Whitaker, and Storey was conducted in something of a Hollywood manner. Old soldiers were mobilized and brought to court to be photographed. Bitter and noisy attacks were made upon the defendants. The judge denounced them in a patriotic and religious oration. He was supposed to have said in effect that this was a holy war of God, that the United States was fighting at the command of God, and that anyone who resisted the state opposed God.[17] He was also reported to have said that criticism of the President and of Government policies could not be permitted in wartime anywhere or under any circumstances.[18] The defendants claimed that the prosecution was granted amazing license by the Court. The judge told the jury that if any remarks made by Storey at the meeting tended, in its judgment, to incite revolution or anarchy, then the meeting was an "unlawful assembly." [19] The prosecution also intimidated the jurors. The trio were found guilty and each was sentenced to six months in jail and fined fifteen hundred dollars.[20] The judge declared that the people of Los Angeles were giving notice through the courts that no peace meetings would be tolerated and these men would be a public example "to deter others from preaching their pernicious doctrines there." [21] The case was decided more on the basis of the local state of mind than on any testimony offered. A writer for the *Nation* declared that the situation in Los Angeles indicated that "war hysteria has reached a height at which sane men must stand aghast. Press, pulpit, people, and courts, even, seem equally mad with war-frenzy." [22]

The principal clerical opposition to the war was not found in the popular churches. It was the smaller, poorer churches that stood most steadfastly against war. These organizations, considered by many to be on the fringe of religious respectability, were the ones which caused the most irritation among nationalists. For instance, a Pentecostal minister by the name of William Reid was arrested because he was reported by the *Sacramento Bee*, December 21, 1917, to have said that "the present war was brought on by all of the nations and that none was more deserving of punishment than this country for its arrogance." The police chief told him, according to the *Bee*, "You should be lined up against a brick wall and shot."

An important case of opposition to war by clergymen involved the Reverend Clarence H. Waldron, a Pentecostal minister of Windsor, Vermont. Believing that war was contrary to the teachings of Christ, he was reported to have told his Bible Class that "a Christian can take no part in the war." Then he added, "Don't shed your precious blood for your country." He was also accused of distributing a religious pamphlet, *The Word of the Cross*, which said, "Surely, if Christians were forbidden to fight to preserve the Person of their Lord and Master, they may not fight to preserve themselves, or any city they should happen to dwell in. Christ has no kingdom here. His servants must not fight." [23] For the various remarks attributed to him and for distributing this pamphlet he was arrested and charged with violating the Espionage Act.

Waldron's case first received publicity on October 21, 1917, when he failed to include patriotic exercises in his morning worship service. This was "Liberty Loan Sunday." Some people in the community charged him with disloyalty. Even though Waldron sang the "Star-Spangled Banner" with a flag draped around him, he was still under suspicion, and local citizens reported him to the federal authorities. He was arrested and tried in an atmosphere of strong hostility. He was unable to get an attorney to take his case. One lawyer said that "the only defense was insanity or absolute denial of everything." Finally, a court-appointed attorney defended Waldron. During the trial Waldron's Christian spirit so manifested itself that he won many friends and the outcome was a hung jury.[24] However, the Government prosecuted the case again, with the assistance of ministers from the Methodist and Baptist churches who resented Waldron's proselyting members of their congregations. Waldron was a former Baptist. In his charge to the jury the judge said, "The defendant's evidence tends to show that the only intention which he had was to serve God." But, the judge added, even if Waldron's motive was good, that should "not excuse him, if you find that he also intended to cause insubordination, disloyalty, or refusal of duty." [25] The jury found that this had been Waldron's intention. It returned a verdict of guilty, and the judge sentenced him to fifteen years at Atlanta Penitentiary, although he was pardoned about a year later. The Attorney General reported that this case was an "effective deterrent against a very dangerous type of antiwar propaganda." [26]

In Rockford, Illinois, the Reverend David Gerdes of the Church of the Brethren was arrested for his opposition to the war. Gerdes was accused of having recommended that his followers refuse to purchase Liberty bonds because, he felt, this was equivalent to shooting bullets at Germans. The case was tried under Judge K. M. Landis, who brought forth the old and ridiculous question, "What would you do if a Hun were to attack the honor of your daughter?" This same question was asked of Gerdes' brother and a member of the congregation. The *Chicago Daily News*, November 20, 1918, reported as follows:

Both said that in such a case they would plead that in God's name their daughter be spared. To kill a man, though a brute, would be to imperil their souls. "Is your soul worth more than your daughter's honor?" asked the court . . . . "It is worth more than all," was the reply. "Take them out of the courtroom!" shouted Judge Landis to a bailiff. "These men hold their measly little shriveled souls of more importance than they do the honor of their mother, wife, or daughter."

Although the Armistice had already been signed when this case came before him, Landis sentenced this minister to ten years in Leavenworth Penitentiary. The term was later commuted to one year and a day.

One religious group which was stridently opposed to war went under, among other names, that of Russellites, or later, Jehovah's Witnesses. Pastor Charles T. Russell, the founder, died in 1916. After his death the work was headed by Joseph T. Rutherford. This sect had many zealous and devoted followers. One of the main tenets of this minor religious group was a belief that war was un-Christian.[27] *The Finished Mystery,* a book written by Russell, was the immediate cause of much trouble for the Society. This book dealt with the Russellite doctrine which opposed any killing of human beings. The passages which angered the governments of Canada and the United States were outspokenly against war. In one place *The Finished Mystery* stated:

> Nowhere in the New Testament is patriotism (a narrow-minded hatred of other peoples) encouraged. Everywhere and always murder in its every form is forbidden. And yet, under the guise of patriotism, the civil governments of the earth demand of peace-loving men the sacrifice of themselves and their loved ones and the butchery of their fellows, and hail it as a duty demanded by the laws of heaven.[28]

In another place the book claimed that Satan created three great untruths, "human immortality, the Anti-Christ, and a certain delusion which is best described by the word patriotism, but which is in reality murder." Consequently:

> If you say that this war is a last resort in a situation which every other method, patiently tried, has failed to meet, I must answer that this is not true . . . . In its ultimate causes this war is the natural product of our unChristian civilization . . . . There is not a question raised, an issue involved, a cause at stake, which is worth the life of one bluejacket on the sea or one khaki coat in the trenches.[29]

There then followed a harsh attack on the clergy as recruiting agents.

Distribution of *The Finished Mystery* began on January 17, 1917, before the war started. Because of government objections, Rutherford stopped the printing in March, 1918. At the same time, arrests began to be made under the Espionage Act for the publication and distribution of the book. In New York City raids were made on the church's headquarters. Immediately afterwards there were similar raids in Pennsylvania, Texas, Ohio, Missouri, and California. Wherever the publication was being circulated, or wherever it was found, arrests were made. Convictions usually followed on the basis that the book obstructed recruiting and enlistment.[30] On June 22, 1918, the *New York Times* editorialized that freedom of religion was not unlimited. The writer declared that the status of liberty was perhaps not what it should be, but, he added, it must be that way.

Judge Rutherford and six other defendants in New York City were sentenced to twenty years in the penitentiary. After the war, however, the conviction of Rutherford was reversed. On May 14, 1919, in an appellate court, Judge Henry C. Ward gave his opinion that "the defendants . . . did not have the temperate and impartial trial to which they were entitled." [31]

The "purification" process in the movies, the press, the schools, and the churches removed and suppressed criticism of the war in places where it might have been important and helpful in clarifying the nation's wartime objectives. It also destroyed the respect of some Americans for the idea of freedom. Part of the result was described by Herbert Croly in a letter to President Wilson on October 19, 1917:

> The tendency at present is to build up a body of public opinion which is either pro-war or anti-war and which has not any intelligent grasp of the way in which the war can be made to serve the purposes which your Administration wishes to make it serve. The propagandists connected with the American [i.e., National] Security League and the American Defense Society, who are setting themselves up at the present time as the only true arbiters of loyalty and who are gaining a great deal of prestige from the fact, are the very people who will subsequently make the task of realizing the constructive purposes which lie behind American fighting excessively and unnecessarily difficult . . . . The war propaganda is being conducted in such a way that militarists like Mr. Roosevelt are allowed to appropriate it.[32]

~~~~~~

"Render unto Caesar"

THE CONSCIENTIOUS OBJECTOR

The entire antiwar movement was conspicuously exemplified by the conscientious objectors. Among these were found representatives of each type of opponent of war. There were the religious objectors, the alien objectors, the humanitarian or liberal objectors, and, finally, the political objectors. The first, the traditional conscientious objectors, opposed all wars, all human killing. The aliens were objectors for personal or nationalistic reasons. They did not want to fight against or kill their own people. The humanitarian or liberal objectors held that all men were brothers and that fraternal blood should not be shed. Among the political objectors there were many radicals, anarchists, syndicalists, and Socialists, men and women profoundly dissatisfied with the current state of society in the United States. Many of these people were quite willing to go to war and to kill, but they objected to participating in a "capitalist" war. It cannot be denied, however, that many of the political and humanitarian objectors were, as Congressman Carl Hayden of Arizona pointed out in 1917, "just as firm in their convictions as those who oppose war from motives of religion." [1]

The problem of conscientious objectors was an old and difficult one. It raised the important question of the relationship between the state and a man's conscience. Actually, there has been little reason to believe that the problem ever will be solved. During the time of Diocletian, 298 A.D., Marcellus, a Roman centurion stationed in the province of Asturias in Spain, threw down his arms and refused to take the oath of allegiance to the Emperor. Declaring that he could obey no one but Jesus Christ, Marcellus renounced forever the use of "carnal weapons" in serving an "idolatrous master." Sentence was at once pronounced, and Marcellus was beheaded the same day.[2] It was a case such as this which is reported to have prompted the Emperor to say, "These pitiful wretches enjoy the peace and splendor of Rome but will not move a finger to protect or to extend either."[3] But there were to be many more Marcelluses and Diocletians, even in the twentieth century.

Congress did not give sufficient attention to the matter of conscientious objection in writing the Selective Service Act. The only provision made for conscientious objectors was that military exemptions would be given, provided the objector belonged to a religious body which opposed war. In keeping with the law, President Wilson ordered on June 30, 1917, that a member of "a well recognized religious sect or organization" whose creed forbade members to engage in war would not have to serve as a combatant if he held religious convictions against fighting, and if he could substantiate his claim before the local draft board.[4] However, no man would be exempted from service in any noncombatant category which the President might designate. The main trouble with the law and the President's executive order was that they did not take into consideration those who had conscientious objections to war on other than religious grounds. Furthermore, objectors were left under military control, a relationship which was certain to breed trouble.

The point varied at which the conflict between the individual objector and the federal Government came to a head. It might be when the conscientious objector was ordered to register. Sometimes it occurred when he was ordered to appear for a physical examination or when his draft board called him to entrain for camp. Most often, however, the conflict came after he arrived at a military base and became subject to military orders.

As mentioned earlier, only a relatively small number of draft age men failed to register. Even most of those who opposed the principles of the Selective Service Act, including the American Union Against Militarism, urged men to register. But some conscientious objectors refused to be drafted. In Providence, Rhode Island, John T. Dunn, an Irish Catholic, Adolph F. Yanyar, a German Socialist, and Theodore Hiller, a Russian-German Socialist, refused to register. When government authorities registered them, they refused to serve. They were then tried by a military court-martial, found guilty of desertion, and sentenced to twenty years imprisonment.[5] Joseph Coldwell, an elderly Socialist, strongly objected to this kind of treatment for political conscientious objectors. He said they were the "victims of a damnable system of government" and were guilty of no crime except that they had "refused to become uniformed murderers." Coldwell was arrested and sentenced to three years in prison for attempting to stimulate rebellion and disobedience to military law.[6]

Some conscientious objectors took the position that the military had no jurisdiction over them. They turned themselves over to the civil authorities and were prosecuted and sentenced in the civil courts. But in most cases, the men were not permitted to remain under civilian control. If a man had been given a short sentence in the county jail, at the end of the period he was usually sent to a military camp. A notable exception to this general rule was the case of Roger N. Baldwin, director of the National Civil Liberties Bureau. Ordered to report for his physical examination shortly before the war ended, Baldwin ignored the summons and presented himself to the civil authorities for prosecution. He was sentenced to a year in jail.[7]

Between May, 1917, and November, 1918, 64,693 claims were filed for noncombatant service by those who had some scruples against participating in war. Local draft boards recognized 56,830 of these as being sincere, and 20,873 were inducted out of 29,679 who passed the physical examination. There were probably many other conscientious objectors who did not claim exemption and who were inducted.[8]

Those who sought exemption from combat duty because of religious principles had relatively little trouble with their draft boards. This was especially the case if they were Mennonites or Quakers, who had a long and well-known aversion to war. Draft officials generally gave these men exemption certificates which could be presented at the military camp to certify their sincerity. But, as will be shown later, even some of those who belonged to well-known pacifist religious groups came into conflict with the army.

There was a general feeling by members of local draft boards, however, that the nonreligious objectors were not sincere. They were generally considered slackers and cowards. Not only did draft boards take this attitude, but community opinion could not understand the conscientious scruples of a man who did not base his action on religion. That a person might be motivated by sincere ideological or political beliefs which would bar his participation in war was incomprehensible to the average American in 1917. The fact that some objectors in this class were political and economic radicals also militated against their being treated understandingly or tolerantly. A good case in point was that of Louis C. Fraina.

In September, 1917, a group of political radicals held a conscientious objectors' meeting in New York City. Fraina was among the leaders. He complained that the Government recognized only religious conscientious objectors. "But since when must a man necessarily belong to a church, belong to a creed, a recognized creed, before he can have a conscience," Fraina asked. Then he explained that the nonreligious and religious objectors were "distinctly different." He had acquired his objection, Fraina said, "by experience, by thinking, action, and I have felt it flow into my conscience and my life . . . ." Fraina charged that the Government recognized the religious objectors and penalized nonreligious ones "because the system of things that this government represents, the infamous system of capitalism has nothing to fear from the religious conscientious objector . . . ." Then he added, "But it has everything to fear from the nonreligious, from the social conscientious objector, because the nonreligious conscientious objector is not interested in his conscience alone, but interested in his social principle that his conscience represents, and is trying to overthrow a system of things that produces war and produces other evils . . . ." In a pamphlet which Fraina distributed the position was taken that to this class of objectors alternative service was just as objectionable as military duty itself.[9] When political conscientious objectors spoke in this vein it is not hard to see why they received little sympathy from local draft boards. Most of this type of objectors arrived at camp without any certificate which recognized them as conscientious objectors.

Between September, 1917, and March, 1918, the President and Secretary of War issued a series of orders designed to deal with the problem of conscientious objectors. On September 25, Secretary Baker said that Mennonites should not be forced "to wear uniforms as the question of raiment is one of the tenets of their religious faith." About two weeks later the Secretary ordered that army commanders segregate the conscientious objectors and place them under instructors who would treat them with "tact and consideration." On December 19, Baker directed that all men who had "personal scruples against war" should be considered conscientious objectors. This gave official recognition to the nonreligious objector. President Wilson issued an executive order on March 20, 1918, recognizing conscientious objectors who (1) belonged to a religious sect and had been certified by their local draft boards or (2) conscientiously opposed war for other than religious reasons but had no certificates. These men were to be assigned to noncombatant service to the extent to which they could accept it in good conscience.[10]

The orders issued by high civilian officials indicate that the Government's policy toward conscientious objectors was to be more liberal than that envisioned in the Selective Service Act, which recognized only religious exemptions. The National Civil Liberties Bureau referred to President Wilson's order of March 20, 1918, as "a conspicuous contribution to the reconciliation of conscience and the State under conscription."[11] This may have been true in principle, but there was a wide gap between principle and practice in handling conscientious objectors.

It was the army which had to administer the law and carry out the executive orders relating to conscientious objectors. Many army men were intellectually and spiritually unprepared to deal with this problem. Their god was discipline; orders must be obeyed. But conscientious objectors did not believe in military commandments. Thus the determination of army officers to fit the C.O. into military routine was pitted against the stubborn will of the objectors who refused to obey military orders.

The main trouble came in connection with the nonreligious objector. Army personnel had little sympathy for this type of person, especially if he were a political radical. Major Frank S. White, Jr., judge advocate at Camp Funston, wrote, "Camp Funston was selected as a dumping ground for the segregation of a large number of these so-called conscientious objectors." Those who had religious scruples against fighting caused no trouble, he said. But there was a large group of "alleged conscientious objectors," White explained, who had no religious objections to war, but who "pretended to have conscientious objections based upon the view of the obligations which they owed to the country." Many in this class, he said,

> were admittedly Socialists and proven to be pro-Germans, who did not believe in Deity, and whose aim was to spread insidious and treasonable propaganda throughout this country, and were actually caught in disseminating it in this military camp, which was subversive of all discipline and destructive of the morale of our Army . . . .

> They would even refuse to march in orderly formation to and from their mess, but would straggle along as they saw fit, and when being ordered out to mess or exercise they would stand in the doorway and block it so that the guards or other persons could not pass, defying the guards and officers to move them; they refused to take exercise, baths, and keep their bodies and belongings clean and in

a sanitary condition; they refused to be vaccinated or inoculated in order to safeguard themselves as well as their fellow soldiers from sickness and disease. In fact, they refused to obey and apparently took pleasure in letting it be known that they would take no part under the Military Establishment nor obey any military command whatever.[12]

It was not until the President's order of March 20, 1918, that the types of noncombatant service were determined. Meanwhile, conscientious objectors were to be segregated on the basis of Secretary Baker's order of October 10, 1917. But when conscientious objectors arrived at an army camp the general practice was to get as many of them as possible to accept combatant duty. All kinds of pressures were used to break the convictions of the objectors. In some camps they were enticed, jeered, hosed, beaten, placed in solitary confinement and given other rigorous and inhuman treatment. Army officers often looked upon physical punishment and a policy of pressure as the best means of testing the genuineness of a man's convictions. Thousands of conscientious objectors did change their minds, for one reason or another, after they reached camp. The figures confirm this conclusion. Some 20,873 religious objectors had certificates supporting their status when they arrived at camp. There were others who claimed exemption from military duty but did not have certificates from their local draft boards. Of all these men only 3,989 finally refused to accept any kind of military duty.[13] From the army's viewpoint, its tactics were successful because four-fifths, or more, of the men finally accepted some kind of duty. But the means used to achieve this end often bordered on the inhuman.

Draftees began arriving in camp in September, 1917. It was then that army commanders had to deal with the difficult problem of handling conscientious objectors. They were still cursing the problem when the war ended over a year later. All too often officers viewed the C.O. with hostility and tried to force him to obey orders. It was in these cases that the brutalities resulted. However, it would be unfair to condemn the army as a whole. Some of the commanding generals interpreted the orders regarding treatment of conscientious objectors in a liberal, sympathetic, and kindly manner. Even some of the strongest defenders of the conscientious objectors and severest critics of the army admit that the handling of these men was not a uniform policy of mistreatment.[14] However, the treatment given to many conscientious objectors leaves a black mark upon the War Department.

There are abundant sources which testify to the rough and sometimes sadistic ill-treatment of C.O.'s. Norman Thomas has related numerous such incidents in his book, *The Conscientious Objector in America* (1923). Two prominent nonreligious objectors later had their experiences published—Ernest L. Meyer, *Hey! Yellowbacks* (1930), and Harold Studley Gray, *Character "Bad"* (1934). Perhaps the best data, however, are to be found in the files of the American Civil Liberties Union.

A typical case of the objector versus the military was that of Sheldon W. Smith, who refused to put on a uniform or to sign the clothing slip. Smith wrote:

> They put a pen in my hand and held it there to make a mark instead of a signature. Next I was stripped in a violent manner and taken inside and dressed amidst arm twisting, thumping, etc. in the endeavor to have me do it myself. When finally dressed in blue denhams [*sic*], part of the noncommissioned officers took me to the bath house which was soon well occupied with spectators or would-be assistants. They again stripped their victim, put him under a shower and scrubbed him with a broom; then whipped him with their belts; put a rope around his neck and drew it up to a pipe until he could not breathe; all the while renewing their question about giving in. One would cry one thing and one another so they did not stick to one form of punishment very long only the bathing was continued until I was chilled and shook all over, part of the time they had me on my back with face under a faucet and held my mouth open. They got a little flag ordering me to kiss it and kneel down to it.[15]

At Camp Grant in Illinois an "atheist objector" by the name of Tinsky "was upstairs in solitary confinement fed on bread and water. He was handcuffed and made to stand up all day and to sleep in the cuffs at night." In Camp Upton an objector refused to obey orders and was struck and cut across the knees and shins repeatedly with a bayonet. For two hours he was beaten with fists and rifles.[16] From other camps came similar reports.

A soldier wrote to Oswald Garrison Villard, "We had a Russian objector who refused to sign for his equipment; after three days on the coal pile, little food, nobody allowed to talk to him or give him anything, a good shot of the needle, he finally gave in. He is a sick man in the hospital now. Another foreigner said good-bye to his wife last Sunday and then cut his throat; some mess." [17]

Norman Thomas has reported the case of three conscientious objectors at Fort Riley, Herman Kaplan, Benjamin Breger, and Francis Hennessey, who were punished for refusing to perform any combatant or noncombatant duty. They would not even sweep their cells. Quoting the diary of one of the victims, Thomas records that they were taken one at a time into the corridor:

> a hemp rope slung over the railing of the upper tier was put about their necks, hoisting them off their feet until they were at the point of collapse. Meanwhile the officers punched them on their ankles and shins. They were then lowered and the rope was tied to their arms, and again they were hoisted off their feet. This time a garden hose was played on their faces with the nozzle about six inches from them, until they collapsed completely, when they were carried and dumped screaming and moaning into the cage and dumped into bed.[18]

There were numerous cases of brutal treatment of conscientious objectors at Camp Funston. One objector, Emanuel Silver, wrote that with others he was aroused from sleep every two hours during the night for several nights and made to march before the point of a bayonet. He was also put under cold showers, his head was severely beaten, and he received only bread and water. He collapsed from exhaustion on October 12, 1918.[19] Another objector wrote that he and others were given cold showers after which one of the group was "dragged back and forth and viciously belabored until thoroughly exhausted." [20]

Norman Thomas, who studied the matter carefully, believed that General Leonard Wood was largely responsible for the treatment of conscientious objectors at Fort Riley and Camp Funston.[21] Wood, the commanding general, had little sympathy for conscientious objectors and apparently none at all for the nonreligious objectors. It may well be that Wood's attitude was reflected by the officers under his command. In reply to a letter from the father of a mistreated C.O., General Wood wrote that these

> alleged conscientious objectors, conspired together and refused to obey the lawful commands of a superior officer in this camp. They are confined in the provost guardhouse and are now awaiting trial by the general court-martial convened at this camp. While in confinement they have defied the constituted authorities and have been mutinous in their attitude towards the officers in command of them

. . . . Your son and his associates do not come within the purview of the Act . . . affording exemption from military service to sincere religious objectors. They do not claim membership in any church. They are, as shown by their words and acts, avowed enemies of this Government, and are opposing the Government in the efforts which it is making to crush autocracy . . . . Fortunately for the Nation and for our Institutions—men of the type of your son and his associates are rare. If this were not the case our Government would soon cease to exist and we would fall under the sway of the aggressor.[22]

The father replied:

Since you do not deny certain atrocities committed upon conscientious objectors by guards under your command—which if true, out-Prussianize the worst of Prussians—I am forced to the conclusion that your ground of accusing my son of mutinous conduct is based upon his refusal to continuously submit to a ritual of despotic militarism, at once un-American and inhuman . . . . You speak true when you utter a warning lest we should fall under the sway of the aggressor. "Eternal vigilance is the price of liberty." In the past history aggressors have often risen from within, and the heels of oppression were usually worn by those that professed a superior love of country and humanity. Your attack upon my son as a coward easily recoils, because cowards do not stand by principles as does my son, nor does a coward have any principles except that of submission and servility.[23]

Men who refused to obey army orders in spite of harsh treatment left the military in a distressed state of mind. In February, 1918, the commanding officer at Camp Custer, Michigan, appealed to Washington for advice on what to do with those who "refuse to obey orders of any kind and who will do no work . . . . Nothing moves them. They respond to no appeals to their patriotism or to their manhood. They will not even consent to act as janitors in the Y.M.C.A. huts, the K. of C. buildings or the camp library." [24]

It was not possible to keep the public from learning something about the mistreatment of conscientious objectors. As early as November 20, 1917, the Detroit *News* told of objectors being thrown into the guardhouse and suffering other indignities. One group of conscientious objectors signed a petition and managed to smuggle it out of camp. "Conditions," they said, had "become practically intolerable." They referred to cold showers at all times of day and night, to attempts to starve the men into compliance, and to an ironclad censorship. "The guards at all opportunities, have battered and manhandled us very often using their bayonets . . . . Just now matters have become so strained that our health, in fact our very lives are in jeopardy . . . . We are at the complete mercy of the petty officers here." [25] But even when conditions became known, public opinion was surprisingly unconcerned.

The question of whether a man was sincere created a real problem for those who had control over the conscientious objectors. On April 27, 1918, Secretary Baker ordered that any objector whose sincerity was questionable, who engaged in propaganda, or who was "sullen and defiant" should be court-martialed.[26] Under a further order of June 1, a Board of Inquiry was established to determine whether a conscientious objector was sincere. This board was composed of Judge Julian W. Mack, Dean Harlan F. Stone of the Columbia Law School, and Major Walter G. Kellogg.[27] Members of the board went from camp to camp interviewing objectors. Men who belonged to sects like the Quakers or Mennonites were usually questioned only briefly and generally accepted as sincere. They were then recommended for the regular exemptions. Political objectors caused the most trouble for the board. If a man said he might fight in some wars, but not in this particular war, he was usually not considered sincere.[28]

Ernest Meyer, author of *Hey! Yellowbacks!* was one of the most notable of the political objectors. He wrote concerning his appearance before the board:

> Briefly, the bone of contention was the depth and sincerity of my conscientious objection to *force* when I particularly stipulated it was directed against *war*—the difference, in his [Harlan F. Stone's] estimation, being nil. And to attack my position he thundered the old gun of: "What would you do if your wife were attacked or if a burglar entered your home." "Resist him," said I.
>
> He didn't reply. For the life of me—I didn't see the comparison clearly myself—but I wanted him to recognize that my objections to one thing didn't necessarily imply objection to a dozen others. You see, the church brethren were "consistent." Confronted with the "rape your wife" and "burglar" question, they almost invariably replied, "I wouldn't use force or kill him, sir!" While I tried to indicate that I wasn't a passivist but a pacifist. "You fellows," said the Dean once, "have been preaching this pacifism for twenty years." "Yes,"

I replied, "and we hope to preach it for twenty more years and more." He smiled. His attitude throughout was friendly, anything but truculent—only terribly sceptical.[29]

The most recalcitrant conscientious objectors found that they were faced with a court-martial trial. Although it was not until April 22, 1918, that Secretary Baker ordered court-martial trials for C.O.'s who were insincere, defiant, or engaged in propaganda, actually about 40 men were court-martialed between September, 1917, and April, 1918.[30] The usual procedure was to put the objector in a position where he would refuse to obey an order. Then he would be tried for violation of the Articles of War. The resulting court-martial ended with the prisoner giving up his "objections" or accepting a long term in a military penitentiary. Altogether 540 conscientious objectors were court-martialed. Only one man was acquitted. The sentences seem extremely severe in light of the "crime." There were 17 death sentences, 142 life terms, and 345 cases with average sentences of 16½ years. Fifty-three sentences were disapproved and 185 others were mitigated by reviewing authorities. Apparently all of the death sentences were reversed. The effective sentences totaled 450.[31] It seems as though in some cases the men were convicted because of their political beliefs. At Camp Dix a conscientious objector was acquitted, but the verdict was reversed by a judge advocate who wrote on the verdict, "In view of the fact that this man is a Socialist, and, as such, opposed to all law and order, I can not see how he could have been classed as a conscientious objector." [32]

One objector stated that the court-martial trial was not held to discover the truth or sincerity of his objections, but "merely to secure a conviction and to inflict an outrageous and almost unbelievable sentence." [33] In some cases rapid-fire questions were shot at the C.O.'s, and often ridicule and scorn accompanied the questioning. Another objector, Maurice Hess, wrote of the court-martial trials at Camp Funston, "In relation to our court-martial trials, I may say that they did not have the slightest resemblance to justice. They were a mere formality in the carrying out of the policy of the camp commander, Mr. Leonard Wood, or possibly of certain officials at Washington." Hess recalled that a fellow objector had been tried and sentenced "in eighteen minutes." [34] There were instances of a summary court-martial where a single officer acted as judge, jury, and counsel. The officer, it was said, did everything but serve the "time." [35]

The questions asked objectors, the grounds on which they were frequently tried, and the sentences imposed by courts-martial show an unrelieved attempt to compel to orthodoxy the foreigner, the radical, and the religious humanitarian who, for various, highly complex reasons, opposed war. Charles Rodolph, a Y.M.C.A. clerk in Brooklyn, refused to submit to vaccination and was court-martialed at Camp Upton. A member of the court declared: "Your objection to the war as it is conducted now is, as I understand it, that the war is carried on mainly by the working people, that they compose the armies, and the war is not for their benefit directly or indirectly; they may carry on the war and come out with no result to their advantage, is that the idea?" Rodolph replied:

> I think that they are receiving advantages, but they are incidental and aside from the real purpose of the war. I think the purpose of the war is in order to enable the different nations, Germany and England in particular, to fight out which will be the dominant factor in our present society. I think that Germany wants to be the dominant factor and I think that England wants to be the dominant factor, and I think that they have fought themselves so near to death in each instance, that they have inflicted such mortal wounds on each other, that it may be possible that there is in the minds of some Americans the desire now to be the dominant factor. That may be.[36]

Rodolph was found guilty by the court and sent to Alcatraz.

Fred A. Robinson, a conscientious objector, was arrested in Washington State. At the time of his arrest he stated, "I, as an ambassador of Christ, have decided to be loyal to my King. Having considered this question carefully from God's viewpoint . . . and considered the penalties, I cannot conscientiously obey this order of induction into military service." Robinson was classed as a deserter, court-martialed, and sentenced to be shot. This sentence was later commuted to twenty-five years in Alcatraz.[37]

One of the most dramatic incidents surrounded the trial and sentence of Ernest Gellert, an idealistic youth who was drafted late in 1917. He refused to obey military orders and was court-martialed and sentenced to ninety days solitary confinement. While in prison he committed suicide, leaving the following note: "I fear I have not succeeded in convincing the authorities of the sincerity of my scruples against participation in war. I feel that only by my death will I be able to save others from the mental tortures I have gone through. If I succeed, I will give my life willingly." [38] But his death served no purpose. He probably expected that there would be a great deal of publicity which would call attention to the plight of the conscientious objectors, but newspapers were more interested in exploiting the exciting events on the battlefields, and little attention was given to the fate of a solitary war objector. Among others who were court-martialed for defiance, failure to obey orders, or other infractions of army discipline were Fred J. Muhlke, Jacob Rose, William Kantor, Solomon Losofsky, and Ernest Balmer. Several of these men wrote of their bitter experiences before military courts, providing data which are now in the files of the American Civil Liberties Union.

It was some of the religious objectors who perhaps most puzzled military authorities. Although many of them accepted noncombatant duty under the farm furlough program or the Friends Reconstruction Unit in France, there were some who caused the army grief and misery. Probably the Quakers and Mennonites were the best known among the minor sects for their opposition to war. But there were many other groups of which many Americans had not even heard. Among them were Molokans, Dukhobors, Dunkards, Seventh Day Adventists, Christadelphians, Russellites, Hutterite Brethren, Plymouth Brethren, and River Brethren. The Mennonites and the Molokans had come from Russia for the express purpose of avoiding participation in war. Members of some of these sects maintained that they could not even accept noncombatant service so long as it was under military control.

When the Selective Draft Act was passed, some of the Molokans went to Washington to see the President. Tumulty assured them that they would not be bothered. However, members of this religious sect were anxious to make their position clear in regard to a law with which they could not comply. In one case six Molokans went before their local boards and said that the Holy Spirit had forbidden them to register. Then each left his name and address with the draft board. According to Kellogg, "The English-speaking Molokan informed the Board that they did not wish to embarrass the Government in any way but that they could not take any part in the war and could not accept even non-combatant service. They were unwilling to take even a farm furlough because that, too, was under military control." [39]

Another case of the Molokans' passive resistance to the Draft Act occurred a few days after registration day when thirty-four members of the sect trooped into Phoenix, Arizona, and surrendered themselves to authorities. They were accompanied by their families. The Los Angeles *Times* of June 10, 1917, reported: "All marched in procession down the main street with singing of hymns, the men in cord-girted smocks and the women in white. At the court house they dropped to the cement pavement in the broiling sun and, with uplifted hands, prayed a few minutes before gathering in the court room." They had come to Phoenix, the *Times* stated, "prepared for martyrdom as a testimony of devotion to their faith." Inside the courtroom the spectators must have been somewhat startled when these men started singing a hymn "with grotesque accompaniment of rhythmic jumping that jarred the old court house. There was keen pathos in the farewells, as wives and children passed out tearfully . . . ." The men were turned over to the army and court-martialed. Later they appeared at Leavenworth and other prisons, where they and other members of their sect suffered the common misfortunes of conscientious objectors.

At Camp Riley twelve Mennonites refused to obey an order to cut down a sunflower which was growing only ten feet away from their camp. Placed in confinement, they were court-martialed and sentenced to twenty-five years imprisonment for refusing to work.[40] Forty-five conscientious objectors, most of whom were Mennonites from Oklahoma, were sentenced to twenty-five years imprisonment for refusing to wear the army uniform. Their only defense was that they were "of a faith objecting to physical force." [41]

Other religious sects had similar experiences in their opposition to war. Jane Addams tells one story of Dukhobors who clashed with the army:

I found myself appealed to on behalf of a frightened little widow who was at the moment desperately holding at bay the entire military prison system. Her husband had been one of those "obstinate cases who cling to a scriptural text and will not listen to reason." During his long imprisonments he had been treated in all sorts of barbarous ways and finally, after a prolonged ducking under a faucet in the prison yard on a freezing day, had contracted pneumonia and died. He had originally and continuously taken his stand against putting on the uniform, and when his wife arrived at Leavenworth to take away the body, to her horror, she found that body, at last unable to resist, dressed in a soldier's uniform. Her representative who came to see me, with his broken English, could convey but feebly the sense of outrage, of unfairness, of brutal disregard of the things of the spirit, of the ruthless overriding of personality which this incident had aroused among thousands of Doukhobortsi [Dukhobortsky].[42]

Some Hutterite Brethren from Freeman, South Dakota, who would not bend to the military were forcibly uniformed and had their beards cut off. That evening a fellow C.O. found them kneeling by their cots praying. One of them said, as reported by the *Washington Times* on October 26, 1917, "We are asking forgiveness from Christ for having our hair cut and our beards trimmed and for wearing the overalls of the army. It is against our religion to do anything in connection with war or military organizations." There were other incidents of cutting the hair and shaving members of religious groups who opposed these practices. It was sometimes done under a "sanitary order."

These accounts are only a few of the tragic tales which might be told. Further repetition, however, could only serve to emphasize the general outline given here. One thing is certain: a large number of conscientious objectors, both political and religious, were grossly mistreated. If one does not want to accept the words of conscientious objectors, there is abundant evidence of mistreatment by army officers themselves. Major E. C. Desobry at Camp Funston reported on November 17, 1918, that guards there had been "too drastic" in giving C.O.'s cold showers, striking them, compelling them to exercise, feeding them on bread and water, and placing them in solitary confinement. And he added that in order to cover up conditions during an investigation guards were, "in a great many instances, evasive, withheld the truth and undoubtedly gave false testimony." [43]

These facts alone, however, do not automatically condemn the Administration or the army for the handling of this difficult situation. Regardless of how abhorrent one may consider the treatment of conscientious objectors, any reasonable person must admit that the army faced a hard problem. Many of the C.O.'s were of such a character that it was extremely difficult to work with them. They were often religious fanatics, Marxian fanatics, or simply fanatics. In some cases they purposely committed acts to anger the military. Captain E. C. Brisben at Camp Funston wrote that the conscientious objectors had "a very antagonistic feeling toward all military persons, and endeavored from the time they arrived in camp to impose as great a hardship upon those directly over them as was possible in their mind." [44]

Perhaps the most important matter from the military viewpoint was the necessity to maintain order. After all, discipline is important in army life. A weakening of discipline over C.O.'s or a coddling of them might make it more difficult to control the regular recruits. At least this was the army view. Colonel J. W. Barnes wrote that lenient treatment of conscientious objectors had caused regular soldiers to "become disgruntled and dissatisfied in the service." [45] The greatest mistake may have been the policy of requiring the army to handle conscientious objectors at all. In World War II there was much greater civilian control of conscientious objectors under Selective Service.

It might be argued that President Wilson and Secretary Baker had it within their power to remedy the maltreatment of conscientious objectors and yet did nothing. This assumption, however, overlooks a number of important facts. In the first place this was the first time anyone then active in government had had to deal with conscientious objectors under conscription. Furthermore, public opinion was a powerful force that administrators had to consider, and public opinion was extremely hostile to this type of opponents of war. When newspapers mentioned conscientious objectors, they were usually antagonistic. Humanitarian groups and organizations did little to try to awaken the country to the real problem involved. Then it must not be forgotten that fathers and mothers whose sons were on active duty could hardly be expected to sympathize with those who appeared to be shirkers. The clergy was also generally critical of the stand taken by conscientious objectors. An Episcopal bishop in the South declared that "the real conscientious objector is unbalanced. True Christian Churchmen are dying for Christ." Another minister said that the conscientious objector was "a man who uses his religion to cloak a yellow streak." [46]

Theodore Roosevelt was his usual belligerent self. In May, 1917, he recommended sending conscientious objectors to the front where they could be fired upon. In Minneapolis, the following September, he declared:

> We have heard much of the conscientious objectors to military service, the outcry having been loudest among those objectors who are not conscientious at all but who are paid or unpaid agents of the German Government.
>
> It is certain that only a small fraction of the men who call themselves conscientious objectors in this matter are actuated in any way by conscience. The bulk are slackers, pure and simple, or else traitorous pro-Germans. Some are actuated by lazy desire to avoid any duty that interferes with their ease and enjoyment, some by the evil desire to damage the United States and help Germany, some by sheer, simple, physical timidity.[47]

Both President Wilson and Secretary Baker believed that special consideration should be given to nonreligious as well as religious conscientious objectors. However, they became increasingly unsympathetic and impatient with the type of absolutist objector who would not take military orders or accept alternate service. When no seemingly reasonable policy could reach this type of objector, Baker "turned severe in sending to jail those who would neither work nor fight." [48] Baker was subjected to especially heavy pressure from the public. He wrote to Wilson on July 22, 1918, that "we are now doing absolutely all that public opinion will stand in the interest of conscientious objectors . . . ." [49] A couple of months later Wilson wrote, "I have little sympathy with the conscientious objector, but I am sure we all want to avoid unnecessary harshness and injustices of any sort." [50] Yet he did not take vigorous action to protect objectors as some liberals thought he should.

A writer to the editor of the *Brooklyn Daily Eagle* gave a fairly accurate picture of the situation concerning conscientious objectors. He wrote:

> It is extraordinary with what monotonous regularity the prophet escapes honor in his own country. Just now it is the conscientious objector who is so amusing. Meet him in Russia, Germany, France, or England, we have a certain respect for him. Though seldom sharing his views, we grant him honesty and would accord him liberty in their [sic] holding. Here at home, on the other hand, it is quite different. He is uniformly contemptible. If he is American, born of Revolutionary stock, he is a coward; if Russian or German Jew, he is a paid spy. If he goes quietly about his business, he is "trying to hide"; if he speaks up at public meetings or in the press, he is seeking "cheap notoriety." If he is polite to the prosecuting attorney he is "cringing"; if he attempts a full defense, he is defiant. Lucky indeed, that he is not trying to ingratiate himself, for nothing that he has done yet appears to his opponents as other than ridiculous. [51]

Indeed, this was the popular impression in 1917 and 1918.

Some people, however, gradually changed their minds about the objectors. One such person was Major Walter G. Kellogg, who was a member of the Board of Inquiry. He wrote in 1919:

> Although I had never set eyes on a conscientious objector, I firmly believed that they were, as a class, shirkers and cowards. My first

trip as a member of the Board upset most of my ideas regarding the objector. I began to see him in a new light. And an examination of over eight hundred objectors in twenty widely distributed military camps and posts has convinced me that they are, as a rule, sincere —cowards and shirkers, in the commonly accepted sense, they are not.[52]

Conscientious objectors were not entirely without support in 1917 and 1918. The Civil Liberties Bureau, at first a part of the American Union Against Militarism, went to the defense of objectors as well as of other opponents of war. This Bureau shortly became independent. After the war it changed its name to the American Civil Liberties Union, and the parent body passed out of existence. The American Civil Liberties Union sought to preserve in America those things for which the newspapers said the nation was fighting in Europe. The Bureau went to the defense of all kinds of people, regardless of their political or religious beliefs, if their civil rights were being violated. It also acted as a clearinghouse of information for those who wanted to know about the laws which controlled individual freedom. It was almost the only organization, other than the Quaker Church, which tried to help the conscientious objectors. Because it befriended and aided various types of war opponents, Socialists, I.W.W.'s and other radicals, it was—and is— intensely disliked by extremists on the right. During the years of the first World War it was accused of being radical and unpatriotic. At one time the Department of Justice raided its offices.[53]

Nonetheless, throughout the war years this organization gave invaluable aid to those who were threatened by physical and legal violence, and to untutored individuals who were caught in the meshes of the law. A conscientious objector wrote to the Union after the war:

Having been held in thrall, I know the meaning of freedom; and, knowing the meaning of freedom, I appreciate in the highest degree the inestimable work which you have done and still are doing for those who are suffering for conscience sake. It is, indeed, gratifying to recollect that one organization dedicated to liberty proved invincible during the political crisis from which we so recently emerged. Had it not been for the persistency of yourselves and those associated with you in opposition to such as hate liberty and despise law, such dangers to human liberty as would have been frightful to contemplate would—no doubt—have betided to the hapless people of this nation.[54]

LESE MAJESTY

Kings, czars, and kaisers, through lese majesty laws, have made criticism of themselves a criminal act, permitting them to go their ways untroubled by public attack. Impassioned war supporters in the United States during 1917–18 wanted some such restriction on critics of the President, or other high government officials, and of war organizations. To some degree, they had their way.

On February 14, 1917, Congress had passed a law, almost without debate, penalizing anyone who "knowingly and willfully" wrote or spoke in a manner threatening the life of or bodily harm to the President. The punishment for anyone convicted of violating this law was a one-thousand-dollar fine and five years imprisonment.[1] When Wilson later asked for a declaration of war, the public was warned at least in one state that this law was a "very live one" and that prosecutions under it would be pushed.[2] Immediately afterwards in St. Louis a man with a German name "made remarks disparaging to President Wilson," and the police arrested him.[3] The Tulsa *Daily World* of April 5, 1917, reported that a New Jersey man had been sentenced to six months in the workhouse for having attacked Wilson in a public speech. The *Minneapolis Journal* of the next day reported the arrest of a man who allegedly said that "if he could get to Washington he would kill the President." On the same day, P. W. Stickrath said, "President Wilson ought to be killed. It is a wonder someone has not done it already. If I had an opportunity I would do it myself." Stickrath was arrested and sentenced to thirteen months in Atlanta.[4] Although such criticisms were accompanied by no overt acts, they were interpreted to be threats against the President under the law, and stiff sentences were often given.

In the debate over the war declaration, Senator La Follette had said:

> I had supposed until recently that it was the duty of Senators and Representatives in Congress to vote and act according to their convictions on all public matters that came before them for consideration and decision.
>
> Quite another doctrine has recently been promulgated by certain newspapers, which unfortunately seems to have found considerable support elsewhere, and that is the doctrine of "standing back of the President," without inquiring whether the President is right or wrong.[5]

Theodore Roosevelt had also opposed this "stand by the President" cry when he felt it meant keeping out of war. What a number of people objected to was the appearance of the *fuehrer prinzip.*

As the war fever increased additional people were arrested for violently attacking the President. Late in May, 1917, H. E. Kirchner, a West Virginian, got into a sharp argument over the draft law. He claimed that it was unconstitutional. He also said that he did not blame Germany for sinking American vessels, since they had been warned to stay out of the war zone, and that the President and his Cabinet were seeking personal honor and glory. He contended that the Kaiser would rule as justly as President Wilson. Kirchner was sentenced to two years in Atlanta Penitentiary and was not pardoned until April, 1919.[6]

On August 1, 1917, Orville Anderson, a former Socialist candidate for governor of South Dakota, lost his temper and said, according to testimony presented at his trial, that "President Wilson is a murderer in the first degree. He is murdering not only the Germans but his own people, the American people as well and he is violating the constitution of the United States by drafting men and sending them to fight in Europe."[7] He was also accused of favoring the Socialist resolutions adopted at St. Louis. Anderson readily admitted this, but denied that he had made statements against the President which had been attributed to him. Nevertheless, he was sentenced to four years in Leavenworth Penitentiary and fined one thousand dollars. In recommending a pardon for him, the Attorney General wrote later that he was "ordinarily a good citizen."[8] Many South Dakotans who knew Anderson would have agreed with this conclusion. There are indications that he suffered more because he was a Socialist than because he had violated any federal law.

There were numerous other cases of people being imprisoned or fined because they threatened or sharply criticized the President.[9] For example, a Texan was convicted and sent to the penitentiary for saying, "Wilson is a wooden-headed son of a bitch. I wish Wilson was in hell, and if I had the power I would put him there." [10] The judge held that the threat implied the necessary steps to kill the President "because he could not be in the state called hell until life was terminated." [11] In his charge to the jury the judge said that it made no difference whether one planned to carry out such a threat. Even an idle threat, he declared, was illegal.[12] In defending cases of this kind, defense attorneys often argued that their clients had been joking, that they had meant no harm, and really would not hurt anyone. The courts, however, did not usually accept such explanations.[13]

Other cases fitted into this general pattern. Whether critics expressed a desire to kill Wilson, said they wished him in hell, or called him a "damned old hypocrite," the result was likely to be a fine, a jail sentence, or handling by a mob. Under the law of February 14, 1917, dealing with threats against the President, sixty cases had come before the courts by June 6, 1918. Twenty-three of the persons accused pleaded guilty, twelve were convicted after trials, two were dismissed, two were acquitted, and, at that time, twenty-one were still pending.[14] Although this number seems quite small, it did not include people arrested under the act in the latter part of 1918, those who had been charged under the Espionage Act, or those convicted under municipal or state sedition laws or under charges by courts-martial. In some cases judges threw out indictments against critics of the President, especially if the prosecution had built its case around the idea that such statements interfered with the military effort. Several of these cases came before Judge Munger in St. Louis. The worst one man had said was, "To hell with Wilson. I am a Republican." The judge declared that he could not agree that such a statement would keep anyone from enlisting or deter American military success.[15]

Of course, it is inaccurate to leave the impression that President Wilson was completely immune from criticism. Indeed, he and members of his administration were harshly criticized. But it made a difference whether the attack came from a high political figure like Senator Chamberlain or Theodore Roosevelt, or from a Socialist, an I.W.W., or a person with a German accent. People in these groups found their criticisms automatically interpreted as disloyalty. And they were effectively silenced.

The immunity from criticism which was built up around the President soon spread to the point where it was unsafe to criticize the Red Cross, the Y.M.C.A., or other official and quasi official government organizations. The first war loan drive in May, 1917, came too early for hysteria to be much in evidence. However, the second one, in October, 1917, and the two which followed in 1918 were different. Patrioteers cast off all inhibitions. The advertising was "colossal." So was the pressure to force people to buy bonds and to scare critics into silence. In some states the state Councils of Defense used "an extensive scheme for checking up on subscribers." When individuals did not subscribe all that was expected of them, vigorous steps were taken to see that they did.[16] In some instances people were called on during the night—and told that they must buy more bonds.[17] "Rolls of dishonor," or "slacker rolls," were compiled, and threats to publish them were made. A full-page Liberty Loan advertisement of late 1918 was headed "No Mercy for Bond Shirkers." It threatened publicity for those who did not subscribe adequately and stated, "The committee men are clothed with full authority to demand an adequate Fourth Liberty Bond subscription from you . . . . A bond shirker is an enemy to humanity and liberty, a traitor and disgrace to his country." [18]

Of the activities of the state Councils of Defense George Creel has written:

> The state councils of defense did splendid work as a rule, but there were some infamous exceptions, for many of these councils conducted themselves in a manner that would have been lawless in any other than a "patriotic" body. During Liberty Loan drives, for example, it became a habit in certain sections to compel a regular income-tax return from the foreign born. Men claiming authority would insist on a statement of earnings and expenditures, and then calmly announce the amount of the contribution that the dazed victims were expected to make. Anything in the nature of resistance was set down as "disloyalty," and some of the penalties visited were expulsion from the community, personal ill treatment, or some pleasant little attention like painting the house yellow.[19]

The pressure exerted on people in Iowa has been told of by Nathaniel R. Whitney in his book, *The Sale of War Bonds in Iowa*. The editor of the *Iowa Homestead* thought the tactics represented a "reign of terror." "Kangaroo" or "slacker courts" were set up by the super-patriots, and special summonses were sent to people who had not subscribed the imposed quota. Of course, these "courts" had no legal power, but as one Iowan said, "The American people have a power—a God-given power, a power higher and greater than the Constitution or law . . . to save the Government, to save the flag, and to save the law itself from destruction at home as well as abroad." If a farmer pleaded that he could not afford more bonds, the local banker usually offered to loan him money for that purpose. Some persons were threatened with the loss of jobs if they did not subscribe.[20]

There were reports from all over the country of people being coerced into buying bonds. A news item from St. Louis, published in the *New York Tribune*, May 21, 1918, stated that saloon keepers who did not purchase bonds would be denied licenses. On February 27, 1918, the Pittsburgh *Gazette-Times* carried a news item which stated that in one Pennsylvania town several men were tarred and feathered because they did not buy bonds. According to the Seattle *Post-Intelligencer* of April 23, an individual, incorrectly accused of not having bought bonds, had his telephone line cut and yellow paint splashed on his house. A mail carrier in Wentworth, South Dakota, who refused to buy war bonds was horse-whipped. In addition, his hair was cut off, and his head was painted red.[21]

Yellow paint was a typical means of stigmatizing people accused of being remiss in buying bonds. In Arizona a railroad worker was covered with yellow paint. His hands were tied, a rope was placed around his neck, and he was escorted through the business section of the town.[22] Another method of forcing people to buy bonds was to seize and sell their property. An instance of this involved a group of Mennonites who refused to buy bonds because of their religious hostility to war. When they came into town one Saturday morning, "their cars were taken and sold at auction and the proceeds applied to Liberty Bonds." [23] Others who resisted pressure and spoke out against bonds were dealt with more severely.

At Olympia, Washington, a single-taxer, W. H. Kaufman, gave a Labor Day address in 1917 in which he said that the United States "had been buncoed into this war by the munition makers." He added that it was a disgrace to buy bonds which, he declared, were a substitute for a munitions tax. For this speech he was sentenced to McNeil Island Penitentiary for five years.[24] Dr. Frederick O. Balcom of Providence, Rhode Island, was convicted and sentenced to a year in jail for making the following statements: "When you women learn that when you stop paying for wars, you will have no wars. The United States Liberty Bonds are not worth the paper they are written on . . . Liberty Bonds, thrift and war stamps are just so much scrap paper; you might just as well throw your money in the waste basket." [25]

An Oklahoma farmer thought he had subscribed for as many bonds as he could afford. Writing about his situation years later, Mrs. Walter Ferguson stated in the *Daily Oklahoman*, "Knowing his reputation for stubbornness, the local patriots were not surprised one day when they went to call upon him and met his flat footed refusal to take another bond, or give another cent . . . . It would require a book to tell of the devilish ways in which he was hounded afterward. Merchants refused to sell him groceries, women cut his wife dead in church; neighbors set fire to his barn. His own children turned against him." [26] On the same theme, Mrs. Ferguson wrote on another occasion:

> I have lived through the patriotic frenzy of '17 and '18. What crimes were committed in the name of patriotism. When our neighbor lay delirious with typhoid, the business men of Cherokee emptied his wheat bins to buy Liberty Bonds. "Said he wouldn't buy none; now, by God, he's got plenty." In the Second Liberty Bond drive, my grandfather refused to buy the excessive quota set by the "white collar guys in the county seat." That Saturday, his new car was sold to the highest bidder and there on the dusty streets of Fairview he was presented with his bonds. He stood there a moment, in his black stetson, Levis and sateen shirt—the typical hard fisted pioneer— then dramatically, he tore those bonds into a thousand pieces and scattered them to the Oklahoma winds. A week later he bought $500 in bonds of his own free will.[27]

One of the most interesting cases of high-pressure bond salesmanship involved John Gerdes, an elderly Nebraskan. Gerdes, a naturalized citizen who was born in Holland, had two sons in the American army and was urging a third to enlist. Although he had bought $1,650 in bonds, the local Liberty Loan committee insisted that Gerdes buy another $650 worth. Gerdes owned property and was considered fairly well-to-do, but the latest bond quota caught him in an embarrassing financial position. He was without ready cash. Members of the committee insisted that he borrow the money and take up his quota. Gerdes, however, refused. Strong language between the old farmer and the leading patriot led to a fist fight. At some point the exasperated Gerdes burst out, "The Government is in with the grocers and millers to rob the poor man . . . . The flour that we have now would not make bread that a —— hog would eat . . . . The farmer that raises his own wheat has a right to grind it up and eat as much as he —— pleases." He also stated, "I don't give a —— what you tell that committee, you can tell them to go to ——." Gerdes was arrested and convicted of violating the Espionage Act. He was fined one thousand dollars and costs.[28] To some Gerdes might have seemed like a stubborn old Dutchman. In any event, he appealed his case to the Nebraska Supreme Court and his conviction was reversed. The court held that a man was perfectly within his rights not to buy bonds and that Gerdes had not violated any law.

In Quincy, Illinois, Theodore B. Pape, a prominent attorney, stated in April, 1918, that he would not buy any bonds. He believed that the war could be brought to an end more quickly if people refused to support it financially. A local committee called at his home and asked why his name was not on the lists of patriotic contributors. He explained his position and firmly refused to subscribe. Local patriots had him hauled into court for interfering with the war effort. However, the judge discharged the defendant after declaring, "It is clear to this court that a criminal prosecution cannot be based upon the failure of a citizen to subscribe to . . . patriotic funds, so long as he does not endeavor to get others to do likewise, with intent to interfere with the operation and success of the military establishment . . . ."[29] Senator L. Y. Sherman of Illinois told his colleagues that Pape was one who "can not adjust himself to the newly organized forces of democracy."[30]

Many of those who got into trouble over the question of buying war bonds were not opponents of war at all. They simply resented the tremendous extralegal pressures put upon them by local patriots. With some it was a question of whether they would run their own financial business or have it partially handled by community bond committees. But, other than those who conscientiously opposed the war, only a few hardy individualists tried to resist the strong pressure to buy bonds.

The Red Cross campaigns to raise funds were carried on in much the same way. It was considered not only unpatriotic but also disloyal not to contribute. Local patriotic leaders were quick to single out those who spoke disparagingly of, or refused to give to, the Red Cross. The official historian for the American Protective League has stated that "during the 'drives' of the Red Cross, many rumors and derogatory statements concerning the work of the Red Cross were spread broadcast through the country. A.P.L. ran down hundreds of complaints, secured many convictions, and handled the entire investigation of the Red Cross until quite recently . . . ."[31]

Many specific examples could be cited of such activities. For instance, an elderly man by the name of Jacob W. Oswald had a large family. Two of his sons were in the army and two more were preparing to enter the service. One of his boys had been injured in the service, and Oswald felt that he had not been given good care. When he was approached for a contribution to the Red Cross, he spoke about the way his son had been treated and said that "before he would be forced to give he would declare himself a Hun." When this was told to his fellow workmen, a mob was formed, and Oswald was doused with a bucket of yellow paint. The old man was then ridden on a rail out of the plant. He brought out his service flag in order to demonstrate his patriotism, but at this point he was so mad he used the flag to wipe the paint off his clothes and face. Oswald was then discharged from his job.[32]

Louis B. Nagler got into a violent argument over the Red Cross and the war. He refused to contribute, stating, "I am through contributing to your private grafts. There is too much graft in these subscriptions. No, I do not believe in the work of the YMCA or the Red Cross, for I think they are nothing but a bunch of grafters." A few days later he stated, "Who is this Government? Who is running this war? A bunch of capitalists composed of the steel trust and munition makers."[33] Nagler, who was the Assistant Secretary of State in Wisconsin, was sentenced to thirty months in Leavenworth Penitentiary. The conviction was based on the argument that attacks upon quasi-governmental agencies assisting the war effort were intended to obstruct and impede the military forces. The defendant argued that if the Red Cross and Y.M.C.A. could not be attacked because they were considered part of the military establishment, it would logically follow that one could not attack or criticize other social and relief organizations assisting in the war. The judge agreed with this logic and added, "Not only would it be a violation of the law to interfere with the drives conducted for the raising of funds for the YMCA, but it would likewise be a similar offense if the opposition was directed to the work of those engaged in raising funds for the Knights of Columbus, the Jewish Relief, or the Salvation Army."[34] Although he was specifically referring only to their war activities, this broad declaration seemed to carry the interpretation of what constituted "military forces" beyond the realm of common sense. Nonetheless, the idea was generally accepted. Judge Munger in St. Louis, referring to failure to buy bonds, declared that "whatever chills or retards the support of the war by the people of the nation at home also tends to defeat the operation and success of the army and navy in its actions on the field of battle."[35]

It is important to note, however, that after the armistice some judges had a complete change of view. Henry C. Koenig was tried before Judge Munger in St. Louis on November 12, 1918. He reportedly said that "they [Red Cross] are a lot of thieves and grafters" and that "the head men of the YMCA are a bunch of grafters and thieves." Now that the war was over, Judge Munger said that this was merely a matter of personal opinion and did not interfere with the success of the military or naval forces! [36]

Some courts recognized the distinction between a person who publicly denounced the Red Cross and one who simply refused to contribute. A Minnesota farmer, William Ludemann, would not give to a Red Cross drive and was called on by the local committee who explained that the Red Cross was assisting the war effort. To this plea Ludemann replied, "I don't care anything about the war; the Government got us into it and let the Government get us out of it." He added that he was "damn sick of it anyhow" and would give nothing. He was convicted for using this strong language, but on appeal the State Supreme Court reversed the judgment. The court held that a man could legally make such statements in the sanctity of his own home. [37] This made sense to those concerned with freedom of speech, but by that time the war was over.

As has been suggested earlier, some of the reluctance to buy bonds and contribute to such agencies as the Red Cross resulted from undue pressures exerted by solicitors. Also, it cannot be overlooked that these organizations were generally headed by bankers and businessmen— people who were disliked by the dissenters as reactionaries, enemies of farmers and labor, and opponents of reform.

A WINTER'S TALE
October, 1917–February, 1918

By the winter of 1917 the effects of the war were felt throughout the nation. Some American soldiers were already overseas; others were in training camps or about to be called. There were wheatless, meatless, and fuelless days. The Government took over the railroads and extended control over other industries. For five days in January, 1918, nonessential industries throughout the nation were closed to save fuel. There were ceaseless appeals for money—for war bonds, for the Red Cross, and for numerous other causes. And the war against the opponents of the war, the cynical, the unbelieving, the "seditious," went on uninterrupted.

By this time, the conventional interpretation of the war—the "war party line"—had been worked out. What was orthodoxy and what was heresy were clearly established. Also, the nationalist organizations to enforce this interpretation were in full operation. The societies, committees, leagues, and councils were moving against all dissidents. They had cleaned out, or were in the process of cleaning out, heretics in the schools, the churches, and the press. Conscientious objectors were being turned over to the army. The opponents of war, conservative, liberal, and radical, were being silenced by criticism, threats of force, mob action, or by indictments, arrests, and even imprisonment.

Incitement to mob action or to arrests continued. Theodore Roosevelt was calling opponents of war "copperheads" and unhung traitors.[1] Secretary of the Treasury McAdoo was reported in October to have said, "America intends that those well-meaning but misguided people who talk inopportunely of peace . . . shall be silenced. I want to say here and now and with due deliberation that every pacifist speech in this country made at this inopportune and improper time is in effect traitorous." [2] Just before some Espionage Act cases came up in Minnesota a prominent judge there charged a grand jury with the task of punishing "sedition" to the limit.[3]

November also had its quota of such remarks. As previously mentioned, it was then that Attorney General Gregory gave his benediction to dissenters: "May God have mercy on them for they need expect none from an outraged people and an avenging Government." [4] Editorializing on Gregory's comments, the *New York Times* said that "the patience of the Government and the country has snapped." [5] James W. Gerard attracted widespread attention when he was quoted in the *New York Tribune,* November 14, 1917, as saying that "we should 'hog-tie' every disloyal German-American, feed every pacifist raw meat, and hang every traitor to a lamp post to insure success in this war." The prolific writer, Dr. Henry Van Dyke, while he did not advocate mob violence, said that "a man who by speech or action endeavors to impede America's efficiency in this righteous war should be judged by the law, and if convicted, promptly executed." [6]

And December revealed no letup in the war against the opponents of war. Major Stanley Washburn was quoted in the *Muncie Evening News,* December 5, 1917, as having said:

> The men who go about the land in the guise of pacifists urging the war be ended are your personal enemies as much as if they had knives in their hands and were stabbing your sons "over there" in the back. What is the antidote for this poison? Action! Swift and crushing. The pacifists must go; they must be effectually muzzled or exterminated, preferably the latter . . . . They should be tried by court-martial and shot with their backs against a wall.

Governor Burnquist of Minnesota was reported by the *Minneapolis Journal* of December 11 to be in favor of disfranchisement of "disloyalists." And Ray Stannard Baker confided to his notebook that some of the "patriots" he was meeting were "all for skewering Germans on bayonets and then twisting the bayonets . . . . Dear gentle John Burroughs is reported in the paper this morning as wanting to wipe out ruthlessly all things German. Half the ministers of the country are in the same mood." [7]

On January 3, 1918, the *New York Herald* ran a cartoon showing eight figures hanging from a gibbet. They included a fire bug, a bomb thrower, a ground glass fiend, a spy, an I.W.W., an exemption shark, an ammunition fixer, and a sedition monger. Above the gibbet were the words, "To Make the World Safe for Democracy"; below it came the

Birds of a feather. —Chapin in the St. Louis *Republic* as reproduced in *Literary Digest*, LV (Aug. 18, 1917), 12.

advice, "The Only Way." On January 20, the *Herald* had another cartoon called "The Spy within our Gates" which carried the suggestion, "Make an Example of Him!" Samuel Gompers' dictum, "Opposition to the war declared by constituted authority becomes treason," was duly published in the *New York Times* on January 2, 1918. The Seattle *Post-Intelligencer* reported on January 27 that many opponents of war were "still at large" and commented, "The gentlemen of the secret service are very properly detaining them." The next day, the *Post-Intelligencer* said that "pro-Germans and others in the state who have been opposed to the United States participating in the war will find it advisable to keep their opinions to themselves from now on." An individual in Kansas City wrote, "Prejudice and bias is at fever heat in this part of the country." [8]

President Wilson admitted that the country was in the midst of "a lot of hysteria." [9] He told delegates to the American Federation of Labor in Buffalo that he was "very much distressed" at the mob spirit which had sometimes been displayed. "I have no sympathy with what some men are saying," he declared, "but I have no sympathy with men who take their punishment into their own hands . . . ." [10]

The spirit of the times was reflected in the drastic actions taken against those who, for some reason, opposed the war. Local, state, and national wartime agencies continued active in this campaign, as did public officials and police officers. In Missouri, some of the county Councils of Defense sent out "red, white and blue cards of warning" to people accused of uttering antiwar sentiments. The results, as the State Council reported, were gratifying.

> The person to whom the first warning card is sent, generally takes it as a warning that they [*sic*] are being watched and immediately become very careful in their expressions. It has been found necessary in only a few cases to send a blue card to anyone and the red card has never been sent. The red card is simply a statement from the Council of Defense that the recipient will be reported immediately to the United States Secret Service. [11]

Other councils were also active in suppressing "seditious" utterances. [12] The Kansas Council issued a speaker's handbook containing a collection of atrocity stories and carrying this notation: "If any individual or family offers destructive criticism of the Government, questions its purpose, talks against it and against the war, report the fact immediately . . . . Put your heel on the vipers!" [13]

In some places it seemed to be the policy of patriotic organizations and newspapers not to publicize the point of view of those charged with "seditious" utterances. At least one Department of Justice official was reported to have told some newsmen "that any publicity given to the victim's side in such cases hurts the work of the Government secret service agents." Secrecy might also prevent popular action against suspected disloyal men, he added. [14] To cap the climax of snooping, it was at this time that children, ten or more years old, were organized to listen for antiwar comments. These young detectives—a thousand units of them in the country according to the *New York Tribune* of January 22, 1918—were called the Anti-Yellow Dog League.

Judge W. T. Burns of Texas personified the rabid intolerance so characteristic of the super-patriots. He declared that "traitors" in Congress should be shot. The judge said he favored administering the law fairly, but added, "I have a conviction, as strong as life, that this country should stand them up against an adobe wall tomorrow and give them what they deserve." He would like to pay for the ammunition, said the judge.[15] Senator La Follette, one of the "traitors" in Burns's opinion, bitterly criticized this type of attack. "The mandate seems to have gone forth to the sovereign people of this country," he said, "that they must be silent while those things are being done by their government which most vitally concern their well being." Then the Wisconsin Senator continued, "It appears to be the purpose of those conducting this campaign to throw the country into a state of terror, to coerce public opinion, to stifle criticism, and suppress discussion of the great issues involved in this war."[16] La Follette insisted that the people had a fundamental right to discuss all aspects of the war.

La Follette and other spokesmen favored harsh treatment for the genuine spy or saboteur. The trouble was, however, that little, if any, distinction existed in the public mind between a person who really threatened the country's security and one who opposed war in principle or who demanded a statement of peace objectives. From the viewpoint of individual and personal freedom the situation was distressing because of this lack of discrimination between real enemies of the United States and critics of economic or war policies. The winter campaign was directed against every type of war opponent. There were people who appeared actually to be pro-German; there was the garden variety of opponent who objected to entering the war; there were those who opposed conscription and those who opposed being conscripted; there were left-wingers, including agrarian reformers, Socialists, and, of course, I.W.W.'s. These opponents of war must be silenced, it was said.

Examples of how these opponents of war were treated could be multiplied at great length. For example, on a night in January, 1918, a group of men surrounded the house of a young man by the name of Maximilian von Hoegen in Connecticut. According to the press, von Hoegen had written on his draft questionnaire *Deutschland über alles* and a number of other pro-German sentiments. The vigilantes rushed the house, dragged the young man away from his protesting family to a nearby square, and read to him the various answers which he had written on his questionnaire. Whenever he admitted the accuracy of the reply he was struck in the face. Before he was released he was forced to kiss the flag and sing "The Star-Spangled Banner."[17] As was usually the case in such circumstances, no effort was made to catch those who

took the law into their own hands. At Osakis, Minnesota, E. H. Strate-
meyer, a naturalized German, was given a coat of tar and feathers for
alleged disloyal statements.[18] In March, 1918, five businessmen at Del-
phos, Ohio, were taken by a mob of almost 400 people to the center of
the lighted street and there forced to kiss the flag under the threat of
being hanged.[19]

The courts seemed to take the attitude that an opponent of war was
guilty unless proved innocent. Julius Rhuberg, an elderly man in Oregon,
was alleged to have remarked privately that the moneyed interests had
led us into the war, that Germany was right, that the draftees should
surrender, and that the United States had no business in the war. At
least one man of military age heard these remarks, although he testified
that they had no influence on his not enlisting. Nonetheless, Rhuberg
was sentenced to fifteen months imprisonment in McNeil Island Penitentiary for violating the Espionage Act.[20]

Many people continued to criticize the conscription act. Especial
trouble, however, awaited those who attempted to resist it. This was
true not only of conscientious objectors, as mentioned previously, but
of all others. Troy Deason, a young Texan, was classified 1-A by his
draft board in spite of his claim for exemption. Deason threatened to
"beat up" the people on the board. For this he was sentenced to eighteen
months in Leavenworth Penitentiary.[21] Another Texas case involved Ger-
hardt Wessels, who was supposed to have advised a Negro how to avoid
being drafted. The idea was that the Negro should pretend to be unable
to read the letters on the doctor's eye chart. Wessels was sentenced to
three years in Leavenworth Penitentiary for "obstructing the recruiting
and enlistment service of the United States." [22] Later the Attorney General
reported that "the evidence in this case appears to have been of a meager
and questionable character." It seems that the principal witness was
very discreditable.[23]

In California Frank T. Howenstine was accused of fitting glasses
to persons liable to the draft in order to distort their vision and of
furnishing them with drops of medicine which would irritate their eyes.
He was assisted by a mentally unbalanced woman, Idell Kennedy. She
was accused of calling the President an Englishman and of saying that
the United States was fighting for an unjust cause.[24] Howenstine and
Mrs. Kennedy were both given heavy sentences, although these were
later commuted.[25]

Some of the draftees continued to be intransigent after they got
into the army. The *New York Times* of February 23, 1918, carried the

news story of four drafted soldiers facing the death penalty because they had "plotted at Tacoma camp to shoot their officers if they ever got into action." On February 24, 1918, the *Columbus Sunday Times* carried the headlines, "Seditious Remark Brings Sailor Ten Years in Prison" and "Blue Jacket Who Said 'Deutschland über Alles' Convicted by Court-martial." On December 22, 1917, the *Minneapolis Journal* published a news item which read: "One hundred American soldiers were court-martialed at Camp Merritt [New Jersey] in the last two months for anti-American utterances and activities. Of these one third were sentenced to federal penitentiaries. The others, whose guilt seemed the result of lack of good sense, have been dishonorably discharged." The officer who issued the story remarked, "Usually we say nothing of these things for publication." Possibly it was thought that objectors coming up for induction needed a warning.

The campaign against agrarian reformers continued during the winter, although the physical violence which had characterized it earlier diminished somewhat. In October, 1917, former Populist Senator R. F. Pettigrew of South Dakota was indicted for having told a reporter, "There is no excuse for this war. We should back right out of it. We never should have gone into a war to help the Schwabs make forty million dollars per year." [26] When the case was ready for trial, a continuance was granted because of Pettigrew's ill health. In November, 1919, the case was dropped. Clarence S. Darrow was to have appeared for the defense. Earlier, while Pettigrew was still under indictment, his Sioux Falls office was painted yellow by a mob. [27]

An Iowan was sent to the penitentiary for quoting one of Tom Watson's bitterly antiwar speeches made in June, 1917. Although Watson had not been prosecuted, it proved dangerous for others to repeat his sentiments. Since this speech is an interesting expression of antiwar feelings, it is worth a brief summary. Watson had declared that Washington was "a carnival, a wild extravagance; an orgy of prodigal waste, a Bacchanalian revel of men who act as though they were drunk on power and had lost every sense of shame, duty, and responsibility." He argued that "huge appropriations made will accrue to the benefit of the classes" and that "it is absurd to say that we are menaced by a German danger." Watson said that the people had been pushed into war without their consent and that "ten million free American citizens [were] suddenly and peremptorily ordered to quit their vocations and to attend a newly constituted tribune to be registered like a lot of dumb cattle." He further declared that editors had been silenced and that the Constitution had been suspended. Furthermore, Watson said:

> Upon the pretext of waging war against Prussianism in Europe, the purpose of Prussianizing this country has been avowed in Congress, with brutal frankness, by a spokesman of the administration.
>
> On the pretext of sending armies to Europe, to crush militarism there, we first enthrone it here.
>
> On the pretext of carrying to all the nations of the world the liberties won by the heroic lifeblood of our forefathers, we first deprive our own people of liberties they inherited as a birthright.
>
> On the pretext of unchaining the enslaved people of other lands, we first chain our own people with preposterous and unprecedented measures, knowing full well that usurpations of power, once submitted to, will never hereafter be voluntarily restored to the people.[28]

David T. Blodgett printed Watson's speech, along with a plea not to re-elect eight Iowa congressmen who had voted in favor of the Selective Service Act. Blodgett was sentenced to twenty years in the penitentiary. The charge was made that this pamphlet tended to cause "insubordination, mutiny, and disloyalty in the military forces of the United States" and to interfere with "enlistment and recruiting." [29]

There was, of course, no letup in the drive against the Nonpartisan League. Opposition was especially strong in Minnesota, where the League was trying to gain a political foothold. In October at least four meetings were forbidden or broken up in Minnesota. On October 3, Louis Keane, Secretary of the Otter Tail County Public Safety Association of Fergus Falls, wrote to Townley that the Association would not tolerate any talk disrespectful of the flag. "So you will construe this notice as an invitation *not to come*," Keane said. Then he explained that if Townley persisted in speaking in that community orders had been given to the police not "to interfere if small boys (or others) use ancient eggs and other missiles wherewith to punctuate your discourse." [30]

In the village of Rock Creek, two League organizers were kidnapped, threatened with lynching, and then driven out of town.[31] Throughout January and February, 1918, disruption of League meetings increased. Sheriffs and other officials, backed by local patriots, broke up meetings all over the state.[32]

Late in February Townley and Joseph Gilbert, League organization manager, were arrested for hindering enlistments.[33] Townley was accused of saying that the United States had been dragged into the war by pluto-crats who were coining exorbitant profits from the blood of young Ameri-cans. He denied having made any such statements, but true or not, the accusations were widely repeated as a means of discrediting the League and its leadership. The arrest of Townley and Gilbert on rather flimsy evidence was quite obviously part of the move by anti-League forces in Minnesota to destroy the organization before it gained much political power. *The Nonpartisan Leader* declared that the powerful economic interests "with which the farmers are at grips in Minnesota have sought to wrap themselves in the American flag and make it appear that to turn the present office holders out in favor of others, indorsed by the farmers and labor, would be highly seditious and treasonable." [34]

Indeed, this was the strategy to be used against the League. Farmers' contributions to war charities and their subscriptions for war bonds left no room for criticism, despite the fact that many farmers may not have liked the war. Thus conservatives tried to show that dislike and criticism of themselves were synonymous with disloyalty and sedition. As will be shown subsequently, this campaign against the League in Minnesota became very intense as the June, 1918, primary election approached. However, before continuing that story let us see how the Socialists and I.W.W.'s were faring in the winter of 1917–18.

"And how goes the battle today, J. P.?
　　How many thousands were slain?
How many blind eyes lifted up to the skies
　　In pitiful pleading and pain?
And how many curses of hate, J. P.,
　　And how many agonized groans?
And how many dollars were lent today,
　　At how many per cent for the loans? . . .

But what is our life or our death, J. P.,
　　And what are our tears and our moans—
The grief-stricken mother, the life without light—
　　As compared with a great banker's loans?" [1]

FURTHER WAR
ON THE SOCIALISTS

There have been and still are many kinds of economic reformers in the United States. They may be classified roughly on a graduated scale according to the amount of control they wish to give governments over economic and, ultimately, over social and political matters. Some leftists, such as the agrarian radicals, merely wanted to deprive business interests of special privileges and extend governmental powers over the economy in a limited way. Some liberals have proposed that government own public utilities—post offices, railroads, telegraph systems, etc. Beyond these are the radicals, such as Socialists, who believe in government ownership and operation of basic industries. This would mean government ownership and operation of mines, factories, and mills, as well as public utilities. At the extreme left are those radicals who wish the government in the name of the proletariat to own all producers' and consumers' goods.

157

Inevitably, this means dictatorship over other aspects of economic and political life.

In November, 1917, the most radical of these groups, the Bolsheviki or Communists, took over the government of Russia. Some American economic reformers temporarily approved this development while radicals were openly elated. Conservatives, on the other hand, were dismayed and frightened. It now became apparent that many economic reformers did not fully realize the differences between the groups left of center. They apparently believed what the rightists said, that all leftists were alike. What some reformers and liberals did not realize was that communism was not liberalism. They failed to see that although the Communists would eliminate the capitalists, they would also eliminate the liberals. The Communists would take economic power away from "capitalists," but they would also deny economic and political rights to non-capitalists. Communism was as much a counterfeit in the matter of liberalism as nationalism was a counterfeit in the matter of patriotism. There was no similarity of aims or ideals between liberals and Communists, other than that they were both economic reformers. There was a great similarity in method between Communists and reactionaries, or between Communists and monarchists. Both wanted all power for the government—with themselves as governors; both wanted immunity from criticism for themselves as governors. The monarchists created a paradise for monarchs and nobility; the Communists, for dictators and commissars.

It took several years for some liberals to see that there was an unbridgeable chasm between them and the Communists. At the very outset, in 1917 and 1918, they had great hopes for the "Russian experiment." They defended and apologized for the Communists, thinking that Soviet excesses were the normal violence following the replacement of a tyrannical government. They did not see that all that was happening was the replacement of the blind violence of the right by the blind violence of the left, that for each injustice eliminated several new ones were substituted. Many liberals did not recognize that the tyranny of the Communists was only different from that of the Czars in that the new tyrant was more efficient and more sweepingly intolerant.

Conservatives had no illusions about the beneficence of communism. The Communists had openly named them—the conservatives, the capitalists, the businessmen, and the property owners—as their enemies. They had said they were going to eliminate them. Conservatives took them at their word. When Communists took over in Russia, the conservatives clearly understood that it meant war to the death. It was not a contest with people trying to reform them; it was a contest with people trying to wipe them out. Was it any wonder that excited conservatives tried to smash Communists and everyone of the left who expressed sympathy for them?

The Socialists were to be one of the principal casualties of this new conservative warfare. Newspapers quite regularly lumped Socialists together with Bolsheviks and said that they were identical. On their part the Socialists continued to express sympathy for the Bolsheviks. For example, on November 9, 1917, the New York *Call* carried a large headline, "Kerenski, Deposed by Bolsheviki, Flees as Radicals Rule Russia." Then the *Call* spoke approvingly of the peace aims of the Reds. Also, Socialists did not buckle under and say they had been wrong about the war. They spoke out, boldly condemning American participation. They continued to condemn conscription and profiteering. They criticized the repressive movement in America and said it was undemocratic, un-American, and unconstitutional. One Socialist said that the United States was at that time "one of the least democratic of all countries." [2]

The *New York Times* on December 13, 1917, thundered:

Thanks to Russian Socialism, the Germans now outnumber the French and the British on the Western Front . . . . We do not speak of the kind of Socialism that is to be found in Germany, for that Socialism is nationalistic and patriotic, and is warmly supported by the Kaiser . . . . We speak of the kind of Socialism to be found in Russia and the United States. In this country it has been powerless to change the steady and resolved course of the nation, but in Russia it has gained the ascendant and there it has been an infinite cause of disaster to liberty.

A little later, on February 1, 1918, the *Times* advocated a Congress made up of "100 per cent Americans" and inveighed against electing in the fall elections any "Socialist or Pro-German candidate opposed to the purposes for which we went to war."

In the New York City election in the fall of 1917, Socialists openly asked for the votes of those who were antiwar. Late in September, ten thousand people attended a Party meeting in Madison Square Garden. A report in the *New York Times* of September 24 noted that this audience applauded economic arguments but that such applause "was gentle and tame compared with the outbursts that occurred whenever a speaker shouted a demand for peace and cessation of war." The mayoralty candidate, Morris Hillquit, was quoted by the *Times* on October 30 as saying that a "Socialist victory in the city election will be a clear mandate to open negotiations for a general peace." At another meeting in October he aroused applause by attacking "Government press censors." [3]

It was to be expected that incumbent John P. Mitchel would aim his attack at Socialist Hillquit by trying to show that he was pro-German and disloyal. However, Mitchel did not stop there. He also accused the Tammany candidate, John F. Hylan, of questionable loyalty. The extent to which the super-patriots would go to try to prove disloyalty is indicated by the fact that Mitchel attacked Hylan's patriotism and loyalty because he had attended a mass meeting sponsored by the Friends of Peace in June, 1915. Hylan's name had also been used on the letterheads of this organization. Here a person was being accused of disloyalty on the basis of actions taken nearly two years before the United States entered the war. In any event, Hylan was forced to repeat time and again that he was loyal and would, if elected, support President Wilson and the war effort.[4]

Shortly before election day, attacks upon Hylan became vicious. "Mayor reveals Hylan as a member of the German propaganda here," the *Times* of October 31 reported. The *New York Herald* of November 3 stated, "New York wants no mayor in City Hall to whom enemy spies would have access." On November 6, the *Herald* ran a cartoon of Hylan and Hillquit entitled "For Mayor of Berlin." Under it were the words, "only a step from pacifism to treason." Theodore Roosevelt described Hillquit as a traitor and Hylan as a dupe. A vote for Mitchel, he said, was a vote for the nation.[5]

Despite a campaign in which the national loyalty of Hylan and Hillquit was seriously questioned, Hylan won by a large plurality. The *New York Times* on November 7 carried the stories, "Judge Hylan Sweeps City"; "Hylan Has Every Vote in the Board of Estimate"; "Socialists Show Big Increase." Hillquit ran third, but he polled 142,178 votes, only 7,129 fewer than second place Mitchel.

New York was a strong center of American interventionists. Yet in that city the Socialist candidate, openly opposing war, and the winning candidate, accused of disloyalty in the war effort, together garnered about 440,000 votes compared with Mitchel's approximately 150,000. Furthermore, the Socialists gained strength in the city government and in the state assembly. From this one might conclude that in other parts of the country a vote for peace might have been enormous. Actually it would probably have been quite small. The nationalists elsewhere tended to be more violent. Pacifist ideas were effectively suppressed.

The fortunes of Socialists elsewhere are somewhat typified by the following story from Klamath Falls, Oregon. Mrs. Anna Blachly, a poor working housewife with two children, was told by two local men that she must buy war bonds. "One of them threatened with the possibility of being hung by the neck if I refused to sign," she wrote. Then she added that the Klamath Falls "vigilance committee" had "resolved to get rid of all Socialists and undesirables. A number of us had orders to leave at a stated time and I was included." Later Mrs. Blachly and some others were arrested and taken to Portland for questioning. There they were released. Her letter concluded, "We are now living in Portland and glad to be out of such a barbarious [*sic*] community." [6]

The state chairman of the Socialist party of South Dakota, Ingmar M. Iverson, registered as a conscientious objector and told his draft board that he "could not and would not engage in the slaughter of fellow workers of this or any other land." Iverson was arrested on a technical charge of desertion and was sentenced to twenty years in the penitentiary. His sister claimed that he had good grounds for exemption as "head of the family and a frail mother's provider since [his] father's death many years ago. The local Board is well aware of these facts but political prejudice against a . . . Socialist blinded all their sense of justice." [7] Incidentally, when the Socialists tried to hold a state convention at Mitchell, South Dakota, on January 22, 1918, police ordered the meeting broken up. One of the delegates was forcibly taken out of town and warned not to return. [8]

In Nevada, Socialist Al Shidler was active and successful in agitating for increased wages. He ran for county clerk on the Socialist ticket and came within a few votes of being elected. Soon afterwards he was discharged by the mining company for which he worked. He was then arrested and accused of having said that the war between the United States and the Imperial German Government "was nothing but a capitalistic war, and if it was not for the graft and money to be made by the capitalists the United States would never have gone into war." He was also charged with having said that "the draft law is the rottenest piece of injustice that was ever railroaded upon the American people; I will fight conscription as long as I have breath left in my body." [9] For these remarks he was fined three hundred dollars and sentenced to two years in McNeil Island Penitentiary.

In Alaska, Bruce Rogers, editor of a Socialist newspaper who had been extremely active in campaigning for the eight-hour day, was haled into court for making the statement, "We must make the world safe for democracy if we have to 'bean' the Goddess of Liberty to do it." He was arrested in December, 1917, and fined three hundred dollars with an alternative of 150 days in jail.[10]

Louise Olivereau, a Socialist and perhaps a theoretical Anarchist, worked as a stenographer for an I.W.W. union in the state of Washington. Influenced by her dislike of war, she made certain anticonscription statements and mailed "violent and frank" anticonscription circulars through the mail.[11] "We do not counsel resistance. We counsel one thing— obedience to your own conscience . . . . We urge you to stand by your own convictions, to maintain your rights as a free individual. If you regard the draft as an infringement upon your individual rights and the rights of your class in society, for your own sake and for the sake of your own class, resist." [12]

For this she was arrested and accused of violating the Espionage Act. Her defense included the following remarks to the jury:

> It does not make an atom of difference whether you decide that I am innocent of any violation of the law or guilty of a crime. America will be a country without dignity, without peace, and an offense to human kind, if a policy of tyrannical oppression and suppression is maintained. So long as the people are denied the right to take counsel together, the right to make their wants and desires known to the governing bodies they elect, and the right to demand that those governing bodies act in accordance with the wants and desires of the people who elect them; so long as hysteria is our motive force rather than reason; so long as tyranny and force are used against the many for the aggrandizement of the law—just so long will America be a proper subject for scorn and abhorrence with all thinking people . . . .[13]

After deliberating only about half an hour, the jury returned a verdict of guilty, and Miss Olivereau was sentenced to ten years in the penitentiary.[14]

The city of Milwaukee had become a Socialist stronghold and much of the organization's power in that area came from the leadership of Victor Berger. Born in Austria in 1860, he came to the United States in

1878 and helped organize the Socialist party. He became editor of the *Milwaukee Leader*, served in Congress from 1911 to 1913, becoming the first Socialist congressman. The more radical Socialists looked upon Berger with some distrust and considered him a "bourgeois member of the party." However, he had strongly opposed American entry into the war, had signed the antiwar resolutions passed at the St. Louis convention in April, 1917, and had written many sharp antiwar editorials and articles which appeared in the *Leader*.

On March 29, 1917, just before war was declared, Berger, John M. Work, and Adolph Germer had written to members of Congress urging them to oppose a declaration of war, or at least require that the question be decided by a public referendum. Even though this was before the war started, a later critic of Berger in Congress recalled these letters to show "the beginning of Berger's disloyal intent." [15]

After the United States entered the war Berger became more and more outspoken against American policies. According to the attorney general, he distributed "enormous quantities" of antiwar literature.[16] He condemned the repressive policies of the Government, criticized those Socialists who had jumped on the war bandwagon, and charged the financial interests with promoting the war. A typical Berger editorial stated, "And we repeat that the war was caused by the struggle between Great Britain and Germany for commercial supremacy of the world's trade. The Social-Democracy of the world stands for and demands peace! If this be treason—let them make the most of it." [17] A few days later he editorialized:

> This is the time when the Congress of the United States is simply a rubber stamp of Mr. Woodrow Wilson and of the Wall Street Clique that is behind Wilson and directs his actions—the time when Congressmen give whispered opinions in quiet corners, which opinions convey the exact contrary to their votes—when Congressmen hardly dare to attack barefaced graft in government contracts for fear that they will be put down as pro-Germans and as friends of Bill the Kaiser.[18]

Berger constantly denounced the draft law as unconstitutional, called the United States a plutocratic republic, and labeled Congress a rubber stamp of an autocratic president. He also published a pamphlet which one congressman called "the crowning infamy." [19] Even though he did not advise anyone against registering for the draft—in fact, he told one Socialist conscientious objector to enlist—Berger was one of the outstanding opponents of war in the United States.[20]

On September 22, 1917, Postmaster Burleson stepped in and barred the *Leader* from the mails. This was in line with the general policy of muzzling Socialist and other radical papers. Then Socialist meetings began to be broken up.[21] On February 25, 1918, the Socialist state executive committee named Berger as a candidate for the United States Senate. He promised to work "for an immediate, general, and permanent peace." [22] He also backed the Milwaukee Socialist candidates whose platform stated: "The American people did not want and do not want this war. They were plunged into this abyss by the treachery of the ruling class of the country—its demagogic agitators, its bought press, its sensational photoplays." [23]

Other candidates seeking the Wisconsin senatorial seat were Republican Congressman Irvine Lenroot and Democrat Joseph E. Davies who had resigned from the Federal Trade Commission to make the race. The Democratic high command was very desirous of winning this election, and President Wilson was not above imputing disloyalty to Davies' opponents in order to gain votes. The President's call for a Democratic Congress in the fall elections is well known, but actually he had followed the same policy early in the year with similar unsuccessful results.

President Wilson praised Davies' patriotism and cast reflections on the position of Lenroot. "The McLemore resolution, the embargo issue, and the armed neutrality measure presented the first opportunities to apply the acid test in our country to disclose true loyalty and genuine Americanism," Wilson wrote.[24] On March 15, Wilson explained to Vice-President Marshall that, while the great body of citizens in Wisconsin were loyal, the election of Lenroot "would by no means demonstrate that loyalty." He added that Lenroot's record had been one of "questionable support of the dignity and rights of the country on some test occasions." [25]

Wilson asked Marshall to go to Wisconsin and speak for Davies. On March 27 Marshall told a Madison audience that, regardless of how loyal Lenroot might be, he was bidding for the votes of traitors, pro-Germans, seditionists, and pacifists.[26] Senator Lewis of Illinois told an Appleton crowd that the President "at this crisis is entitled to one of his party organization . . . ." [27]

The main battle was between Davies and Lenroot, but as the election approached Berger's strength seemed to grow to menacing proportions. On February 2, Berger was indicted for violating the Espionage Act.

However, it was not made public until March 9 during the heat of the campaign. When the district attorney in Chicago was asked why the indictment had been suppressed for over a month, he replied that "the government felt that the announcement should be made at this time to develop other angles of the case." Berger charged, probably in truth, that "it is a political move, pure and simple." [28] Despite this handicap, the Socialist candidate continued to campaign on the principle of "100 per cent for peace." The day before the election he wrote that "the issue is clear—heaven or hell, peace or war, Socialists or profiteers." [29]

Lenroot, like Berger, was on the defensive where the loyalty issue was involved because of the positions he had taken before 1917. However, just a few days before the election which was held on April 2, Lenroot and other Republicans launched an all-out attack on the Wilson Administration. This proved to be good strategy. As it turned out, President Wilson's attempt to identify the Democratic party with superior patriotism failed miserably from a political standpoint. Lenroot defeated Davies by a small margin, and Berger polled over 100,000 votes. In Milwaukee the Socialists elected a mayor. Lenroot's victory should have been a warning to the Administration. The bold emphasis upon the need of Democrats to carry on the war successfully was probably poor strategy. Republican Senator Sherman strongly resented the implications of Wilson's stand and told his colleagues that "I insist on electing men of my own political persuasion as one of the proper means of carrying on the war . . . ." [30]

Berger and four other Socialists,[31] who were indicted at the same time, were not brought to trial until late in 1918 after the war had ended. They were charged with conspiracy in writing and circulating seditious and pro-German literature. Some of Berger's strong antiwar editorials were cited as evidence against him.[32] Berger and his comrades denied any conspiracy and argued that they simply all held the traditional Socialist views on war.[33]

The trial was held before Judge Landis in Chicago. Berger's attorney asked for a change of venue, charging that Landis was prejudiced against Socialists. Landis denied this request. However, the defendants felt as though the whole atmosphere was hostile to them. The Reverend Irwin St. John Tucker declared, "I lost interest in this trial when the second day was half through. No good sportsman cares to play a game where the dice are loaded and the deck is cold, and the opponent neither knows or cares nothing about the rules of the game and even the ordinary rules of decency and honor." [34]

The five men were found guilty, and Judge Landis sentenced each of them in February, 1919, to twenty years in the penitentiary. After the conviction Berger declared that he and his comrades were not guilty of conspiracy but had simply expressed the "position of the International Socialist movement." "Now," he said, "if this teaching of Socialism is a crime, then we are criminals . . . . This is the reason why my comrades and I were indicted. This was a political trial. The Socialist party was on trial. This fact is admitted by everybody who knows anything about our political and economic conditions." [35]

Berger appealed his sentence to the United States Supreme Court, which ruled in 1921 that Judge Landis should have granted a change of venue.[36] As a result of this decision, the case was dismissed and the charges were finally officially dropped by the Government in February, 1923.

Meanwhile, in November, 1918, before his trial, Berger was elected to Congress. After long consideration, however, the House of Representatives, with only one dissenting vote, refused to seat him on November 10, 1919. As one congressman said, "The one and only issue in this case is that of Americanism." [37] A special election in December, 1919, saw Berger defeat a fusion candidate, but in January, 1920, he was again denied his seat in the House. Finally, in November, 1922, after having lost the congressional race in November, 1920, Berger was elected a third time. By that time the national hysteria had abated and he was allowed to take his place in Congress.

▄▄

"It is no time to waste money on trials and continuances and things like that."

CONTINUED WAR
ON THE I.W.W.

It was against the I.W.W. and its members that the conservatives
continued to direct their heaviest fire. In the minds of many citizens the
doctrines of the I.W.W. had even more in common with those of the
Bolsheviks than did those of the Socialists. To make matters worse,
I.W.W. leaders openly praised the Russian radicals.

As mentioned before, almost immediately after the Bolsheviki
grabbed power in November, 1917, newspapers and magazines in the
United States began to connect American radicalism, especially the
I.W.W., with the Russian Reds. When a meeting was held on December
2, 1917, in New York City to celebrate the Bolsheviki triumph, the *Times*
reported the next day that the crowd had been composed of Anarchists,
Socialists, I.W.W.'s, and other radicals. On December 26, the *New York
Times* headed a story, "See Worldwide Anarchist Plot," with a subhead,
"Washington Officials Connect I.W.W., Bolsheviki, and Revolutionaries
in Many Lands."

The following February, Ralph Easley, chairman of the Executive
Council of the National Civic Federation, told an audience that Bolshevism, I.W.W., and Anarchism were synonymous.[1] Three days later Senator
Poindexter said the Bolshevik movement in the United States was typified
by the I.W.W.[2] A writer for *Forum* magazine declared that Bolshevism
in America was "so closely allied to the I.W.W. that if you prick one
the other bleeds." [3]

Assuming then, as many people did, that the I.W.W. was the American counterpart of the Russian Reds, it followed that safety for current economic and social arrangements demanded the organization's death. One observer declared that the I.W.W. was no ordinary trade union. "The whole social and industrial fabric is threatened, nothing less. Such a dangerous influence is not to be trifled with." Any delay in destroying the organization, said this writer, would be dangerous.[4] Thus throughout the fall and winter of 1917–18, the campaign to exterminate the I.W.W. reached a new high. The I.W.W. seemed more dangerous than ever in light of unfolding events in Petrograd.

In a dozen or more western states a vigorous and unrelenting battle against I.W.W. members was carried on by commercial clubs, safety committees, loyalty leagues, and others. One I.W.W. wrote that "lumber workers, on strike throughout the Northwest states for the eight-hour day, felt the concerted effort of all means of repression. Without show of legality, martial or civil, halls were raided, hundreds arrested, denied right of attorney, thrown into 'bull-pens,' starved, beaten, and shot." [5]

On one occasion, two companies of the Third Oregon Infantry were dispatched to Elum, Washington, where they threw pickets into a stockade. These men were held for months without formal charges. Reports to the American Civil Liberties Union stated that hundreds of I.W.W.'s were arrested in the vicinity of Yakima and Pasco. Workers who tried to meet at Pasco were beaten and drenched with the fire hose.[6] Local trainmen who only expressed sympathy for the strikers were taken from their trains by militia at Pasco and sent to bull-pens incommunicado.[7] An I.W.W. organizer by the name of "Roughneck Jack" was driven out of a small town in Nevada.[8] During the month of February, 1918, soldiers in one of the Washington army camps discovered that some workmen were I.W.W's. Twenty of them were driven out of the camp into the cold, rain, sleet, and snow.[9]

Seattle was encountering a great deal of labor unrest, and employers were anxious to use the excuse of patriotism to wipe out the radical labor movement. One night early in January, 1918, two civilians and about twenty sailors mobbed the Piggott Printing Company plant in Seattle. This company printed the Socialist *Daily Call* and the *Industrial Worker,* an I.W.W. publication. After employees of the plant were forced to lie down on the floor, the mob stuck timbers and iron bars into the running presses. Type cases and cabinets were upset, and type forms for several publications were hopelessly "pied." "You have been running some pretty bad dope," one of the mob was reported by the *Tacoma Tribune,* January

5, 1918, to have remarked after the wrecking had been finished. "Tell your boss that he's about through." The Seattle *Post-Intelligencer* quoted the leader of the mob as saying, "We'll let you off easy this time, but the next time it will mean death." Damage was estimated at fifteen thousand dollars.[10]

According to the *New York Evening Call* of May 20, 1918, the Piggott Printing Company "was told that if it continued doing work for the I.W.W. the plant would be destroyed and the owners physically assaulted. The banks also refused to do business with the printing company, and the paper mills refused to sell paper to the printing shop." On January 26, 1918, the Seattle *Industrial Worker* reported that G. Merle Gordon, ringleader of the mob, had been released from the county jail after eleven members of the Elks' Lodge had posted his thousand-dollar bail. The *Post-Intelligencer* reported on April 24, 1918, that Gordon was released on his plea of "mental irresponsibility" caused by the seditious articles published by this press. A patriotic party followed Gordon's acquittal.

Regular visits were made once a month to the Idaho lumber camps to look for I.W.W.'s. When frequent raids on I.W.W. halls did not break the winter strike, members of the "home guard" were sent early in 1918 to search workers for I.W.W. cards.[11] At Butte, Montana, there were raids on the I.W.W. hall "by employers' agents, and soldiers duly officered, who acted without warrant or process and beat and bayoneted union members by order of the commanding officer." [12] In February, 1918, an I.W.W. by the name of Mell Hathaway was horsewhipped and driven from town. Antonin Gualberti got three years in the penitentiary for distributing antidraft literature.[13]

Red Lodge, Montana, was the scene of several mob actions against I.W.W. members. Jalmar Wintturi, a Finnish worker, swore that on the evening of November 19, 1917, he was forcibly taken from his home by several men, one of them foreman at the Northwestern Improvement Company, and given a third degree quizzing at the courthouse about the I.W.W. After a while the head of the group said, "What will we do with this fellow. We do not want to stay here any longer." Both shooting and hanging were suggested. Then the head man declared, "All the fellows that want to hang Jalmar Wintturi say 'Aye,' and they all yelled 'Aye.' Then he hammered on the table and said 'That is all.'" At that point Wintturi protested that he had done nothing to deserve such treatment. "My ideas may be different from yours," he continued, "but that is no reason why you should hang me." Members of the group replied, "Belonging to the I.W.W. is enough to hang a man for." Then Wintturi was taken to the cellar and a rope was put around his neck. Again he was asked if he belonged to the I.W.W. and he denied it. The rope was alternately tightened and slackened as Wintturi was queried about the I.W.W., but he refused to give any information. Finally, according to his account, "the rope was tightened again and I hung for about ten or fifteen minutes and then when the rope was loosened I fell to the floor. He [one of the men] kept kicking me and asking if I belonged to the I.W.W. Finally I said yes, I belonged to the I.W.W." Then one of Wintturi's captors said, "What the hell is the matter with you, why didn't you say that before?" Under threat of further hanging, Wintturi was forced to reveal the names of other I.W.W. members and to promise that he would help locate specific individuals sought by the vigilantes. All the while he was being questioned the rope was around his neck. When he hesitated to answer, the rope would be tightened. He was made to promise that he would leave the I.W.W. and to "swear to honor the flag." Following this ordeal, three of the men took Wintturi home to his crying wife and children. It was then about 4:30 A.M. After he gave his I.W.W. card to the vigilantes, they left. Wintturi's first reaction was "to see Jack Ollila and tell him I had told them he was a member of the I.W.W." But he found that Ollila had received similar treatment. The two men then "figured on how we could best leave Red Lodge." [14]

Other workers around Red Lodge also felt the harsh hand of extra-legal punishment. Emil Koski, secretary of the Finnish Workers' Club, was shamefully mistreated, and John U. Heliste was lashed with a black-snake whip because he supposedly made derogatory statements regarding the Government.[15] In March, 1918, a large group of Finnish miners were arrested in a raid on the I.W.W. hall.[16]

Elsewhere the story was much the same. At Cedar Rapids, Iowa, an I.W.W. organizer, Joseph Selzer, was arrested, apparently because he had antiwar literature in his possession. Sentiment against the I.W.W. was so strong that Selzer felt it would be useless to hire a lawyer. Besides, he lacked the money. He was fined one thousand dollars for "unlawful organization" and was sentenced to one year in jail.[17] The presiding judge, Milo P. Smith, said, "It pleases me to impose this sentence upon you. I regret that the law did not permit me to order you stood up against the wall and shot." [18]

Indictments against members of the I.W.W. were often supported by the most flimsy evidence. For example, an uneducated I.W.W. laborer, William M. Collins of Montesano, Washington, was arraigned for reportedly having made critical remarks about conditions at Camp Lewis. He was sentenced to fifteen months in the McNeil Island Penitentiary on the grounds that his remarks were designed to interfere with the success of American military forces. In October, 1918, the Circuit Court of Appeals reversed this decision because there had been insufficient evidence to support the indictment.[19]

At the same time, the Circuit Court of Appeals reversed the conviction of Leonard Foster. Foster, an I.W.W., was another civilian worker at Camp Lewis. It was charged that he and other I.W.W.'s had spread dissatisfaction and discontent among workers and soldiers. They were accused of intentionally trying to cause insubordination in the army and of interfering with the military and naval success of the United States. In reversing Foster's conviction, which had been a five-year penitentiary sentence, the court said the indictment had been too general. The charges, said the judge, were vague and meaningless.[20]

Some of the most violent attacks against the I.W.W. occurred in Oklahoma. Following the Green Corn Rebellion in August, many Oklahomans were nearly hysterical about the activities of the I.W.W. John B. Meserve, a member of the Oklahoma Council of Defense, reported to Washington that the I.W.W. had sent several of its most vigorous organizers into the Tulsa District. He claimed that they intended "to destroy the waterworks system, and simultaneously place incendiary bombs in various parts of the city." [21] An Enid citizen was quoted as saying that two million I.W.W.'s were plotting to loot, destroy, and overthrow the Government.[22] The mere mention of the I.W.W. seemed to bring visions of impending revolution.

On October 29, a bomb exploded in the home of oilman J. Edgar Pew in Tulsa. Urged on by exaggerated newspaper stories, a nervous public immediately jumped to the conclusion that this dastardly act was the work of direct-action, revolutionary I.W.W.'s. The following morning the Tulsa *Daily World* headline stated, "I.W.W. Plot Breaks Prematurely in Blowing Up of Pew Residence." Based on "unimpeachable sources," the claim was made by the *World* that a general strike, destruction of property, and other heinous acts were a part of a general conspiracy by the I.W.W. Just what evidence he had to back this charge, the writer did not disclose. In any event, a front-page message "to all loyal Tulsans" called for 250 men "to complete Tulsa Home Guards."

Shortly after the bombing, W. J. Powers was picked up in the railroad yards and accused of being the I.W.W. responsible for the job. But no evidence was produced against him other than that he was a member of the I.W.W. The police were unable to break him under a thorough questioning.

October 30 found Tulsa charged with fear and excitement. By the end of the day 200 men had joined the Home Guard. The *World* editorialized that "Tulsa is apprehensive that other acts of wanton destruction will occur . . . . The I.W.W., German bought and German controlled, seems bent upon . . . sparing neither life nor property." The editor quoted an anonymous Civil War veteran as saying, "I will be one of a committee of citizens who will knot the rope and pull it over a tree when one of the disreputable wretches is found." "This, then to the assassins," concluded the editor, "your worthless lives will be made more wretched at any attempt to inaugurate the reign of terror you have contemplated . . . . There is no tribunal to which you can appeal for clemency; there is no official but will sustain the true citizenship in keeping civilization uppermost and in upholding the nation in its work to be done."

On November 5, police raided the I.W.W. hall in Tulsa and eleven men were arrested. The men readily admitted that they were members of the I.W.W. They even boasted of it. Without any show of resistance or argument with the officers they were taken to jail. In the I.W.W. hall copies of *Solidarity* and other "seditious literature" were found, according to the Tulsa *Daily World* of November 6. Since there was no evidence to connect the men with dynamiting Pew's residence, they were held on vagrancy charges. Police Captain Wilkerson said that "we are going to arrest every man who is found loitering about the I.W.W. headquarters. If they get out of jail and go back there we will arrest them again, and again and again." Then Wilkerson added, "Tulsa is not big enough to hold any traitors during our Government's crisis and the sooner these fellows get out of town the better for them."

One of the eleven, Bernard Johnson, was placed on trial November 8, and it was agreed that the decision in his case should apply to the other ten. Because he had been in Tulsa only three days he was a poor suspect in the Pew bombing of ten days before. The trial was continued the next day, November 9. There was contradictory testimony about the arrested men's character, but no specific incidents of misconduct were shown. In fact, none of the men had a police record. The prosecution rested its case mainly on the fact that the men were members of the I.W.W. Great effort was made to determine their attitude toward the war and the Government. The trial ended about 10:30 P.M. and Judge T. D. Evans found seventeen men guilty. Six persons had come to testify for the defendants and they, too, were arrested, tried, and convicted. In fining each man one hundred dollars, Judge Evans said, "These are no ordinary times." [23]

Meanwhile, Tulsa newspapers openly advocated direct-action methods against the I.W.W. In an editorial entitled "Down with the Agitators," published November 7, the *World* stated, "The one remedy for the vicious agitator is to ride him on a rail. If he seriously objects to that he might be used for decoration for a telephone pole." On the morning before the trial ended, the *World* editor became even more belligerent. In his editorial, "Get Out the Rope," he not only attacked the I.W.W., but revealed the basis of his true fears, namely, effective organized labor in the oil fields. "The oil industry can take care of its own troubles," said the writer. "It does not need the I.W.W. There is not a man in the field who does not know that whatever grievance he may have does not need the arbitrament of a labor union to solve." Then he added:

If the I.W.W. . . . gets busy in your neighborhood, kindly take occasion to decrease the supply of hemp. A knowledge of how to tie a knot that will stick might come handy in a few days. It is no time to dally with the enemies of the country . . . . The first step in the whipping of Germany is to strangle the I.W.W.'s. Kill 'em just as you would any other kind of a snake. Don't scotch 'em: kill 'em! And kill 'em dead! It is no time to waste money on trials and continuances and things like that.[24]

Later in the evening, this advice was to be followed.

It was about eleven P.M. that the vigilantes took action. One of the arrested I.W.W.'s said later, "The turnkey came and called, 'Get ready to go out you I.W.W. men.'" The men grabbed their belongings and "were immediately ordered into automobiles waiting in the alley." One report said that they were to be turned loose on the condition that they would leave Tulsa immediately. But when they reached the north part of town, a masked mob, known as the Knights of Liberty, stopped the cars and ordered everyone to throw up his hands.

We were then bound, some with hands in front, some with hands behind, and others bound with arms hanging down their sides, the rope being wrapped around the body. Then the police were ordered to "beat it" which they did, running, and we started for the place of execution . . . .

When we arrived there a company of gowned and masked gunmen were there to meet us standing at "present arms." We were ordered out of the autos, told to get in line in front of these gunmen and another bunch of men with automatics and pistols lined up between us. Our hands were still held up, and those who were bound, in front. Then a masked man walked down the line and slashed the ropes that bound us, and we were ordered to strip to the waist, which we did.[25]

Then each prisoner in turn was tied to a tree and, while the others looked on, was lashed until his back ran with blood. Then a coat of hot tar was applied to the bleeding backs and feathers were applied. According to the Tulsa *Daily World* account, "with each stroke of the brush the blackrobed man in charge of the ceremony uttered the words: 'In the name of the outraged women and children of Belgium.' " An elderly victim pleaded for mercy, saying, "I have lived here for eighteen years and have raised a large family. I am not an I.W.W. I am as patriotic as any man here." [26] But since the speaker had been arrested at I.W.W. headquarters, he received the same treatment as the others. The men's clothing and other possessions which had been returned by the police were then thrown into a pile, gasoline was poured over them, and they were set afire. The Tulsa *Daily World* reporter wrote, "As the last man was loosed from the whipping post they were all lined up with their faces toward the west. 'Let this be a warning to all I.W.W.'s never to come to Tulsa again,' said the ringleader. 'Now get!' " [27] Some revolver shots were fired in the air and the bloody, tarred, and feathered victims ran stumbling into the dark. The next day, November 11, reporters from the Tulsa *Daily World* at the scene found "pieces of clothing and flesh and a profusion of feathers . . . entangled on the fence wires."

The victims of this highhanded and illegal action got no public or open sympathy in Tulsa or elsewhere in the state. An examination of editorials in the Tulsa *Daily World* reveals something of the local state of mind. In fact, the *Daily World* on November 12 justified the whole gory action by laying the blame on the I.W.W. "The man who lives by the sword must die by the sword," wrote the editor. I.W.W.'s had taken the law into their own hands and had been dealt with by that "sterling element of citizenship, that class of taxpaying and orderly people who are most of all interested and committed in and to the observance of law." The writer concluded that Tulsa citizens could now go about their daily tasks free and unfearful, knowing that Tulsa was a place "where men and women can live unmolested in their daily occupations and that anarchy has no place or position here." There were at least seventeen men who must have bitterly resented this hypocrisy.

Other editorials and news stories followed the same theme. On November 11 an account was published which said that "I.W.W. danger in Tulsa [is] not ended . . . officials look for further depredations and more 'night parties.'" Two days later the Knights of Liberty were referred to as a "patriotic body" and the editor warned that "it is up to the people of every community to protect itself." On the sixteenth the editor wrote, "The time has come for every citizen of Tulsa to constitute himself a secret service committee of one. Look up your neighbors, be careful with whom you converse, and always let the other fellow do the talking unless you are absolutely sure of his patriotism." The next day a *World* editorial admonished local citizens, "Watch your neighbor. If he is not doing everything in his power to help the nation in this crisis, see that he is reported to the proper authorities."

This frantic and unreasoning attitude was also reflected in Oklahoma City. The *Daily Oklahoman* editorialized on November 12 that the Tulsa incident was "a rather highhanded proceeding," but added that it was entirely possible "to understand it and to say amen to it." The *Daily Oklahoman* said that I.W.W. "treason is common knowledge. The black treachery of it defies words." "The *Oklahoman*," wrote the editor, "always has opposed lawlessness of every kind. But this is war." Then the writer concluded, "Along with tar and feathers, there are trees in this state and rope in plenty and the will to use them."

Later in the month a representative of the I.W.W. appeared in Tulsa to investigate. He was arrested, sent first to Chicago, and then later tried with other I.W.W.'s in the Wichita case. The Tulsa *Daily World* of November 11, 1917, reported that Government agents "were making no apparent effort to discover the identity of the fifty black-robed and hooded men." In fact, one Government agent advised that "every reliable citizen should carry a gun." The *New York Evening Call* of May 6, 1918, reported, "Six months' efforts by the National Civil Liberties Bureau to secure the arrest of members of the Knights of Liberty mob that took seventeen I.W.W. prisoners from the police and whipped and tarred them . . . have failed."

This state of mind found in Tulsa spread to other parts of the state. In Drumright, Bartlesville, and elsewhere, I.W.W.'s were arrested or run out of town. The Tulsa *Daily World* of November 16 reported that the Sapulpa police chief shot and killed an I.W.W. suspect when the prisoner attacked him with a knife. On November 24, according to the *World,* the I.W.W.'s had set fire to a railroad station at Henryetta. Two days later, the *World* attributed a wreck on the Frisco Railroad to the I.W.W. Three people were killed. Two days later the same paper admitted that boys had been responsible for the wreck. Patrick S. Nagle, one of the state's Socialist leaders, described the situation as "a reign of terror" which was being upheld by the state's press and the "Democratic machine." [28]

In December, 1917, a visiting minister in Tulsa declared that "Socialists, I.W.W.'s, pro-Huns, and pacifists" were all "undesirable citizens." He remarked, "We are fighting to uproot autocracy that the world may be safe for democracy. We must also guarantee that safety by destroying Socialism. It is but another form of autocracy." [29]

Three days after Christmas, 1917, a Tulsa laborer, Charles Krieger, was arrested and imprisoned on the charge of having dynamited the Pew residence. Krieger was brought to trial in October, 1918. The state introduced prisoners from Leavenworth Penitentiary "who were to swear that Krieger had blown up the house and had confided in them prior to their conviction." However, when two of the men testified for the prosecution they swore they had never heard Krieger say anything about it. But a third man swore that Krieger had planned the explosion and had sent the three of them to blow up Pew's house.[30] Krieger was finally acquitted in May, 1920, but for twenty-two months he had been confined in jail awaiting the outcome of his trial. It seems that he was luckier than many other I.W.W.'s because of the fairmindedness and impartiality of Judge R. S. Cole. Some judges refused to bow to the popular hysteria. In Oklahoma and elsewhere, however, there was a general state of mind reminiscent of the attitude of King James I, who said about the Puritans, "I will make them conform or I will harry them out of the land."

Californians were not to be outdone by Oklahomans in striking at I.W.W.'s. Early in the fall of 1917, about 125 I.W.W.'s were arrested in Fresno. Forty of them were held without any formal charges, but were freed about two weeks later on a writ of habeas corpus. On November 21, twenty-five men, including the I.W.W. secretaries in Los Angeles, San Pedro, and Sacramento, were indicted for conspiring to intimidate employers by threatening to strike unless their wage demands were met.[31] This indictment, however, was later dismissed.

On December 17 a bomb exploded on the back porch of Governor Stephens' residence in Sacramento. Fortunately, no one was hurt. As had been true at Tulsa, it was immediately suggested that I.W.W.'s were responsible and police began making arrests.[32] According to a report to

President Wilson from Simon J. Lubin, President of the California State Commission of Immigration and Housing:

> The local police in Sacramento, to make a showing, rounded up some sixty men in and around the I.W.W. headquarters. Then, they did not know what to do with them. At first the police appealed to the special agent in charge of the bureau of investigation of the Department of Justice to take the men over; but he refused. A committee of local citizens then in some way got in touch with certain authorities here, who, we are told, instructed the United States Marshal in San Francisco to hold the prisoners.[33]

This quotation has been marked "false" on the copy in the Wilson files but, nonetheless, it seems to coincide with local newspaper comment. On December 29, the *Sacramento Bee* said that a representative of the Department of Justice had not found enough evidence for federal officials to hold the prisoners. Consequently, this report said, the city was holding them. Two days later the *Bee* reported that "felony charges" had been placed against the men. On January 1, 1918, the *Bee* stated that federal warrants had been obtained.

In his report to Wilson, dated March 29, 1918, Lubin declared that

> from what we learned in the grand jury room, and from what the federal attorney told us, we doubt that they have any stronger evidence against fifty-five of the sixty men than this; that they swore and blasphemed and pounded upon the cell walls, after they were arrested. The situation at this moment is bad. If the men were now released, it is more than likely that some of them will be lynched, or at least very badly handled. If they are held, there is more than good ground for agitation to gain their release; and we doubt whether any jury would bring in a conviction.[34]

In his account of the situation published in the *New York Times* on April 19, 1918, V. S. McClatchy, editor of the *Sacramento Bee*, declared that a vigilante committee of "responsible, reliable, temperate, but resolute citizens" would have taken direct action against the I.W.W.'s if they had been freed.

In seeking grounds to sentence the men, officials dropped the original charge of bombing the Governor's mansion. Instead, on February 8, 1918, the forty-six men still jailed in Sacramento, and the nine others from other parts of the state, were indicted for violating the Espionage Act.[35] As will be seen later, they were not brought to trial until December.

The Sacramento bombing incident encouraged a further wild and inflammatory campaign against the I.W.W., although nothing had been presented to show that the I.W.W. had actually been responsible. There were stories of firing haystacks, burning factories, and poisoning sheep.[36] On December 27, 1917, a cartoon in the *Sacramento Bee* showed men in front of a firing squad. The caption read, "A Swift Cure for I.W.W.

A SWIFT CURE FOR I.W.W. POISON. —Buel in the *Sacramento Bee*, December 27, 1917.

Poison." Two days later this paper editorialized, "The *Bee* recommends an organization of responsible citizens that will act in this matter with determination and deliberation, and will use *any necessary means* to suppress disloyalty and disorder." [37] On January 7, 1918, the *Bee* stated, "Germany through members of the I.W.W. organization is financing a gigantic plot to destroy industrial plants and crops of the Pacific Coast." This was the sort of unsubstantiated story which commonly appeared in the press of this period. On January 21 a letter was reported to have come from the Tulsa Chamber of Commerce suggesting that Sacramento emulate Tulsa in handling I.W.W.'s. Try tar and feathers, was the word from Oklahoma.[38] The head of the Sacramento Chamber of Commerce was reported to have said, "I am for prompt use of the rope." [39] On February 9, 1918, the *Sacramento Bee* headline read, "Evidence Shows Discontents Planned Reign of Terror and Hoped to Destroy All War Plants on Pacific Coast." This story was attributed to the Department of Justice by the Seattle *Post-Intelligencer* of the same day. On February 16, the *Post-Intelligencer* quoted a sheriff as saying that the I.W.W. menace was growing more serious and that state laws were inadequate to cover the situation.

A pamphlet published by the Civil Liberties Bureau stated that "a constant stream of false stories against the I.W.W. deliberately planned to create hatred and mob violence" had appeared after the summer of 1917. These stories, it was charged, occupied leading positions and were well-timed so as to appear about the time of arrests or indictments. If the stories were later denied, the denials or corrections were "invariably in small type with no display and inconspicuous positions." [40] The Spokane Labor Council issued a statement in the *Seattle Union-Record,* September 1, 1917, which said that if the press had not "fomented prejudice, stirred up class hatreds, by publication of the wildest rumors" concerning I.W.W. activity, "rumors which had no foundation in fact," the organization would have died out.

It was suggested at various times that all I.W.W.'s should be interned. But when the matter was presented to President Wilson, he replied, "There is no legal authority for such internment as you suggest except in the case of alien enemies, and the proportion of alien enemies among the class referred to is, of course, very small." [41]

Early in April, 1918, Wilson wrote to his Attorney General:

> You will remember that a Mr. Bell came here with great excitement from the Pacific Coast, delegated by certain of the Western Governors to propose some rather radical things to us for the purpose of suppressing the I.W.W.'s who certainly are worthy of being suppressed. He has been followed now by a Mr. Lubin . . . . Will you not be kind enough to have it carefully read in your department with a view to seeing whether anything is proposed which it is feasible and wise for us to do? [42]

But while government officials were pondering the problem, local citizens continued to rely on direct-action methods. One thing became increasingly clear as the months passed by; neither antiwar statements nor overt acts against the war effort by I.W.W.'s were necessary to bring demands to crush the organization. Just being a member of the I.W.W., or associating with members—one of the seventeen men tarred and feathered at Tulsa was not an I.W.W.—was considered disloyal and un-American.

▄▄▄

"AH TO BE INDICTED
IN THE SPRING"
March, April, and May, 1918

For opponents of war indicted under the Espionage Act or other wartime measures, the rigors of the law did not begin with a penitentiary sentence or some other punishment. The accusation, the indictment, the trial, all carried with them misery and suffering. Arthur Garfield Hays commented later that he had always been quite philosophical about indictments when they affected his clients. But he experienced an "appalling shock," he said, when "the dreaded word 'indictment'" was used against him where loyalty was involved.[1] In some instances an indictment meant that one would be avoided by friends and acquaintances; in other cases the indicted one avoided them. Sometimes it meant the loss of a job. Then there was the trial itself with additional personal questioning, attacks, and humiliations. Also, there were expenses. Legal fees mounted rapidly. Periods when a person was held in jail awaiting trial, as well as the trial itself, meant loss of wages. For the poor man, such expenses were tragic, not only for himself but for his family who also suffered humiliation, scorn, privation.

During World War I, public feelings were whipped up to such an extent that a mere accusation of disloyalty was sometimes nearly enough to send a man to prison. Occasionally the accused would be let off with a humiliating lecture or a small fine, but often this result would be accomplished only when a high-priced lawyer had been engaged. When the accused was also a well-known reformer or radical, he generally found that he was being tried by conservative judges and lawyers, conservative juries, and a conservative press. Looking back at the trials of conspicuous dissenters from the vantage point of 1922, Representative Huddleston of Alabama declared: "In such cases a trial is more or less a farce. It is sort of legalized mob action. The rich, influential, and ably defended, of course, go free. The weak, the undefended, and the friendless are convicted of course. To be an alien, radical or labor agitator is to go to jail." [2] There was some overstatement in this, but not much.

Appellate courts reversed convictions many times where the evidence of bias was obvious. The number of these reversals in themselves constitute a damning indictment of some of the trials. One judge had his decision overruled because he barred defense testimony which should have been admitted and because his charge to the jury was "seriously misleading and prejudicial." [3] Often higher courts reversed decisions because of insufficient evidence or other irregularities in the procedure. The Berger case was remanded by the Supreme Court because, it said, Judge Landis should not have presided when the defendants were absolutely convinced of his bias. Landis had said, "One must have a very judicial mind, indeed, not to be prejudiced against the German Americans in this country. Their hearts are reeking with disloyalty." [4]

After the trials and prison terms were over, the troubles of the victims were still unfinished. In the middle of 1919, Bruce Rogers wrote to a friend, "I am boycotted and blacklisted for all employment, and entirely without means." [5] Another individual wrote, "I am in bad health, without any income, my position and good chance for promotion is lost, my family is broken up, my reputation tarnished and I am living in Detroit in a small room by myself on the bounty of a friend." [6] These instances indicate the particular problems of dissenters who were poor.

In this spring of 1918, the nationalists followed very closely the pattern which they had set in the previous months. There were accusations, arrests, trials, fines, and sentences. The Attorney General reported: "Not infrequently as many as 1500 complaints reach the Department of Justice in a single day. It is safe to say that there is nothing whatever in 95 per cent of these cases, and yet all are thoroughly investigated in order that we may cull out the small number which justify prosecution." [7] Thus people continued to be arrested—and convicted.

There were times when perfectly loyal people got into trouble under the most ridiculous circumstances. Early in the year a middle westerner went to Florida where he found the weather unseasonably cold. As he came in from a fishing trip he was heard to say, "Damn such a country as this." He was arrested by a local deputy and charged with violating the Espionage Act. The man had to hire a lawyer to gain his release. In telling of this incident Senator Sherman deplored the fact that there were "hordes" of marshals around the country trying to distinguish themselves by making arrests.[8]

In March, as the Germans won some victories in France, Chicago police rounded up a great many individuals of German birth living in the city. The *Chicago Daily News,* March 25, 1918, reported that "a steady stream of handcuffed men" was hauled into the jails for gloating over German successes.

Two soldiers received sentences of thirty years in the penitentiary and a third was given fifteen years at hard labor for making antiwar statements.[9] Some ex-soldiers, veterans of earlier wars, got into trouble for the same reason. People who criticized soldiers as educated savages, spineless creatures, or "damned bums" also ended up in jail.[10] As before, they were sent to the penitentiary.[11] Then there was the Ohio farmer, John White, who said that soldiers in American camps "were dying off like flies" and that the "murder of innocent women and children by the German soldiers was no worse than the United States' soldiers did in the Philippines." He was sentenced to twenty-one months in the penitentiary.[12] People of German blood who made friendly remarks about the Germans were also indicted and punished. Charles G. Schulze was sentenced to fifteen years in the penitentiary for such remarks.[13]

Two Americans who had enlisted in the Canadian army were told that they were fools. W. E. Mead, an I.W.W. organizer who was partially intoxicated, said to them, "This is a capitalistic war started by England because she is afraid of Germany corraling commerce." [14] Mead was sentenced to five years in the penitentiary, although he was pardoned after serving two years and four months. In recommending a pardon the Attorney General said that Mead had a good reputation as a law-abiding citizen and "was evidently a poor workingman with apparently no one to intervene in his behalf." [15] The case was of special interest because Mead had not even been charged with interfering with the military forces of the United States, but with those of an ally.

In a little pamphlet entitled *Pure Common Sense,* Andre Boutin said: "War is pure ignorance . . . . It shows on its face that we are worse than savage . . . . Just as long as the fancy class teaches that it is right, that it is patriotic to fight (murder) for your country, just so long will war reign." He was convicted of violating the Espionage Act.[16]

A number of Socialists were indicted and sentenced for disloyalty in the spring of 1918. Jacob O. Bentall, who had been a Socialist candidate for governor of Minnesota, was accused of trying to discourage a young man from registering for the draft. He also opposed sending men overseas and reportedly said that the war had been caused by the Morgans, Carnegies, and Schwabs. He was sentenced to five years in the penitentiary.[17] In reporting this case the Attorney General said that Bentall's conviction had been due to his continued statements that the war had been caused by big business and financial interests.[18] In sentencing Bentall the judge was quoted by the *Minneapolis Journal* of April 19, 1918, as saying, "Upon the President's recommendation, Congress declared war in April of last year. After that declaration the hour of discussion passed."

James A. Peterson, who had been a Socialist candidate for the United States Senate in Minnesota, was also haled into court. He was indicted for publishing an article entitled "The U.S. Senate and Our Country's War Aims." Among other things, Peterson wrote that thousands of young Americans were being sacrificed in order to achieve the territorial ambitions of the European allies. He was convicted and sentenced to four years at Leavenworth.[19]

Another Socialist politician, William Peregrin, had taken part in the move to get the conscription act repealed. Department of Justice operatives got on his trail. After considering what had happened in the courts to other Socialists and opponents of conscription, he was convinced that he had no chance. Rather than be sent to Leavenworth, he decided to place a piece of dynamite in his mouth and light the fuse. He was survived by a wife and daughter.[20]

The American Socialist Society and Scott Nearing were indicted jointly in March, 1918, for publishing a pamphlet called *The Great Madness*. This had been written by Nearing of the People's Council who, after having been fired from the University of Pennsylvania and Toledo University, was then connected with the Rand School of Social Science in New York. The views expressed in *The Great Madness* and other pamphlets written by Nearing contained the traditional Socialist ideas regarding war. "The 'plutocracy,' . . . finding its hold upon the political and economic life of the nation endangered by changes in public opinion, seized upon the instinctive martial responsiveness of the people to rehabilitate its falling power," Nearing wrote. "There was no cause

at issue which could in the least concern the interests of the people . . . .
It fastened upon America that militarism which the capitalists who
contrived the war affected to condemn. It was a victory for 'plutocracy,'
which was at once reflected in the acclaim of their venal press." [21] It
was charged that *The Great Madness* tended to cause insubordination
and disloyalty in the military forces of the United States and that
Nearing and the American Socialist Society, which published the
pamphlet, had conspired to obstruct recruiting and enlistment. The
Society was found guilty and fined three thousand dollars. Oddly enough,
Nearing was acquitted.[22]

A Socialist in Everett, Washington, was arrested for some violation
of the Espionage Act. Emil Herman, state secretary of the party, appeared as a defense witness. Immediately afterwards Herman was arrested. His arrest was based on the fact that some disloyal books and
stickers were found in his office. Among the books were *The Great
Madness, Mental Dynamite,* and *The Menace of Militarism.* On the
stickers were printed some antimilitaristic remarks falsely attributed to
Jack London. The statements were in part: "Young Man! The lowest aim
in your life is to be a good soldier. The 'good soldier' never tries to
distinguish right from wrong. He never thinks, never reasons; he only
obeys . . . . A good soldier is a blind, heartless, murderous machine . . . . No man can fall lower than a soldier—it is a depth beneath
which we cannot go. Young Man Don't Be a Soldier, Be a Man." [23]
Herman was sentenced to ten years in the penitentiary. A similar case,
involving the same quotations, occurred a little later in Oregon.[24]

One of the most prominent Socialists indicted in the spring of 1918
was Rose Pastor Stokes. On March 20, the Kansas City *Star* ran an
article which stated that Mrs. Stokes opposed the war but favored the
Government. Mrs. Stokes wrote to the editor stoutly denying this report
and asked that her denial be printed. She said: "In the interview . . .
I am quoted as having said, 'I believe the Government of the United
States should have the unqualified support of every citizen in its war
aims.' I made no such statement, and I believe no such thing. No government which is for the profiteers can also be for the people, and I am
for the people, while the Government is for the profiteers." Earlier she
had said that American soldiers would some day learn "that they were
not fighting for democracy but for the protection and safeguarding of
Morgan's millions." [25]

Mrs. Stokes denied some of the statements attributed to her and
declared that part of the convicting testimony was false, but the court

was antagonistic and she was found guilty and sentenced to ten years in the penitentiary. Judge Van Valkenburgh was quoted as saying that "anything which lowers the morale of our forces, which serves to chill enthusiasm, extinguish confidence, and retard cooperation may very well cause insubordination, disloyalty or mutiny." [26] When President Wilson learned of the Stokes case, he wrote to his Attorney General: "I have had a good many people speak to me recently about the fact of the (very just) conviction of Rose Pastor Stokes and at the same time the apparent injustice of convicting her when the editor of the Kansas City *Star* seems to be, to say the least, a direct participant in her offense. Don't you think that there is some way in which we could bring this editor to book?" [27] Of course, no action was taken against the powerful *Star*.

By the time Mrs. Stokes was convicted the Espionage Act had been revised and strengthened. The *Literary Digest* commented that her conviction was generally "taken by the press as a proof that the new Espionage Law has teeth in it." The writer agreed that this was a timely warning "to the whole tribe of pacifists and obstructionists." Yet, he added, "there are many regrets that the first notable victim should not have been a more dangerous enemy." [28] In any event, the Circuit Court of Appeals reversed the conviction and the Justice Department dropped the case in 1921.

Among the radicals who continued to receive rough treatment were members of the Nonpartisan League. As explained earlier, the League, especially its leaders, had been under heavy attack since the early fall of 1917. In September, Senator La Follette's strong antiwar speech in St. Paul, given under League auspices, had brought the organization further embarrassment and criticism. Throughout the winter of 1917–18, the campaign against the League was intensified and charges of disloyalty were widely publicized in the conservative press. League meetings were broken up in several Minnesota localities. The February arrest of Townley and Gilbert for "discouraging enlistments" seemed like the culmination of the effort to discredit the League.

But actually this was only the beginning. The most bitter fight against the League, based mostly on the charge that it was disloyal, occurred in the spring and early summer of 1918. The main struggle was in Minnesota, where the League was trying to capture the state government, as it had done in North Dakota. But all the way from Minnesota to Texas, and from Texas to Washington State, anti-League forces were up in arms as the farmers' organization sought to build its strength. While the expressed reason for opposing the League was its alleged disloyalty, the real factor which caused alarm was its radical economic program. Conservative, propertied interests shuddered at the League's demand for antiprofiteering legislation and the confiscation of large fortunes to pay for the war, to say nothing of the state-enterprise objectives.

Early in 1918 League organizers were busy in Texas. When some of them first went to the town of Mineola, they were met by the sheriff, a lawyer, and several other citizens. When questioned in an unfriendly manner by these local officials, the League supporters insisted that they had a perfect right to hold organization meetings in that vicinity. One Leaguer declared, "You know the law about interfering with the constitutional rights of citizens like us; if not, I will read it to you." The Mineola lawyer reportedly replied, "I don't give a damn about the law; this is war time." [29]

Apparently there were others in the community who did not "give a damn about the law." On April 4, three League representatives were arrested and jailed. When M. M. Offut, state office manager, protested, he was seized and had his hair and beard cut off with sheep shears before he was driven out of town. The other three men were taken by a mob and given a severe whipping. The Greenville (Texas) *Banner* said this was evidence that "Americanism is not to be tampered with around Mineola." [30]

In other states where the League was trying to organize farmers the reaction was much the same. In Montana, J. A. McGlynn had a hall closed to him at Terry, even after he had tried to prove his patriotism by signing affidavits showing how many war bonds he had purchased and how much he had contributed to the Red Cross. The mayor told McGlynn that he could not say anything that would stir up class hatred. McGlynn asked if advocating lower interest rates for farmers would be considered as doing so. The mayor replied that it would, and McGlynn then left town. [31] In Washington a state Grange meeting was broken up at Walla Walla because State Master William Bouck endorsed the Non-partisan League. [32]

As might be expected, League leaders looked upon nearby South Dakota as a fertile political field to be cultivated. Many of the same farm problems which had given rise to the League in North Dakota existed in the sister state to the south. By late 1917 the League had started a concerted campaign to recruit members in South Dakota, looking toward the elections of 1918. Republican politicians, including Governor Peter Norbeck, recognized the League as a real threat to their power.

The strategy devised to defeat the League has been frankly stated by W. Harry King, one of Governor Norbeck's close associates. It was "to brand the Nonpartisan League as socialists and then . . . show the disloyalty of the socialist party and socialist propaganda," King wrote.[33] Opponents of the League in South Dakota hesitated to brand the organization's rank and file members as disloyal. In fact, King wrote that the membership "of the Nonpartisan League in this state is loyal; there is no doubt of that."[34] Good proof that charges of disloyalty were only for political effect is found in Norbeck's letter of May 2, 1918, in which he wrote, "I wish some publicity would be given to the disloyalty of League members but this should not be overdone."[35]

Following the pattern in other states, League meetings were prohibited in several localities by supercharged patriots who had fallen under the spell of their own propaganda. In February, 1918, the League was not permitted to hold a meeting in Madison. Upon hearing of this undemocratic action, Governor Norbeck notified the county sheriff that "no political organization should be interfered with." But he qualified this position by adding, "None should be prevented except such as are held for the purpose of embarrassing the government in the prosecution of the war."[36]

The next month local citizens at Gregory beat up several League organizers and then put one on a train headed for Nebraska. Governor Norbeck again declared that civil rights in South Dakota would be protected and that the guilty persons at Gregory would be prosecuted. But local opinion was in no mood to tolerate fair play or freedom of speech. The editor of the *Rosebud Investor* said that Norbeck's action in connection with the League "has of late been distasteful to loyal citizens. He has insisted on their rights to spread their unpatriotic propaganda, so long as they do not violate the letter of some motheaten law made for us in time of peace." Then the writer belligerently challenged the Governor by saying that it made no difference what he wanted; "no unpatriotic move will be tolerated in this part of the state, and he isn't man enough, hasn't backing enough, nor influence enough to compel it."[37]

The campaign against the League continued unabated and in the November election Norbeck badly defeated Mark Bates, the League candidate for governor. Norbeck showed more concern for free speech than a number of other governors—once he made a 250-mile trip to personally assure that a League meeting was not molested at Bonesteel. But local sentiment, partially fanned by Norbeck's political machine, resulted in grave limitations on the activities of League organizers, and in some cases they were handled roughly.[38]

Though the experience of League organizers in other states was harrowing, it was in Minnesota that the League was fought most belligerently. In the spring of 1918 the League chose Charles A. Lindbergh as its candidate for governor. Lindbergh was highly popular among Minnesota farmers and had served in Congress between 1907 and 1917. He had opposed American entry into the war and was an outspoken critic of big business. His nomination threw a real scare into the state's conservative political interests.

Lindbergh foresaw the attack which would be leveled against him by the supporters of his Republican opponent, incumbent J. A. A. Burnquist. In accepting the nomination, he said, "These profiteers and politicians, as pretended guardians of loyalty, seek to perpetuate themselves in special privilege and in office." There was no real question of loyalty, he added, but he realistically admitted that he expected his opponents to accuse him and his supporters of disloyalty.[39]

The Nonpartisan League found that it was fighting a defensive battle all the way. County attorneys, local grand juries, and the courts played an important part in placing a brand of disloyalty on the League. The indictment of Townley and Gilbert by a Martin County grand jury on the grounds of "discouraging enlistments" provided ideal political ammunition for the anti-League forces. In March the League was further embarrassed when a Goodhue County grand jury indicted Gilbert for disloyal statements. About two months later, right in the midst of the Lindbergh-Burnquist race, Gilbert was convicted and sentenced to a year in jail and fined five hundred dollars. He did get a stay of sentence pending his appeal. Throughout the campaign these and other indictments were cited—Townley and Gilbert were indicted by a Jackson County grand jury in May—by opponents of the League as proof that the organization's leadership was unpatriotic and disloyal.[40]

Under these circumstances the Nonpartisan League failed completely in its attempt to wage a campaign on the basis of economic reform. Enemies of the organization did everything possible to avoid economic issues and focus public attention on the loyalty question. When the League seemed to be gaining strength, even under charges of disloyalty and pro-Germanism, more positive action was taken. League meetings were stopped or broken up in many parts of the state. Early in March a League official at Pipestone was fined one hundred dollars with the alternative of thirty days in jail for having attempted "to conduct a meeting forbidden by county officials." By the middle of the month nineteen out of eighty-seven counties had prohibited League meetings.[41] Of 250 meetings scheduled by League officials in the winter and spring of 1917–18, some forty had to be cancelled.[42]

On one occasion a meeting had just begun when the county sheriff appeared with about thirty townsmen, who had been sworn in as special deputies. They marched to the platform and announced that no League meeting could be held in that county under any circumstances. Lindbergh could not speak, they said. Annoyed at this interference, the farmers became somewhat belligerent and it appeared as though serious trouble might result. Then Lindbergh stood up and raised his hands. "Friends," he declared,

> we are a peace-loving people. We are governed by laws and cer-
> tain men are chosen to enforce laws, and among those so selected
> is the sheriff here. While I think these officers are wrong in their
> action of wilfully suppressing free speech, a discussion of the
> serious economic issues confronting us, nevertheless it would do
> our cause more harm than good to have riot and possible bloodshed
> here. I suggest that we adjourn a few miles south into the State of
> Iowa which still seems to be part of these United States.[43]

A farmer announced that his place was available and in ninety minutes the thousands of automobiles and occupants had been transported to the neighboring state. The meeting was then held without further trouble.

Lindbergh drew tremendous crowds. But many of the meetings had to be held outdoors as "townspeople were so bitterly hostile against League candidates that halls could not be rented at any price." [44] Both local and state officials gave open support to the extralegal actions of the anti-League groups.[45]

The intense feeling against the League was perhaps best personified by John F. McGee, head of the State Public Safety Commission. In May, 1918, he went to Washington to support a court-martial bill as a method of handling disloyalty. He argued that "where we made a mistake was in not establishing a firing squad in the first days of the war. We should now get busy and have the firing squad working overtime." [46] Later he complained that Minnesota law enforcement officers had been too lenient with the League. "A Non-Partisan League lecturer is a traitor every time," he said. "In other words, no matter what he says or does, a League worker is a traitor." [47]

A little more than a week before the election, Congressman Clarence B. Miller of Minnesota took time out from his regular labors to fire a verbal volley at the League and its gubernatorial candidate. League leaders, he said, "are socialists, and nothing but socialists. Some of them appear to be positively anarchists." These officials had given the organization "a distinctly seditious direction," he declared, which had a "sinister influence in our national life." Then he added that membership in the League came chiefly from "those of pro-German sympathies." [48] The same day Miller spoke, newspapers reported that the Nebraska State Council of Defense had told League leaders to stop their organizational activity there.[49] And so the attack continued.

Conditions had become so bad in Minnesota that the League's executive committee memorialized Congress on the situation. The memorial, a 120-page booklet, included copies of affidavits showing treatment given League organizers and speakers, reproductions of telegrams from sheriffs who refused to permit League meetings, instances of lawlessness and other outrages.[50]

But appeals for protection and fair play got nowhere. League leaders did everything possible to counteract accusations of disloyalty. Townley appeared before the Senate Military Affairs Committee on May 1 and strongly denied that members or officials of the League were disloyal.[51] Resolutions passed by the League in support of the war effort were circulated as widely as possible. And continued unsuccessful attempts were made to emphasize the economic issues at stake.

George Creel's letter to John Simpson, president of the Oklahoma Farmers' Union, disclaiming the charge that the federal Government considered the League disloyal, did no good. On May 13, Creel wrote to Simpson that the Government did not consider it "an act of disloyalty to be a member of this League." Then he added that the League had "by resolution and organized effort" given pledges of loyalty.[52] Even President Wilson wrote to Gregory that "since the war began the League has rendered consistent assistance and very effective assistance where it could to the cause of the war." [53]

The vicious campaign was climaxed on June 16, when the voters gave Burnquist 199,325 votes to only 150,626 for Lindbergh.[54] The League candidate had polled a surprisingly large vote in light of the type of campaign which had been waged against him.

Of course, this did not settle the question of the League's loyalty. About a month after the election the State Supreme Court dismissed the indictments against Townley and Gilbert. The basis of the indictments had been found in a series of resolutions passed by the League on June 7, 1917, which were given wide distribution in pamphlet form. While the League had pledged to stand by the country "right or wrong as against foreign governments," it had urged conscription of war profits and government control over consumer and producer prices. Jobbers and speculators were condemned, and, according to the League position, the war had been caused by commercial monopolists who were contesting for markets. The resolution read:

> The moving cause of this world war was and is political autocracy used to perpetuate and extend industrial autocracy. It is the struggle of political overlords to extend and perpetuate their power to rob and exploit their fellowmen. Autocratic rulers who have robbed and exploited the fathers and mothers now slaughter the children for the single purpose of further entrenching themselves in their infamous position and securing and legalizing their possession of the fruits of others' toil and thrusting the world under the yoke of political autocracy, which is ever the shield and mask of industrial autocracy.[55]

The League had also asked for the abolition of secret diplomacy and demanded that America's European allies state their peace terms without "indemnities, contributions, or interference with the right of any nation to live and manage its own internal affairs."[56]

The court said that there was nothing in these resolutions that violated the law. As a whole, they appeared "nothing more serious than a rhetorical, and somewhat flamboyant, platform upon which a certain class of citizens are solicited to join an organization whose avowed purpose is the amelioration of the alleged evils of present economic conditions."[57]

A favorable decision from the Supreme Court, however, could do little good in July. The election was over and the most had already been made of the false accusations. Creel later wrote that, in his opinion, the Republicans and Democrats did not want the League to establish a reputation for loyalty. "They preferred that the Nonpartisan League should be disloyal rather than loyal," he wrote, "in order that they might be provided with a campaign weapon."[58]

Those who had called the League leaders disloyal finally had the satisfaction of seeing Townley and Gilbert convicted and sentenced. In December, 1918, Gilbert's conviction and sentence to a year in jail in Goodhue County were affirmed by the State Supreme Court.[59] Then in June of 1919, Townley's and Gilbert's appeal from the district court of Jackson County to the State Supreme Court failed. They moved for a new trial but the motion was denied in April, 1921.[60] The United States Supreme Court denied a petition for a writ of certiorari later in the year.[61] Townley began serving a ninety-day sentence in the Jackson County jail in November, 1921.

The conviction of Gilbert and Townley had been based on the belief that they had intended to discourage enlistments and to interfere with the war effort. F. A. Teigan, a former disgruntled League organizer, gave some of the most damaging testimony. He quoted Townley as having once said, "We are against this Goddamned war, but we can't afford to advertise it." [62]

In the numerous harsh and illegal attacks on League organizers and their supporters, it was not often charged that the individuals involved had made any disloyal or seditious statements. They were not accused of opposing the war by any overt acts or in any specific ways, although there were general and constant references to lack of patriotism. The "crime" of most Leaguers was that they were members of an organization which was trying to organize farmers and wrest political and economic power from those then in control. A writer for *The Public* said that the extralegal action against the League was "merely a repetition of what we have seen at Homestead, Ludlow and Bisbee." The "essential truth," he continued, was "that the inspiration and the dominant motive is the desire to protect the established economic order." [63] In any event, charges of disloyalty proved to be an excellent means of keeping the Nonpartisan League from extending its power beyond the bounds of North Dakota.

▬▬▬▬▬▬▬▬▬▬▬▬▬▬▬▬▬▬▬▬▬▬▬▬▬▬▬▬▬▬▬▬▬

"Happy were the fools and the thoughtless men of action in those days."

George Bernard Shaw

THE AMERICAN REIGN
OF TERROR

Spring, 1918, in the United States was a time when strident voices filled the air, when mobs swarmed through the streets, when violence of all kinds was practiced upon the opponents of the war. The words and actions were not unlike those of earlier months, but the tones were heightened, the tempo accelerated.

A preacher was quoted by the *Detroit Free Press* on March 4, 1918, as saying, "The person who claims to be neutral ought to be exported, jailed, interned, labeled, or . . . rendered powerless." An editor exclaimed, "For goodness sake, when is the firing squad to get busy." [1] Other editors spoke of firing squads, stone walls at sunrise, and telegraph poles.[2] There were even those who almost regretted the "passing of the boiling-in-oil period of administering reprisal to traitors to their country." [3] On August 3, 1918, The *New Republic* declared, "This [hysterical] state of mind is being assiduously cultivated by many of our newspapers, many of our respected fellow citizens, and certain public officials. Those who do not encourage it certainly fail to protest against it." [4]

To guarantee orthodoxy, the prying into people's opinions continued unabated. An army official in South Carolina invited civilians to report to him any suspicious and disloyal activity, as well as any signs of sympathy for the enemy.[5] The state Councils of Defense were flooded with complaints against individuals of doubted loyalty. In Nebraska, for example, it was at first the practice of the Council to have a representative call on the accused, question him, and warn or threaten him if that seemed necessary. But the complaints grew so numerous that this procedure had to be changed and offenders were forced to come before the Council. An official of this body reported, "When we summon offenders before our committee . . . we do not permit them to be represented by attorneys, and we do not reveal to them the names of the men who make the complaints." The writer added, "We are partial to the tender touch, to the educational process, and as I have said we find that in most cases it works successfully. But we have had cases—many of them—where the 'iron hand' was necessary, and we have not hesitated to use it." [6]

The Councils of Defense in some other states carried on in much the same way. At one time in South Dakota, some thirty-five people were subpoenaed in order to find out if they were loyally supporting the war. A farmer and his wife, suspected of "anti-American" activities, fainted when the sheriff read the subpoena to them.[7] Suspects in a Florida town were made to repeat a catechism of loyalty.[8]

From the very beginning of the war there had been attacks upon things German. Now the cries of hate rose to a crescendo. Names of towns and individuals were changed. The lowly hamburger became the liberty sandwich, and sauerkraut was called liberty cabbage. Hymns, symphonies, and operas of German origin were looked upon with suspicion. And then, of course, there was hatred of the German language.

During the winter of 1917–18, there was a strong drive to abolish the teaching of German in the country's schools. Theodore Roosevelt backed it.[9] So did the state Councils of Defense. The American Defense Society urged the mayor of New York to discontinue teaching the "Kaiser's tongue" in the city schools.[10] At a national meeting on illiteracy, much of the session was given over to attacks upon the teaching of German.[11] The argument was advanced that the German language had no cultural or practical value and that to teach it gave aid and comfort to the enemy. *The Manufacturers Record* said that German had been emphasized not because of its "intrinsic value" but because it was part of the "political propaganda intended to wean the people of this country away from Anglo-Saxon and Anglo-Celtic origins and ideals and divide the national interest and national sympathy." [12] Professor Knight Dunlap of Johns Hopkins declared that the German language was a "barbarous tongue," lacking in cultural worth and without commercial importance.[13]

With these sentiments predominating, the desired results were soon obtained. The use of the German language was forbidden in the pulpits and schools of Montana. In Iowa, the Governor ruled that German could not be used on streetcars, over the telephone, or anywhere else in public.[14] News stories from all sections of the nation told of individual cities outlawing the use of German in public places and forbidding its teaching in the schools. On March 26, 1918, the Seattle *Post-Intelligencer* announced, "German Barred from Spokane's Public Schools." Again on April 9, the *Post-Intelligencer* headed a story, "Speech of Hated Hun Forbidden." As the Oklahoma schools dropped German from their curricula, the Tulsa *Daily World* declared, "German Deader than Latin Now."[15] On the basis of a poll taken by the *Literary Digest,* 149 schools had discontinued German language study by March, 1918.[16] Others were to follow.

On the same intellectual level was the move to burn German books. In Lewiston, Montana, a committee marched on the local high school and burned all the German textbooks it could find.[17] A book-burning was announced as a part of a Fourth of July celebration in Shawnee, Oklahoma.[18] Another was promised in Spartanburg, South Carolina.[19] In a small Indiana town, German books were thrown into a muddy ditch.[20]

A common punishment devised for people suspected of disloyalty or sedition was that of kissing the flag. The riot in Boston on July 4, 1917, was accompanied by flag-kissing. In December, a young man in Arkansas was compelled to wrap a flag about him, kiss it, and then salute army recruiting officers.[21] By 1918 flag-kissing had become so frequent that it was hardly first-rate news. In Trenton, New Jersey, two sisters working in a pottery plant were reported to have made disparaging remarks about American soldiers. Other workers gave them the choice of being ducked in a canal or kissing the flag and pledging allegiance to the United States. The two chose the flag-kissing punishment.[22] In California, the police forced a Russian to kiss the flag.[23] A foreigner in New York was arrested for failing to register. He swore that he would be a "slacker as long as he lived." He was forced to kiss the flag several times and then wave it above his head as he paraded up and down the corridor.[24] In New Jersey a man who refused to subscribe for a Liberty bond was compelled to go to his knees and kiss the flag.[25]

A young man in Montana, E. V. Starr, fell into the hands of a mob bent upon vindicating its peculiar standard of patriotism by compelling him to kiss the flag. In the heat of the argument, Starr remarked, "What is this thing anyway? Nothing but a piece of cotton with a little paint on it and some other marks in the corner there. I will not kiss that thing. It might be covered with microbes."[26] Starr was arrested under the state sedition act for using language "calculated to bring the flag into contempt and disrepute." He was fined five hundred dollars and costs, and given a long penitentiary sentence. In denying Starr a writ of habeas corpus, the district court said that he had been "more sinned against than sinning." The members of the mob, not Starr, "should have been punished," said the court. The judge then sharply criticized that brand of patriotism which descended to fanaticism.[27] But the court held that Starr had no legal recourse, except to apply for a pardon.

Along with flag-kissing came a great sensitiveness about respect for the national anthem. A Croatian by the name of Frank Horrath failed to stand in a Pittsburgh theater when the anthem was played. A policeman took him away from an angry mob and put him in jail. He was charged with disorderly conduct and fined ten dollars.[28] In Chicago an individual was fined fifty dollars for failing to stand when the "Star-Spangled Banner" was played.[29] Similar incidents occurred elsewhere.

As mentioned before, yellow paint was customarily used to single out those who were considered disloyal. Sometimes homes, offices, and churches were marked with it. Frequently, even individuals were painted.[30] For example, when some Nebraskans refused to participate in a Liberty Loan rally they were painted yellow,[31] as were three men who made adverse comments about the loans in Kansas City.[32] A grain elevator in Little Rock, Iowa, was painted yellow because the proprietor was accused of pro-Germanism. When he tried to locate those who had done the painting job by using bloodhounds to follow them, "loyal citizens" beat him and drove him out of town.[33]

Unique forms of violence were often devised by mobs to punish those charged with disloyalty or pro-Germanism. For instance, in San Rafael, California, a man had his hair clipped in the form of a cross, after which he was tied to a tree on the courthouse lawn.[34] A person of German birth in Salt Lake City was thrown into a bin of dough where he almost suffocated.[35] In Pennsylvania a man was taken from a hotel room, "severely beaten, made to walk up and down the street with a dog chain around his neck, forced to kiss the flag and doused into a large watering trough."[36] At LaSalle, Illinois, Dr. J. C. Biemann, a pioneer physician, was ducked in a canal by several hundred men and boys. Then he was forced to kiss the flag and warned to leave the city. His "crime" was that he was supposed to have called Secretary of War Baker a "fat head."[37]

In Berkeley, California, a large canvas tabernacle used by the

Church of the Living God was burned down by a mob of men and boys. The pastor, the Reverend Joshua Sykes, and two elders were ducked in the baptismal tank. Along with other leaders, they were shortly arrested for their pacifist activities. They were accused of having told members of their church that they were citizens of God's kingdom and not of the United States, and that they should not assist with the war. Sykes and others were also accused of urging members not to contribute to the Red Cross, to buy Liberty bonds, to display the American flag, or to participate in war work. They were sentenced to various terms in McNeil Island Penitentiary.[38]

Ernest Votaw, a Quaker and an outstanding opponent of militarism, was appointed real estate assessor in a small Pennsylvania town. However, when he appeared to take his job, a "committee" informed him he would have to resign or else be tarred and feathered and ridden out of town on a rail. Votaw resigned.[39] Dr. James P. Warbasse was expelled from a county medical society in the same state because of his pacifist leanings. Later, however, he was restored to the roster.[40]

Opponents of war often felt the pain of mob beatings. A man distributed handbills which advocated conscripting all incomes over five thousand dollars in order to finance the war. He had to be rescued from a mob.[41] A Lithuanian woman packing-house worker, who supposedly made disloyal remarks, was badly beaten by other women when she refused to wear an American flag which they had pushed upon her.[42] In Pocahontas, Arkansas, the sheriff gave a young man permission to "beat up" a worker in a button factory who had "hoped Germany would whip the entire world." The beaten employee was then made to kiss a Wilson button and salute the flag. Of course, he lost his job.[43] A chap with a German name was severely beaten in a San Francisco saloon for saying that the United States "is not democratic. This Government is nothing but a hypocrite. There is no difference between it and any other government." He was also sentenced to sixty days in jail.[44]

During the spring of 1918 news stories from all sections of the country told of people being beaten by mobs of super-patriots. Sometimes it was for not displaying a flag, for objecting to the draft law, for criticizing American soldiers, or even soldiers of the associated powers; perhaps it was for not buying bonds, or for other reasons. But whatever the cause, the safest policy for one's physical well-being in many communities was to remain silent. Criticism of war aims and policies would not be tolerated.[45]

Besides beating their victims, American mobs frequently resorted to the use of tar and feathers. There were a number of such cases in the fall of 1917. Perhaps the most notable incident was that of the seventeen I.W.W.'s at Tulsa. But throughout the late winter and spring of 1918, there was a veritable rash of tar and feather incidents. A few examples from various sections of the nation will illustrate the situation.

Joe Polaras, a Mexican living in Seattle, was tarred and feathered because he was supposedly unpatriotic.[46] In Reno, Nevada, Elmer White was tied to a stake, lashed with a cat-o-nine-tails, tarred and feathered, and ordered out of town.[47] A superintendent of schools in a Colorado town was given a coat of grease and feathers—a slight variation.[48] At Emerson, Nebraska, Rudolph Schopke was tarred and feathered because he refused to contribute to the Red Cross.[49] In Oklahoma O. F. Westbrook, a farmer living near Altus, was dragged from his bed by a masked and heavily armed mob and taken to a wooded area. There he was forced to kiss the flag and take the oath of "eternal allegiance to the Knights of Liberty." He was then lashed with a blacksnake whip and given a coat of tar and feathers.[50] Similar incidents were reported in or near Muskogee, Wynnewood, Elk City, and Henryetta—all in Oklahoma. At Electra, Texas, a confectioner by the name of George Geanapolus was tarred and feathered and driven out of town by some two hundred businessmen.[51]

Students at Rutgers University approached one of their fellow students, Samuel H. Chovenson, an antiwar Socialist, and demanded that he speak at their Liberty Loan rally. When Chovenson refused, he was "stripped, covered with molasses and feathers, then blindfolded, and paraded through the streets of the town." Signs carried at the head of the procession bore the inscriptions, "This is what we do with pro-Germans!" "He's a Bolsheviki!" "He is against the Liberty Loan and the U.S.A."[52]

The Milwaukee *Free Press* reported that in its section of the country mobs were "riding roughshod over law and order to punish instances of alleged disloyalty."[53] And this was happening all over the nation. Furthermore, almost everywhere there was vicious, slanderous gossiping about people who did not accept the conventional view of the war.

Mobs had not been on the march long before they threatened the very lives of their victims. A Pennsylvania mob, composed of women munition workers, attempted to lynch a man who was supposed to have made seditious remarks.[54] An Oregon supporter of the Russellites distributed a circular criticizing persons said to have suppressed the circulation of *The Finished Mystery*. For this a mob threatened to lynch him.[55]

When an Austrian employee of the Erie Railroad was accused of a lack of patriotism, he was "hauled thirty feet above ground at the end of a rope . . . and a fire hose was played upon him. He was cut down an hour later by friends who found him alive." [56]

Those who committed such acts quite naturally prepared the way for other mobs to kill their victims. The precedent for mob killings was, of course, present in the United States. In the first six months of 1918 alone, there were thirty-five such events. The states of Alabama and Louisiana led in number of killings with eight each. [57] But these were mostly racial killings. The new mob killings were to be "patriotic" affairs; they were murder in the name of liberty and democracy.

On March 24, 1918, in the small town of Hickory, Oklahoma, a Bulgarian was shot and killed by a policeman. It was alleged that he had said something "seditious," and, according to the policeman, the victim had fired first. [58] On the same date an "operative" of the County Council of Defense in Tulsa shot and killed Joe Spring, a waiter in a restaurant. He accused Spring of making pro-German remarks. [59] Two days later the County Council of Defense issued a statement declaring that "any person or persons who utter disloyal or unpatriotic statements do so at their own peril and cannot expect the protection of the loyal citizenship of this nation." [60] On March 27, the Tulsa *Daily World* reported, "It wasn't S. L. Miller that was on trial for murdering Joe Spring yesterday . . . . It was the patriotism of Tulsa and the principle of a new unwritten law that makes it justifiable for a man to slay one who speaks out against the country that shelters and nurtures him." Miller was found not guilty. "The decision was received with cheers, and men, women, and children rushed to Miller to congratulate him, both for his patriotism and the outcome of the trial." On April 14, the *Daily World* reported that the policeman who had killed the Bulgarian was also acquitted. The presiding judge released the officer "after making a patriotic talk and warning pro-Germans not to speak their sentiments against the United States."

Southern Illinois was one of the most mob-ridden parts of the country. There was widespread discontent and unrest in the coal fields. Conflicts between employers and workmen were common. It was in this region that a labor lawyer and a union leader were tarred and feathered and driven out of town because they were causing "dissension among several thousand coal miners near Staunton." [61] At the same time, according to an account in the files of the American Civil Liberties Union, "more than one hundred persons were made to sign pledges of loyalty." This news stimulated stern measures in Worden, Mount Olive, Gillespie,

Williamson, Hillsboro, and several other small towns. There were numerous instances of people being taken from their homes and forced to make public professions of loyalty. Some were forced to kiss the flag; others had to sing the national anthem or play patriotic tunes on musical instruments. To protest such actions was in itself considered disloyal. It was said that the American Defense Society was trying to make the district "100 per cent American." [62]

In the town of Christopher, a Polish Catholic priest, the Reverend John Kovalsky, was accused of having remarked that "God is with the Kaiser and the Kaiser will win the war." In spite of his fervent denials he was taken by a mob, and, with three other men, was tarred and feathered. What the others were accused of was not specified.[63] In Benton Mrs. Frances Bergen got into an argument and apparently said some uncomplimentary things about President Wilson. Both Mrs. Bergen and Henry Baker, with whom she had argued, were arrested. While Baker's fine was paid by public subscription, the Loyalty League took Mrs. Bergen through town on a rail, forcing her to wave the American flag. One account stated, "At frequent intervals the procession paused, while Mrs. Bergen was compelled to shout praise for President Wilson." [64]

Labor organizers were especially unpopular. At Hillsboro three union organizers, L. B. (Dad) Irvin, and Frank and Joseph Zib, had done effective work with the laborers. Among other things they had helped to bring about a large increase in the accident compensation received by injured miners. After the draft was passed, the Zib brothers registered as conscientious objectors. Although the questionnaires were supposed to have been private, the local editor immediately wrote a scathing article against them, and the private information was made public. Within a short time a group of citizens decided to take action against Irvin and the Zibs. On March 8, 1918, the vigilantes assembled, prepared tar and straw, and went in search of their intended victims. A report to the Civil Liberties Union stated: "Not finding the Zibs or Irvin at home after all their preparations, they became more enraged and with that frantically seized every possession—clothing, trunks, furniture, typewriter—their library, everything, and pulled them down the steps into the street where they offered them, in the name of freedom, to the flames prepared by the others of the group." Continuing their search, members of the mob descended in force upon a house where Irvin was believed to be hiding. When they knocked on the door—the occupants of the house apparently did not understand the purpose of a visit from the mob—a shot was fired, and a wild melee followed. Four men were wounded, including policeman Seaton Emory and a young man named Clifford Donaldson. Donaldson died later. He was twenty-four years old and had just enlisted in the navy.[65]

The hysteria of the area spread into the small town of Collinsville just east of St. Louis. The local Council of Defense advocated "loyalty pledges," and there was severe criticism of a Baptist minister who felt that the church should not be used for Thrift Stamp meetings.[66] Miners expressed uneasiness because some of their fellow workers were of foreign birth. Conservative elements were disturbed by union agitation. Members of a Loyalty committee began to agitate for the suppression of "disloyalty." Loud accusations were made against Robert Paul Prager, a young man of German birth. A registered enemy alien, Prager was employed in a local bakery. He had applied for membership in a local miners' union at which time he was supposed to have talked to the men on the virtues of Socialism.[67] However, so far as is known, he was not guilty of directly opposing the war. He had made no seditious statements and no incidents had occurred. In fact, he had tried to enlist in the navy but was rejected because he had one glass eye.

Because of wild and irresponsible talk about disloyalty, the mayor ordered the saloons closed on April 4, thus throwing a group of idle, half-drunken men onto the streets. They began a search for Prager. When they found him, "his shoes were stripped off and members of the mob began pulling off his clothes, when someone produced an American flag. It was wrapped around him and tied." [68] In this condition, with only a flag to cover him, he was dragged barefooted, stumbling through the streets.

At this point, the police rescued Prager and placed him in the city jail. But the mob soon broke into the jail and took its victim out of town in search of a convenient tree. This may have happened after the police "insisted no violence be done inside the city limits." [69] Prager was asked if he were a German spy, and "if he had tried to blow up the Maryville mine." One member of the mob was reported to have struck Prager on the head and knocked him down. A participant in the mob action, Joseph Riegel, was quoted as saying, "All the time the crowd kept getting more excited and angry. Someone shouted, 'Well if he won't come in with anything, string him up.' A boy produced a handkerchief and his hands were tied. I might have been the man who did the tying. I was drunk, and because I had been in the army the crowd made me the big man in the affair, and I guess I was sort of puffed over that." [70] Before they hanged Prager, he was allowed to write a note to his mother and father. "Dear Parents:" he said, "I must this day, the fourth of April, 1918, die. Please, my dear parents, pray for me. This is my last letter or testament. Robert Paul." [71] He was then given a few minutes to fall on his knees and pray before members of the mob pulled him high in the air where he gasped his last breath. As a report in the *New York Call* of April 16, 1918, expressed it, "He was one, his pursuers were five hundred, who, after baiting him to their heart's content, deliberately murdered him." The *New York Times* of April 11 reported that his last request was to be buried with an American flag over him.

At last the excesses of the super-patriots had reached such heights that some people were jolted into realizing, for the first time, how serious mob actions in the name of loyalty had become. That Prager had been guilty of no crime, or of any overt acts of disloyalty, made the deed even more dastardly. In referring to the case, Attorney General Gregory declared, "From all the facts I have been able to gather concerning the lynching of the man in Illinois, I doubt his having been guilty of any offense." [72]

There was widespread condemnation of the lynching, even by those who had previously spoken out most strongly against all aspects of disloyalty. Theodore Roosevelt and William Howard Taft both immediately condemned the action. The most outspoken critic was Senator Sherman of Illinois. He referred to the mob and to city officials as follows: "The police followed this drunken mob to the edge of the city . . . . There are four policemen in that town to preserve the peace. That magnificent constabulary followed to the city limits; they said they had no jurisdiction beyond it; and the mob was allowed to wreak its bloody purpose upon the helpless victim." [73] He also called the mayor a "poltroon" and a "renegade in public office." [74]

The *New York Call* editorialized on April 16, 1918, "It is our national purpose to stand before the world as a clean and honorable nation. We do not want our Allies to be burdened with the necessity of apologizing for our Kultur." The Oklahoma City *Daily Oklahoman* printed a fine denunciation of mob law on April 22. It was a good article, but it was tardy—very tardy. On April 11, the *Chicago Herald* recommended "punishment of the guilty crew." The *Detroit Free Press* of April 6 carried a strong and forthright condemnation of mob lynchings. The *New York Times* said editorially that "a fouler wrong could hardly be done America." The editor declared that, in light of United States war aims, "we shall be denounced as a nation of odious hypocrites." The *Times* also called for punishment of those responsible.[75]

Some papers, however, were quite reserved in their criticisms. This was probably because they did not want to take a position which might be interpreted as in any way lacking in patriotism. Their attitude, however, indicates a fundamental problem posed by modern nationalism. How can one safely attack an evil action when it is clothed in "patriotism"? It is quite apparent that many papers felt it could, and perhaps should, not be done. After the Prager lynching nationalists tried to lay the blame for mob actions on the victims themselves. Some elements of the press even seemed to approve the action.[76] On April 12 the *Washington Post* commented, "In the East the public mind toward the war was much earlier divested of errors." Then it added, "In spite of excesses such as lynching, it is a healthful and wholesome awakening in the interior of the country."

Eventually a number of the leaders of the mob were indicted and tried. There was great difficulty in obtaining a jury, and the trial was a most unjudicial affair. Defendants wore red, white, and blue ribbons, and occasionally a band would play patriotic airs in the courthouse. The defense attorney's statement to the jury "was almost entirely a loyalty plea, mingled with an attack on the State for conducting the prosecution."[77] The defense argued that Prager's lynching was a "patriotic murder" which served as a means of home protection.[78] The jury returned the usual mob verdict of not guilty in twenty-five minutes. Those in the courtroom congratulated the defendants. There was cheering and handclapping, and one juryman shouted, "Well, I guess nobody can say we aren't loyal now."[79] But he was wrong. The New York *Evening Post* of June 3, 1918, said that the verdict was a "gross miscarriage of justice." Indeed, it was.

The sentiment of local patriots, however, was expressed in a story from Edwardsville, Illinois. It reported a feeling of "grim satisfaction" by the public in southern Illinois. Continuing, the account stated, "Having lynched an undesirable resident and escaped without unpleasant consequences, Madison County is ready for the next comer. Hanging is not an agreeable business and it may not be necessary to hang anybody else. That is entirely up to the other fellow. If a deserving victim should happen along there are other trees and plenty of unused rope."[80] The "unhung traitors" idea had gained wide popularity and acceptance. On April 13, the *Seattle Union-Record* ran an editorial which stated ironically, "If you don't like your neighbor, shoot him! . . . Then declare he made seditious or pro-German statements and rely on the patriotism of the people to see that you are not punished. That is, in effect, the advice of the yellow press." After referring to certain local newspapers, the editorial in the *Union-Record* continued, "As a result of similar utterances we have had during the past few weeks a regular terror of tar and featherings, hangings, and even burnings of alleged traitors." Such was the spirit and action of early 1918.

Prager's hanging capped the climax of violence performed under the guise of patriotism. But even this ghastly incident did not bring people to their senses. It did not create a popular demand which might say in effect, mob law will no longer be tolerated. It did not end further patriotic excesses.[81] Instances of violence in late April and early May of 1918 continued to be reported in all sections of the United States. When a Kentucky citizen later protested to President Wilson about "the persecution of a naturalized German-American in his town," a man who had bought war bonds liberally, Wilson commented to Tumulty, "I have no doubt that there are hundreds of cases like it." [82]

The Prager affair, as well as the less violent actions by nationalists, seemed to call for vigorous action by the federal Government to protect innocent people against lawless and irresponsible mobs. Many moderate Americans, and even some of the super-patriots, objected and were publicly critical of current happenings. Also, stinging criticism of what was called American barbarism began coming from abroad. The German Government lodged an official protest through the Swiss legation, and even offered to pay Prager's funeral expenses.[83] Needless to say, this offer was not accepted.

But President Wilson was distressingly slow in taking any forthright action. The Prager murder was discussed at the regular Cabinet meeting on the afternoon of April 5. Apparently, the President and his advisers decided to sidestep this touchy issue. The *New York Times* reported on April 6 that "from what was said after the meeting it was apparent that the President and his advisers decided that the federal Government had no warrant for interference." Speaking after the meeting, Attorney General Gregory said that it was a problem for Illinois to handle. To refuse to accept responsibility may have been an easy way out, but it did not satisfy a great many people.

On April 18 John Lord O'Brian of the Department of Justice prepared a memorandum which was sent to Wilson suggesting that some sort of statement should be issued by the Government "for the purpose of reassuring the people, quieting their apprehensions, and preventing so far as possible the spread of mob violence, evidence of which is now appearing in all parts of the country." [84] Still Wilson held off. He did write on April 22 that he was "very deeply concerned" about the treatment of people "whose offense is merely one of opinion." Wilson added that he had "a very great passion for the principle that we must respect opinion even when it is hostile . . . ."[85] But his silent concern did little good.

On June 11, a bulletin was issued by the Council of National Defense warning its local representatives against undertaking any repression unless they were "expressly requested or authorized by the . . . Department of Justice."[86] It was not until July 26, after the "patriotic" jury in Illinois had proclaimed members of the mob innocent, and after other incidents had occurred, that Wilson finally spoke out. A few days earlier, he had asked Creel to prepare the way for his statement. "My only object," he told Creel, "is to fix the attention of the people on this protest of mine in the way that will give it the greatest possible emphasis."[87] One observer stated that Wilson acted because of the "use made of the Prager case in the German Reichstag."[88]

The President's statement said:

There have been many lynchings, and every one of them has been a blow at the heart of ordered law and humane justice. No man who loves America, no man who really cares for her fame and honor and character, or who is truly loyal to her institutions, can justify mob action while the courts of justice are open . . . .

We proudly claim to be the champions of democracy. If we really are, in deed and truth, let us see to it that we do not discredit our own. I say plainly that every American who takes part in the action of a mob or gives any sort of countenance is no true son of this great democracy, but its betrayer, and does more to discredit her by that single disloyalty to her standards of law and right, than the words of her statesmen or the sacrifices of her heroic boys in the trenches can do to make suffering peoples believe her to be their savior. How shall we commend democracy to the acceptance of other peoples if we disgrace our own by proving that it is, after all, no protection to the weak? Every mob contributes to German lies about the United States, what her most gifted liars cannot improve upon by the way of calumny. They can at least say that such things cannot happen in Germany except in times of revolution, when law is swept away!

I therefore very earnestly and solemnly beg that the Governors of all the States, the law officers of every community, and, above all, the men and women of every community . . . will co-operate . . . to make an end of this disgraceful evil.[89]

The President spoke noble sentiments and, as usual, spoke them well. But his statement came too late to be very effective. Had he spoken out boldly a day or two after the Prager lynching, the weight of his words might have been felt. As it was, little was accomplished. It was only page seven news in the *New York Times.*

Referring to the Wilson proclamation, the *New Republic* commented:

The facts upon which the President's protest is based are notorious. Yet they meet with comparatively little reprobation or even notice either from the newspapers or from public speakers. There is no indication that the great majority of those people who do most to mould public opinion in this country are particularly shocked at the presence of mob violence and other evidences of collective moral disintegration.[90]

A writer for the *New York Call* said on July 29, "The reaction of the press of our native von Bissings to the personal statement of the President in condemnation of lynching and terrorism is a sorry spectacle. Some papers have nothing to say in their editorial columns, while others come forward with a 'me too,' generally hedged with some 'ifs, buts, perhapses,' and other qualifications."

This condition, however, was by no means universal. The *New York Times* severely condemned the "mob mind" and expressed hope that the President's statement would help to curb the excesses of super-patriots. Yet even the *Times* praised the people's great patience and the "almost saintlike patience of the Government" in dealing with "disloyal agitators."[91] Probably the *New Republic* was right in its judgment that leaders of public opinion were not especially "shocked at the presence of mob violence."

THE SEDITION ACT
Legalizing Intolerance

Violence and intolerance are cancerous growths. They feed and expand on violence and intolerance. The more violence was practiced in 1917–18 without being curbed or scarcely even criticized, the more its practitioners were encouraged to increase its scope and intensity. The fact that high officials were constantly making loose attacks on undefined "disloyalty" seemed to make mob attitudes and actions appear almost admirable. Now, in the spring of 1918, the proponents of repression wanted even more severe laws to hit at people they disliked, laws which would extend the mantle of legality—and respectability—over all their hatreds and demands for conformity of thought and action. The hysteria that accompanied flag-kissings, tarring and featherings, and even lynchings, was reflected in this new campaign of the nationalists for more stringent and repressive laws.

Incitement continued to appear in the press and in public statements. The old-line interventionist, James M. Beck, spoke of the "heavenly vision of punitive justice." [1] The Council of National Defense, meeting in Washington with a group of governors, demanded stronger laws against "spies" and "disloyalty," and declared, "Traitors should be summarily dealt with. A few good examples of death sentences would have a salutary effect in stopping their activities." [2] When the *Christian Science Monitor* reported views expressed by Senator Overman, the story was headlined, "Extreme Penalty For Spies Urged." [3]

—Photo by Harris & Ewing, Washington, D.C.

VICTOR L. BERGER

As had been true during the previous months, little or no distinction was made between a spy or dangerous traitor, and one who simply criticized American war policies, opposed war on principle, or advocated peace. The great majority of war opponents did not create any physical threat or danger to the country; yet, because they were lumped in the public mind with the actual perpetrators of violence and sabotage, they suffered increasing difficulties.

The position of the extreme nationalists is well shown by Vice-President Marshall's recommendation for legislation that would annul the citizenship of every American not "heartily in support of the Government in this crisis." He also advocated confiscating the property of such people. "This is no time for the pacifists to be running loose," Marshall said.[4] Senator Williams of Mississippi went even further in demanding uniformity. He told his colleagues: "There is no Democratic Party and there is no Republican Party here any more. There is a loyalist, pro-American, aggressively and if necessary offensively pro-American party, and a party which is pro-German or lukewarm in its Americanism. Those who are not with us are against us, and let them take their medicine; and if the law does not give them their medicine the people will . . . ."[5]

One justification for more repressive laws was the increasing incidence of actual or alleged sabotage by German agents. Senator Lodge stated that enemy representatives had been engaged in "dynamiting factories, in starting great incendiary fires, in attempting to destroy railroad bridges, in poisoning food, and in mixing glass with bread."[6] Senator Overman complained that "the country is full of traitors, scoundrels, and spies . . . ."[7] Somewhat later, Congressman Edward E. Robbins had printed in the *Congressional Record* an itemized list of such "crimes committed by German sympathizers against our Government . . . since war was declared." The following are typical examples:

> July 19, 1917: Three men arrested in Kansas City for selling poisoned courtplaster saturated with Tetanus germs.
>
> July 19, 1917: San Antonio reports discovery of liquid poison made for Germans in Mexico . . . .
>
> August 22, 1917: Gov. Cox sees plot in Ohio coal-mine strike; investigation started.
>
> August 20, 1917: Rosenwasser blames strike in his shoe factory to German influence . . . .

> October 28, 1917: Army mules have been disabled in Vancouver
> by insertion of needles in their joints.

Many of the items were "reports" or "accusations." He ended with a huge list of "incendiary enemy fire losses for nine months." [8]

Robbins then told the story of Israel Putnam who caught a British spy in the American Revolution. Putnam notified the British commander, "I have caught one of your command within the American lines. He was arrested as a spy, he will be tried as a spy, and if convicted he will be hanged as a spy. P.S. He was hanged at 4 o'clock today." Robbins was applauded when he said the United States needed more Putnams. Senator Lodge accused the Administration of "dealing too lightly with German agents." He said that "the only way to treat them was to shoot them down." Senator Chamberlain also "urged the shooting of German agents" and said that such cases should be dealt with under the military code.[9]

However, the desire to punish spies and saboteurs was not the real reason senators and congressmen favored new and more restrictive laws. The talk about spies was largely for the effect it would have in gaining support for additional "loyalty" legislation. It was a camouflage for other motives. Even the most ardent nationalists knew that laws already on the statute books were entirely sufficient to punish wartime spies and traitors. The main idea was to clamp down on traitorous speech and ideas.

In this regard, it was argued that additional legislation on loyalty was needed because the Espionage Act was completely inadequate. Congress and judges, it was said, had taken the teeth out of it. Attorney General Gregory declared that Congress had deleted sections of the original espionage bill which the Department of Justice had deemed essential. He also complained because some district judges had instructed acquittal when Gregory thought the defendant's guilt was obvious.[10]

What the nationalists wanted was a law that would bite deep into the neck of any and every opponent of the war. They claimed that the Espionage Act had not resulted in enough indictments, to say nothing of convictions. They wanted complete repression and were not satisfied that hundreds of persons had been convicted under the original Espionage Act. According to Cummings and McFarland, "of the one hundred and eighty tried prior to January 1, [1918] . . . only six were acquitted." Also, of the "nine hundred and eighty-one persons tried for violation of the Selective Service Act only seventeen had been acquitted." [11] But the nationalists wanted no acquittals.

A case which aroused particular interest was that of Ves Hall, a young man in Montana. In a small, isolated village of about sixty people,

OVER THERE—OVER HERE!
—Cassel in the New York *Evening World* as reproduced in *Literary Digest*, LVII (Apr. 20, 1918), 7.

Hall had said that he would not go to war, that Germany would win, that President Wilson was crooked, and that the war was being fought for the benefit of Wall Street millionaires. Hall was acquitted in district court on the grounds that his statements could not possibly have interfered with the success of the army and navy as defined in the Espionage Act. The judge said that it was a mistake to assume that anyone making slanderous or disloyal remarks could be convicted under the 1917 law. In effect, he held that there must be some relation between the act and the results of the act. The Espionage Act, in other words, was not one for unlimited suppression of free speech. [12]

Senator Walsh was distressed over this decision, as were many others. Walsh called the Hall case "the most startling" and "possibly the most notorious" proof of the weakness of the 1917 law. People in Montana, he declared, were highly indignant. [13] Members of the American war party had adopted what seemed to them a logical view; support of the war was patriotic and any opposition to the war was treasonable.

The most common argument advanced to justify additional legislation to insure loyalty was that it was essential to stop mob violence. Mob actions were blamed on the lack of firm action by the federal Government in fighting disloyalty and sedition. When the Government did not protect the people, it was said, they would take the law into their own hands. This had the effect of saying that opponents of war must be sent to the penitentiary to save them from impetuous and furious mobs. Nonetheless, high administrative officials, congressmen and senators, governors, and people at large, all supported more rigorous and repressive laws on this basis.

On the afternoon following Prager's hanging, members of the cabinet were reported to have said that one of the main reasons the lynching occurred was that Congress had been slow in passing a stronger sedition law.[14] A few days later Attorney General Gregory declared that "most of the disorder throughout the country is caused by lack of laws relating to disloyal utterances." [15] Senators took the same position. Lodge said that if the law did not cover seditious cases they would be "dealt with by lynch law." [16] Senator Jones of Washington, referring to the tarring and feathering of an I.W.W. by Yakima citizens, said the people were desperate and "intend to take the law into their own hands to suppress traitorous conduct." [17] "The people," said Senator Fall, "will take the law into their own hands with Judge Lynch unless Congress enacts the needed laws." [18]

The Prager lynching prompted Governor Lowden to state his position. He said he deplored seeing patriotism used as a cloak for crime, but added that there had been "provocation" for such lawless deeds. More vigorous federal prosecution of disloyalty was Lowden's formula to restore calm. "I believe," he said, "that we have been too lax." [19] A prominent leader of the American Defense Society also blamed the Prager hanging on lax laws. He declared that mobs had "assembled and righted the wrongs which neither the local nor the federal authorities have dealt with." [20] And the mayor of Collinsville, Illinois, got in his two cents worth. He sent a telegram to Senator Overman saying that a stronger espionage law "would have a wholesome effect on those tending to be disloyal." [21]

Newspaper editors took the same attitude. In sampling opinion throughout the country, the *Literary Digest* found editors blaming mob action on lack of sufficient laws and weak court actions.[22] Along this line the conservative *Christian Science Monitor* editorialized on May 4, "The most regrettable thing about the whole matter [mob actions] is that, owing to the failure of the state and federal courts to deal adequately with the problem, private citizens are left, in self-protection, to take the law into their own hands."

Here then were arguments for stiffer loyalty legislation. But this was by no means all. Probably the chief and underlying reason why many people supported a sedition law was to curb the I.W.W. and other radical labor groups. There were frequent charges, especially by senators and representatives from the northwestern states, that the I.W.W. had been coddled.[23] Some way must be found to jail more I.W.W.'s. Radical labor movements must have their vocal cords cut. Senator Hardwick, who opposed a sedition law, declared, "I understand that the real—in fact, practically the only—object of [part of the bill] is to get some men called I.W.W.'s, who are operating in a few of the Northwestern States . . . ." [24] It is important to note that the model for a federal sedition law was the anti-I.W.W. Montana statute enacted in February, 1918.

But how could practically every antiwar statement or action be made treasonable or illegal? Opposition to war could not be called treason. The Constitution defines treason, and political opinions do not come within its scope. The answer was found in the word sedition, which meant to excite discontent against the Government or to disturb the public tranquillity through inflammatory language. Only a few opponents of war resisted lawful authority, but it might be considered that they excited discontent against the Government, although even the latter was an old and honored American custom. Nevertheless, sedition, broadly defined, would be a means of further throttling free speech—as long, at least, as the courts and public opinion were sympathetic.

Under pressure from local patriots, some states did not wait for the federal Government to pass a sedition law. Late in February, 1918, Montana enacted a statute which provided a twenty-thousand-dollar fine and a twenty-year penitentiary sentence for anyone convicted of using "disloyal, profane, scurrilous, contemptuous, or abusive language" about the American form of government, the flag, the Constitution, or military personnel and their uniforms.[25]

In other states—and in cities—this movement was taken up.[26] In California, bills were introduced which would have given the death penalty to some kinds of war opponents through court-martial proceedings. It was hoped to obtain laws which would "reach the I.W.W." [27] Nebraska legislators passed a bill providing a ten-thousand-dollar fine and a twenty-year jail sentence for individuals convicted of disloyal acts or utterances.[28] This act was "intended to catch the I.W.W. tramps and pool hall habitués," said its author. "It provides that persons habitually idle and refusing to work are liable to prosecution." [29] A Texas law provided punishment of twenty-five years in prison for offenses such as those mentioned in the Montana statute. In addition, any "disloyal" or "abusive" language concerning "the entry or continuance of the United States of America in the war" was prohibited. [30] It appeared, under this law, that it would be illegal even to discuss whether or not it had been wise for the United States to enter the war. Opposition to discussing why the United States went to war, however, was not confined to Texas. Senator Swanson told his colleagues that a sedition law was necessary because of the "insidious and treasonable propaganda being conducted in this country, grossly misrepresenting the causes which impelled this country to wage war against Germany . . . ." [31]

Inspired by what the states were doing, or were about to do, and pushed by popular demand, Congress turned its attention to a national sedition bill. Congressman Webb introduced the measure, which had been prepared in the Department of Justice, on January 16, 1918. After a few minutes of debate on March 4, it was passed by an unrecorded vote. [32] But even during this brief discussion, it was clear that members of the House wanted legislation, not so much to strike at spies as to silence hostile opinion about the war, and to curb radical labor elements, especially the I.W.W.

Representative William E. Cox of Indiana declared that "we ought to have some wider and broader and deeper legislation in this country that would reach out and take hold of the men who are uttering seditious statements against this Government, criticizing the President right and left, and talking about a revolution to come." [33] Congressman Clarence B. Miller of Minnesota was also deeply concerned with the spread of bad ideas. He explained that the I.W.W. had sinister plans to cut agricultural production in the northwestern states. The man who burned a haystack or an elevator, Miller continued, could be punished under the present laws. But, he added, "that crime is mild compared to that of an individual who goes among farm hands and pours into their ears the worst kind of seditious stuff quietly and privately and forms them into an organization that will cause them to strike and demand impossible conditions about the time the harvests are on." [34]

The Senate Judiciary Committee studied the House bill and favorably reported a somewhat revised measure on April 2. Senator Overman, who had charge of it, told his colleagues that the bill should be speeded through the Senate immediately so that it could become law before

April 6 when the Liberty Loan drive was to begin.[35] When more extended debate began on April 4, Overman again asked the Senators to move quickly. However, Senator Lodge and others refused to be hurried, a situation which caused Overman to declare impatiently, "Senators can do as they please about delaying this bill. The people of this country are taking the law in their own hand on the ground that Congress is not doing its duty. In numerous cases it is said that men are being mobbed all over the country because Congress does not pass laws under which the guilty ones can be adequately punished." Then the North Carolina Senator reminded his colleagues that the bill not only had the support of the Judiciary Committee, "but it is copied from the laws of States in the great West, which were not satisfied with what Congress had done in respect to the enactment of Federal law." [36]

Despite Overman's insistence, the Senate chose to look this gift horse in the mouth. Many were interested in its teeth. Just what sort of legislation was being advocated?

Actually, the bill, an amendment to the Espionage Act of 1917, included many things. Heavy punishment—up to twenty-year prison terms and twenty-thousand-dollar fines—was in store for people who made false statements that might hinder successful operation of the military forces. It was illegal to make false statements that would obstruct the sale of war bonds, to incite disloyalty, and to obstruct enlistments. The most sweeping infringement upon free speech, however, was the provision for punishment of anyone who, in wartime, "shall willfully utter, print, write, or publish any disloyal, profane, scurrilous, or abusive language about the form of government of the United States, or the Constitution of the United States, or the military or naval forces of the United States, or the flag of the United States, or the uniform of the Army or Navy," or any language intended to bring these institutions "into contempt, scorn, contumely, or disrepute." [37]

There were two other provisions of the amendment which were highly restrictive. One of these was aimed directly at the I.W.W. It made it illegal to utter, write, print, publish, speak, "urge, incite or advocate any curtailment of production in this country of any thing or things, product or products, necessary or essential to the prosecution of the war." Finally, the powers of the Postmaster General were to be expanded so that he could order mail returned to the sender if he thought it violated provisions of the Espionage Act. Such mail was to be marked "Undeliverable Under Espionage Act." The Postmaster General could do this merely "upon evidence satisfactory to him."

It is clear that dissent of nearly every imaginable form was to be silenced or punished under this bill. Freedom of speech and of the press were subjected to the severest restrictions in American history. Still, there were those who thought the amendment did not go far enough. Congressman W. B. Walton of New Mexico complained that it was too mild. "I would have voted for it much more readily," he said, "if it carried the death penalty for the offenses which it is designed to prevent." [38] Senator Chamberlain also favored handling what he considered spies and traitors by military court.[39] And Senator Fall said that, if necessary, the President could follow Lincoln's example and suspend the writ of *habeas corpus*. Then, he explained, military law could apply.[40]

Some of the extreme nationalists became highly enthusiastic in trying to take sedition cases out of the civil courts. Judge McGee of Minnesota was quoted as saying, "What we need is a court that can't be fooled with a lot of technicality and red tape." Then he added significantly, "You can't fool a military court." [41] Attorney General Gregory admitted that "from every section of the country comes up the cry that the disloyal and seditious should be tried by military courts-martial and promptly shot." [42] In fact, an assistant in Gregory's office prepared a bill which would have given control of disloyalty cases to military courts. But this was disavowed by both Gregory and President Wilson.[43]

However, for a time those deeply concerned with questions of civil rights feared that military courts might be empowered to try loyalty cases. Roger N. Baldwin wrote that "the newspapers here are so full of material showing the necessity of military trials for all offenses under the Espionage Act that it looks to me as if it would be difficult to defeat the legislation." [44] Previously Lawrence Todd had referred to the movement as "the last word in war frenzy." [45] Another writer said that provisions of the Chamberlain court-martial resolution "meant the firing squad for brain and conscience." [46]

There was never any doubt that the sedition amendment would be approved. However, its consideration in the Senate provided a good view of the wartime attitudes on freedom of speech and expression. Among the bill's most effective opponents were Senators Johnson of California, Gore of Oklahoma, Vardaman of Mississippi, and Hardwick of Georgia. La Follette took little part.

Various implications of the measure were revealed in the Senate debate. Senator Cummins, for example, asked if the bill would penalize "criticism or censure of the President of the United States or of the conduct of the Government." Even though the office of president was not mentioned in the amendment, Senator Charles S. Thomas of Colorado replied that, in his judgment, it would.[47] At this point, Theodore Roosevelt entered the controversy and hurriedly wrote an editorial on the subject for the Kansas City *Star*. He exploded at the thought of being prevented from using "contemptuous and slurring language about the President." This idea, Roosevelt stormed, was "sheer treason to the United States." The old Bull Mooser charged that such an interpretation of the proposed law would be unconstitutional. Roosevelt said that he would not be muzzled.[48] However, he made no plea for the principle of freedom of speech.

Senator Hardwick contended that the sedition measure would prevent public discussion of peace terms and that the time would no doubt come when such discussion would be highly desirable. He declared that "even the President was not exempt from the most drastic criticism because he discussed these matters." If the bill passed, Hardwick said, "free speech in a free country will simply mean that one man is perfectly free to advocate war to the end of eternity and another man can not advocate peace without putting himself in a dungeon." He was particularly disturbed at the thought of what some extremist judges would do with the law. When you have a law, he argued, "that is capable of almost any construction and that can be used as an engine of persecution where perfectly loyal men who have honest difference of opinion may be punished, I tell you I halt and hesitate and gag over it. I tell you I can not vote for it." [49]

Hiram Johnson spoke at length against the bill on several occasions. "The language of the bill demonstrates the fact," he declared, "that this is a bill not for the punishment of disloyalty or of treason, but it is a bill to suppress the freedom of the press . . . , and to prevent any man, no matter who he is, from indulging in fair and decent expression, or voicing legitimate criticism concerning the present Government, the present administration, or any department in respect to the war." Not only was the measure designed "to throttle honest and legitimate discussion or criticism," Johnson continued, "but it even purports to prevent one from thinking as he wishes to think." The main sections of the bill, he said, meant that "you shall not criticize anything or anybody in this Government any longer or you shall go to jail" and "that you shall not think critically of anything or anybody in this Government hereafter or you shall go to jail." [50]

Johnson said that he could not justify such a repressive law simply because the United States was involved in war. In reply to Senator

Fall, who argued that different standards of freedom must prevail because of the war, Johnson said, "It is war . . . . But, good God, Mr.
President, when did it become war upon the American people?" [51] Johnson said measures like that under discussion resulted from "a peculiar
sort of mental hysteria that comes when people are forced to face great
struggles and great attacks." Then he added, "Measures such as this do
not unite a people; they breed discontent; they cause suspicion to stalk
all through the land; they make the one man the spy upon the other;
they take a great virile, brave people and make that people timid and
fearful."

Discussing this state of mind further, Johnson said there would be
"distrust of neighbors, insidious suspicion skulking all over the land,
and finally the very discontent that every one of us would avoid." He
illustrated his argument by telling of a recent conversation with a businessman about a bill designed to expand presidential powers. The man
said, "Good God, if you pass such a law we might just as well be in
Prussia." Johnson said he warned his acquaintance to keep quiet because
he might be sent to the penitentiary for such a statement if the sedition
bill passed. "A brave man does not have to boast, and a patriot does not
have to protest his loyalty," Johnson declared. "This bill puts a premium
upon hypocrisy; this bill makes the man with the loudest vocal vocifera-
tion of his own virtues and his own patriotism the greatest man among
us." [52]

In essence, leading opponents of the bill took the position that
there was more strength in freedom than in repression, the idea that is
at the very core of free, democratic government. Senator Gore, already
hated by the extreme nationalists because of his prewar activities, declared that "the guaranties in favor of freedom of thought and freedom
of speech . . . . did not work as much mischief as the intolerance and
the despotism which undertook to cut the tongues out of the throats
of men who sought to give utterances to honest convictions." [53]

Senator Vardaman argued along the same line. "You can rely upon
the inherent patriotism and the individual good judgment of the citizen
to take the grains of wisdom from the talks of men and . . . cast aside
the chaff. The people can take care of themselves." He continued, "I believe in an hour like the present that the fullest and freest discussion
should be permitted." Vardaman thought that, even in wartime, the
"rights and privileges guaranteed by the Constitution should be upheld
and scrupulously respected." Then he added, "When we are going around

sharp curves or crossing the breakers under a full head of steam, all the headlights should be turned on." [54]

Senator Reed of Missouri agreed with the general purposes of the legislation, but, like others, he thought it was far too drastic. "Frequently men fail to accomplish their purpose by attempting measures too extreme," he said. Reed agreed that Montana might need such a law, but it was entirely unnecessary "to fasten such a law upon the entire United States." [55] It was far worse, he complained, than the hated Alien and Sedition Acts of 1798.

While the Senate had the measure under consideration, Senator France of Maryland introduced an amendment which caused sharp discussion. France proposed that "nothing in this act shall be construed as limiting the liberty or impairing the right of any individual to publish or speak what is true, with good motives, and for justifiable ends." [56] This may have seemed harmless on the surface, simply a restatement of existing constitutional guarantees both state and national, but a move was quickly made to eliminate the restriction. The Attorney General's office bitterly opposed it, as did the army. John Lord O'Brian wrote to Congressman Webb that the proviso "would very seriously interfere with the successful prosecution of cases" arising under the proposed law. O'Brian said that some of the most dangerous type of "propaganda" "on its face generally shows a motive entirely legitimate." The Espionage Act had been fairly successful against "propaganda," O'Brian wrote, "and if amended as requested . . . there is every reason to prove that it will be thoroughly effective. Its effectiveness for the purpose of killing propaganda, however, has come from the principle that motives prompting propaganda are irrelevant . . . ." The France amendment, O'Brian claimed, "would make the question of motive not only relevant but essential, and would introduce an element of proof which would greatly increase the condition of successful prosecution and greatly decrease the value of the espionage act as a deterrent of propaganda."

O'Brian was especially concerned with the problem of motive in handling religious objectors to war. In cases of religious pacifism, where the Bible was cited as authority, proof of bad motives would be especially difficult, he explained. A few days later O'Brian wrote to Senator Overman on the same theme. He said that the "greatest danger to the country, internally, to-day is the use of different sorts of seditious propaganda, particularly the false pacifist propaganda." As a lawyer, O'Brian told Overman that he should understand "what a cloud of confusing legal technicalities can be stirred up by introducing collateral questions as to what are justifiable ends, the personal motives of the defendant, etc." [57] In short, the Department of Justice did not want the responsibility of having to prove bad motives. In that case there might not be many convictions.

Some heated debate centered around the France amendment. It was passed by the Senate but fell before a Senate-House conference committee never to be revived. Senator Fall said that France's amendment would emasculate the legislation, and, if it were included, he was then ready to support Senator Chamberlain's court-martial resolution. [58]

The enlarged powers granted to the Postmaster General in the sedition amendment also came in for sharp criticism, especially by Senators Johnson and Hardwick. To grant Burleson this extreme and broad administrative power over the delivery of mail, Johnson said, was a further infringement upon free speech and expression. Hardwick also attacked such arbitrary power and said the language was far too inclusive. [59] Senator Lodge complained that it would now likely be impossible to even criticize "our deplorable Post Service" and that any newspaper criticizing the Government might be barred from the mails. [60] But this section could not be defeated.

At one point in the debate, Senator Lodge, who voted against the bill although he favored its general objectives, pointed out its essentially false nature as an amendment to the Espionage Act. It was not directed against espionage at all, he argued; it would not touch "a single spy or a single German agent." "The spies or agents," he said, "do not go around uttering, publishing, and writing. The dangerous men keep quiet." [61] Later in the debate, he said that spies "probably pretend to be loyal to the United States in order to cover their opposition." Then he added, "To state it very broadly, it is aimed at certain classes of agitators who exist in different parts of the country." [62] On every hand there was open admission that this was the case. Senator Watson not only wanted to curb criticism of the Government and its officials in wartime, but showed his resentment of such criticism in peacetime as well. [63]

Senator Poindexter, who was deeply worried about the I.W.W.'s in his state, declared that "this legislation is a product of the times. Many of the things that are proposed to be punished by this bill might very well go unnoticed and be of trivial public importance in times of peace . . . ." [64] Yet, he said, he could not understand why opponents of the bill placed so much importance on the right of free speech. "Why [do] they attach so much more importance to . . . the right to talk," he asked, than to men's property and lives which were being taken? [65]

To this Senator Hardwick replied, "If we are fighting freedom's battles, let us fight in a cause worthy of freedom. Let us preserve the ancient and immemorial rights of freemen as they come down to us . . . ." Hardwick argued further that the country would be stronger by maintaining its basic freedoms than by surrendering or hedging them "on every occasion." It was ridiculous, he continued, to act as if the American people were disloyal simply because they did not unanimously approve all of the methods and plans of those in power. [66]

The sedition amendment passed the Senate on April 10. Differences in the Senate and House version necessitated agreement in a conference committee. The conference committee reported back to the Senate on April 22 with, as mentioned earlier, the France amendment eliminated. On May 4 the Senate adopted the conference report by a vote of 48 to 26, with 21 not voting. [67] Three days later, the House approved it by the overwhelming margin of 293 to 1. [68] The single negative vote was cast by Socialist Meyer London of New York. The amendment was signed by the President and became law on May 16.

Passage of the sedition amendment immeasurably sharpened the Espionage Act as a tool to strike at disloyal and unpopular opinions. The *Atlanta Constitution* said it was just what the country needed. Countering the argument that the law was extreme and unwise, the editorial stated, "How any measure can be 'too drastic' in its applications to traitors and disloyalists . . . in time of war it will be hard to make the red-blooded, 100 per cent American members of society understand." [69] But the *Milwaukee Leader* advised its readers, "Your best course is not to talk about the war at all." [70] Before long, quite a number of people must have concluded that the Socialist editor was right.

THE LEGAL DRAGNET

June through November, 1918

It is true that national unity had been largely achieved in the United States by the summer of 1918. Yet a surprising number of people were still either silently or openly critical of the war. Neither censorship nor propaganda nor mob violence nor jailings could end the smouldering opposition to the war among some Americans. Not even killings, such as that of Prager, or laws, such as the revised Espionage Act, could force complete acquiescence. Many critics, of course, were frightened into silence, but there were others who continued to speak out regardless of the dangers involved. The conflict on the home front went on with neither side changing its beliefs or its conduct.

Opponents of the war continued to express their stubborn disbelief, and strident nationalists demanded the strangling of all such criticisms. There was still mob violence. There were still indictments, trials, and harsh sentences. The dismal parade of people going to prison continued. Conscientious objectors held firm to their faiths, and the military used harsh measures to make them yield. And then, of course, there were those thousands outside the army who evaded, or tried to evade, conscription. The story of an internal war among the American people could be seen by anyone who closely watched the newspapers or read the court decisions.

The incitements to repression appeared somewhat more restrained after the outbreaks of violence in April and May, but they did not disappear. On June 3, 1918, the *Atlanta Constitution* praised the Sedition

Act and intimated that criticism of the war effort should not be permitted. Theodore Roosevelt was quoted by the *Minneapolis Journal* on August 26 as saying that internationalism was "treason to the nation" and that pacifism gave aid to the Hun. The American Defense Society and other "patriotic" organizations continued as before. A St. Louis newspaper reported in August of 1918 that "orders were issued to the St. Louis police today to arrest any person who publicly criticized the United States for entering the war, or who questions the constitutionality of the selective draft. Those arrested will be held for the Federal Department of Justice." This order resulted from a request by the American Defense Society asking the police to "wage relentless war on pacifists who conduct their propaganda under the guise of innocent arguments against the nation's entry into the war." Those utterances and sentiments were considered seditious.[1]

After a flag-kissing in Georgia, W. F. Dorsey, a former mayor, was quoted by the *Atlanta Constitution* on June 1, 1918, as saying that "hereafter disloyalists might expect to be branded on the forehead and on either cheek, and the rope would be the end of traitors, in legal process of law or otherwise." In one town, placards warned that the Loyalty Committee had been organized to "put the fear of God in your souls or wring the life from your detestable bodies." Then this warning added, "The hemp and torch are ready and waiting."[2]

But the Sedition Act made use of "the hemp and the torch" much less necessary. Now more than sufficient legal authority existed to silence antiwar critics. The Attorney General had asked for a "liberal construction" of the new law, and he got it. Convictions were obtained, and there was little criticism. Lawyers often avoided going to the defense of those accused of "sedition." One writer commented that "any lawyer who dares to defend such persons [political prisoners] is cut and condemned by members of his profession."[3] An attorney wrote to the Civil Liberties Bureau, "I do not know an available lawyer at or near Huntsville, Alabama, who would care to represent the indicted Socialists. Most of the lawyers refuse to handle such cases for fear of ruining their professional reputations."[4]

Meanwhile, the volume of accusations increased enormously. The Department of Justice was flooded with thousands of complaints, demanding that suspects, even neighbors and friends, be punished to the limit of the law. According to Cummings and McFarland, by late 1918 "the volume of prosecutions for all sorts of utterances became so great that . . . a circular was issued directing that no more sedition cases be presented to grand juries until the facts had been submitted to the Department of Justice." [5] But even then prosecutions continued in some districts.

In Michigan Louis Jasick threatened the President by reportedly saying that "if he got a chance he would shoot President Wilson." [6] Jasick was given a long prison term. A similar case involved a cantankerous and argumentative old Ohioan, J. Herman Dierkes. Dierkes was a member of several war committees but still did not like the war. He referred to Wilson as "the poor slob" and said, "I feel sorry for him. I would rather serve a term in the penitentiary than wear a uniform in Wilson's Wall Street war." He was also accused of saying, "It is a great mistake to carry on this war; those s.o.b.'s in Washington will be sorry." He called it a "moneyed war" and said that one might as well throw his funds away as to buy Liberty bonds. Dierkes was sentenced to five years in Atlanta Penitentiary, although he did not serve the full term. [7]

The new law was effective against those who attempted to interfere with the war loan campaigns. After William Powell of Lansing, Michigan, had been forced to buy a Liberty bond, he declared, "The East End gang forced me to buy a fifty dollar bond. I hope the Government goes to hell so it will be of no value." He was also reported to have said that the atrocity stories were lies. "This is a rich man's war and the United States is simply fighting for money," he said. [8] These remarks were made during an argument with a relative who reported Powell to the police. Powell apparently did not take the matter seriously and did not even hire a lawyer. The jury, however, found him guilty, and Judge Arthur Tuttle sentenced him to twenty years in the penitentiary and fined him ten thousand dollars. By selling his property he managed to raise five thousand dollars, to which figure the judge reduced the fine. Powell, who had a wife and five small children, wrote to the Civil Liberties Bureau, "In the name of God and Humanity what can there be done for me for an unintentional error." [9] When the mayor of Lansing criticized the sentence, the judge promptly cited him for contempt. However, the mayor apologized to the court and was let off with a reprimand. [10]

The Sedition Act was especially effective in dealing with people of foreign birth. Peter Wimmer, an obscure old man, was quoted as saying that "America did not have a chance to win this war; that President Wilson started the war to protect the Wall Street brokers who had purchased English and French securities; that President Wilson was a friend of the rich man . . . and that the Kaiser was always a friend of the poor man." He was fined five hundred dollars and sentenced to six months in jail for these seditious statements.[11]

The extent to which people's privacy was invaded to guarantee loyalty and conformity is well illustrated by a situation at Covington, Kentucky. There, among a fairly large German element, lived C. B. Shoborg, Henry Feltman, and J. Henry Kruse. Shoborg, a former policeman and member of the city council, was a man of sixty-six who ran a shoe shop. He was a quiet, law-abiding person who had lived there since childhood, although he had been born in Germany. Sixty-five-year-old Feltman had been born in Kentucky and had a banking and tobacco business. Kruse, a man over fifty-five and a Kentuckian by birth, was a brewer. These three men were close friends and had been accustomed for years to meet in the shoemaker's shop to discuss current affairs.

There was considerable local feeling that quite a number of people in Covington were disloyal. When Shoborg and his friends were suspected of disloyalty, a detective agency was employed to place a dictograph in Shoborg's shop so that private conversations of the three men could be heard. Between March and July, 1918, detectives reported that Shoborg, Feltman, and Kruse were critical of the Red Cross, called Theodore Roosevelt a "damned agitator," and expressed pleasure at German military successes.[12] The charges could not be corroborated because not more than one detective at a time could listen over the dictaphone.[13] The three were indicted on September 13, 1918, for favoring the German cause and opposing the United States. Shoborg was sentenced to ten years in the penitentiary, Feltman to seven years, and Kruse to five years. Feltman, apparently because he was wealthy, was fined forty thousand dollars.[14]

Although it was not shown that the discussions of Shoborg, Feltman, and Kruse had interfered with the war in any way, it was held that "disloyalty, extreme, pervasive, and constant, . . . shown by words only, could hardly be conceived in more typical and complete form." The court maintained that since others were sometimes present, the discussions were not private. "The influence of such a center would radiate through an appreciable part of the community," said the court.[15]

Andrew P. Lockhart, an individualistic and irritable ex-tailor, lived in Tennessee. In 1918, he was nearly sixty years old. Having lost his savings, he had become a milk peddler in Chattanooga. Lockhart was a man of small education, and at the time of his arrest in October, 1918, he was ill. His dislike of war was reflected in his reported statement that he would kill his son if he joined the army. However, the boy did enlist. He also was quoted as saying that Germany would win the war, that he wanted it that way, and that the United States had made a grave mistake in going to war against Germany. For these remarks, he was sentenced to a year and a day in Atlanta and fined one thousand dollars.[16]

The bad tendency doctrine was recognized by the court in this decision, as well as in numerous others. Statements made by Lockhart before the United States entered the war in 1917 were readily admitted in evidence. In fact, some of the most damaging testimony was based upon Lockhart's prewar talk. Evidence of disloyal statements after the passage of the Sedition Act, said the court, "is somewhat vague and uncertain." "Yet," the judge added, "the record tends to show a more or less consistent and continuous course of speech from the time before the United States entered the war until the defendant's arrest." [17]

An even better example of the bad tendency idea is found in the case of Henry Albers. Born in Germany, he had migrated to Oregon where he built up an extensive business, employing over 1,000 men, many of whom he had encouraged to enlist. He was a large contributor to war charities, and his company had purchased $300,000 worth of Liberty bonds. Albers was accused of having made various seditious remarks while on a passenger train going to Portland, Oregon, on October 8, 1918. He was drunk at the time. After some heckling, he became loud and profane, and reportedly said, "I am a German and don't deny it— once a German always a German . . . . To hell with America." Albers continued his drunken tirade by calling Secretary McAdoo "a s—— of a b——," and by declaring that "I have helped Germany in this war, and I would give every cent I have to defeat the United States." He also said the United States was not a free country—not as free as Germany.[18] Government prosecutors took the position that whiskey had unsealed Albers' lips and made him say what he really thought. Going back as far as 1914 and 1915, evidence was introduced to show that Albers had been friendly to Germany in the war with England. When the defense objected to admitting such evidence as having no relevancy under the Sedition Act, the court held it was admissible "to show the bent of the defendant's mind." [19] On that basis he was sentenced to three years in the penitentiary and fined ten thousand dollars.

Stephen Binder, a New York butcher, strongly opposed the war. He published a booklet entitled *Light and Truth* in which he wrote that "this book was written and published as a defiance to our Government's misrule and as the bold assertion of the injustice of America's entrance into the world's war." He declared that, under the pretext of preserving American rights, the United States went to war to save England and her allies. "It was to bolster up the dwindling hopes of big American financiers who had great fortunes at stake in the war gamble on England's side," he argued.[20] Binder also made other antiwar statements. He was convicted and sentenced to a two-year prison term largely on the basis that his remarks were designed "to arouse dissatisfaction with the war." [21]

Thomas E. Moore, alias Jacques Mamaux, was arrested for drunkenness and put in the county jail at Pomeroy, Ohio, on the evening of June 25, 1918. During the night a fight broke out in the jail and Mamaux was badly beaten. When the deputy sheriff appeared the next morning, he asked Mamaux about his nationality. Mamaux refused to answer, and according to his story, the deputy said, "Before you get out of this jail you will have a nationality." On this point Jacques eventually yielded and said that he was a Swede.

The conversation then turned to the war. Mamaux told the officer, "If you are so damned intelligent, I suppose you can tell me who started this war." Then answering his own question, Mamaux replied, "John D. Rockefeller, a s—— of a ——, and a capitalist started this war . . . . It is a God damned capitalist's war." The deputy sheriff then told him that a man in uniform had tried to get him out of jail the night before. Mamaux's response to this was that "the whole United States Army is only a God damned legalized murder machine." [22] The outcome of the affair was Mamaux's indictment under the Espionage Act for uttering "disloyal, profane, scurrilous, and abusive language about the military forces of the United States." He was sentenced to two and a half years in Atlanta.[23]

A case where the defendants were convicted largely on the basis of bad ideas was that of Jacob Abrams and four associates in New York. Poverty-stricken young Russian immigrants in their twenties, they were all Anarchists except Samuel Lipman, a Socialist. Abrams and his friends bitterly opposed sending American expeditionary forces to Russia and published several radical leaflets denouncing United States policy.

On August 23, a number of workmen at Houston and Crosby streets in New York picked up some leaflets which had been thrown from a nearby upper story window. Some were written in Yiddish, others in English. Seeing that the leaflets were belligerently critical of governmental policy, the workers notified the proper authorities. Before long H. Rosansky, who later admitted throwing the leaflets out the window, was arrested. Shortly afterwards Abrams and five others, including a young woman, Molly Steimer, were also arrested.[24]

The leaflets which aroused so much attention carried radical demands for the cessation of American intervention in Russia. One leaflet referred to the "hypocrisy of the United States and her allies." President Wilson, it said, "with his beautiful phraseology, has hypnotized the people of America to such an extent that they do not see his hypocrisy." According to the writer, the President's "shameful, cowardly silence about the intervention in Russia reveals the hypocrisy of the plutocratic gang in Washington and vicinity." Militarism and capitalism were crushing the Russian Revolution, it was argued, and "The Russian Revolution cries: 'Workers of the World! Awake! Rise! Put down your enemy and mine.'" [25] Despite the harsh attack on President Wilson and capitalism, the leaflets did not indicate that the writers were pro-German. One statement read, "We hate and despise German militarism more than do your hypocritical tyrants."

Another leaflet, entitled "Workers—Wake Up," charged that American intervention in Russia was designed not to help further the war against Germany but to defeat the Bolsheviki. Money loaned to make munitions, the argument went, "will make bullets not only for the Germans but also for the Workers Soviets of Russia." The workers, it was said, must answer the "barbaric intervention" by a general strike.[26]

There were conflicting reports on how the young radicals were treated after their arrest. One of the defendants declared that the police fiercely beat him and his friends. Two of the men were described as "a terrible sight. Lachowsky's clothes were dirty, torn and in blood; his face was in blood and all blue, his hair missing from his head in a number of places. Prober's condition was the same." [27] It was also charged that police administered a verbal third degree—asking the defendants about their attitudes toward the war and the President, and whether they were Bolsheviki. Chafee says that although the Assistant District Attorney, who showed the prisoners great consideration, was convinced that no violence was used, "charges of brutality seemed disquietingly specific and sincere." [28] Data in the American Civil Liberty Union files seem to substantiate this opinion.[29]

The Abrams case was not tried before any of the New York judges who had had experience with important espionage cases. Instead, Judge

Henry D. Clayton of Alabama was assigned to the case because of the crowded New York dockets. Clayton came from an area where dissent against the war was rare and where revolutionists were practically unknown.

The defense attorney tried to prove that American intervention in Russia was not anti-German and therefore opposition to such a policy could not logically interfere with the war against Germany. However, this testimony was excluded by Judge Clayton with the judicial statement, "The flowers that bloom in the spring, tra la, have nothing to do with the case." [30] Judge Clayton took the position that it was illegal for the defendants to try to create public opinion hostile to the Government of the United States, so as to "prevent the Government from recognizing that faction of the Government of Russia, which the Government has recognized, and to force the Government of the United States to recognize that faction of the Government in Russia to which these people were friendly." "Now," the judge added, "they cannot do that. No man can do that, and that is the theory that I have of this case, and we might as well have it out in the beginning." [31] Although Clayton's statement was not part of the evidence, certainly, so far as the jury was concerned, the harm had been done.

Five of those originally arrested were found guilty of violating the Espionage Act. Three of them, including Abrams, were given twenty-year prison terms. Molly Steimer was sentenced to fifteen, and Rosansky to three years. When Lipman was sentenced, he declared, "I did not expect anything better," to which the judge replied, "And may I add, that you do not deserve anything better." [32]

The *New York Times* praised Judge Clayton and the outcome of the trial. The editor did not believe that Clayton considered the defendants "particularly dangerous to the country or its institutions." Yet, he said, Clayton "was evidently determined that they, and especially others suffering from the same delusion of persecution, should be made to realize that 'freedom,' as it exists in the United States, is a very different thing from the liberty claimed and exercised by their Bolshevist friends in unhappy Russia." [33]

The Abrams decision was upheld by the United States Supreme Court. The majority argued that the real purpose of the alien radicals was to interfere with American military success in Europe. Their language, said the court, "intended" to encourage disloyalty and resistance to the United States in wartime.

Justice Holmes, however, wrote a strong dissent. He declared that "it is evident from the beginning to the end that the only object of the paper is to help Russia and stop American intervention there against the popular government—not to impede the United States in the war that it was carrying on." Then after raising other questions, Holmes said, "Even if I am technically wrong and enough can be squeezed from these poor and puny anonymities to turn the color of legal litmus paper . . . the most nominal punishment seems to me all that possibly could be inflicted, unless the defendants are to be made to suffer not for what the indictment alleges but for the creed that they avow." [34]

The Abrams case was important, not for the personalities involved, but for the principle upheld. That they were, in many respects, low characters, there is little doubt. But this does not excuse the type of trial they received. The chief importance of the case lies in the fact that Abrams and his friends were convicted not for pacifist or pro-German activities but because they agitated against the Government's policy in Russia. There were, it is true, vague threats to American munitions plants, but this did not play a prominent part in the trial. Furthermore, the Abrams case shows how far the courts were willing to go in the summer and fall of 1918 to throttle bad ideas. It was undoubtedly one of the most important cases arising under the revised Espionage Act of 1918.

The conviction of persons like Abrams, Albers, Shoborg, and Lockhart, individuals of no particular standing or influence, indicated the extent to which the extreme nationalists were committed to stamping out dissent. And there was an increasing tendency in these trials to look, not so much for overt acts, but for the bent of the defendant's thinking. Men's minds were explored more fully to try to ferret out unpatriotic thoughts and words.

The expanded use of the Espionage Act to eliminate spoken opposition to the war was now paralleled by more vigorous enforcement of the Selective Service Act to catch draft evaders. The police and federal officials were constantly picking up individuals who had failed to register or who had not reported for duty. A surprisingly large number were reported by neighbors and acquaintances. In spite of this, it was common knowledge that thousands were successfully evading service. In order to pull these slackers into the army, it was decided that some dragnet system was necessary. The idea was to check or apprehend all men who appeared to be of draft age. This would be done in a particular area at a given time. Then those found avoiding the draft could be held for military authorities, and those whose registration was in order or who were unqualified for service could be released. Such was the plan.

Between April and September drives to round up slackers were made in many cities. Some of the principal raids were staged in Minneapolis, Chicago, Detroit, Cleveland, Atlantic City, and New York. According to the *Minneapolis Journal* of April 27, hundreds of men were held for several hours in order to check their registration cards. On July 11 over 500 persons were apprehended at a Chicago ball park where detectives and federal agents stopped them at the gates.[35] A day later some 10,000 men were checked for their draft registration and classification. Over 1,000 of them spent the night at the police station and other places of detention when they could not produce proper identification.[36]

In August, the raids continued. On the 15th some three hundred police, detectives, federal agents, and members of the American Protective League raided the piers, boardwalks, and cafes at Atlantic City looking for slackers.[37] Three days later a dragnet was thrown over Tulsa and thousands were made to prove their loyalty and to show that they were not draft delinquents.[38] The American Protective League played a leading role in the slacker raids. During the Chicago drive, according to Emerson Hough, "A.L.P. operatives met every incoming railway train and were at the gate of every train leaving the city." [39] As the Government cracked down on draft evaders, stories appeared telling of men hiding out in the hills of Alabama, Mississippi, Arkansas, and other states. In Arkansas there was a reported battle between police and draft dodgers in which three were killed.[40]

The greatest raids, and the ones causing most popular excitement, were staged in New York City and vicinity. There one thousand sailors, seven hundred and fifty soldiers, and hundreds of A.P.L. men and police took part. Senator Frelinghuysen, who happened to see some of the activity, has left one of the many contemporary descriptions: "I stood on a street corner and saw soldiers armed with rifles, with bayonets fixed, hold up citizens, compel them to stand waiting while there were crowds around jeering at them, and when they failed to produce their registration cards," he said, men "were put in motor trucks and driven through the streets amid the jeers and scoffs of the crowd; they were sent to the armories and there held for hours without food, practically without opportunity of communicating with their relatives and friends in order to procure the evidence demanded by the authorities." [41]

Senator William M. Calder told his colleagues that "in one place I saw a street car stopped and an armed sailor go into the car and take men out of it, in some cases where they were escorting ladies. Men were stopped in the street. They were taken out of their places of business and crowded into vans, perhaps 50 or 60 packed in like sardines and sent to the police station houses." [42]

The estimates varied widely on the number of persons who were either held or forced to prove that they were not slackers. The *New York Times* set the figure at 20,000.[43] Some guesses went as high as 60,000. In any event, the Department of Justice considered the raids successful. The Attorney General reported that, over a three-day period in Manhattan and the Bronx, more than 11,652 men were apprehended and held. Of these, he said, "about 300 were inducted into military service and at least 1,500 were turned over to their local draft boards as delinquents." [44]

The Department of Justice and the army may have been pleased with the slacker raids, but angry protests soon reached Washington. Men who were not subject to the draft law reported to their senators and representatives that they had been held without excuse or cause, that they had been embarrassed, humiliated, and highly inconvenienced by the proceedings. Revelation that even the most elementary civil rights had been violated without shame or hesitation produced both surprise and sharp criticism.

The New York *World* led off with a scathing editorial, charging that whoever ordered the raids acted in "defiance of the spirit of American law." Arrests, continued the writer, had been made without warrants, and by "men destitute of official standing"—a reference no doubt to the A.P.L. operatives. "There is no record in all the history of New York of such another lawless proceeding," said the editor. To seize thousands of men merely on suspicion was "a shameful abuse of power." [45]

Editor Frank Cobb did not stop with this. He wrote to Tumulty, "Please call the President's attention to the shocking and lawless methods taken in New York in the so-called slacker raids. If he could see what I have seen his blood would boil with indignation." Cobb added that "I can think of nothing that will have a worse effect on public opinion and war sentiment in this city than this action of . . . arresting tens of thousands of patriotic and law-abiding citizens at the point of the bayonet and driving them through the streets under armed guards to remain under arrest until they prove their innocence." This was a "shameful spectacle," Cobb concluded, "which I would not have believed could happen outside a conquered province under Prussian military control." [46]

Even the *New York Times,* which often followed the official government line, said the campaign had been made "with more zeal than judgment." The manner in which it had been planned and executed "has no sensible man's approval." Looking at the broader issue, the *Times* editor wrote that "the appearance of infringing on personal liberty should be sedulously avoided." [47]

Senator Hiram Johnson stormed his disapproval. It was unbelievable, he said, that such things could happen "in free America." The New York ordeal had been nothing short of "terrorism," Johnson complained. The California Senator, incensed at the danger to freedom and liberty, said that "the only place left in all this land where liberty finally may have its fight made for it, and where freedom may be protected, is right here in this body." [48] Senator Sherman asked if the writ of habeas corpus had been suspended, and Johnson replied that when such an event as the New York raids was possible it "has been in fact suspended." [49] Even Senator Fall joined the critics: "Never in the history of Germany, until military rule was declared, could such acts as this have been committed. Never in the history of any civilized country under the heavens, except in the history of Russia, could such acts have been committed." [50] Senator Chamberlain, normally not sensitive about civil rights in wartime, said there was absolutely no authority for such action in the Selective Service Act,[51] and Senator Frelinghuysen argued that the law was not to be enforced "by press-gang methods." [52] Chamberlain said that slackers should be reached by due process of law. The country, he continued, "will not stand it to have innocent young men rounded up and imprisoned." [53]

However, there were those both inside and outside of Congress who approved the use of dragonnades. Senator Kirby told his colleagues not to get "unduly excited" over the methods used to enforce the conscription law. It is better, he said, that "some individuals are inconvenienced or individual rights are infringed or invaded more or less . . . than that the law shall not be enforced." Senator Jones resented the criticism of some of his colleagues. "Instead of trying to cast aspersions or to unfavorably criticize such efforts," he said, "we should commend these actions as patriotic American citizens." [54] On the same theme the editor of the Tulsa *Daily World* wrote on September 9, "It seems to the *World* that there is no occasion and little justification for the torrent of criticism by Senators upon Government officials for the slacker raids."

The Senate gave brief consideration to investigating conditions surrounding the slacker raids, but dropped the idea when President Wilson asked Attorney General Gregory to report on the matter. Gregory wrote to the President on September 9 that he accepted full responsibility for the raids. He explained that his orders against using military personnel and members of the American Protective League had been ignored, and that arrests by such persons had been illegal and "ill-judged." But he denied the practicality of trying to round up large numbers of draft dodgers individually. "Some form of dragnet process," he said, "within the law of course, was absolutely essential." Gregory said he planned to continue the procedure unless Wilson directed otherwise.[55]

Since the war was nearly over, such vigorous and extensive roundups as that in New York were not repeated. But the apprehension of evaders did not stop. Brief news items continued to appear in different parts of the country, telling of individual attempts to avoid the hated conscription. Some brothers in Wisconsin objected to registering on religious grounds. A posse went after them and a pitched battle resulted. Two were killed, others were wounded, a barn was burned, and excitement —locally—was high.[56] Such stories were told in other areas. As late as 1920 there was talk of another general roundup of draft dodgers in New York, but it was never carried out. At that time the War Department had a record of 173,911 draft evaders or delinquents, of whom 7,500 were in the Empire State.[57] Altogether, there were 337,649 evaders or delinquents of one kind or another, including 163,738 who had been apprehended or whose cases had been disposed of before July 15, 1919.[58] Many of this class of war opponent, however, were never caught or punished.

THE I.W.W. ON TRIAL

As already indicated, members of the I.W.W. were probably subjected to more severe treatment than any other category of war opponents. This was true not only because I.W.W.'s opposed the war, but
also because members of the organization were the victims of a determined conservative campaign to stamp out radical social and economic
ideas. Conservatives may be among the first to deny class feeling, but
this drive had all the earmarks of a class war.

Throughout 1918 and 1919 three great mass trials were held involving I.W.W.'s who had been arrested in late 1917 or early 1918. The
best known and most important case concerned William D. Haywood
and 112 other defendants at Chicago. The other leading cases were decided at Sacramento and Kansas City. The latter trial did not end until
December 18, 1919, over a year after the armistice.

In reviewing these cases, it is essential to remember that, by the
time the trials were held, public opinion against the I.W.W. had been
whipped up to a fever pitch in many localities. Moreover, attacks against
individual members and the organization in general continued during
the trials, making it difficult, if not impossible, for jurors to reach unbiased decisions based strictly on the evidence.

While the Chicago case was getting under way in the spring of
1918, there were frequent reports of beatings, jailings, and indictments
against I.W.W.'s in many parts of the country. For example, on May 1
a raid on the I.W.W. in Detroit resulted in the arrest of some 1,200 persons.[1] The following day members of the union were arrested in Seattle.
The Seattle *Post-Intelligencer* said on May 3, "Reds Hall Cleaned Up and

Locked." This was part of Mayor Ole Hanson's campaign to wipe out the organization in Seattle. "All were arrested," continued the *Post-Intelligencer* story, "who, in the opinion of the chief [of police] did not come up to the mark exacted by Uncle Sam of its loyal citizens during the present trying times." Most of the men were soon released, but that was not front-page news.

On May 16 the *Post-Intelligencer* reported the arrest of a man who was trying to raise defense funds for those in jail. A few weeks later, when members of the I.W.W. tried to hold a meeting outside of town in a nearby woods, police broke it up. The police chief told the Seattle "Minute Men" not to allow any I.W.W. gatherings in that vicinity.[2] Early in June at Susanville, California, an I.W.W. was arrested and jailed for thirty days when he disregarded orders to leave town.[3] And the press kept up a constant attack. The *Sacramento Bee* editorialized on July 1, 1918, "There must be no leniency to the damnable I.W.W. They are traitors to the Government. There is evidence that they are in the pay of Germany. They fomented strikes during the darkest hour of the nation's peril and the safety of the nation itself demands their extermination."

This attitude was also reflected in Montana. There an I.W.W. remarked with appropriate epithets, "We are going to win the [Chicago] case." He was promptly arrested and convicted of sedition, although the decision was subsequently reversed.[4] The *New Republic* carried an advertisement signed by John Dewey, Thorstein Veblen, Carlton J. H. Hayes, Helen Keller, and others asking for assurance of a fair trial for the I.W.W.'s. The magazine was advised by an agent of the Department of Justice not to reprint it, under threat of getting into difficulty with the law.[5]

In April, while the trial was still in its preliminary stages, the American Civil Liberties Union published a pamphlet, *The Truth About the I.W.W.* Among the editors were John Graham Brooks, Robert W. Bruere, and Carleton H. Parker. The purpose, it was said, was to present to a wider public the results of various government investigations of the I.W.W. which had been made during the war. The Department of Justice even took steps to hamper the distribution of this little booklet.

Enemies of the I.W.W. were quick to take up the cudgels in defense of righteousness and respectability. In July a pamphlet was written by T. Everett Harré entitled *The I.W.W.: An Auxiliary of the German Espionage System*, with an introduction by Ralph M. Easley. This was given wide circulation in order to counteract the American Civil Liberties

Union pamphlet. Easley said there was an organized attempt to influence the Government's effort to convict the I.W.W.'s at Chicago. "This intensely partisan, mushy and grotesque attempt to paint this criminal organization in the hues of a lily," Easley said, was designed to confuse the public mind.[6] Harré wrote that the I.W.W. must be "stamped out; made impotent or utterly destroyed." [7]

Worst of all from the viewpoint of the defendants was the pernicious and constant interference by federal agents, the post office department, and local authorities with those trying to help in the I.W.W. defense. A memorandum in the American Civil Liberties Union files noted that Department of Justice agents "arrested the active members of I.W.W. defense committees at many points in the country, stopped their meetings, and seized their funds. This was done at Seattle, New York City, San Francisco and other places." The report continued, "First class mail from the general defense committee was held up in such quantities in Chicago in the months of January and February, 1918, that the defense committee was obliged to resort to subterfuge to get its matter into the mails." [8] In fact, Senator King said during the debate on the Sedition Bill that he favored giving the Postmaster General increased powers for this very reason. "Thousands of dollars are being sent to Mr. Haywood and other leaders of the Industrial Workers of the World," he said. The Sedition Act, King declared, would keep those who published disloyal literature from receiving contributions through the mails.[9] Such was the atmosphere in which the Chicago trial opened in April before Judge K. M. Landis.

Following the government raids on various I.W.W. offices on September 5, 1917, some 166 men had been arrested. The names of all these persons had been included in the original indictment, but 53 of the defendants were finally dismissed on lack of evidence, including Arturo Giovannitti, one of the editors of the *Masses*.[10] This left 113 to stand trial.

The general charge against the defendants was conspiracy against the war program of the United States. The first count accused them of conspiring to obstruct, hinder, and delay by strikes and acts of violence the production and transportation of certain war supplies. The second count charged the defendants with conspiracy to intimidate and to interfere with persons in their free right to execute certain contracts. The prosecution introduced much evidence in an attempt to substantiate these two industrial counts.

The third and fourth counts were based upon written or oral opposition to conscription or to the war. The third count charged the defendants with being members of the I.W.W. and conspiring to commit thousands of offenses against the United States, each consisting of unlawfully inducing and aiding young men of military age not to register or to desert after their induction into the military forces of the United States. The fourth count accused the I.W.W.'s of conspiracy to cause insubordination in American military and naval forces, and of obstructing recruiting and enlistment by speeches and articles. A fifth count, charging the defendants with illegal use of the mails, was thrown out before the case went to the jury.[11]

After some 29 days had been spent examining veniremen, the trial really got started on May 1. Although it had been announced by government attorneys that the I.W.W. as an organization was not on trial, it soon became apparent that the prosecution was basing its case on much more than specific and provable acts of law violation. When the trial opened, the Government's chief counsel, Frank K. Nebeker, alluded to specific illegal offenses. But he also assailed the entire organization, its principles, and objectives. When it became difficult to prove that various defendants had committed specific unlawful acts, the prosecution introduced voluminous evidence—pamphlets, editorials, letters, etc.—to prove that I.W.W. members were engaged in a great conspiracy against the Government. Files and data taken from I.W.W. offices on and after September 5, 1917, furnished a vast supply of material on which to draw.

The revolutionary philosophy of the I.W.W. was given prominent attention by the prosecution. The I.W.W. preamble, criticisms of the capitalist class, advocacy of the general strike, and talk of sabotage were held up as proof of disloyalty, along with scores of pamphlets and statements denouncing the war.[12]

Much of the written evidence introduced by the Government antedated the entry of the United States into war. Letters referring to sabotaging railroads and burning threshing machines were as old as 1913 and 1914.[13] George F. Vanderveer, principal attorney for the defendants, strenuously objected to admitting such evidence. But Judge Landis permitted it in order to show the frame of mind or the intent of the I.W.W. Vanderveer also was overruled when he objected to questions which, in light of the charges, seemed irrelevant. "Do you believe in the ceremony of marriage?" one defendant was asked. "I believe in the ceremony of marriage," he replied. "Is that the common belief of the members of your organization?" continued the prosecutor. Landis did not agree to Vanderveer's objection that such questioning was not permissible cross-examination.[14] It was evident that this line of questioning was designed to create prejudice in the minds of jurors by trying to show that I.W.W.'s opposed marriage and favored free love.

A number of letters written either by or to Haywood were introduced in evidence. For instance, Haywood wrote on July 7, 1917, in reply to an inquiry on registering for the draft, that "while no official stand has been taken by the organization on the question of registration . . . still nothing has been left undone to help out the boys arrested for evading registration." [15] Some pamphlets and articles became part of the record even though they had not been written by any of the defendants. This, of course, was to buttress the indictment with as many data as possible on the revolutionary characteristics of the I.W.W. [16]

Perhaps the most damaging evidence against the defendants, although it could have related only to a few of them, was a piece of paper purported to contain the formal antiwar position of the I.W.W.'s executive board. While the statement had not been distributed as an official document, an editorial had appeared in *Solidarity* which was very similar in thought and expression. It declared opposition to all wars and threatened to oust any member of the I.W.W. who joined the American military forces. The statement warned against letting "the masters of industry, under the cloak of 'military expediency' " destroy the I.W.W. organization. Referring to the right to organize and the rights of free speech and press, the statement continued, "These tyrannical acts and usurpations of power, we can not and shall not tolerate without protest and resistance by all methods within our power." [17]

Writings in the I.W.W. paper, *Solidarity*, were introduced to give further support to the indictments. On May 12, 1917, *Solidarity* had carried a bitter attack on the proposed Selective Service Act. This, said the writer, was the "rankest, rawest, crudest piece of work that was ever attempted to be 'put over' in the interests of Big Business underlying the mask of 'patriotism.' " [18] Evidence was also presented to show that some of the defendants had advocated sabotage.

For their part, the defendants frankly admitted that they had written and spoken against the war and against conscription. They denied, however, that any conspiracy had existed. They argued that their criticism of government policy was spontaneous, as was that of many other people. The strikes in which the I.W.W. had engaged were not designed to cripple war production, it was said, but to remedy economic grievances of long standing. [19] Defense counsel contended that there was no specific evidence against a number of the men, except that they were members of the I.W.W.

After weeks of argument and counterargument the case finally went to the jury. The Government had presented 144 witnesses and the defense 184, 84 of whom were the defendants themselves.[20]

Although it was common knowledge that Judge Landis was hostile to all radical groups, it was generally conceded that he had conducted the case in a fairly judicious manner with the possible exception of permitting questionable cross-examination. His charge to the jury appeared unbiased. Landis told the jurors, "Now, our industrial society is not on trial here . . . . Organized labor is not on trial." He emphasized that passive knowledge of criminal or illegal acts was not enough to warrant conviction and that it was necessary to show active and individual participation. Landis explained that he had admitted prewar evidence only "to enable the jury to come to an understanding of the frame of mind of the men accused here as conspirators." [21]

On August 30, after deliberating only fifty-five minutes, the jury brought in a verdict of guilty on all counts for ninety-six men. The sentences which followed ranged from one year in prison and a thirty-thousand-dollar fine for the unknown Charles R. Jacobs to twenty years and a thirty-thousand-dollar fine for Haywood. Fourteen of the defendants were given twenty years in the penitentiary along with twenty- or thirty-thousand-dollar fines; thirty-three were given ten years; another thirty-three, five years; twelve, one year; one, eighteen months; and two, only a few days.[22] Some of the sentences were unusual and appeared unbalanced, for example, the combination of one year in jail and a thirty-thousand-dollar fine. The heaviest fines and longest prison terms were given to the I.W.W. leaders and to the aliens.

If Judge Landis had been restrained during the trial, he shed his judicial composure when he pronounced the sentences. Landis declared that the jury could not possibly have reached any other conclusion. The defendants, he said, were guilty beyond doubt. "In times of peace," Landis advised, "you have a legal right to oppose, by free speech, preparations for war. But when once war is declared, that right ceases." [23]

As Judge Landis read off the sentences there was weeping and an occasional groan. Some of the defendants paled; others tried to get to their wives or other relatives. The wholesale convictions and stiff sentences were obviously unexpected. The result of the trial, Haywood was quoted as saying, "was a great surprise. I can't understand how some of us were not acquitted at a moment's notice. I rather looked for a hung jury on some of us." [24]

The convictions were widely hailed throughout the country, and they

BILL HAYWOOD
HEAD OF I.W.W.

—Photo by Harris & Ewing, Washington, D.C.

Eugene V. Debs

aroused an even more clamorous demand for the Government to stamp out the I.W.W. forever. The trial, said the *Boston Transcript,* would "stamp the organization with infamy in the minds of citizens." According to the *Kansas City Journal,* the I.W.W. had been revealed in all its "hellish character as the Bolsheviki of America." The time had come, said the writer, for the Government to "wipe out the I.W.W., the Non-Partisan League, the radical Socialists, and all other Un-American and anti-American organizations on this continent." The *Pittsburgh Post* advised that, since the I.W.W. had been proved treacherous, the country should wage war against the organization until it was crushed. In Los Angeles, the *Times* warned that anyone who might yet sympathize with the I.W.W. "ought to be either on trial himself or else held under mighty close watch." [25] The *Christian Science Monitor* editorialized on September 4 that every sentence in a certain I.W.W. publication printed in February, 1917, was treasonable. The I.W.W. could have reversed its policy after the war began, the editor continued, but "it rushed headlong into treachery, sedition, and treason."

Occasionally, however, other viewpoints were expressed. The Springfield *Republican* agreed that justice had been done, but added, "Let even the Haywoods teach us something. Let us counteract their passion for anarchy with our own passion for democracy and justice. By reaching down to the depths and rescuing from exploitation and oppression the humblest and most helpless of wage earners we may put the revolutionary I.W.W. out of business—but not before." [26] To a later generation of Americans this advice made sense, but in 1918 it was generally considered nonsense. As the Tulsa *Daily World* had said earlier, the way to deal with a snake was not to scotch it, but to kill it. Regardless of public opinion, the Attorney General could report that he believed the trial would "have a beneficial effect in checking the unlawful features of the activities of this organization." [27]

In retrospect, the I.W.W. trial in Chicago seems to have been a weird combination of justice and injustice. There was no doubt that some of the individuals on trial had violated specific provisions of the Espionage Act. These men deserved punishment. The principal objection to the trial was the careless inclusion of people against whom no serious evidence was presented other than that they were members of the I.W.W. At least two of the defendants were not even affiliated with that organization. Later the Attorney General frankly admitted this situation. Referring to defendant Charles Ashleigh, he wrote, "He was a writer and speaker of some note, and while there was no proof of overt act on his part, he cooperated with leading I.W.W.'s up to, and immediately following, the declaration of war by this country. . . . Very little . . . was shown concerning his activities after the war began." [28] Almost the same words were used in regard to Jack Law and Vincent St. John. When he recommended commuting Clyde Hough's sentence, the Attorney General wrote, "It appeared . . . with regard to the espionage act, for violation of which he was also convicted, that the applicant was confined in jail for nine days before that act was passed and continuously thereafter and accordingly had had no opportunity to violate the provisions of that act." [29]

In light of such statements, it seems clear that the I.W.W. as an organization was on trial—and was convicted. As explained earlier, much of the evidence did not deal with specific acts of individual lawlessness, but with I.W.W. philosophy and objectives. It is not likely that people not members of the I.W.W. would have been convicted on the same type of evidence.[30]

Haywood and the other defendants appealed the decision, but with only minor success. Defense counsel argued that seizure of material in I.W.W. offices which was later used against the defendants was in effect making them testify against themselves in violation of the Fourth Amendment. But the Court held that this was not the case. I.W.W. lawyers also maintained that evidence submitted on discouraging enlistments antedated the Espionage Act and the Sedition Act and therefore was not admissible. But the Appellate Court decided that it was legal to admit such evidence "as bearing on defendants' possession and knowledge of the use of the means by which these felonies could be committed." It bore directly on "criminal intent," said the Court.[31]

The appeal judges, however, did modify the trial court's decision by dismissing the convictions on the first two counts. But this did not affect the sentences or the fines. Convictions on counts three and four were enough to provide the maximum sentence, since the sentences ran concurrently on all counts. For example, Haywood was given six and ten years respectively on counts one and two, and two and twenty years on counts three and four.[32] But the decision of the higher court did mean that the convictions were based mainly upon written and spoken opposition to the war and to conscription. The case did not go beyond the circuit court as the Supreme Court denied an appeal for a writ of certiorari.

The next mass trial resulted from arrests of I.W.W.'s around Fresno and Sacramento, California, both before and after the bombing of Governor Stephens' residence in December, 1917.[33] Within a few weeks, over fifty men were being held at Sacramento and indictments were brought in February, 1918.

Yet there was no move for an immediate trial. While waiting for the slow wheels of justice to turn, the prisoners were sometimes confined in a space so small that some of them had to stand or sit up in order to make room for the others to lie down to sleep. They had to sleep on the floor, even in winter, without sufficient coverings. The food was poor and medical treatment virtually nonexistent. According to Dowell, "five of the defendants died in jail, one from tuberculosis and four from the influenza epidemic." [34]

The indictment against the California I.W.W.'s was similar to that used in the Chicago trial. The four counts included charges of conspiring to prevent and delay the execution of certain laws passed to prosecute the war; interference with those furnishing supplies for the war effort; influencing men not to enlist in the army and navy; and violation of the Espionage Act by interfering with the military and naval forces of the United States.[35] There was nothing in the indictment about dynamiting the Governor's mansion. The charges were based mainly on writings found in the personal possession of the accused or in I.W.W. offices. One of the defendants was accused of transporting nine sticks of dynamite under "false and deceptive markings." [36]

In preparing their defense, the I.W.W. met unrelenting resistance. Because of high feeling locally against the I.W.W., it was impossible to set up a defense office in Sacramento. A defense committee office was established in San Francisco, but even there the office was raided seven times in six months. Secretary A. L. Fox was arrested for vagrancy fifteen times in four months. Some of those who were active in defending the prisoners were also indicted.[37] Theodora Pollock was arrested when she sought to bail out one of the defendants, James Price, and the thousand dollars found on her was impounded for a long time when it was badly needed for defense expenses.[38]

Frederick Esmond, an I.W.W. publicity man, was arrested, let out on bail, and then rearrested after he began exposing jail conditions in Sacramento.[39] On February 1, 1918, A. L. Fox sent a telegram to the United States District Attorney in which he said, "Today registering strong remonstrance . . . inhuman treatment I.W.W. Federal prisoners your custody Sacramento." He also denounced the District Attorney's personal conduct and the "lying press stories." Strange as it may seem, this and similar telegrams protesting prison conditions were later incorporated in the charges against some of the defendants.[40]

The inclusion of Miss Pollock among the defendants aroused some criticism. The main charge against her was that she had written an antiwar poem some time before April, 1917. Late in September, 1918, but before the trial started, a Californian explained to President Wilson that she was "a young woman of good antecedents and position" and was a former social worker in California. Having become interested in, and concerned over, the conditions of seasonal workers in California, she had joined the I.W.W. and had become a member of its Defense Committee at the time of the Mooney prosecution. Actually, said the writer, there was nothing against Miss Pollock except "that she is a member of the I.W.W. organization." This charge, he said, was "tantamount to conviction in California."[41] On October 3, 1918, William Kent wrote to Wilson, "No one denies the gentle character of this lady, and no one has any fear of her action or influence. That she should be indicted for writing a fool poem that never was published and which was unobjectionable . . . adds absurdity to a situation otherwise horribly tragic."[42]

Perhaps because of these letters, Wilson asked Gregory for information. The Attorney General sent him a report from an agent in California which stated that Miss Pollock was dangerous. He reported she was an internationalist, indifferent to the Government and to war, and that she favored abolishing the wage system. After studying this report, Wilson wrote, "I have now gone very carefully over the case of Miss Pollock with the Attorney General, and am sorry to tell you that I think you have got the wrong impression about the evidence against her. It is very considerable in volume and very serious in character."[43]

At last, on December 7, 1918, after spending about a year in jail, forty-six defendants stood trial. As had been true at Chicago, the prosecuting attorneys directed their main attack at the entire I.W.W. organization. Again much was made of the I.W.W. preamble, articles from *Solidarity*,[44] and booklets and pamphlets which had been published and distributed by the I.W.W. Evidence was also presented in an effort to connect the defendants with fires and other reported acts of sabotage. Witnesses for the prosecution, reported one observer, displayed amazing memories.[45]

Most of the defendants were convinced that a fair trial was impossible. Justice, they said, could not be obtained. Therefore, forty-three of the forty-six under indictment entered a "silent defense," refusing to testify or acknowledge the existence of the court. A reporter was told by one of the accused: "When one has been arrested fifteen times in four months as a 'vagrant,' although actively employed and under salary all that time; when one has been repeatedly arrested, held for days and then dismissed without trial, only to be re-arrested the following day; when the crimes charged against one multiply overnight, is it to be wondered at that the defendants wearily say, 'What's the use?' " [46]

Describing the trial, one defendant wrote that the courtroom was closed because of fear of influence "from the organization." Then he continued:

> The few reporters and an occasional visitor, admitted by officials as they choose, sit at a table at the side of the room . . . . Theo [Pollock] sits at the table with the two lawyers and I sit just behind her with the 44 men defendants to either side and behind me. They listen, read occasionally from books carried in their pockets, smile or chuckle occasionally . . . . The guards sit behind and to either side of the prisoners—a lot of them—great huskies. The prisoners are ragged, unkempt, unshaven. The sheriff gives them no razors, of course, and charges them a dollar, I am told, for a shave. And, naturally, they haven't the dollar. Their clothes are worn and thin— summer underwear and not enough. Their cells get no sunlight—are chill. They—*we all*, including Theo and me—have colds and coughs, as has the judge, as have some of the lawyers . . . . I can't hear the witnesses, because of the coughing. We are not consenting to be depressed, but just ready—for anything. Anything, that is, except that Theo should be the martyr the prosecution longs to make her . . . . I am reading President Wilson's *New Freedom*. I confess I'm absolutely at sea. I *can't* understand.[47]

On January 16, 1919, all forty-six were found guilty. The three defendants who had attorneys received light sentences of two months in the San Francisco jail, and, in the case of Theodora Pollock, a hundred-dollar fine. Those who maintained a defiant attitude—the silent defenders—were made to pay for their intransigent disrespect for the court. Ten-year sentences were given to twenty-four, three got five years each, and the rest were given lesser prison terms. An appeal, heard in 1921, failed to alter the trial court's decision.[48]

Mass conviction of I.W.W.'s in Chicago and Sacramento still left another large group awaiting trial in Kansas. In November, 1917, there was a general roundup of I.W.W.'s in parts of Oklahoma and Kansas. This followed the mob action at Tulsa. Between thirty and forty men were arrested, and in March, 1918, they were indicted for violating the Espionage Act. While waiting to stand trial the men were placed in jails at Hutchinson, Wichita, Topeka, and other Kansas towns. In September, shortly before the armistice, a motion was upheld to quash the indictment, but the same day a new indictment was made. Attorneys for the I.W.W. then asked that the new indictment be quashed and Judge John C. Pollock of the United States District Court sustained the motion on June 7, 1919.[49] By that time fifty-two I.W.W.'s were being held.

In order to keep the men from being released, Fred Robertson, United States District Attorney, successfully moved to have them reindicted. Nonetheless, attorneys did get some of the defendants freed on bail. The legal battle continued until December 1, 1919, when thirty-three members of the I.W.W. were finally placed on trial at Kansas City.

Meanwhile, a vigorous effort was being made to run all I.W.W.'s out of Kansas. Five alleged I.W.W.'s were arrested at Hutchinson on June 12 and charged with "fomenting revolution." Robertson was quoted as saying, "We are not going to waste a minute with these trouble makers." [50] Gripped with fright by the Big Red Scare, people, if anything, were even more hysterical in 1919 than they had been during the war. Early in May, Seattle's Red baiter, Ole Hanson, requested mayors of American cities "to close all I.W.W. halls" and "throw the teachers of force and violence in jail." [51]

The Kansas City trial followed the general pattern laid down in Chicago and Sacramento. About the same charges and arguments were made.[52] Twenty-six defendants, some of whom had been in jail for about two years, were found guilty and given sentences ranging from three to six years.[53] The case was appealed to the Circuit Court which, in May, 1921, threw out the first count of the indictment. This had charged that the defendants had conspired "by force to prevent, hinder or delay the execution" of certain United States laws. The evidence, said the court, was not sufficient to sustain this count.[54] As a result of this decision, nineteen men were released since their conviction had been based largely on the first count of the indictment.

Altogether, 168 I.W.W.'s were convicted during the three mass trials. Evidence of violating specific laws was clear and unmistakable against some individuals. In other cases, the evidence was fuzzy and of such a nature that it was difficult to be certain about the defendants' innocence or guilt. In still other cases, the charges were so vague and the evidence so meager that one must conclude that some men were convicted primarily because they were members of the I.W.W. The cases were not settled so much by the fine points of law as by the atmosphere of the times. A reporter for the *New York Times*, probably unwittingly, summarized the situation quite accurately. When he began his story of the Kansas City trial, he wrote, "The I.W.W. as an organization was placed on trial here today." [55]

▄▄▄

"The master class has always declared the wars; the
subject class has always fought the battles."

THE UNITED STATES
V. EUGENE V. DEBS

As radicals throughout the land were imprisoned for opposing the
war, the outstanding radical of them all, Eugene V. Debs, was still at
large. Perhaps the Administration did not want to move against him, for
Debs was an important and influential person, a man with a large and
loyal following. He had a strange and unique personal charm which
drew men to him. As one admirer expressed it, to meet him was a sacra-
ment. Indeed, many of his followers sounded more like converts than
like members of a political party.[1]

For years Debs had opposed war. The platform on which he made
his first race for president in 1900 had denounced it. Yet it must be said
that Debs had little real understanding of international affairs. Like most
other Socialists, he opposed war because he believed that it resulted
from capitalist greed and rivalry. From the beginning Debs had opposed
the moves which finally led the United States into actual participation
in the European holocaust. By 1918 he had long since parted intellectual
company with such propreparedness and prowar Socialists as Charles Edward Russell and Upton Sinclair. Debs had repeatedly said that he
favored only one war—the "world-wide war of the social revolution."[2]

As his Socialist friends were arrested and jailed for speaking out
against the war, Debs became outraged. He assailed the mob violence,
some of which occurred in his home town of Terre Haute. But throughout 1917 Debs had not taken a leading part in fighting conscription, the
Liberty Loan drives, or any of the policies which made the war possible.

He was, as Ray Ginger has written, "hesitant and floundering." [3] He held numerous meetings in Ohio during 1917, mostly in the homes of friends, but they were poorly attended and went virtually without notice.

By late 1917 and early 1918, however, Debs was becoming more militant. The conviction of his beloved Comrade Kate Richards O'Hare in December, 1917, had aroused his deep and bitter indignation. In his speeches throughout early 1918, he defended with increasing boldness those who had been convicted for violating the Espionage Act. Also, he was becoming impatient and distressed with some Socialists who were either partially or wholly supporting President Wilson's peace aims. He denounced them in strong terms.

By the summer of 1918, Debs had decided that he must abandon any appearance of restraint and assail the war with even greater vigor. He deliberately intended to use extreme language in order to dramatize his position and stir up more opposition to the war. By using militant words, he would also dare the government authorities to arrest and place him on trial. "Debs was determined either to open the prison gates or to swing them shut behind himself." [4] He had no right to be free, Debs thought, when others were in prison for saying what he believed. In December, 1917, he had written to Kate O'Hare, "I cannot yet believe that they will ever dare to send you to prison for exercising your constitutional rights of free speech, but if they do . . . I shall feel guilty to be at large." [5]

Debs chose to make his stand at Canton, Ohio, where he spoke before the Ohio State Socialist convention on June 16, 1918. During the preceding weeks he had attacked the President, denounced federal officials, and criticized the war. Yet he had not been arrested. At Canton, however, he became even more outspoken and talked himself into a place of top leadership among the opponents of war. Undoubtedly Debs was aroused by his visit, just before starting his address, with Alfred Wagenknecht, Charles E. Ruthenberg, and Charles Baker, prominent Ohio Socialists who were then in the Stark County Workhouse across the street from where he spoke. These friends had been convicted for violating the Selective Service Act.

Debs began by ironically observing that it was "extremely dangerous to exercise the constitutional right of free speech in a country fighting to make democracy safe in the world." But he was not to be deterred by any such dangers. "I would rather a thousand times be a free soul in jail than to be a sycophant and coward in the streets," he continued. When the shouts and applause subsided, he said, "They may put those

boys in jail—and some of the rest of us in jail—but they can not put
the Socialist movement in jail."

Then for two hours Debs proceeded to praise the Socialist movement, to predict its ultimate success, and to indict American capitalist
society in the most scathing terms. For the most part, the speech was a
determined and rousing bid for Socialist support. Debs said things
that he had said many times before. But parts of the speech went further.

The old Socialist denied that, just because they opposed the war,
Socialists favored German militarism. The Socialists, he said, had been
fighting German militarism "since the day the Socialist movement was
born." And he added that thousands of Socialists "have languished in
the jails of Germany because of their heroic warfare upon the despotic
ruling class of that country." Then Debs continued by recalling how
Theodore Roosevelt had "visited all the capitals of Europe, and . . . was
wined and dined, dignified and glorified by all the Kaisers and Czars
and Emperors of the old world." He declared that "while Roosevelt was
being entertained royally by the German Kaiser, that same Kaiser was
putting the leaders of the Socialist Party in jail for fighting the Kaiser
and Junkers of Germany. Roosevelt was the guest of honor in the White
House of the Kaiser, while the Socialists were in the jails of the Kaiser,
for fighting the Kaiser. Who was fighting for democracy? Roosevelt?"
Answering his own question, Debs said: "I challenge you to find any
Socialist who was ever the guest of the Kaiser, except as one of his prison
wards . . . . Do not imagine for one moment that all the plutocrats and
Junkers are in Germany; we have them here in our own country, and
those want to keep our eyes focused upon the Junkers in Germany so
we won't see those within our own border."

After excoriating the "Wall Street Junkers," Debs said: "These are
the gentry who are today wrapped up in the American flag, who shout
their claim from the housetops that they are the only patriots, and who
have their magnifying glasses in hand, scanning the country for evidence of disloyalty, eager to apply the brand of treason to the men who
dare to even whisper their opposition to junker rule in the United States."

During his address, Debs defended Tom Mooney, charging that
Mooney was the innocent victim of the "powerful and corrupt corpora-
tions" in California. And he did not overlook the I.W.W. then on trial
in Chicago. "There are few men who have the courage to say a word
in favor of the I.W.W. I have," Debs said. Judges and the courts were
not spared, as Debs ranged the field of what he considered corrupt capi-

talist institutions. Referring to a recent five to four decision of the Supreme Court in the child labor case, he called it "a kind of craps game."

In contrast, Debs overflowed with praise of the Russian Revolution. "All our hearts now throb as one great heart responsive to the battle-cry of the social revolution," he said. "Here, in this alert and inspiring assemblage our hearts are with the Bolsheviki of Russia." At that time, Debs hoped that the Russian radicals would share his ideals. He also had the practical desire to keep Russian and pro-Russian elements satisfied within the American Socialist party. In both cases he was to be disappointed. The Bolsheviki tyranny was far removed from Debs' humanitarianism, and the radical elements among the Socialists were to withdraw and form the Communist Labor party in September, 1919.

Debs did not limit his remarks to a general attack on the capitalist class. He tied it closely to wars, their causes, and destruction. "The master class has always declared the wars; the subject class has always fought the battles. The master class has had all to gain and nothing to lose, while the subject class has had nothing to gain and all to lose— especially their lives," Debs shouted. Aiming his blows at the cowardly press and subservient clergy, Debs declared, "When Wall Street says war the press says war and the pulpit promptly follows with its *Amen.*"

Perhaps government agents were most annoyed at Debs' open and emphatic expression of sympathy for war opponents then in jail. Referring to Rose Pastor Stokes, he declared, "Why the other day they sent a woman to Wichita Penitentiary for ten years. Just think of sentencing a woman to the penitentiary for talking." Then he added that "the United States under the rule of the plutocrats is the only country which would send a woman to the penitentiary for ten years for exercising the right of free speech. If this be treason, let them make the most of it." [6]

As Debs had spoken a government stenographer had taken down his speech. At the same time, agents of the Department of Justice went through the crowd demanding to see the draft registration cards of the young men present. It had been an orderly meeting, but as the cheering Socialists left two things were clear: Debs had emphatically stated his antiwar position; and he would undoubtedly suffer the consequences. [7]

About two weeks later, on June 29, Debs was indicted for violating the Espionage Act. He was accused of attempting to incite insubordination, disloyalty, and mutiny in the American military and naval forces; of having obstructed recruiting; of having uttered and published language intended to provoke and encourage resistance to the United States;

and of having "feloniously" made certain false statements intended to promote the success of Germany.[8]

The trial began on September 9 in Cleveland, Ohio, before Judge D. C. Westenhaver, a former law partner of Newton D. Baker.[9] It was a short and dramatic affair, lasting only from the ninth to the twelfth of September. There was no long debate over evidence, no squabble over the suitability of jurors, or any of the other things that had characterized the trials of so many other antiwar radicals.

When the prosecution opened its case, it became clear that Assistant District Attorney F. B. Kavanaugh considered Debs' conviction of utmost importance. Pointing at the defendant, he said, "This man is the palpitating pulse of the sedition crusade."[10] One of the main witnesses for the prosecution was Clyde R. Miller, a Cleveland newspaper reporter. He testified to the accuracy of the Canton speech and also about interviews which he had held with Debs. Other witnesses told of Debs' earlier antiwar statements. Joseph Triner, whose memory was notably vague, recalled that Debs had said a few weeks before: "A working man has no place in a capitalist's war such as this. The only war in which I have any interest is that of the workers against the capitalists. They may call me a disloyalist and brand me a traitor, but I shall stick to my principles. The master class is pretending to wage this war for democracy, but by persecuting us they have branded this pretension a lie."[11] Despite the introduction of such statements, the different versions of Debs' Canton speech formed the principal evidence against him. It was sufficiently established that Debs had made antiwar statements and that men of military age were in the audience.

In his opening argument, Seymour Stedman of Debs' counsel asked if a court would "indict Woodrow Wilson because he wrote in his book *The New Freedom* that wars are brought about by the rulers and not by the people."[12] At this and other statements, some of Debs' friends in the courtroom began clapping. Judge Westenhaver immediately ordered them to be arrested, including Rose Pastor Stokes who was attending the trial while awaiting the decision in her own appeal to the Supreme Court. Mrs. Stokes and several others were fined.[13]

To the great surprise of many, when the prosecution rested its case the defense called no witnesses. Debs was ready to admit the facts presented by his prosecutors. It was agreed, however, that he should speak in his own behalf. Describing the circumstances, Max Eastman wrote: "It was dark when [Debs] began speaking, though only two o'clock in the afternoon, and as he continued it grew steadily darker, . . . and the windows looking black as at night-time with gathering thunder-clouds. His utterance became more clear and piercing against that impending shadow, and it made the simplicity of his faith seem almost like a portent in this time of terrible and dark events." [14]

Debs frankly admitted making the Canton speech, but he denied there was anything in it "to warrant the charges set out in the indictment." He said that he had nothing to retract. "When great changes occur in history, when great principles are involved," he said, "as a rule the majority are wrong." [15] Debs further admitted that he had expressed sympathy for his convicted Socialist friends and that he had praised the Bolsheviki. "I have been accused of having obstructed the war," he said. "I admit it. Gentlemen, I abhor war." Pointing to history, Debs reminded the jury that Christ had been crucified because the money changers, the high priests, and businessmen said he was preaching dangerous doctrine and inciting the people. Christ's enemies said of him "just what the ruling class says of the Socialist today," Debs continued.

Appealing for the right of free speech under the First Amendment, Debs declared: "I believe in the right of free speech, in war as well as in peace . . . . I would under no circumstances suppress free speech. It is far more dangerous to attempt to gag the people than to allow them to speak freely what is in their hearts." [16]

After Debs finished speaking, District Attorney Edwin S. Wertz reviewed the case for the prosecution. Charging that Debs had wilfully sought to obstruct the recruiting of military personnel, Wertz argued that it made no difference what Debs thought about the war. Congress had set the policies for all to follow. Wertz accused Debs of wanting to bring Bolshevism, anarchy, and misrule to the United States. The defendant did not want the Socialist party to change its views on the war, Wertz argued. Then the District Attorney declared that Debs and his kind had never produced anything except devilment and trouble, like the Bolsheviki in Russia. Whoever advocated such teaching, in Wertz' judgment, was a traitor and should be jailed or shot if the laws permitted. Referring to Debs as "an old ewe," Wertz ridiculed the defendant's idea of international friendship of all peoples. "I'll tell you what internationalism is," he exclaimed. "Pitch all the nations into one pot with the Socialists on top and you've got internationalism." [17]

After the arguments and speeches were over, it remained for the jury to decide the fate of Debs. It was a foregone conclusion, however, that he would be found guilty. The jury was made up of men averaging about seventy years of age whose average wealth was $50,000 or more. The economic problems about which Debs had spoken did not seem so real to them.

Before Debs was sentenced, he turned to the Court and said with his usual earnestness:

> Your honor, years ago I recognized my kinship with all living beings, and I made up my mind that I was not one bit better than the meanest on earth. I said then, and I say now, that while there is a lower class, I am in it, while there is a criminal element I am of it, and while there is a soul in prison, I am not free. I listened to all that was said in this court in support and justification of this prosecution, but my mind remains unchanged. I look upon the Espionage Law as a despotic enactment in flagrant conflict with democratic principles and with the spirit of free institutions.

Debs then added: "I ask no mercy, and I plead for no immunity. I realize that finally the right must prevail. I never so clearly comprehended as now the great struggle between the powers of greed and exploitation on the one hand and upon the other the rising hosts of industrial freedom and social justice." [18]

Debs was given a ten-year prison term. Before he began to serve his sentence, however, the case was appealed to the Supreme Court. As *amicus curiae,* Gilbert E. Roe filed a comprehensive brief attacking the constitutionality of the Espionage Act. He maintained that the law was never intended "to convert into a criminal act such discussion of public matters as is contained in the articles set forth in the indictment in this case." Referring to the Kentucky and Virginia Resolutions, he said: "The test is not whether the matter is true or false, or the motive good or bad. Intention has nothing to do with it . . . . It is time enough for the rightful purpose of civil government for its officers to interfere when principles break out into overt acts against peace and good order." He quoted Professor St. George Tucker, writing in 1803: "Every individual certainly has a right to speak or publish his sentiment on the measures of government; to do this without restraint, control or fear of punishment for so doing, is that which constitutes the genuine freedom of the press." Roe argued that unless this was right, "the free speech and free press clause of the Constitution is absolutely valueless." If a "jury is permitted to penalize public discussion of the measures of government," he continued, "because of the intent which the jury may find animated the discussion or the results which the jury is permitted to find [in the absence of evidence of any specific result], such discussion caused, then the constitutional guarantee of free speech and free press is wiped out." [19]

The Supreme Court decision was written by Justice Holmes and delivered on March 10, 1919. Two counts of the indictment remained against Debs. One charged him with attempting to incite insubordination and disloyalty in the military forces. The other accused him of obstructing the recruiting of troops. Holmes explained that the main theme of Debs' Canton speech had been the growth and development of Socialism. With that, he said, the Court was unconcerned. "But if a part of the manifest intent of the more general utterances was to encourage those present to obstruct the recruiting service . . . the immunity of the general theme may not be enough to protect the speech," Holmes wrote. Holmes quoted a number of antiwar statements by Debs, including his remark, "I have been accused of obstructing the war. I admit it. Gentlemen, I abhor war." Debs' strong opposition to the war was so expressed, Holmes continued, that the jury was convinced "its natural and intended effect would be to obstruct recruiting.[20] With this position the Court agreed, although it seemed inconsistent with the "clear and present danger" doctrine which Holmes himself had recently pronounced.

Within about a month Debs was on his way to the state penitentiary at Moundsville, West Virginia. After a short stay there, he was moved to Atlanta. The outstanding opponent of war had been silenced.

The *Nation* reported that Debs had gone to prison for an ancient and high cause—"the fundamental rights of man." A great person had been wronged, continued the writer, and "the hearts of true and independent men everywhere follow him with thankfulness as he goes to his high office." [21] However, the *New York Times* editorialized: "There is no reason for sympathy with Debs, except such as goes to a fighter who asks no odds. The law defines certain acts as crimes. These acts Debs proudly confessed." The *Times* editor denied the "impossible doctrine that he had full liberty to overturn the Constitution, but that the Government had no power to stay him." [22]

The trial and conviction of Debs emphasized the fact that, although the war was nearly over, the Government was in no mood to let up on opponents of war. The conviction of Debs under the Espionage Act, said a writer in *Survey*, "constitutes perhaps the highest point reached by the government in its efforts to punish violators of that act." [23]

▬▬▬▬▬▬▬▬▬▬▬▬▬▬▬▬▬▬▬▬▬▬▬▬▬▬▬▬▬▬▬▬▬▬▬

"Quit your crying, baby, lonely little waif,
Papa's in an iron cage to make your future safe.
All the other daddies have gone and left their wives,
And all the kids on our street are playing with their
    knives." [1]

A PRISON
FOR YOUR THOUGHTS

The California minister who wrote the above lines was one from
the new classes of people who suddenly had dealings with American
courts, jails, and penitentiaries. Their crime was not housebreaking,
arson, larceny, or murder, but opposition to war, to conscription, to repression. Although many of these people were political, economic, or
religious nonconformists, normally they had not had previous trouble
with the law. They had found, however, that wartime made a difference
with law and constitutional rights. How much more important seemed
prosecuting attorneys, judges, juries, bailiffs, lawyers, wardens—and
money. Most of these people were not men and women of substance,
and, quite probably, money itself assumed a new standing in their eyes.

The real ordeal for many war opponents was to be found in the city
jails, guardhouses, and penitentiaries. These cesspools of society contained about all the moral filth that could be accumulated in one place,
and it is doubtful if anyone came out of them entirely unmarked. Secretary of War Baker could write that conscientious objectors would be
imprisoned in Leavenworth "where the men have a wholesome outdoor
life and are kept busy upon things that are worth doing." [2] Some of the
objectors probably wished that Mr. Baker had a better understanding of
some of the conditions which existed at Fort Leavenworth. Even in the
best of the jails there was crudeness, dirt, and brutality—and Leavenworth was not the best.

It would be unrealistic and inaccurate to give a wholesale indictment of the conditions under which opponents of war were held. The reports of prisoners were, to be sure, generally highly critical of their treatment. Conditions of brutality described by some prisoners, even when discounted for exaggeration, almost defy the imagination of civilized people. It must be remembered, however, that the accounts of those in prison were prejudiced and often aimed at arousing sympathy from outsiders. Yet, despite all of this, there is abundant evidence that opponents of war, especially conscientious objectors, were often horribly treated. The files of the American Civil Liberties Union hold numerous accounts of such ill-treatment and in some cases record the death of prisoners.

As might be expected, some of the imprisoned Socialists complained bitterly because they had to work virtually without pay. This, they said, was an example of the extremes to which greedy capitalism would go in search of profits. For example, Kate Richards O'Hare, a mother and member of a fine family, made overalls, as did other women prisoners at the Missouri State Penitentiary. She and the others were being exploited, Mrs. O'Hare wrote, and the "profits from these chattel slaves are enormous. The state provides the building, heat, light, power, and convict labour, and the contractor pays the state a pittance for the right to exploit the prisoners and the taxpayers." Mrs. O'Hare claimed that she earned, even at nonunion sweatshop wages, from $4.80 to $5.20 a day. At that rate, she calculated her earnings at about $1,800 during her imprisonment, but she was paid only $10.50. She declared that "the difference between the wealth I created and the pittance paid me went, not into the treasury of the nation I was presumed to have injured, not into the treasury of the State of Missouri, but into the pockets of the prison contractor as profits." [3] Mrs. O'Hare charged that the prison was rife with petty graft. "I saw all manner of punishments and heartsickening brutalities," she said, "and in every single instance, except one, the fact that profits were threatened was the cause of the punishment." [4]

Mrs. O'Hare also complained about prison officials. The shop overseer, she said, "was coarse, vulgar, egotistical, bigoted, intolerant, and a sadist. In the prison shops his word was law, and any woman could be made the victim of his vicious temper and uncurbed brutality. His vocabulary was rich in unspeakably vile epithets and lurid profanity, and his favorite pastime was subjecting the women to his degenerate vulgarity, which they of course dared not resent." Pressure of work and the monotony of prison routine, she wrote, were "just about enough to wear a woman out physically and send her back to society fit only for the human scrap-heap or the potter's field." [5] Mrs. O'Hare also wrote about the "criminally stupid mixing of clean women with the frightfully syphilitic." She could never forget, she said, being forced to live "in constant danger of contamination from the most loathsome of all diseases because I held opinions contrary to the opinions of the party in power." [6]

There were many other types of complaints by the political prisoners. One radical opponent of war at Atlanta Penitentiary wrote on March 24, 1918: "The Warden [has held up] any literature favoring Tom Mooney and San Francisco cases. He told me in an interview recently that 'I will put you in the hole, yes in the dungeon, for all the rest of your time and you will lose good time, too, where you will not see a God damn person, if I hear of you saying anything in favor of Socialism or against the war.'" The writer stated further: "The warden personally reads all mail of we [sic] radicals. Our letters are returned upon the slightest pretext. He will not allow [Alexander] Berkman to talk to any of the prisoners—a guard watches him every minute." The report also referred to privileges being taken from men because it was believed that they had read forbidden newspapers. An old Virginia mountaineer who had been sentenced to Atlanta for five years for opposing the draft had "been in solitary confinement since January 16," the report continued.[7] Debs, on the other hand, who was admittedly given special consideration at both Moundsville and Atlanta, had no such complaints. He spoke favorably of the warden. Debs received numerous favors, including permission to receive radical newspapers.[8]

Complaints by imprisoned opponents of war included brutality, solitary confinement, poor food, dirt and filth, forced association with sex perverts, lack of medical treatment, and unreasonable rules and regulations. Some of the worst experiences of war opponents were found in the local jails. In some instances, members of the I.W.W. were held for months, and in a few cases for about two years, awaiting trial. Especially in California and Kansas, I.W.W.'s suffered from the worst abuses of an outmoded, ill-administered, and sometimes corrupt jail system, plus a determined effort by some officials to punish them even before their trial. As mentioned earlier, over fifty I.W.W.'s were jammed into a small, filthy, disease-ridden jail in Sacramento where some of them died awaiting trial.[9]

In Kansas I.W.W.'s were held at Topeka, Wichita, Kansas City, and other towns. Winthrop D. Lane of the *Survey* staff visited a number of these places early in 1919. At Topeka he found ten I.W.W.'s crowded in a dark unhealthy cell where they were plagued by incessant noise, filth, bugs and vermin, and poor food. He was shown the "dungeon," a place of punishment reminiscent of the Dark Ages. The situation was much the same at Kansas City, and, if anything, worse at Wichita. Part of the difficulty was, to be sure, an outgrowth of the jail system itself. Too, the jails had not usually been built to take care of mass arrests which caused overcrowding and a demand for facilities that could not be met without additional money and effort, neither of which abounded around most city or county jails. I.W.W.'s, feared and hated in most local communities, were likely to suffer even more than most prisoners.[10] But it is pleasant to be able to record exceptions to the general pattern. At Hutchinson, Kansas, for example, the sheriff permitted I.W.W. prisoners to go outside on hot days and sit under shade trees, and showed them humane consideration in other ways.[11]

The most vivid picture of jail conditions and the most sordid treatment of war opponents was to be found in the cases of conscientious objectors. Reference has already been made to conditions at Camp Funston and Fort Riley under General Leonard Wood.[12] Much the same conditions, however, were found at other places. For instance, two C.O.'s, Sterenstein and Eichel, were imprisoned at Fort Jay on Governor's Island, New York. Two visitors reported as follows:

> Major Ward informed us that most solitary confinement cells are in the cellars of the prison . . . . They are small and all but completely dark. Light and air come in from a very small opening on the top, and through a small iron grating . . . . The door of Sterenstein's cell was opened first. We found him with his wrists shackled to the iron bars of the small opening in the door. He was in his underwear and in bare feet. There was no pail in his cell. The only thing in the cell was a blanket. When Eichel's cell was opened, we found him shackled in the same way to the bars of the grating in the door. He was in his underclothes and had on one stocking. There was a pail in his cell.

These men, Major Ward explained, had been put in solitary confinement for refusing to work and to obey instructions.

> They were shackled to the bars of the grating from 7:30 A.M., to 11:30 A.M., and then from 12:30 P.M., to 4:30 P.M.—the theory being that this is equivalent to an eight-hour working day. They are given

two slices of bread three times a day and a pitcher of water three times a day. They are given no water with which to wash. If they wish to wash they must use some of their drinking water. They are not permitted a toothbrush. They are taken on Saturday night and given a shower bath.

After 14 days of such confinement, the prisoners are released into the prison yard for 14 days. They are given raw food, an ax for chopping wood, cooking utensils, and shelter at night. Otherwise they are regarded as men on a desert island, bound to shift for themselves. If, after these 14 days of desert island life, they are still unwilling to yield their conscientious convictions, they are placed in solitary confinement again for another 14 days. This can go on indefinitely for the term of 20 or 30 years, to which these men have been sentenced, or until they are broken, either physically or mentally.[13]

The same system was used at the United States Disciplinary Barracks at Leavenworth where many of the C.O.'s were held at one time or another. If a C.O. refused to work, he was put in solitary confinement and made to stand manacled to the bars for nine hours a day. This system, which Secretary Baker ordered halted on December 6, 1918, has been described by Colonel Sedgwick Rice in a letter to a mother who had inquired about her son. "I am sorry to inform you that your son is still in solitary confinement and that he still maintains that he cannot work while in this institution," Rice wrote. "While in confinement, his hands are fastened in such a manner as to make sure that he will stand during the working hours, (9 hours per day), that is to say, he is handcuffed to the bars in such a manner as to entail the least possible constraint. The rest of the time he has the freedom of his cell." Then the commandant concluded: "If at the end of his 14-day sentence he still persists in his refusal to work, it is very probable that another period of confinement will follow. Of course, you understand that he may terminate his punishment at any day or hour that he decides to work . . . . You may rest assured that if he breaks down in any way . . . he will be given proper medical care and removed to the hospital if necessary." [14] About two months later this young man, Evan Thomas, was released.

After he was freed Thomas wrote a well-balanced account of his experiences for *Survey* magazine. He told of being chained to the bars, of poor food, and of inadequate quarters. But he admitted that some of the conditions were not so bad. The greatest burden, he wrote, was the "unspeakable moral filth and vice to which one is constantly exposed." [15] At a New York meeting sponsored by the National Civil Liberties Bureau Thomas said that he did not condemn the prison or the officials so much as the system.[16] Another Leavenworth prisoner described conditions as follows: "The hole is our jail you know, a black, cold place in the sub-basement. The men hang there chained by their wrists to their cell doors nine hours a day. They sleep on a cold cement floor between foul blankets and are given bread and water if they will eat at all." Beatings, cold showers, and other brutality were common. "Several Russians— Holy Jumpers from Arizona—have been hunger striking in the Hole," continued the prison account. "Two of them were beaten so bestially that even the authorities were shocked and the sentry is to be court martialed. The sentry is being tried, however, only because he exceeded his authority." Then the writer concluded:

> These Russians were so weak at the end of six days that two of them had to be taken to the hospital—veritable ghosts. The others finally accepted a bowl and a half of cornflakes and milk daily in preference to forcible feeding . . . . They are ready to die in this dungeon. Their courage, so firm and beautiful, shames the others of us.[17]

In November, 1918, the Hofer brothers and Jacob Wipf were removed from Alcatraz to Leavenworth. According to Hershberger, "when they arrived they were forced to walk through the streets of the city, from the railway station to the prison, at the points of bayonets. When they arrived at the prison, wet with sweat, they were forced to remove their outer clothing and to stand outside in the cold for two hours in the middle of the night. At five o'clock in the morning they were again compelled to stand in the cold until Joseph and Michael Hofer became ill and were taken to the hospital, where they died a few days later." [18] The body of one of the brothers was sent home in a military uniform. The remaining members of this group, David Hofer and Jacob Wipf, were fed on bread and water and manacled to bars nine hours a day for several weeks.[19]

One prisoner reported after his release that "the 'old order' Mennonites were having the hardest time at the time I was there. One was still in the g.h. and the two others who had just been released, had been handled very rough by guards; tied by their thumbs, cut with bayonets, etc." [20] Of the 360 religious objectors court-martialed and sentenced, 138 were Mennonites.[21]

Benjamin Salmon, a violent antiwar C.O. at Leavenworth, charged that prison authorities were grafters and "that they were not furnishing the prisoners one-third of the food they were entitled to." [22] Salmon was then placed in close confinement for infraction of prison rules.

> He refused to work, was put in a solitary cell for two weeks, (on bread and water) the prison authorities say that he had organized a hunger strike in the prison in which he had gotten 700 others to join; they have threatened him with a court-martial; he defies them to court-martial him, says that they dare not do so, threatens to have some of the prominent officials sent to the penitentiary and says he will succeed without a doubt. [23]

After this he was placed in an insane ward and forcibly fed. He wrote to President Wilson asking to be killed outright rather than by this slow torture of forcible feeding. [24] Salmon was an excellent example of the political prisoner who, although badly treated, brought much of his difficulty upon himself. He was an unco-operative and incorrigible individual of the braggart type whose actions would have tried the patience of a Job, to say nothing of an army officer. Even his lawyer admitted to Walter Nelles that Salmon was a real problem to him, as well as to the army. [25]

What has been said of Fort Jay and Leavenworth was equally true at Alcatraz. Hershberger has described the treatment given to the Hofer brothers. These men had been court-martialed and sentenced to twenty years imprisonment. Although they were harmless religious pacifists, they were taken to Alcatraz chained in pairs and under armed guard. "Upon arrival," Hershberger recorded, "when they again refused to wear the military uniform, they were stripped of all clothing except light underwear and placed in a dark and filthy dungeon where they had to sleep on a cold concrete floor without blankets. For four and one-half days the only food they received was one-half glass of water every twenty-four hours." After this ordeal they had their hands manacled to the bars in such a way that their feet scarcely touched the floor. This lasted for a day and a half. Then "they were beaten with clubs until one of them became unconscious. They were then kept in solitary confinement in their cells for four months, being given only one hour for exercise on Sundays." [26] While they were held in solitary, military uniforms were placed beside them on the floor as a reminder that they could avoid their ordeal if they would give in. Jacob Wipf said afterwards, "We had decided that to wear the uniform was not what God would have us do. It was a question of doing our religious duty, not one of living or dying, and we never wore the uniform." [27]

The following account of this island prison has been given by Clark Getts: "At Alcatraz there are about thirty C.O.'s. Five are refusing to work —Grosser, Rodolf, Harderson, Dart, Simmons. They have all served three periods of solitary confinement." Getts then told of the system of compulsory church attendance: "If a prisoner refuses, he is dragged from his cell and taken to church. If he resists he is taken to solitary. The story of the chaplain beating three religious objectors last December—with his own fists, after they had been dragged to the chapel—is known to you, I suppose. The episode has not been repeated, but the worthy's attitude is quite unchanged, and no one doubts that if a prisoner repeated the Hofers' performance he would be treated to the same experience."

At another time Getts described the "hole." "The 'hole' here is particularly bad," he wrote. "Even the best of cells is damp, foul, smelly, cold, and comfortless . . . . There is but one small window to give light for the whole row of cells, which are consequently so dark one cannot see one's hand in front of one's eyes. The prisoner must sleep on the damp floor (some of the floors being concrete, but others bed rock), and is provided with two blankets—insufficient for this climate . . . ." According to Getts, "the place is infested with vermin as at Leavenworth, and large rats are numerous. Grosser has sense of humor enough to lie awake nights and play with them, he says—but men are known to go insane in the dungeon, and the reason is self-evident. The food allowance is 18 ounces of bread and a pitcher of water per day." [28]

Claude O. Grant, another C.O., absolutely refused to work under any military orders. He was held at Alcatraz for four months. Most of the time he was given only one meal each day. There were instances where he did not even receive that. He was finally sent to a hospital after being declared temporarily insane.[29]

In 1919, a conscientious objector by the name of Frederick W. Leighton was sent to Alcatraz. A member of the prison "hard busy"—a prisoner's gang—ordered him out, and when he went on eating he was struck in the face. Then, according to a letter from a fellow prisoner: "He sat up, folded his arms, and allowed the fellow to go on beating him. Finally he walked out but was met at the door and beaten again. He was knocked flat. When I met him a few minutes later he had lost a front tooth—his face was a huge swollen pulpy mass and his lip was puffed and bleeding. Leighton is still a pacifist, strange to say." [30]

The treatment of political prisoners was by no means always bad. For example, despite the ill-treatment of the Hofers at Alcatraz, they were "treated fairly well," according to Thomas, after a time of great suffering.[31] Clark Getts spoke of Alcatraz as not a model prison, but added, "In the event of another war I should choose it for confinement before any other I know." [32] Getts also told of friendly and sympathetic guards who smuggled the prisoners tobacco and candy.[33] But, as explained more fully in Chapter Twelve, conscientious objectors were known to have suffered terribly. Other opponents of war were also mistreated because of their opposition to war on principle or to World War I in particular.

▄▄▄▄▄▄▄▄▄▄▄▄▄▄▄▄▄▄▄▄▄▄▄▄▄▄▄▄▄▄▄▄▄▄▄▄▄

"Mourn not your captive comrades who must dwell,
  Too strong to strive,
Within each steel-bound coffin of a cell,
  Buried alive.
But rather mourn the apathetic throng—
  The cowed, and meek—
Who see the world's great anguish and its wrong
And dare not speak!" [1]

"LET OUR PEOPLE GO"

Peace did not end the trials and tribulations of opponents of war. Even though the enemy had been defeated and the excuses for suppression were gone, those who had favored stiff wartime restrictions did not demonstrate generosity or forgiveness. President Wilson, Theodore Roosevelt, Judge Landis, Attorney General Gregory, and others held to the belief that opponents of war must pay the penalty for their unpatriotic errors. The drive for amnesty found no recruits among this group. And what about the nation's intellectual and religious leaders? They too, for the most part, were silent—at least until it was no longer particularly unpopular to advocate amnesty for violators of the wartime Espionage Act. As for the great American press, it took months, and even years, after the war before there was more than an occasional demand for tolerance. There were exceptions, but they were rare.

Nonetheless, there were those who, even before the armistice, were willing to be called pro-German or Red in order to undo some of the worst injustices of the war years. Early in February, 1918, Louis F. Post, Assistant Secretary of Labor, wrote to Wilson: "Now that the conscription law has been vindicated, would it not be desirable in the public interest, voluntarily to grant a blanket pardon to such of the persons early convicted under its provisions as were not consciously disloyal in their opposition to the execution of the conscription law?" Post felt that the step could be explained by saying "the law was a novelty to them," and that it "seemed inconsistent with their notions of American democracy." Such a step, he said, "would have a stimulating effect upon a large body of confused but nevertheless patriotic sentiment." Wilson replied that it was an appealing suggestion, but added, "Perhaps it is unwise to show clemency until we have got such a grip on the whole conduct of the war as will remove all doubts and counteract all cross currents." [2]

"For the period of the war."
—Harding in the Brooklyn *Eagle* as reproduced in *Literary Digest*, LVII (June 29, 1918), 19.

Even after the armistice, President Wilson did not believe that the cross currents had been sufficiently counteracted. In fact, Wilson's reply to Post revealed a pattern of thought about the opponents of war which was to become more fixed in later months and years. Regardless of the President's liberal tendencies in other directions, he could not find it in his soul to forgive pacifists, Socialists, I.W.W.'s, and others who had opposed the war. These people who had been skeptical of both the announced causes and aims of the Great Crusade to which Wilson was so devoted, were, in his judgment, nothing short of outright traitors. They would get no sympathy from him. Until Wilson left the White House on March 4, 1921, the amnesty campaign was thwarted by this stern and stubborn man.

Immediately after the armistice there were sporadic and undirected efforts made to free the prisoners who were confined largely because of verbal or written opposition to the war. It was argued that wartime conditions were no longer present, that the offenses had been mostly expressions of political and economic opinion, that trials had taken place in a hostile atmosphere, especially where the I.W.W. was involved, and that many of the men had served long enough to pay for their mistakes.

On November 30, 1918, thousands of stickers suddenly appeared at Camp Lewis, Washington, saying, "We demand the immediate release of all political prisoners." [3] This reflected the beginning of a national campaign for amnesty. A few days later Gilbert E. Roe, prominent New York barrister, spoke before the Civic Club of New York City and urged that all political prisoners should be freed. "The President spoke eloquently yesterday concerning the wrongs of the unfortunate people of Belgium and France, but I did not observe that he said anything about the wrongs of our own people," Roe declared. In a critical tone, he continued, "When the President arrives in Europe let us hope that he will learn that political prisoners have been freed over there, and this may perhaps remind him of hundreds of his fellow countrymen who are deprived of their liberty here for political offenses." The armistice had freed business, Roe commented, but nothing had been done about unhaltering free speech. [4]

Later in December, *Dial* published a letter which described the conditions under which some of the conscientious objectors were being held at Fort Leavenworth. [5] The writer demanded that they all be pardoned and released. Then shortly before Christmas a committee representing the families of conscientious objectors called upon Secretary of War Baker. It presented Baker with a petition containing some 15,000 signatures and asked him to recommend a general amnesty so that the men could enjoy the holiday season at home. Baker, however, refused. [6] But as the demand became more insistent, some of the opponents of war were released on an individual basis. On January 16, 1919, orders were given to release 113 conscientious objectors at Fort Leavenworth. Members of the Board of Inquiry had gone over the men's records and found them to be "sincere objectors." The *Official Bulletin* said this action reflected the War Department's policy of "returning to civil life at the earliest practicable moment such conscientious objectors as are not serving court-martial sentences." [7] This action was later to bring stinging criticism from the American Legion, which proposed that Congress should investigate the War Department's policy of releasing C.O.'s. [8]

By early 1919 amnesty committees were being formed in various cities to work for the release of political prisoners. In March, 249 sailors and soldiers sent a petition to Secretary Baker, asking that political prisoners be freed at once. The League for Amnesty of Political Prisoners appealed to all governors to take similar action for those persons held under state laws.[9] In April, the Washington, D.C., Citizens' Amnesty Committee requested President Wilson to release the prisoners.[10] The American Civil Liberties Union was especially active in aiding jailed opponents of war, and some of the labor unions gave a helping hand. At an Atlantic City meeting of the American Federation of Labor in June, a delegation from the International Ladies' Garment Workers Union introduced a resolution asking for the release of all those convicted under the emergency wartime laws.[11]

Some of the liberal periodicals also took a stand. The editors of *Dial* wrote in January: "The war is over. The nation should follow the historic example offered even by autocracies in the past, and set free those prisoners for whose detention a national crisis no longer offers excuse. It should act fully, generously, immediately." Whether wartime restrictions on freedom of speech had been desirable was not then the question, they wrote. "In any case they have done their work. No further gain can be anticipated by keeping their violators in prison." [12] A few months later the *New Republic* argued that there was much less reason to keep the conscientious objectors "out of their liberty than the railway owners out of their property." Those C.O.'s still in jail should be released at once, said the writer.[13] The amnesty campaign also began to gain a sprinkling of newspaper support, and families of the imprisoned men wrote to their congressmen asking for help. Thus the move to free the political prisoners gained momentum.

Another factor that added strength to the amnesty drive was the strike among military prisoners at Fort Leavenworth in February, 1919. The broader question involving the justice of many court-martial sentences began making front-page news. "Military justice has become the livest question growing out of the war," commented the New York *World* on February 10, 1919. "Every mail that comes to Washington brings an echo of it to members of Congress and to the authorities in the War Department." Acting Advocate General Samuel T. Ansell played an important part in publicizing how military prisoners had been tried and sentenced. Consequently, Ansell was demoted to the rank of Lieutenant Colonel, although Secretary Baker denied that Ansell's demotion had anything to do with his opposition to severe court-martial sentences.[14] Discussion of the court-martial system and the fate of military prisoners stimulated interest in the political prisoners, especially in some of the C.O.'s who had received court-martial sentences.

As pressures developed to release opponents of war, the Wilson

Administration took the position that there were, after all, no real political prisoners. Attorney General Gregory said on April 11, 1919, that no individuals were in prison "because of the expression of their views on social, economic or political questions including the war." [15] Every convicted person had broken some specific law. Thus the Administration insisted that no general amnesty was feasible and that every man's case must be studied separately and individually.

In a letter to all federal attorneys on February 1, 1919, Gregory wrote, "You are undoubtedly aware of an agitation now current demanding a 'general amnesty for all political prisoners.'" Gregory then explained that the Department of Justice did not recognize any class of persons as "political offenders" and that the Department did not favor "any general amnesty." "Nevertheless," he continued, "it may be that during the war some individuals in close cases have been convicted upon inadequate evidence of their willful intent to interfere with the war program, and others have undoubtedly received sentences unduly severe." Then Gregory asked the federal attorneys to "send the department a frank and informal expression of your views upon the justice of the verdict and sentence in each case of conviction under this section where the term of the sentence remains unexpired." [16]

Gregory kept Wilson fully informed about the demands for amnesty. He wrote that he could not recommend "an indiscriminate pardon of these persons," but, he added, "that injustice did result in certain cases of this type must be conceded—it could hardly be otherwise." Because of "intense patriotism and aroused emotions on the part of jurors," Gregory explained, "it is apparent that in certain individual cases the severity of the sentences imposed would sometimes be out of proportion to the intrinsic character of the offense committed." On the whole, however, Gregory thought justice had been done. Yet he did recommend to Wilson that certain sentences under the Espionage Act be commuted.[17]

As the problem was shuffled back and forth between various Washington departments, the agitation to release the prisoners continued with no letup. The National Women's Trade Union League meeting in Philadelphia and the Workers Defense Union which met in New York passed resolutions in June, 1919, urging that all restraints be removed on free speech, press, and assemblage.[18] The American Federation of Labor passed a resolution demanding that all wartime laws which infringed upon freedom of speech and press be repealed immediately after a peace treaty had been signed. However, at its 1919 gathering the A.F. of L. failed to pass a resolution recommending pardon for all of those in jail for political or conscientious reasons. In June the Amnesty Committee of Chicago wrote to Secretary Baker, asking that he prevail upon President Wilson to release the conscientious objectors. Baker replied somewhat curtly that he would call the President's attention to the request, but that future peace was more likely to be achieved by those who gave their lives in war rather than by those who stayed at home for conscience' sake.[19] Baker's position was given warm praise by the editor of the *New York Times*.[20]

President Wilson encountered the amnesty movement when he toured the country in September, 1919, seeking support for the League of Nations. As the throngs turned out to see the President in Seattle, a large number of I.W.W.'s and other radicals wore hatbands and held streamers bearing the words, "Release Political Prisoners." In an area where the I.W.W.'s had taken up positions along the sidewalk, lack of enthusiasm for the President was embarrassingly conspicuous. Although it was contrary to the wishes of the local arrangements committee, Wilson invited a delegation from the radical labor movement headed by James A. Duncan, secretary of the Central Labor Council, to meet with him the next day. "Social unrest" was reported to be the main topic of conversation, but Wilson was also asked to pardon the political prisoners. The I.W.W.'s in Seattle were especially concerned about the release of Hulet M. Wells, Sam Sadler, and other radicals who had been arrested and convicted in that area.[21]

The promoters of amnesty naturally turned the spotlight upon the release of Eugene V. Debs. It was believed that his freedom might set a pattern for the release of others. Super-patriots, realizing the same thing, mustered all their strength to keep Debs in prison. His imprisonment was to them a symbol of the entire movement for repression and typified the drive to make the country safe from radicalism. Wilson's new Attorney General, A. Mitchell Palmer, explained to the President that Debs' release "would be bitterly resented by a very large portion of the population who consider him a dangerous leader in the ultra-radical class war movement." [22] Because of the intense fear of radicalism and bolshevism in 1919, some people were more determined than ever that the radical opponents of war should not be released. That would only add to the nation's troubles, it was said.

On July 30, Attorney General Palmer wrote to Wilson that "Debs' sentence of ten years is too long and ought to be commuted, but I am firmly of the opinion that the time is not yet ripe for such action." [23] Palmer explained that Debs "has been in prison only a couple of months, is absolutely unrepentant, will not personally make any application for clemency," and that many people would resent releasing a prominent radical. "We should wait until the peace treaty is ratified and conditions in the country have settled down somewhat before we seriously consider executive clemency," Palmer concluded.[24] Wilson replied that he agreed with this judgment.[25]

Much importance was attached to a confession of guilt and admission of error by the political prisoners. It is clear from Palmer's memorandum, and from other statements, that high administration officials were especially rankled by the refusal of some war opponents to admit that they had been wrong. Later the Attorney General recommended clemency for a political prisoner because, he said, the individual was "deeply penitent, had renounced his affiliations with the I.W.W., and promised obedience to the laws of the United States in the future." [26]

When word reached Debs that his situation might be improved if he would repent, he exploded: "Repent! Repent! Repent for standing like a man! For having a conviction about a public question, and standing by it for the cause! Why, before I would don the sackcloth and get down into the ashes before the Attorney General or any other man on earth for having a principle I would gladly walk to the gallows or the stake." [27]

Secretary of Labor William B. Wilson was among those who asked for Debs' release. But he could not alter the position of his chief. The President wrote, "I am sorry that my judgment differs from yours in the matter and that I do not deem it wise to pardon him." [28] Oswald Garrison Villard, who was ridiculously accused of Red leanings during the Bolshevik hysteria in 1919 and early 1920, prevailed on Secretary Lansing to work for Debs' freedom. "I wonder whether you can privately hold out any hope for the early release of Eugene Debs? You were good enough to say to me in Paris that you thought he ought to be released and would be as soon as he had served a little while," Villard wrote. "I am wondering whether the Cabinet has any conception of the tremendous feeling of bitterness throughout the country among people who have never known Mr. Debs, and who, like myself, have never even heard him speak and do not belong to his Socialist Party," he continued. "I think it would do as much to allay the prevailing unrest, as perhaps no second Industrial Conference could, if he and other political prisoners like Kate Richards O'Hare who are in prison solely because of their opinions, were released." [29] But no amount of pleading could move the Wilson administration to free Debs or to deviate from the policy of freeing only an occasional political prisoner on an individual basis.

Some of the more outspoken proponents of amnesty even got into difficulty with the law. In Syracuse, New York, Charles W. Steene, Frank L. Preston, and William Hotze sought to gain the release of political prisoners by playing up the brutal treatment received by some prisoners. They published and distributed a leaflet in November, 1919, which showed a prisoner hanging by his wrists. The caption read, "Hung by the wrists from ceiling for 8 hours a day. McNeil's Island, Washington." Another picture showed a prisoner being hit with a baseball bat, an event reputed to have happened at Leavenworth. The leaflet had other pictures or cartoons of this nature, along with the announcement of a Socialist sponsored meeting where it was planned to seek a remedy for these conditions. "Mr. President—let our people go. American citizens charged with no crimes against persons or property and guilty only of expressing their political, industrial, and religious beliefs, are subjected to these tortures in your prisons," said the writer. "The war is over," continued the announcement; "in the name of liberty and justice we demand the release of all prisoners whose alleged crimes consisted in the peaceable expression and maintenance of their political opinions, industrial activities, or religious beliefs." [30]

When Steene and his friends attempted to hold an amnesty meeting, it was stopped and the three men were arrested. They were charged with violating the Espionage Act and of uttering disloyal and scurrilous language about the United States and the American form of government. Indicted on January 12, 1920, more than a year after the armistice, Steene, Preston, and Hotze were found guilty and sentenced to eighteen months in prison. The pictures in their leaflet implied that justice could not be obtained, the Court held, thus bringing disrepute on the United States Government. Likewise, the military forces which were allegedly responsible for the brutalities were also degraded. Certain provisions of the Espionage Act, said the Court, "are obviously for the purpose of preventing the sort of abuse of the form of government which . . . is calculated to inflame and arouse the ignorant and vicious to an actual attempt to bring about open disloyalty." [31]

On Christmas Day, 1919, a Fifth Avenue amnesty parade was planned in New York City. When it started, the police intervened and arrested a number of the participants. It was reported that the police clubbed some of the marchers. Those arrested, however, were freed by the Court and the police were censured. There was even talk of an investigation of police behavior. Criticism of the police instead of jail sentences for the demonstrators indicated a significant change in public sentiment. However, in late 1919 several amnesty meetings were broken up by super-patriots.[32]

By 1920, after a year of effort, it was clear that a growing tide of public opinion favored release of the political prisoners. Senator Owen told a New York audience that wartime animosities must be forgotten. He expressed opposition to any new restrictive laws and recommended that at least certain categories of political prisoners be freed.[33] A delegation from the American Federation of Labor went to Washington in February to discuss the release of conscientious objectors with Secretary Baker. Senator France told the A.F. of L. group that he was ready to introduce a resolution recommending presidential clemency for those still held.[34] On March 10 Senator France did introduce such a resolution. Referring to this action, the New York *American* wrote on March 16: "Freedom of opinion is the cornerstone of American democracy . . . . It does not mean merely freedom of sound opinion, freedom to say what the majority approves. It means freedom to err, to differ from the majority and even to believe what is not true."

In May, a committee of Socialists called on Attorney General Palmer, appealing for the release of political prisoners, especially Debs and O'Hare. Palmer, reported the *New York Call* on May 15, gave the impression "that the Wilson Administration would be happy to liberate all those whom it has imprisoned for *lese majesty* if that could be done without a confession of guilt by the Administration." The Attorney General, it was said, "appeared very solicitous of the judiciary, saying it might be held as a reflection upon the courts if the executive power should now turn loose those whom the courts had duly put in prison." The Socialist callers were convinced that the Administration had a "gnawing hunger for apologies as a basis for pardon." Palmer asked why the petitioners did not follow the regular legal processes and formally apply for a pardon. To this Seymour Stedman replied that there was a significant difference between amnesty and pardon. Amnesty, he said, "was formal recognition by the authorities that the crisis no longer existed during which it had been held unsafe to let citizens express their right to criticize, and took the form of restored liberty for all those who had been restrained during the alleged emergency. Pardon, on the other hand, involved a stultifying declaration by prisoners that they had done wrong when they adhered to conscientious scruples and practices." The Socialists won no general amnesty but they were encouraged by the release of Kate O'Hare about two weeks later.[35]

To a slight extent the amnesty drive got tangled in politics during the 1920 presidential campaign. After announcing that he favored amnesty, Parley P. Christensen, candidate of the Farmer-Labor party, asked Republican Warren G. Harding to state his position. Harding replied that he approved "generous amnesty for political prisoners," but said he could not offer an opinion on the Debs case without further study.[36] But Harding soon reversed himself. Seeing that amnesty was unpopular among the conservative interests, he restated his stand in a speech at Omaha in October. He expressed opposition to what he termed "Czarism" and "Terrorism," but said that general amnesty "to political prisoners is no more justified than a general grant of amnesty to yeggmen." No differences existed, Harding said, between ordinary crimes and political crimes; or between ordinary prisoners and "political prisoners." [37]

Despite Harding's position, it was obvious by the fall of 1920 that the amnesty campaign was bearing fruit. There were frequent reports of individual political prisoners being quietly released. The decline of the Big Red Scare operated in their favor, since most of those held were political radicals. Furthermore, the press was showing more sympathy toward the imprisoned war opponents. The *Literary Digest* reported that even many of the more conservative papers were taking the attitude of letting bygones be bygones. There were some editors, however, who still agreed with one Washington newspaper which opposed dumping the "crowd of marplots and conspirators" upon "an already outraged nation." [38] Others argued that the prisoners, if released, would join the Red agitators and cause even more trouble. The weight of this argument in late 1920, however, was not so strong as it had been a year earlier. As explained before, there is no doubt that the abnormal fear of radicalism during 1919 and early 1920 militated against more rapid release of political prisoners.

The failure of war opponents to repent also continued to irk some editors. The Philadelphia *Bulletin* said it would not be so bad to release the offenders if they had learned anything about citizenship. But, continued the writer, "there are no proofs of repentance offered." Mercy would be warranted, wrote the editor of the Washington *Post*, "where the offender admits his wrong-doing and expresses sincere regret." However, that was not the case, he added, with Debs or Berger.[39]

But the bitter-enders were fighting a losing battle. On November 23, 1920, Secretary Baker ordered the last thirty-three conscientious objectors released so that they could be home by Thanksgiving. Even though this was two years after the armistice and after most political prisoners had been released abroad, Baker and the President were still due for some harsh criticism. The *American Legion Weekly,* the *Grand Rapids Press,* and the Washington *Post* were among the publications which bitterly assailed the Government's policy. To the *Press* these men were "shirkers, skulkers, and ingrates," and the Washington *Post* referred to them as "cringing, skulking cowards." [40]

The cautiousness with which the Administration moved in freeing political prisoners can be explained partly by the strong forces pulling in opposite directions. Press reactions reflect the crosscurrents and pressures under which the Government had to operate. When such powerful organizations as the American Legion and the American Federation of Labor took conflicting positions on the question of freeing political prisoners, it would have taken a bold and forthright administration indeed to openly flaunt one or the other. Thus, in the final analysis, the policy of releasing an individual or small group of war opponents at various intervals was one of expediency.

There was always the question of what should be done with certain individuals, and the Justice Department gave considerable attention to some particular cases. Late in 1920 Palmer wrote to Wilson asking for an opinion on whether the Government should again prosecute Rose Pastor Stokes. It will be recalled that she had been tried, convicted, and sentenced for violating the Espionage Act in 1918. The Circuit Court of Appeals, however, had reversed the judgment because the trial judge's charge to the jury had been inflammatory and prejudicial to the defendant's rights. "The question is, shall we try Mrs. Stokes again?" Palmer asked. He concluded:

> In view of the great pressure on behalf of so-called political prisoners and because the defendant is a woman and the war is over for all practical purposes, I am very strongly inclined to think that we ought to drop the case; but as it involves a question of policy which will affect the disposition of other indictments pending against other persons not yet tried, I would appreciate it if I could have your view as to what ought to be done.

Wilson replied that he considered Mrs. Stokes one of the "dangerous influences of the country." The President said that he hesitated "to advise that the suit against her be dropped, but I feel the embarrassment of pressing the suits now which we began under the authority of the Espionage Act, because I think the country feels that the time for that is past. I hope, therefore, that you will not make an exception of Mrs.

Stokes' case, but rather put it on the same footing that you are putting all others that have arisen in the same way." [41] The Justice Department did not press the Stokes case, however, and on November 15, 1921, action was dropped.[42] The public's growing desire for moderation was obviously affecting government policy.

Samuel Gompers continued to work both publicly and privately for the release of Debs and other political prisoners. He appealed to the President for general amnesty "to those political prisoners whose conviction and imprisonment was not because of moral turpitude." He made a special plea for Debs. "I have had serious differences with Mr. Debs," Gompers wrote. But, he added, "I never have held that Mr. Debs gave voice to any utterance through insincerity or that he was a traitor to his country. His was, I firmly believe, a mistaken conviction, but it was a conviction." Reminding Wilson that the American Federation of Labor meeting at Montreal had adopted resolutions "urging the granting of amnesty of the prisoners held for political offenses during the war," Gompers concluded that amnesty would "exemplify the spirit of mercy" typical of the Christmas season.[43] Still Wilson was not moved.

There were reports that Wilson refused executive clemency for Debs because it might encourage others to oppose the Government in event of another war.[44] Upon hearing this, Debs said he would be ashamed to be free under "the chaotic conditions of society." He expressed the hope that his case would be the last to be considered.[45]

F. W. Galbraith, National Commander of the American Legion, praised the President's stand. "Your decision not to pardon Eugene V. Debs as recently reported in the press heartily concurred in by Department Adjutants of the American Legion," Galbraith wrote. "The American Legion," he continued, "views with heartfelt satisfaction this vital act in support of the fundamental doctrines of the Constitution." There must be no "compromise for the enemies in our midst who would overthrow the Government by force," concluded Galbraith.[46]

Even after the presidential election, Wilson continued to watch the Debs situation closely. Tumulty recalled that when a recommendation for pardoning Debs arrived at the White House, Wilson examined it carefully and exclaimed, "I will never consent to the pardon of this man." If he did so, Wilson said he could never face the mothers who had sent their sons into battle. "While the flower of American youth was pouring out its blood to vindicate the cause of civilization," Wilson told Tumulty, "Debs stood behind the lines sniping, attacking, and denouncing them. Before the war he had a perfect right to exercise his freedom of speech to express his own opinion, but once the Congress of the United States declared war, silence on his part would have been the proper course to pursue." Still bitter, Wilson said: "I know there will be a great deal of denunciation of me for refusing this pardon. They will say I am cold-blooded and indifferent, but it will make no impression on me. This man was a traitor to his country and he will never be pardoned during my administration." [47] And Woodrow Wilson was a man of his word. On February 12, only a few days before leaving office, Palmer recommended that Debs be pardoned. Wilson scratched only one word across the recommendation—"denied." [48]

March 4, 1921, brought a marked change to the Washington scene. The Puritan Moralist had been evicted and the easy-going Warren G. Harding moved into the White House. His friend Harry Daugherty took over the Department of Justice. The amnesty committees got more sympathy from leaders of the new Administration. Also, members of Congress began to show greater concern for the remaining political prisoners. For example, Tom Watson of Georgia introduced a resolution requesting a pardon for David T. Blodgett, the Iowan who had been sentenced to ten years in Atlanta for printing excerpts from one of Watson's antiwar speeches. "Should he be in the Senate and I in the penitentiary?" Watson asked. "He did not say any more in Iowa than I have said here in the Senate." [49] Meyer London, Socialist Congressman from New York, presented resolutions, petitions, and memorials from Socialist, Labor, and other groups, all asking for the release of political prisoners. One of the petitions stated: "According to our information there are confined in various Federal prisons 147 men serving sentences, some of which run as high as 20 years. All of these men were convicted of practically the same supposed offense, namely, of written and spoken opposition to the war or of using language construed by the courts to be in opposition to the war." Then it added that "whatever may have been demanded by exigencies of war, hostilities, in fact, ceased three years ago . . . . There no longer exists the slightest justification for the continued incarceration of these men." [50]

On April 4, 1921, Gompers and Congressman London, along with others, called on Harding and urged that he grant a general amnesty to all political prisoners. Harding was amiable, but promised nothing.[51] The *New York Times* editorialized that the proposal for amnesty "is of impudence and unreason all compact" and called Gompers' position "unintelligible." [52]

But now it would be only a matter of time until the remaining

political offenders would be released. Approval of the formal peace proclamation on November 14, 1921, was an especially favorable factor. As
mentioned before, the very next day the Department of Justice dropped
its case against Rose Pastor Stokes, and there were reliable rumors that
Debs would soon be freed.[53] On November 23 the *New York Times*
reported that, the day before, the Cabinet had considered at some length
the problem of freeing political prisoners. Again, the report stated, there
was a feeling that several political prisoners, including Debs, would
be released by Christmas. The *Times* editorialized a few weeks later that
probably no one would become "violently excited" if all political prisoners
were released, but what galled the editor was that "they show no sign
of repentance." [54]

Attorney General Daugherty presented Harding with a lengthy
review of the Debs case on December 23, 1921. He wrote: "An overwhelming mass of letters, petitions, and resolutions, the latter passed by
various labor and other organizations throughout the country, have been
received requesting and urging the release of Debs as a matter of right
and justice, it being asserted that he has violated no law, has been
wrongfully convicted, and is being illegally imprisoned for daring to
exercise his constitutional right of free speech." Daugherty continued that
Debs had not applied for "executive clemency and therefore no action
would be taken in his case were it not for the enormous mass of communications received in his behalf by people who clearly regarded Debs
as a martyr to the cause of freedom of speech and the most conspicuous
example of the illegal prosecution, and even persecution, of those who
differed with the policy of this Government and the course pursued by
it in the late war in Europe."

But, said the Attorney General, "it is wise . . . and I think expedient, that the Government should take note of the misapprehension
and misunderstanding existing among a portion of our people who believe
that constitutional rights have been invaded by prosecutions under the
espionage law, and that we should examine their contentions and by some
act or pronouncement indicate the attitude of the Government and its
reasons therefor." Daugherty explained further that "Socialists throughout the country, and others who are requesting Debs' release, still maintain, in defiance of the decision of the Supreme Court, that the acts
complained of are within the constitutional rights of the individual, and
they demand that Debs and all similar offenders be released forthwith."
The attitude of these people, he continued, "is not that of a misguided
and mistaken individual who, now that he knows the law, yields ready

obedience and regrets his misstep, but it is one of defiance and refusal to accept the laws of the country as finally and judicially determined. Debs, also, is one of the same general attitude, though not so rampant in his utterances."

Debs was an old man and in bad health, Daugherty went on to say, "and he is not a normal man, mentally, on this particular subject, his obsession clearly preventing him from acquiescing in the final decision of the courts respecting the limitations of freedom of speech as guaranteed by the Constitution. He is a man of much personal charm and impressive personality." Yet, wrote the Attorney General, those very qualities made Debs "a very dangerous man, calculated to mislead the unthinking and afford an excuse for those with criminal intent. So far as he thinks correctly he may be conscientious, but he does not think correctly, and apparently can not do so on the questions involved in this case, and it must not be overlooked that under our form of government his theories, which are in conflict with the highest constituted authority, are wrong and treasonable." [55]

Although Daugherty had many objections to Debs, he argued that it would be best to release him. On December 23, 1921, it was officially announced that President Harding would free Debs and twenty-three other political prisoners on Christmas Day.[56] When Harding was later congratulated for granting clemency to some of the opponents of war, he explained, "I couldn't do anything else . . . . Those fellows didn't mean any harm. It was a cruel punishment." [57] This sounded more like the agreeable and pleasant Harding the boys liked to play poker with all Saturday night.

The release of Debs was still not followed by a general amnesty, but more and more individual prisoners were pardoned or had their sentences commuted. Congress became sufficiently concerned in early 1922 so that both houses held hearings on the question of amnesty for political prisoners. Albert De Silver, head of the National Civil Liberties Bureau, described to the House committee the circumstances under which the prisoners had been arrested and convicted, how mobs had run unchecked, and how public hysteria had operated against obtaining fair trials. A majority of the committee members, however, found no difficulty in justifying the continued imprisonment of the remaining 113 men.[58]

There was no letup in the effort to get these last political prisoners freed. Friends and relatives of the imprisoned men took every opportunity to dramatize the situation. Late in April, 1922, children of men at

Leavenworth, led by Kate Richards O'Hare, staged an amnesty crusade. Twenty-five children paraded in Philadelphia on April 27 carrying placards, "I Want My Daddy," and "Debs Is Free—Why Not My Daddy." [59] Going on to Washington, the group picketed the White House and carried signs which read, "My Daddy Never Saw Me" and "No Profiteer Went To Prison." The thirty-five women and children did not see Harding, but they did discuss the problem of amnesty with a presidential secretary. Later they saw Daugherty.[60] Over a month later Mrs. O'Hare was still in Washington, complaining that the President had turned away representatives of the group "twenty times without any good reason." She said that "we will not leave Washington until we have succeeded in getting the Administration to meet this issue squarely." [61]

At the time of the Washington Disarmament Conference, when everyone seemed to be talking about peace and good will, Congressman London reminded his colleagues: "Now that you are all singing the praises of those who love peace, of those who advocate international concord, of those who seek the abolition of war, the question of amnesty for men who had the courage to speak their true convictions about war during the war" should be considered. "Everyone can be a hero now," London said. "Everyone can bravely proclaim his love of peace. I want to submit to you the cases of those men and women to whom the love of peace was a life passion, to whom it was a religion, to whom it was the meaning of their existence—the case of men and women who believed that it was their mission to preach peace on earth when men were killing one another."

Pointing out that 113 political offenders were still in the federal penitentiaries, with hundreds more in state prisons, London argued that the Espionage Law was "wicked" and that it "copied the worst features" of the Alien and Sedition Acts of 1798. He charged that during the war it had been "impossible for a man to get a square deal when charged with a violation of the Espionage Law, if it was known that he had at one time or another opposed the entry of the United States into the war." Even worse, London explained, "if in addition to that the man happened to be an advocate of an unpopular economic doctrine, if in addition to that the jury was composed of employers of labor, if the prisoner at the bar chanced to be a member of a union which had conducted a strike in the locality, he had no chance on earth." Warming to his subject, the New York Socialist said that "there is nothing more dangerous than the theory that the mere declaration of war deprives one of the right to criticize." [62]

Congressman John Miller of Washington asked London if he were trying "to defend the principles of Trotski and Lenin in the Congress of the United States." Although this was 1922, the bogey of bolshevism was very much alive. Miller's question illustrates how the amnesty question had become entangled with the fear of postwar radicalism. Representative Hersey of Maine said that the "propaganda" and "agitation" on behalf of "socialistic draft evaders, conscientious objectors," and others who violated the Espionage Act must be answered. Hersey declared that "Socialism, the father of bolshevism, can never ascend to power in the United States through the efforts of the gentleman from New York or the picketing of the White House by the children of convicts." He said it was time for Congress to accept the challenge and "meet the issue squarely of socialism against civilization." [63]

London expressed surprise that Hersey would resort to "denouncing the amnesty movement as socialism, Bolshevism, and anarchism." He argued that

it requires courage in ordinary times to be in a minority, but when the world is mad with the fury of war, the man who has the courage to proclaim a principle which is true for all time is the first victim of the mob. The patriotic fervor during the war was such that it was utterly impossible for any judge or jury to do justice in the ordinary sense of the word . . . . I am a pacifist at heart. I detest war, but many a time during the war I found rising within me hatreds such as I thought myself incapable of. I can see how the average juror would find it practically impossible to give a square deal to a man who was charged with having made a strong radical statement which appeared to him, the juror, as opposition to the Government and as endangering the country.[64]

Further debate in Congress was set off a few months later by the death of the Mexican Anarchist, Ricardo Flores Magon, who had been convicted of violating the Espionage Act by publishing revolutionary material in his Spanish language paper, *Regeneracion,* at Los Angeles.[65] It was now argued that Magon had not really interfered with the war effort and that his radical statements had been designed to gain revolutionary support in his native Mexico. Friends claimed that he had been the victim of war hysteria and, besides, he was in bad health. The Justice Department, however, denied all pleas for Magon's release and he died at Leavenworth on November 21, 1922.[66] Magon had been freed, commented the Baltimore *Sun,* but by death rather than by the Justice Department. Magon had been no threat to American security, said the editor. "The articles in the little paper which he published in Los Angeles were in the Spanish tongue and as little likely to 'discourage recruiting' as a Dutch edition of the New Testament." [67]

To head off the demands for general amnesty, the American Defense Society circularized members of Congress and others with a statement which said: "The Joint Amnesty League, members of Congress, and others who are thus apologists for criminals should not be allowed to get away with the idea that these prisoners are languishing in jail simply because they violated the American right of free speech. They are murderers and destructionists and the I.W.W.'s themselves have not had the hardihood to claim that they are illegally confined." [68]

Congressman George Huddleston of Alabama, taking note of this, commented that over sixty men were still in federal prisons who had been convicted under laws no longer in effect. "I know of no better name for these persons than 'political prisoners,'" he declared, "because that is exactly what they are. Their offenses were not against persons but directed against the Government by opposing measures relating to carrying on the war." This situation, Huddleston said, was a "disgrace to our country." Criticizing the Department of Justice, he continued, "Whenever pardon for them is mentioned the department emits a smoke screen and attempts to divert attention from the true issue by reckless statements that the prisoners are 'anarchists,' 'communists,' or even murderers." There was no law in the United States, he argued, that made it a crime for a "man to be an I.W.W., a communist, an atheist, or to hold any other belief, no matter how wild and subversive it may be, nor is it a crime for men to belong to an organization, no matter what purpose it may have. Our laws are aimed at men's actions, not at a frame of mind or a belief." He charged that it had not been violent deeds which had brought convictions, but the use of certain words. There were those "influential groups in this country [who] do not sincerely believe in free speech or other constitutional guarantees," he added. Huddleston said that the "reactionary and selfish interests" not only insisted on holding political offenders in jail, "but promptly vent their spleen upon all who may advocate their release." [69]

Opponents of amnesty were in the last trenches, but they would go down with flags flying. Congressman Walter F. Lineberger of California replied to Huddleston that most members of the House proposed "to fight this wholesale amnesty movement to the finish . . . and we throw down the gauntlet to those who so deeply sympathize with those who would upset the Government and institutions for which our comrades fought and bled and died on Flanders Field in 1917 and in 1918. We will keep the faith, buddies, never fear." [70]

Lineberger and others may have kept faith, but all the time political prisoners were being released. On December 30, 1922, President Harding promised freedom to eight I.W.W.'s convicted in the Chicago trial, provided they would leave the United States. By early 1923 church leaders, governors, college presidents, prominent journalists, including William Allen White, and many others were lending support to the amnesty campaign.[71] Important organizations working in the same cause were the Federal Council of Churches, the Methodist Federation of Social Service, and the Women's Industrial League. The Baltimore *Evening Sun* wrote that "profiteers have recently been pardoned and German spies . . . have had their liberty restored, but the radical talkers are still in durance vile. It would appear that the most heinous crime in this country is to say what one thinks." [72] That was an exaggeration, but it helped awaken people to the cause of amnesty.

In June, 1923, President Harding offered freedom to twenty-four I.W.W.'s at Leavenworth. The conditions were such, however, that ten or eleven of the men said the price of freedom was too high. Part of the requirement for release was a promise that they would be "law-abiding." This, the men said, was tantamount to a confession of guilt. They argued that they had not been disloyal and therefore did not have to promise loyalty.[73]

By November, 1923, as one labor paper expressed it, "few people except the American Legion and Attorney General Daugherty" opposed amnesty.[74] Senator Borah demanded that the last political prisoners be released. "I do not believe that laws of repression, laws which deny the right to discuss political questions are any more necessary in time of war than in time of peace and I do not believe they are constitutional either in time of war or in time of peace," he declared. "If we cannot, as a free people," Borah said, "be free to discuss political problems which involve limb and life, even in time of war, our Government rests upon a very brittle foundation indeed." [75] On November 19 the New York *World* sent Coolidge an open letter reminding him that the war had been over for five years, and that political prisoners in foreign countries had been released. How much longer, Coolidge was asked, would American political offenders be held?

It would not be much longer. Coolidge had already—about the

middle of November—appointed a three-man commission headed by former Secretary of War Baker to investigate the problem of releasing political prisoners under federal control. At that time there were seven I.W.W.'s at Leavenworth who had been convicted at the Chicago trial, men who had refused President Harding's conditional commutation. The largest group still held, however, was nineteen of those convicted at Sacramento.[76]

The same news story which told of the President's commission also carried a statement made the previous July by Judge Frank H. Rudkin of San Francisco who had presided at the Sacramento trial. Judge Rudkin said he would recommend "immediate and unconditional" release if the Justice Department should again ask for his opinion. "The state of public opinion was such at the time of the Sacramento trial," he said, "that an indictment was tantamount to a conviction." [77]

On December 15, President Coolidge, acting on the advice of his special commission, commuted the terms of the last thirty-one political prisoners. The *New York Times* the next day headed its story, "Coolidge Releases All War Offenders As Christmas Gift." Senator Borah, who had been active in seeking this result, exclaimed somewhat caustically, "I am delighted that a President of the United States has discovered the First Amendment to the Constitution and has the courage to announce the discovery." [78] Borah charged that "intolerance, bigotry [and] prejudice" had kept the men confined for years and that their release was "a vindication of the right of free speech and free press." The New York *World* said on December 17 that Coolidge deserved "a vote of thanks for wiping out at one stroke the national disgrace of political prisoners held five years after the end of the war."

But the bitter-enders were not happy. The *New York Times* editorialized that "free speech" was not involved.[79] Judge Landis denounced Coolidge's action,[80] and John R. Quinn, Commander of the American Legion, scored the President for releasing "thirty-one criminals." [81] It had taken five long years of constant and strenuous effort to gain freedom for men and women who had opposed war in 1917 and 1918. The hates and passions generated by national conflict died slowly.

"Survival of war psychology is an unaccountable thing; it constitutes a new indictment, if one were needed, of the devastating effects of war upon human character." [1]

POSTWAR REPRESSION

The year 1919 saw the beginning of a period of cynicism and disillusionment. It was the morning after the Great Crusade, and in the postwar dawn much of the wartime idealism looked like tinsel. That which had been publicized as pure gold now looked suspiciously like fool's gold. Hoping to forget the war and its problems, the American people started to rush furiously after amusement and excitement. But wartime attitudes and emotions continued despite the search for normalcy.

The pattern of repression set during the war years did not end in November, 1918. The slowness with which political prisoners were released was only one minor reflection of this. Under the momentum already established, curbs on free speech and press, along with popular intolerance and mob actions, continued without much noticeable slackening. Wartime repression would no doubt have lost its force much more quickly had it not received a powerful boost by the haunting fear of radicalism and bolshevism. The intolerance and hate which had fed and nurtured on war was now to feed and grow on radicalism.

As mentioned earlier, the campaign against radicals in the United States had been intensified after the Russian Revolution in the fall of 1917. By 1919, however, the menace of bolshevism seemed to have become much more serious. The Reds had not only consolidated their position in Russia, but they were spreading their influence to other parts of Europe. Fed by irresponsible and exaggerated news stories, many Americans suddenly concluded that the United States was to be the next victim of revolution.

The fear of radicalism in 1919 replaced war as an excuse for repression. The old Devil had been the Kaiser; the new Satan was bolshevism. And bolshevism for many came to be interpreted as about everything that was not conservative. During the war pro-Germanism had been synonymous with treason. Now, in the minds of many Americans, bolshevism and treason were cut from the same cloth.[2]

By the spring of 1919 the American press was filled with the most lurid stories describing the awfulness of bolshevism and expressing the fear of its imminent threat to America and its institutions. These highly exaggerated accounts of radical power and influence seemed convincing as left wing radicals in the United States praised developments in Russia and recommended the same thing for America. Revolutionary propaganda emanating from the Third International and distributed through an increasingly militant left wing press caused frightened conservatives—and even some liberals—to demand that radicals be silenced or deported.[3] There was just enough fire behind the smoke of radicalism to provide conservatives with ammunition to attack not only radicals but all nonconformists. Thus radicalism was substituted for opposition to war as the cloak to protect intolerance and repression.

Just a few days after the armistice, Attorney General Gregory wrote that the country still needed the services of organizations like the American Protective League. "Illegal activities harmful to the public morale during the discussion of peace terms must be watched for and reported," he wrote. "Violations of the war statutes, all of which are still in force, must be prosecuted. Pending investigations must be continued and others instituted," he concluded.[4] And Gregory was not to be disappointed. The American Protective League and the National Defense Society continued active in 1919, but these organizations no longer concerned themselves with war or defense, or even with loyalty. They turned to help save the nation from radicalism.

In line with nationalist desires, repressive wartime laws continued to be enforced. The trials of I.W.W.'s at Sacramento and Kansas City were completed and the defendants convicted. Debs was sent to Atlanta six months after the war was over. Convictions under state conspiracy and sedition laws continued.

A series of events in 1919, occurring in an atmosphere already rife with unrest, stimulated the new demands for repression. In February a general strike in Seattle became the focus of national attention. Pictured by the press and by Mayor Ole Hanson as a conflict between bolshevism and Americanism, rather than as a typical labor-management dispute, the strike, people from coast to coast were led to believe, was Bolshevik inspired and operated.[5]

Excitement created by the Seattle strike had not yet died down when news was headlined in most of the nation's press that bombs had been sent to such prominent individuals as Ole Hanson, Senators Hardwick and Overman, Supreme Court Justice Oliver Wendell Holmes, Judge Landis, Postmaster General Burleson, and Attorney General Palmer. Most of the so-called May Day bombs were intercepted, although one which exploded at the Hardwick home wounded a maid and burned Mrs. Hardwick.[6] Anti-radical feeling now reached a fever pitch, but it was even further intensified by May Day riots and disturbances in New York, Boston, and Cleveland. Surely, it was said, radicalism had reached grave and dangerous proportions. But worse was yet to come. On June 2 explosions occurred simultaneously in several cities, destroying property and taking two lives. The bombing of Attorney General Palmer's house in Washington, D.C., was the most spectacular and widely described of these explosions.

The Red Scare by mid-1919 had reached such proportions that Congress, the Justice Department, and patriotic societies like the American Legion and the American Defense Society joined forces to curb radicalism both real and imagined. The Justice Department strengthened its Bureau of Investigation and Congress appropriated liberal sums for the Department's anti-Red campaign.[7]

A move had already gained headway to keep radical literature out of circulation by denying it mailing privileges. "Treasonable matter," it was said, must not be permitted to pollute the public mind. Early in February Senator Borah, working in the opposite direction now that the war was over, sought to repeal the sections of the Espionage Act which gave the Postmaster General power to exclude certain publications from the mail. Borah argued that "there ought not to be any restraint upon the minds of the American people in any way, shape, or form." [8]

Senator Knute Nelson of Minnesota expressed the typical ideas of those who favored not only a continuation of wartime repression, but an enlargement of it. Citing examples of radical writings which he said were flooding the country, he declared, "We need now, even more than we did during the days of the war, legislation to protect the people of the United States against the circulation of dangerous literature through the mails." Nelson argued that "emissaries from the Russian Bolsheviki, furnished with money from that country, have come over here to preach the Bolshevik propaganda in our own midst." [9] Instead of repealing any of the espionage legislation, Nelson thought it should be extended "in order to stem this most iniquitous propaganda." He saw bad days ahead for his beloved Republic unless "the wicked tide of anarchy and bolshevism" was stopped. Nelson argued that it was the duty of Congress "to protect the American people against this poisonous spirit of anarchy and sedition. The Constitution never was intended for the protection of people of that kind. To my mind it is idle to invoke the liberty of the press for those classes of people. They are outside of the pale of constitutional or any other law," he concluded.[10]

The constitutional doctrine expounded by the senator from Minnesota seemed to strike a sour discord with strong and generally accepted American traditions. Nonetheless, it had widespread support. Senator Borah, however, challenged this nationalistic-reactionary interpretation and warned that such a doctrine should never be permitted to take root in the United States. It was that precise idea, he said, "upon which bolshevism and I.W.W.ism are founded, to wit, that the man who disagrees with you is entitled to no protection other than that which force may, in its beneficence, see fit to grant." No man in America, Borah argued, was "beyond the pale of the law." [11]

Not only was there a popular demand to keep radical literature out of the mails, but some members of Congress saw a pressing need for a peacetime sedition law. Shortly after the Seattle strike, Senator Jones of Washington introduced a bill which would prohibit any speaking or writing aimed at inciting resistance to law by force or violence, or advocating any change in the form of government except by constitutional means.[12] The Jones bill died a lingering death in committee, and, except for some discussion in June, the question of a federal sedition law remained relatively dormant until autumn.

Critics of Congress, however, could take heart because the states were working overtime to pass measures to curb evil-thinking and to protect the public mind from pollution. Again, it had been the wartime legislation of 1917 and 1918 which set the pattern for peacetime action in the states. It will be recalled that Idaho and Minnesota passed criminal syndicalism laws in 1917. Arizona, Montana, and South Dakota followed the next year. But now in 1919, there was a veritable rash of criminal syndicalism, Red flag, and sedition measures enacted by the state legislatures.[13] These statutes were aimed at those who sought to overthrow the Government by force or who advocated violence. By early 1920, twenty-eight states and two territories had sedition, syndicalism, or Red flag legislation on their statute books.[14]

The promoters of these laws knew well enough that a few radicals were not going to overthrow the Government of the United States. But they used this as an excuse to put legal curbs on radical and disaffected individuals who wanted basic changes in the economic, social, or political organizations of the country. If the laws could be used against moderate reformers and labor organizers, so much the better.

Other wartime attitudes also found support and acceptance during this period. One important development along this line was the demand for peacetime conscription. This seemed contradictory to the idea of a war to end wars, but nonetheless universal military training won considerable support. In August, 1919, Secretary of War Baker presented Congress with bills which would require three months service for all qualified young men eighteen and nineteen years of age. Congress considered a number of different universal military training bills over a period of several months before the whole question was finally defeated in April, 1920.[15]

Also, extralegal action by mobs, as well as pressures for conformity by teachers and preachers, continued long after the war ended.[16] I.W.W. and Socialist meetings were regularly broken up and halls were closed in numerous cities. A group broke into a Socialist hall in Cincinnati and burned a quantity of literature in a street bonfire. Socialist meetings were prohibited in Philadelphia when it was said that "no radical meetings" would be allowed.[17]

One of the outstanding instances of mob action involved former Congressman Ernest Lundeen of Minnesota when he tried to make a speech against the League of Nations at Ortonville, Minnesota. Before he began his talk, the local sheriff told Lundeen that "you can't talk here." Lundeen informed the sheriff of his constitutional rights, but this made no difference. When he said that he proposed to discuss the League of Nations, a member of the American Legion replied, "Like hell you are." Just as Lundeen commenced to speak, he was seized by the sheriff, the head of the local American Legion post, and others, and escorted to the railroad depot where a train was just leaving. He was locked in a refrigerator car. At Appleton he was released when the train crew heard his shouts for help.[18] This was the area where mobs had been accustomed to attacking the Nonpartisan League.

By the fall of 1919 additional events had taken place which prompted Congress to give renewed and more serious consideration to federal sedition legislation. The fear of bolshevism was again played for all it was worth when the Boston police strike occurred in September.[19] The police strike had not even ended before it was announced that within a few days a steel strike would begin. As if this were not enough, a coal strike began on November 1. The press and public officials laid these labor disturbances directly at the door of the radicals.

Meanwhile, Attorney General Palmer had been preparing for more direct action against the Reds. On November 7, his agents rounded up hundreds of radicals, including about 200 members and officers of the Union of Russian Workers in New York City. The Lusk Committee, a New York group commissioned to investigate and ferret out radicalism in that state, also staged a series of raids and seized several hundred individuals and a large amount of literature.[20] After considerable sifting, the federal and local raids netted 246 alien radicals who were liable for deportation.

Attorney General Palmer was still receiving plaudits for his daring raids on supposedly dangerous radicals when another event far across the continent shocked the nation. On Armistice Day, American Legionnaires and members of other groups at Centralia, Washington, staged a patriotic parade to celebrate the victory over Germany. The parade route ran directly in front of the I.W.W. hall. Fearing they might be attacked, as they had been in the past, the I.W.W.'s prepared to defend their hall against any eventuality. After passing the I.W.W. headquarters peacefully, the marchers for some reason retraced their course. When it appeared that some Legion members moved toward the hall, they were met by gunfire which before it ended had killed four Legionnaires. During the night, a mob broke into the jail, seized Wesley Everest, a member of the I.W.W., and hanged him on a bridge trestle at the edge of town.[21]

Brief mention has been made of the major strikes, the Palmer raids, and the Centralia Massacre—all between September and November— only to show the atmosphere in which a renewed effort was made to pass a peacetime sedition law. On October 27, even before these events had so aroused public opinion, Senator Thomas Sterling of South Dakota had introduced a bill to "prohibit and punish certain seditious acts," a measure which had the approval of the Judiciary Committee.[22] Then on November 17, Congressmen John W. Summers and Lindley L. Hadley, both of Washington, and Martin L. Davey of Ohio all introduced sedition bills.[23]

Representative Summers warned his colleagues that "anarchy, sedition, disloyalty, I.W.W.ism, Bolshevism, radicalism and un-Americanism in all their various forms" must be stamped out. Citing Attorney General Palmer's report that 327 radical newspapers were being published and distributed in the United States, Summers said that action to suppress radical publications was imperative. "Our citizens must not be polluted by these doctrines," he said. Urging his colleagues to move with unusual legislative speed, he concluded that there remained little time to talk. "The House is burning. I beg for immediate consideration and favorable action on the bill." [24]

Attorney General Palmer gave his full support to sedition legislation. In fact, the Davey bill had been prepared in his office. Apparently Palmer thought that America could be saved from internal destruction only by a policy of repression. Even President Wilson arose from his sickbed to lend support to Palmer and lawmakers who were supporting repressive legislation. In his message to Congress in December, Wilson said: "With the free expression of opinion and with the advocacy of orderly political change, however fundamental, there must be no interference, but towards passion and malevolence tending to incite crime and insurrection under guise of political evolution there should be no leniency." Legislation which had been recommended by the Attorney General, Wilson remarked, should be passed.[25] The fear of radical ideas and utterances is well reflected in the fact that some seventy different sedition bills were proposed in Congress during the latter part of 1919 and early weeks of 1920.[26]

On January 10, 1920, the Senate took up the Sterling bill. This measure would have made it "unlawful for any person to advocate or advise the overthrow, or to write or knowingly to print, publish, utter, sell, or distribute any document, book, circular, paper, journal, or other written or printed communication, in or by which there is advised the overthrow, by force or violence" of the Government of the United States. Furthermore, any literature which advocated destruction of persons or property as a means of accomplishing "economic, industrial, or political changes" was to be nonmailable.[27]

Senator France regretted that the Senate had permitted "this repressive and destructive legislation" to crowd bills into the background which he considered much more important. As was to be expected, Senator Borah attacked the provision dealing with keeping certain literature from the mails, and he was successful in getting an amendment more favorable to the accused. The protests of a few senators, however, were in vain. The Red Scare at that very time was reaching its height and the Senate meant to do what it could to aid Attorney General Palmer in silencing or ridding the country of Reds.

Less than three weeks before, on December 21, 1919, the Justice Department had deported 249 aliens on the *Buford,* popularly known as the "Soviet Ark." Then on January 2 over 4,000 radicals, Communists, members of the Communist Labor party, and other suspected radicals were corralled in various parts of the country,[28] and frantic demands arose for the Government to fit out more Soviet Arks. Many arrests were made without cause or excuse, and civil rights were shamefully violated and abused, but this was of little concern to those who would save America by physical or legal repression.

It was in this atmosphere that a poorly attended Senate passed the Sterling bill by a voice vote on January 10, 1920.[29] The most interesting aspect of the debate just prior to the bill's passage was Senator McKellar's demand to make the measure even more restrictive and repressive. The McKellar amendment asked that every citizen who either spoke or wrote to other persons "with the intent, either peaceably or by violence," to overthrow the Government of the United States should be fined and imprisoned, or "in the discretion of the judge, be deported permanently to the Island of Guam" or to any of the Philippine Islands. If Senator McKellar could have had his way the United States would have established its own Siberia.[30]

The Sterling bill now went to the House, where it was amalgamated with the one being pushed by George S. Graham of Pennsylvania. The lower chamber considered the Sterling-Graham measure with utmost seriousness, but it was never passed much to the disgust of strong nationalists. People were about to recover their sanity and balance despite the continued preachings of Palmer, some congressmen and senators, elements of the press, and members of the general public, that destructive revolution was imminent.

Many factors accounted for the rather sudden decline of the Red Scare.[31] There had been those, of course, who had urged an end to repression both during and immediately after the war. The influence of these individuals gradually gained more weight. In the closing days of the war, George Creel had written to Wilson suggesting that "as soon as possible steps should be taken to demobilize the Council of National Defense so that the chauvinistic, reactionary state organizations may be put out of business."[32] Dudley Field Malone was reported by the New York *World* on February 17, 1919, as saying that Americans were being frightened by government detective agencies and spies. "If I were returning, as President Wilson is," Field said, "to put into effect a great idea, I would drag the detective reports out, I would let the press speak again for liberty, I would abolish the Espionage Law and Burleson with it."

But these and other demands to end legal repression were less important than the fact that people finally came to realize that there had been no real danger from the Bolsheviks in the first place. Furthermore, communism seemed to be losing ground in parts of Europe. People's attention was being increasingly devoted to other things such as prohibition, woman suffrage, and the coming presidential election. Of greater importance, as Murray has pointed out, "was the fact that at last the temper of war was giving way to the temper of peace." [33] Indeed, it was too much to expect that Americans would for long exhibit wartime hysteria, even when stimulated by the fears of radicalism, when those fears proved to be illusory.

The excesses of extreme nationalists did as much as or more than anything else to bring a reaction against hysteria and extralegalism. The arrest of hundreds of alleged radicals without warrant or cause—merely on suspicion—between November, 1919, and January, 1920, brought protests even from conservatives. However, it was the suspension of five Socialist assemblymen from the New York Legislature on January 7, 1920, which electrified the growing storm of protest.

It was Charles Evans Hughes who took the lead in sounding the alarm. He condemned the assembly's action as being contrary to the "fundamental principles of our government." Could the government be saved, Hughes asked, "at the cost of its own principles." Hughes held no brief for Socialism, but his concern arose out of a desire to "maintain the peaceful processes essential to democracy," and his wish "to see Socialists as well as Republicans and Democrats enjoy their political rights." Even apart from principle, Hughes concluded, such action would "do more to encourage the spirit of revolution and to strengthen the advocates of violence than any conceivable propaganda could accomplish." [34] Hughes not only protested, but he led a move in the New York Bar Association to send a committee to Albany to defend the rights of the ousted Socialists. On January 20, Hughes filed a statement on behalf of the Bar Association which, after reviewing the merits of the case, urged that the Socialists be reseated at once.[35]

The Hughes position received widespread backing, although the Socialists did not regain their seats in the assembly. Summarizing the press comment, the *Literary Digest* said, "Emphatic protest and almost universal condemnation are launched by Republicans, Democrats, and Socialist newspapers alike" at the suspending of five duly elected Socialists. The Springfield *Republican* ridiculed the situation and asked when the Democrats would be suspended by the Republicans, or the Republicans by the Democrats because the others' principles were inimical to the United States.[36] Senator Borah denounced the action, and even Senator Harding criticized it.[37]

However, the *New York Times* would not concede that any wrong had been perpetrated on American democratic principles. It sourly editorialized that the action at Albany should "impress some of our revolutionaries with the strength and the depth of the intention of the great mass of the American people to keep their polity intact against all the efforts of those who would destroy its fundamental principles."[38] Not of least importance was the *Times'* constant harping on the St. Louis antiwar Socialist platform of 1917.[39] But the popular tide had turned.

The ebbing trend of the Red Scare was also seen when the alien deportation policy was modified. There was still strong public support for more "Soviet Arks," but officials in the Labor Department, especially Assistant Secretary Louis F. Post who was responsible for deportation orders, reversed the extreme actions desired by Palmer. Post cancelled hundreds of warrants when he found no real basis for deportation. "In nearly every deportation case," he wrote, "the record disclosed nothing but some variety of proof of mere technical membership in one or another organization which the Secretary of Labor had held to be within the proscription of the alien deportation laws. And in most of those cases it was apparent that the alien had neither suspicion nor cause for suspicion that the organization was unlawful."[40] Post explained that "as a rule, the hearings show the aliens arrested to be working men of good character, who are not anarchists or revolutionists, nor politically or otherwise dangerous in any sense." They had been held and subjected to severe hardships, Post declared, "for nothing more dangerous than affiliating with friends of their own race, country and language, and without the slightest indication of sinister motive, or of any unlawful act within their knowledge and intention."[41]

Post received blistering criticisms for his actions and was widely accused of tenderness toward the Reds. Congressman Davey said that Post's "sympathies evidently are with the enemies of our Government." Davey lamented the fact that "the hand of the Attorney General has been made impotent by that friend of revolutionists and that enemy of our Government, Louis F. Post."[42] There were demands for Post's impeachment, and Representative Homer Hoch of Kansas introduced the necessary resolution on April 15. At the subsequent hearings, Post was at first not asked to testify. However, on May 7 he gave such a brilliant defense and explanation of his action that the impeachment proceedings were soon dropped.[43] In any event, Post's efforts greatly reduced the number of aliens finally deported. He cancelled some 2,202 arrest warrants and finally by June, 1920, only 591 aliens were still subject to deportation.[44]

Most Americans had recovered their equilibrium by the spring of 1920. Yet there were those who continued to assail the supposed Red menace and to demand government repression of economic and political nonconformists. Those who favored a peacetime sedition law died hard. Palmer continued to advocate very drastic legislation to punish peacetime sedition.[45] On January 27, 1920, in a general letter to the nation's press, Palmer concluded, "My one desire is to acquaint people like you with the real menace of evil-thinking which is the foundation of the Red movement." [46]

Congressman Davey, who had introduced one of the severest restrictive measures, passionately urged his colleagues to act. As late as April, 1920, Davey stressed the fact that the United States had no law which would reach the apostles and leaders of revolution. It was absolutely necessary, he said, that "the apostle of this red doctrine, who makes it his business to spread the poison, who incites and fires the gullible dupes of red revolution" be repressed by law. Attacking those who insisted upon freedom to talk, Davey declared, "It makes me suspicious of their real purpose." [47] But the flames of wartime and postwar repression were dying and no amount of fanning by Congressman Davey or persons of like mind could revive them.

Federal peacetime sedition legislation had been beaten by the fair-mindedness and good sense of the American people and of some of their leaders. Senator George W. Norris spoke for a majority when he said that he had "faith enough in the principles of our Government and in its very foundation-stones to believe that it can withstand the attack of crazy nonsensical anarchists and others." Justice Holmes declared that "effervescing opinions" were like champagnes; "the quickest way to let them get flat is to let them get exposed to the air." [48]

The postwar attitudes of the American people can be partly explained by the fact that they were unprepared for the new world in which they found themselves in 1919. Most people had expected that, when the fighting ended, a prewar type of normalcy would be restored. They comfortably expected that with Germany defeated and the Kaiser in exile things would be about the same as they had been in prewar years. But, as is often the case, men's ideas of what was to be and what actually happened were entirely different. Conditions did not turn out as people thought they would. Consequently, they were unprepared for the social unrest, for the strikes and discontent so prevalent in those postwar months.

Americans were puzzled and disturbed. Instead of seeking the real reasons for the trouble, the press, government officials, and citizens in general adopted what Frank I. Cobb called the "medicine man procedure of hunting out the devil upon whom the responsibility could be laid." [49] The new devil, of course, was radicalism. The idea of repressing radicals by jailing them was silly because ideas are not so easily curbed. The way to deal with the problem was to try to remove the causes of discontent and restlessness rather than to suppress manifestations of that unrest. It took over a year after the war for a majority of the American people to recognize this elementary principle. The recovery of national sanity by the summer of 1920 ended a three-year period during which strident nationalism had demanded conformity of thought and action to such an extent that fundamental liberties were openly and unashamedly violated. The best traditions of American democracy had been hit a hard blow. The rights of free speech and free press in the United States never recovered completely from the damage done in those years.

"My heartsickness in politics comes not from the
crook and the rogue, but from the honest and well-
intentioned who blindly stab and destroy with their
good intentions."

Hiram Johnson [1]

THE VALUE OF FREEDOM

The civil strife in the United States in the years 1917–18 was only
an incidental part of a much larger problem. Primarily it was another
chapter in the long story of mankind's bigotry, intolerance, and in-
humanity to man. There was a time when men were imprisoned, tortured, and killed in the name of religion. It was said that these "heretics"
constituted a threat to the true religion and to the church. What was
actually meant was that they constituted a threat to the power, the
opinions, and the programs of the individuals in control of religion and
the church. In our own age there are areas where men are imprisoned,
tortured, and killed, not for their religious beliefs but in the name of the
state. Now it is argued that political heretics constitute a threat to the
nation. Here again what is actually meant is that they constitute a threat
to the power, the opinions, and the programs of the individuals in control
of the state. The attack on civil rights and freedom during World War I
was indeed part of the age-old problem of the relationship between the
individual and the state. The experiences of many opponents of war
showed clearly what can happen to individual freedoms in time of crisis,
even in the United States where the habits and traditions for protecting
those rights were historically strong.

An important question is, did the American people learn anything
from their World War I experiences? Did the widespread violations of
freedom and civil rights teach any lessons? Did the repressions and demand for conformity cause American citizens to vow an eternal war
against the repetition of such events?

If World War I is compared with World War II, it is evident that the latter was fought without the harsh and extensive attacks on freedom of speech and press which were so common in World War I.[2] It is true, of course, that some Americans suffered from government policies of restriction. Thousands of Japanese were interned simply because they were Japanese.[3] Some papers, including Father Coughlin's *Social Justice,* were denied mailing privileges. There were a few incidents in which repressive policies were employed against political and economic radicals, either to the right or the left. These things were all reminiscent of World War I.

However, there were not the lynchings or mob actions; not the convictions of people for criticizing the President; there were not the pressure and charges of disloyalty if one failed to buy bonds or subscribe to the Red Cross; German was not dropped from the curriculum of hundreds of schools and colleges; yellow paint as a mark of disloyalty was seldom if ever seen; tar and feather episodes so common as punishment for disloyalty during World War I were not in evidence; conscientious objectors received much better treatment than in World War I; manifestations of intolerance and repression so characteristic of 1917 and 1918 were much less common. Indeed, the American people seemed more mature, less fearful, and more concerned with the rights and opinions of others.

So far, so good. However, the picture presented here is, unfortunately, much less than the whole story. In fact, since World War II, and even before the United States entered that conflict, there have been successful demands for repression of thought and opinion. The demands for conformity have grown to dangerous proportions. They have arisen out of a popular fear of communism and have been fostered to a considerable degree by professional patriots and demagogs. Pages have been taken directly from the book of World War I, and new chapters of repression have been added. Conformity and loyalty were synonymous in World War I. Now loyalty is associated with the conformity demanded by those who oppose communism. The present attack on individual rights and liberties can be summed up in the legislative investigations of individuals for loyalty, state and federal sedition laws, loyalty oaths for public officials and labor union leaders, acceptance of the principle of guilt by association, and even threats to those who dare to criticize government or its policies, especially those policies relating to loyalty.

These problems have all been dealt with extensively elsewhere and it is not proposed to review them here.[4] However, something must be said of the present laws and actions which show a close relationship to the situation in World War I. A. Mitchell Palmer went to his grave without seeing Congress pass a peacetime sedition law which he so earnestly desired in 1919 and 1920. But his departed spirit could look with complete satisfaction and approval on the Alien Registration Act of 1940, generally known as the Smith Act. Here was the country's first peacetime sedition legislation since 1798.

This law grew out of investigations and hearings conducted by the Un-American Activities Committee of Congress in the late 1930's. These investigators concluded, with considerable popular support, that the country was honeycombed with Communists. The part of the law relating to seditious utterances and writings made it unlawful for any person "to knowingly or willfully advocate, abet, advise, or teach the duty, necessity, desirability, or propriety of overthrowing or destroying any government in the United States by force or violence, or by the assassination of any officer of any such government." Similarly, it was unlawful to "print, publish, edit, issue, circulate, sell, distribute, or publicly display any written or printed matter" with a view to "overthrowing or destroying any government in the United States by force or violence." [5]

The Smith Act was patterned after the Espionage Act of World War I and the various state criminal syndicalism laws. In fact, the states had led the way and the federal Government was only following the examples already established when it acted in 1940. By the end of 1950 thirty-one states and territories had passed laws repressing seditious utterances and writings, and twenty states had criminal syndicalism laws in force. And the cities were not to be outdone, as a number of them passed anti-sedition ordinances. [6]

In 1950 Congress, under a continuing fear of the Communist menace, took another long step down the road of repression when it passed the Internal Security Act, commonly referred to as the McCarran Act. Under this statute it is unlawful for any person to conspire with others "to perform any act which would substantially contribute to the establishment within the United States of a totalitarian dictatorship." [7] Furthermore, in a time of national emergency people may be detained if there is reasonable belief that a person "probably will commit or conspire with others to commit espionage or sabotage." This is a new type of repression which may punish an individual *before* any unlawful act has been committed. These laws, along with other aspects of the federal Government's loyalty program, raise some fundamental questions about civil rights and human freedoms.

Americans who either participated in or approved of the events recorded in the pages of this book believed that they were good patriotic citizens. They felt that their motive of achieving unity behind the war effort was of such supreme importance that they could not be held strictly accountable for the means used to accomplish it. In other words, the end justified the means. They rationalized their conduct by saying that war opponents were trying to injure the nation and thus did not merit the privilege of free speech, nor the physical safety and security that the law and the nation granted to people in normal times. What they were actually doing was repeating the age-old trick of deceiving themselves and others by sanctifying their pet project—a war, an economic fancy, a racial fantasy—by identifying it with God, with religion, or with the nation.

This specious thinking has turned up everywhere in recent times. It has been used to excuse the destruction of freedom within nations and to promote acts which have destroyed the peace between nations. It was the prime justification for those who killed the Archduke Franz Ferdinand, Jean Jaurès, Giacomo Matteotti, and innumerable nameless people in Germany and Russia within the last three decades. These assassins, like those in Butte, Montana, and Collinsville, Illinois, claimed to be patriots. They said that their victims were enemies of the state, had injured the state, or were planning to injure the state. Thus the punishment handed out to them was deserved, and the perpetrators of the acts were patriots. This type of thinking is all too prevalent in mid-twentieth century United States. Now the demand for repression comes in the name of a type of negative loyalty against communism. The test of loyalty is not acts or deeds so much as loud denunciation of communism and the acceptance of certain repressive policies to fight it. One is reminded of the hypocritical Pharisee of Jesus' time who demonstrated his piety by long public prayers.

Excited Americans who made up the vigilante groups, the loyalty leagues, and the defense councils in 1917–18 displayed American traits. They reflected the lurid qualities of the American press and the American theater. They also demonstrated a normal human willingness to sacrifice fundamental principles or long-range benefits in order to gain some immediate advantage.

Since the beginning of modern history there have been people ready to support the autocratic power of rulers and to limit or suppress the rights and freedoms of individual citizens. Supposedly, however, believers in democracy do not accept this principle. In the American democratic system the majority party is given the reins of government, but its authority is neither absolute nor permanent. Ultimate sovereignty remains in the citizenry and not in the government. Thus the business of the public officeholder in this arrangement is not to "rule" but to advance the welfare of all citizens and to protect their freedoms, immunities, and sovereign power. Above all, this means the protection of those citizens in minority groups whose views are opposed to those of the majority.

But, as might be expected, even in democratic countries politicians and pressure groups have sometimes stirred uneasily under such limitations and restrictions. The yearning to get one's way is so strong, regardless of the political traditions of a nation, that some men will seek to break down this system. In times of crisis, such as the 1917–18 period, good people, well-intentioned people, "democratic" people will themselves advocate a policy of repression and the abolition of freedom. They argue that the nation's right to protect itself overrides the citizen's right to express himself.

But freedom is not a handicap placed on a democratic nation to humor people. As Henry Steele Commager has written, "We do not protect freedom to indulge in error. We protect freedom in order to discover truth." [8] Freedom is an advantage given to a nation; it is national life insurance. To prevent individuals from expressing their views, therefore, does not protect a nation; it weakens it.

A country in which there is freedom of expression is one which has freedom of action. Policies are not limited to those suggested by a ruler or a dominant party. They may be initiated or modified by the suggestions of any individual or group. In this way a nation's range of effectiveness is widened and serious errors, even tragic errors, may be avoided. Man is prone to err. No individual, no ruler, no legislature, no political party can avoid making mistakes. But where policies are subject to unrestricted debate, where actions must withstand unlimited criticism, blunders can be avoided. Under such a system protagonists can safely present the good points of their theories, and opponents can safely uncover their faults. As a result, the nation can change its policies at any time; it can make strategic retreats; it can reverse its course. Politics is the art of the pliable. No system other than one of free government allows a nation such flexibility or such stability. To be sure, freedom, as Alan Barth has said, "cannot provide a guarantee against ruinous mistakes; but it can provide a means of correcting mistakes, a means denied to those in a society where dissent is silenced." [9]

But extremists, people excited by hatreds and fears, overlook the fundamental advantages of freedom. They see only dangers arising from differing ideas. They consider freedom a liability rather than an asset and feel safer with blinders on the nation. In their thinking there are only two choices—their way and the wrong way.

The conduct of these individuals is the Achilles heel of modern governments. Such doctrinaires and extremists, hiding behind the shield of patriotism or national loyalty, try to build up support for some program or policy. It may be a war, a reform, opposition to a political doctrine, or something else which claims their passionate support. They are assisted by politicians eager to gain votes, by newspapermen desirous of selling papers, by entertainment people anxious to gain popularity. They all join, perhaps unconsciously, in pandering to fear, hatred, greed, envy, conceit, in spite of the fact that they usually speak in the name of God, religion, justice, democracy, humanity, or any number of other righteous generalizations. When these pressure groups are successful, large segments of the public share their excitement and become equally unbalanced. Thoughtful people are afraid to disagree with them, and extremism dominates the scene. This was true in 1917–18 and has more recently been repeated in the early 1950's in Senator Joseph McCarthy's anti-communism campaign. Democracy and freedom of action, the right to disagree, to dissent, are thus seriously curbed by the popular demand for conformity.

World War I created new national and international problems of great magnitude. Mid-century Americans can understand the feelings of anxiety and uncertainty which prevailed. Yet the violation of civil rights and the mob actions can arouse only condemnation in the minds of liberty-loving citizens. The duty of the supporters of war was to answer the war opponents and not to jail them. Under a democratic system of government, free discussion, not repression, is the way to achieve unity. The power to maltreat or imprison those who entertain dissenting opinions is a tyrannical power. It is the prime characteristic of despotic governments and wherever it has been used it has injured the nation. There certainly is no excuse for its use among free peoples.

Such, however, was not the view of American nationalists in the years 1917 and 1918, or in the 1950's. They felt that because they were "right" in a situation involving loyalty to the Government they were justified in silencing or exterminating those who were "wrong." They apparently believed that their good motives justified their evil actions. They demanded the power to suppress radicals and pacifists, and their endeavor to institute a campaign of repression was successful. They succeeded in installing in the United States the European Continental system of limited or restricted freedom to replace the Jeffersonian system of popular sovereignty. Laws were passed which, in effect, deprived all those who disagreed with the Government in its war policies of the right to express those opinions. Supported by these laws, Government officials and mobs did suppress freedom of speech, freedom of press, and freedom of assembly. The newspapers supported such actions, and some courts approved them.

During the first World War freedom was taken away from the American people and placed in the hands of their lawyers. It ceased to be a constitutional right and became a personal concession of rulers and judges. Here was found a return to the idea of government by men rather than by laws. One judge might permit certain views to be expressed while another might prohibit all ideas not pleasing to him. What one had a right to say or print became a vague and unpredictable thing. A citizen without legal advice certainly could not tell. His only safety lay in silence. Judge Van Valkenburgh probably reached the low point in interpreting freedom of speech when he said it meant "criticism which is made *friendly* to the Government, *friendly* to the war, *friendly* to the policies of the Government." [10] The difference between this view and the views expressed by judges of the Hapsburgs, Hohenzollerns, and Romanovs would be hard to find.

It was customary at the time for defenders of the repressive movement to say that it was justified by the circumstances. But this raises a fundamental question of whether there is more safety in freedom or in repression. Is a nation made stronger by a free system or by a closed system? Are modern Americans willing to admit that the problems of war, hot or cold, labor-capital disputes, conservative-radical political conflicts, and other problems cannot be solved within the framework of freedom? It is certain that if man's big problems are to be solved satisfactorily at all, they will be solved in this framework. History belies any other conclusion. The wrecks and ruins of closed systems of government which demanded conformity and crushed dissent and freedom are strewn along the paths of history from ancient times to the present.

There are those who would even today say that under the repressive policies of 1917 and 1918 freedom still existed in the United States. But a freedom which is hedged about with ifs, buts, and whereases is not freedom. Freedom of speech means the right to express views. It cannot mean the right to express only correct views or intelligent views. Human beings are too fallible. Freedom of speech has to mean the right to express wrong views, and stupid views, yes, and even evil views. The basic idea back of freedom of speech is that divergent views clarify men's thinking and that in the conflict of ideas the right and just views will eventually prevail. People need not be protected from bad ideas. If one does not believe this he should not deceive himself that he believes in freedom of speech and in democratic government. People are either fit to govern or they are unfit. If they are fit and qualified to govern themselves the Government has no responsibility to protect them from undesirable ideas. The people will protect themselves, a fact which is the very core or essence of self-government.

Along with the right to be wrong or stupid, freedom of speech must also include the right to express opposing and dissenting views. Praise for conservative ideas, applause for governmental policies, is permitted under the worst autocrats, kings, duces, czars, and commissars. A democracy, however, is different. In such governments all ideas are subject to questioning and to attack, and governmental policies may be eternally damned. Beyond this, freedom of speech also means the right to speak on important matters, such as war, peace, conscription, militarism, communism, fascism, labor unions, big business, or any other subject. Freedom of speech which is limited to the field of *trivia* is *not* freedom of speech.

Furthermore, freedom of speech has to mean the right to speak in critical times, in times when irrevocable decisions are in the making. One must be able to debate, attack, and condemn national actions and policies in time of war and in other times of tension. To those who contend that the freedom of speech referred to in the Constitution applies only to noncritical times, one must answer in the following words: "The Constitution of the United States is a law for rulers and people, equally in war and in peace, and covers with the shield of its protection all classes of men, at all times, and under all circumstances. No doctrine involving more pernicious consequences was ever invented by the wit of man than that any of its provisions can be suspended during any of the great exigencies of government. Such a doctrine leads directly to anarchy or despotism." [11]

Justice Brandeis had something pertinent to say on this point. Speaking of popular frenzy and hysteria, he said that people in peace as well as in war "may differ widely as to what loyalty to our country demands; and an intolerant majority, swayed by passion or by fear, may be prone . . . to stamp as disloyal opinions with which it disagrees." But he added, "Convictions such as these, besides abridging freedom of speech threaten freedom of thought and of belief." [12]

The problem of maintaining the rights and freedoms of free men is not an easy one. The main problem is an old one, namely, that of trying to reconcile liberty with authority. Freedom is not absolute. Absolute freedom without law or individual responsibility is anarchy. Freedom involves a personal responsibility which ultimately comes from the wisdom and experience of a people who believe it contributes to national strength and individual happiness. Democratic administration and personal freedom cannot be assured by government, even if government were disposed to do so. Freedom and democracy can be strong only when the vast body of citizens maintains individual discipline and responsibility. Thus, in the final analysis, maintenance of freedom depends not upon law but upon the people themselves who have a respect for and appreciation of the law. How well citizens understand the basic meaning and values of freedom will determine its strength and existence. Charles Evans Hughes once said of freedom, "We, the people, are its power, its peril, and its hope." [13]

Freedom is not something which, once obtained, continues to exist automatically. It requires constant surveillance by a people to maintain this valuable heritage. Americans must forever be on guard to keep their freedoms from eroding away under the pressure of chronic crises, legal repression, or the pressure of self-styled patriots who play upon the fears of people in troubled times. The American people may never again be able to enjoy individual freedom to the extent known before World War I. Government must be prepared to act quickly and effectively against crime, violence, and sabotage. But neither the Government nor anything else should ever be permitted to curb differing or dissenting ideas.

Those who would advocate repression and oppose deviation from the accepted standards imply that all truth is already known. But this is a false assumption. All truth is not now and never will be known. Free expression and interchange of all kinds of ideas are the only avenue to truth. Perhaps the most telling contrast between the free, democratic position and that of a closed and uniform system was drawn by columnist Stewart Alsop in a story which he wrote in Moscow in 1955. Talking to some Russians, Alsop said, "In America if there were a dozen Americans talking politics in one place they would soon be arguing loudly with each other. Don't you ever argue with each other about anything?" he asked. A Russian replied, "There is an old saying that argument is the birthplace of truth. But we already know the truth. Therefore, we have no need to argue with each other." [14] God forbid that such an attitude should ever take root and flourish in the United States.

━━━

Chapter 1

1 *New York Times,* February 2, 1917.
2 *Ibid.,* April 3, 1917.
3 Merle Curti, *Peace or War: The American Struggle, 1636–1936* (New York, 1936), p. 252.
4 *Ibid.,* p. 251.
5 David Starr Jordan, *The Days of a Man* (New York, 1922), II, 718–19.
6 *Ibid.,* pp. 727, 729. See also *New York Herald,* April 2, 1917.
7 Curti, *Peace or War,* p. 250.
8 *Cong. Rec.,* 65 Cong., 1 Sess., April 4, 1917, pp. 212, 214.
9 *Ibid.,* p. 234.
10 *Ibid.,* p. 227.
11 *Ibid.,* April 5, 1917, p. 253.
12 *Ibid.,* p. 364.
13 *Ibid.,* April 4, p. 215.
14 *Ibid.,* p. 235.
15 See Jane Addams, *Peace and Bread in Time of War* (New York, 1922), p. 117.
16 *Cong. Rec.,* 65 Cong., 1 Sess., April 4, 1917, p. 209.
17 *Ibid.,* p. 228.
18 *Ibid.,* p. 220.
19 The antiwar vote in the lower house was larger than had been expected and it was said that it would have been even larger if congressmen had voted their convictions. See Robert Lansing to Edward N. Smith, April 7, 1917, Lansing Papers. See also the *New York Post* of April 6, 1917.
20 *Cong. Rec.,* 65 Cong., 1 Sess., May 11, 1917, p. 2088. This document was published in its entirety in the *American Socialist,* April 21, 1917. This official organ of the Socialist party editorialized on January 9, 1915: "Nor should American Socialists favor the German side of this war as against that of the Allies. The claim that the German sword has been drawn in the interests of 'culture' is just as false and hypocritical as the contention that the Allies are fighting for democracy." For a fuller account of the position of the Socialists, see David A. Shannon, *The Socialist Party of America* (New York, 1955), pp. 99–125.
21 Congressman Fred A. Britten of Illinois said, "The truth of the matter is that 90 per cent of your people and mine do not want this declaration of war . . . ." *Cong. Rec.,* 65 Cong., 1 Sess., April 5, 1917, p. 317.
22 Cedric C. Cummins, *Indiana Public Opinion and the World War, 1914–1917* (Indianapolis, 1945), p. 247.
23 Quoted in *ibid.,* p. 251.

24 John C. Crighton, *Missouri and the World War, 1914–1917: A Study in Public Opinion* (Columbia, Mo., 1947), pp. 182–83.

25 *Ibid.*, p. 185. For the situation in North Dakota see Robert P. Wilkins, "North Dakota and the European War, 1914–1917: A Study in Public Opinion" (Doctoral dissertation, University of West Virginia, 1954), pp. 324–34. The attitude of people in Maine has been discussed by Edwin Costrell, *How Maine Viewed the War, 1914–1917* (Orono, Maine, 1940). Costrell concluded that "Maine wanted war when the United States entered upon war; that if the question had been referred to the people of Maine in a national referendum they would have voted for war" (p. 89).

26 A few localities did hold unofficial plebiscites and reported an overwhelming majority. Congressman Lundeen sent out 54,000 ballots in his district. Of 8,000 replies which he had received by April 5, only 10 per cent, or 800, voted for war, he said. These polls, of course, were too limited to mean much. In one town the Secret Service men moved in and the State Attorney General hastily ruled that a referendum could not be held because it was not a local question. *New York Herald*, April 1, 1917. See also *Cong. Rec.*, 65 Cong., 1 Sess., April 5, 1917, p. 362.

27 Merle Curti, *Bryan and World Peace* (Northampton, Mass., 1931), p. 247. There are a few letters on this period in the Bryan papers in the Library of Congress.

28 Jordan, *The Days of a Man*, II, 734.

29 James Oneal, "The Socialists in the War," *American Mercury*, X (April, 1927), 419.

30 Ralph Barton Perry, *The Yale Review*, VII (April, 1918), 670. This statement was made in connection with Perry's review of the books, *My Four Years in Germany*, by James W. Gerard, and *Foes in Our Own Household*, by Theodore Roosevelt.

31 John L. Heaton, *Cobb of "The World"* (New York, 1924), p. 270.

Chapter II

1 See Carlton J. H. Hayes, *Essays on Nationalism* (New York, 1937), p. 6.

2 Addams, *Peace and Bread*, pp. 111 f. ". . . this concerted and deliberate attempt at misrepresentation on the part of newspapers of all shades of opinion was quite new . . . . After the United States entered the war, the press throughout the country systematically undertook to misrepresent and malign pacifists as a recognized part of propaganda and as a patriotic duty." *Ibid.*, pp. 134 f.

3 *New York Times*, August 16, 1917.

4 *Ibid.*

5 *Ibid.*, November 21, 1917.

6 Ray Stannard Baker and William E. Dodd, *The Public Papers of Woodrow Wilson: War and Peace* (New York, 1925–27, 6 vols.), V, 67.

7 American Civil Liberties Union files, XXXV, 106 ff. See also the *Minneapolis Journal,* July 8, 1917.

8 Thomas F. Carroll, "Freedom of Speech and of the Press in Wartime: The Espionage Act," *Michigan Law Review,* XVII (June, 1919), 622.

9 Ernest S. Bates, *This Land of Liberty* (New York, 1930), p. 97.

10 Carroll, "Freedom of Speech and of the Press," pp. 623 ff.

11 *Cong. Rec.,* 65 Cong., 1 Sess., April 30, 1917, p. 1599.

12 *Ibid.,* April 19, 1917, p. 831.

13 C. Vann Woodward, *Tom Watson, Agrarian Rebel* (New York, 1938), p. 454. Quoting the *Jeffersonian,* May 17 and 24, 1917.

14 *Cong. Rec.,* 65 Cong., 1 Sess., April 26, 1917, p. 1167.

15 *Ibid.,* April 30, 1917, p. 1594.

16 *Ibid.,* May 11, 1917, p. 2099.

17 *Ibid.*

18 The *Sacramento Bee,* May 12, 1917, gave Senator Johnson credit for defeating the censorship provision. In place of this section there was still operating the voluntary censorship arrangement established earlier. Under this editors submitted doubtful matter to the Committee on Public Information before publishing it. Carroll, "Freedom of Speech and of the Press," p. 628 n.

19 40 *U.S. Stat.* 230, June 15, 1917. See also *Cong. Rec.,* 65 Cong., 1 Sess., April 30, 1917, p. 1604.

20 *Cong. Rec.,* 65 Cong., 1 Sess., April 30, 1917, p. 1595.

21 *Schenck* v. *United States,* 249 U.S. 47, 39 Sup. Ct. 247, 63 L. Ed. 470 (1919).

22 Zechariah Chafee, Jr., "Sedition," *Encyclopedia of the Social Sciences* (New York, 1931), XIII, 638.

23 For example, see the *Minneapolis Journal,* August 16, 1917.

24 Zechariah Chafee, *Freedom of Speech* (New York, 1920), pp. 110, 399 f. See also Chafee, "Sedition," *Encyclopedia of the Social Sciences,* XIII, 638. Consult further Chester R. Milham, "A History of National Espionage Legislation and Its Operation in the United States During the [First] World War" (Ph.D. thesis, University of Southern California, Los Angeles, May, 1938). Note particularly the treatment of the Trading with the Enemy Act, pp. 95 ff.

25 General Ordinance No. 35, 1917, Indianapolis, Indiana, American Civil Liberties Union files, XXXII, 45.

26 *The Annotated Code of the Public General Laws of Maryland,* ed. George P. Bagby (Baltimore, 1924, 2 vols.), II, 3105–7. There was an attempt to get such a law passed in California. See the *Sacramento Bee,* March 18, 1918. For the Idaho law see the Report of the Idaho State Defense Council, April, 1918, Council of National Defense files.

27 H. D. Craig to George Creel, June 13, 1918, Committee on Public Information files.

28 Carbon copy of letter from "director" (probably Walter S. Gifford) of Council of National Defense to Henry C. Quimby, March 1, 1918, Council of National Defense files. See Bulletin No. 99 of the Council of National Defense on loyalty and sedition, June 11, 1918, *ibid.*

29 George Creel, *Rebel at Large: Recollections of Fifty Crowded Years* (New York, 1947), p. 196.

30 Carbon copy of letter from J.S.C., "Assistant Chief," to the State Council of Defense in Louisville, Kentucky, July 1, 1918, Council of National Defense files. For studies of the commendable work of these councils see Frederick Lewis Allen, "The Forty-Eight Defenders," *Century*, XCV (December, 1917), 261–66; and Waldo G. Leland and Newton D. Mereness, *Introduction to the American Official Sources for the Economic and Social History of the World War* (New Haven, 1926), p. 421.

31 Homer Cummings and Carl McFarland, *Federal Justice: Chapters in the History of Justice and the Federal Executive* (New York, 1937), p. 421.

32 American Economic Foundation, *What Happens to Civil Liberties During Times of War?* (Cleveland, 1942), p. 7.

33 Emerson Hough, *The Web* (Chicago, 1919), p. 163.

34 *Ibid.*, p. 14.

35 Cummings and McFarland, *Federal Justice*, p. 422.

36 Woodrow Wilson to Thomas W. Gregory, June 4, 1917, Wilson Papers. See McAdoo's memo, June 2, 1917, *ibid.* Gregory's reply is in the Wilson Papers marked P. F. Department of Justice.

37 For an excellent account of this organization see O. A. Hilton, "The Minnesota Public Safety Commission in World War I, 1917–1919," Oklahoma Agricultural and Mechanical College, Arts and Sciences Studies *Bulletin*, XLVII (Stillwater, Oklahoma, May 15, 1951), 1–44.

38 *Report of the Minnesota Commission of Public Safety* (Minneapolis, 1919), p. 32 f.

39 *Literary Digest*, LIV (June 9, 1917), 1765.

40 Quoted in Cummings and McFarland, *Federal Justice*, p. 420.

41 William Hard, "Mr. Burleson, Espionagent," *New Republic*, XIX (May 10, 1919), 42.

42 George Creel to A. Bruce Bielaski, October 10, 1918, Committee on Public Information files.

43 See the letters from John Lord O'Brian, July, 1918, Committee on Public Information files.

44. Ray Stannard Baker, *Woodrow Wilson: Life and Letters* (New York, 1927–39, 8 vols.), VIII, 67.

45 Woodrow Wilson to Thomas W. Gregory, August 27, 1917, Wilson Papers.

46 Quoted in Baker, *Wilson: Life and Letters*, VII, 283; Gregory to Wilson, October 6, 1917, Wilson Papers.

47 T. W. Gregory to Gilbert A. Currie, April 12, 1918. In Committee on Public Information, *The Official Bulletin*, Vol. II, No. 285, p. 2.

Chapter III

1 *Cong. Rec.*, 65 Cong., 1 Sess., April 16, 1917, p. 731.

2 *Ibid.*, April 25, p. 1120.

3 *Ibid.*, p. 1094.

4 *Ibid.*, April 27, p. 1355.

5 *Wells et al.* v. *United States*, 257 Fed. 605 (9th Cir. 1919). The circular was offered as evidence at the trial. For other cases involving early opposition to conscription see *United States* v. *Pass*, 256 Fed. 731 (9th Cir. 1919). Consult also the Los Angeles *Times*, May 18, 1917, and the *Seattle Union-Record,* May 19, 1917.

6 Wilson to Eliot, April 11, 1917, Wilson Papers.

7 *New York Times,* April 30, 1917. For a discussion of churches in wartime see Ray H. Abrams, *Preachers Present Arms* (New York, 1933), pp. 127–42. See also *Cong. Rec.*, 65 Cong., 1 Sess., April 25, 1917, p. 1094. For the situation in Indiana see Cedric C. Cummins, *Indiana Public Opinion and the World War,* p. 247.

8 Baker and Dodd, *Public Papers of Woodrow Wilson,* V, 38 f.

9 *New York Times,* May 19, 1917.

10 *Ibid.*, May 23 and 29.

11 Los Angeles *Times,* May 28, 1917; *ibid.*, June 28.

12 *United States* v. *Sugar et al.*, 243 Fed. 423 (E.D. Mich. 1917). See also *Sugar* v. *United States*, 252 Fed. 79 (6th Cir. 1918). See the *Minneapolis Journal* of May 28 and 29, 1917. On the other hand, proponents of war were equally determined. The mayor of Sacramento threatened to have police break up a meeting planned by people of that city to oppose sending troops abroad. *Sacramento Bee,* April 16, 1917. As early as mid-April the police in New York City compelled the owner of a building to break a contract with people desiring to hold an anticonscription meeting. "Police were at the meeting place to turn the crowds away." Meetings in Phillipsburg, New Jersey, and another in Gutenberg, New Jersey, were called off because of threats of the mayors of those towns. Others in Brooklyn, New York City, and Providence, Rhode Island, were cancelled for the same reason. See American Civil Liberties Union files, XXV, 106.

  See Woodrow Wilson's comments on war and labor, quoted in Baker and Dodd, *Public Papers of Woodrow Wilson,* V, 36; *New York Times,* September 3, 1917.

13 *Ruthenberg et al.* v. *United States*, 245 U.S. 480 (1918). Ruthenberg was quoted as saying, "Neither of us knew Schue [the man they were said to have induced not to register]; neither of us heard of him until his name appeared in the indictment against us" (*Milwaukee Leader,* February 2, 1918).

14 *Hammerschmidt et al.* v. *United States*, 287 Fed. 817 (6th Cir. 1923). See *Literary Digest,* LIV (June 16, 1917), 1836–37, for picture.

15 Tulsa *Daily World,* June 1, 1917.

16 *Minneapolis Journal,* May 31, June 1, June 3, 1917.

17 *Kramer et al.* v. *United States*, 245 U.S. 478 (1918).

18 *New York Herald,* June 5, 1917. See also Emma Goldman, *Living My Life* (New York, 1931, 2 vols.), II, 602–3; *Goldman et al.* v. *United States*, 245 U.S. 474 (1918).

19 Goldman, *Living My Life,* II, 606.

20 *Anarchism on Trial: Speeches of Alexander Berkman and Emma Goldman*

before the United States District Court in the City of New York, July 1917, ed. B. L. Reitman (New York, 1918), p. 69. See also the *New York Times,* June 16 and 17, 1917.

21 *Anarchism on Trial,* p. 40. Berkman stated that the Conscription Bill "was signed by the President of the United States at ten o'clock at night, May 18th. The witness of the District Attorney stated here that Miss Goldman spoke on May 18th at 9:15 p.m. and that her speech was finished at 9:45." See also Sen. Exec. Doc. No. 153, 66 Cong., 1 Sess. (1919), *Investigation Activities of the Department of Justice,* pp. 125 ff. Goldman, *Living My Life,* II, 622.

22 Goldman, *Living My Life,* II, 623.

23 Baker to Wilson, May 1, 1917, Wilson Papers.

24 *New York Times,* May 28, 1917.

25 *Ibid.,* June 10.

26 As quoted in the *Literary Digest,* LIV (June 16, 1917), 1831.

27 Jane Addams, *Peace and Bread,* pp. 117 ff.

28 William D. Haywood, *Bill Haywood's Book* (New York, 1929), pp. 297–98. See also the Tulsa *Daily World,* July 6, 1917.

29 American Civil Liberties Union files, XLVI, 22.

30 *Arver* v. *United States,* 245 U.S. 366 (1918).

31 *United States* v. *Wangerin,* 245 U.S. 366 (1918).

32 Wilson to Tumulty, July 27, 1917, Wilson Papers.

Chapter IV

1 By June 15, sixty-seven individuals were in jail at Duluth, Minnesota. A few days later over a hundred warrants were out in Los Angeles. See *Minneapolis Journal,* June 15, 1917; and Los Angeles *Times,* June 22, 1917.

2 *Firth et al.* v. *United States,* 253 Fed. 36 (4th Cir. 1918).

3 *New York Herald,* June 17, 1917.

4 Louis P. Goldberg and Eleanore Levenson, *Lawless Judges* (New York, 1935), p. 169. See also Senator Hardwick's discussion of the incident in *Cong. Rec.,* 65 Cong., 1 Sess., September 7, 1917, p. 6743.

5 Quoted in the *New York Times,* July 9, 1917.

6 *Stilson* v. *United States,* 250 U.S. 583 (1919).

7 *New York Times,* July 6, 1917.

8 *Schenck* v. *United States,* 249 U.S. 47 (1919).

9 *Ibid.*

10 *United States* v. *Schenck et al.,* 253 Fed. 212 (1918).

11 *Schenck* v. *United States,* 249 U.S. 47 (1919).

12 *O'Connell et al.* v. *United States,* 253 U.S. 142 (1920). See also *Report of the Attorney General, 1919,* p. 507.

13 *Report of the Attorney General, 1921,* p. 741. Thomas Carey was given two years in the penitentiary for refusing to be drafted and for advising

others to avail themselves of the legal services of Daniel O'Connell. *Ibid.*, *1922*, p. 414.

14 *Ibid., 1918*, p. 49.

15 Quoted in *United States* v. *Pierce et al.*, 245 Fed. 878 (N.D. N.Y. 1917).

16 *United States* v. *Baker et al.*, 247 Fed. 124 (D. Md. 1917).

17 Department of Justice, *Interpretation of War Statutes*, Bulletin No. 52 (Washington, 1918), p. 27.

18 *Pierce et al* v. *United States*, 252 U.S. 239 (1920). See also *Report of the Attorney General, 1918*, p. 49.

19 *O'Hare* v. *United States,* 253 Fed. 538 (8th Cir. 1918).

20 *Report of the Attorney General, 1918*, p. 49; see quotation in *ibid., 1920*, p. 779.

21 Lawrence Todd to Roger Baldwin, December 28, 1917, American Civil Liberties Union files, VIII, 129.

22 *Report of the Attorney General, 1922*, p. 437.

23 *Daily Argus Leader* (Sioux Falls), August 28, 1917. See also *Report of the Attorney General, 1918*, p. 48.

24 Quoted in *Heynacher* v. *United States,* 257 Fed. 61 (8th Cir. 1919).

25 *Head* v. *United States,* 248 U.S. 593 (1918). Quotation found in New York Bar Association, "Records and Briefs," in the case of *Head* v. *United States,* 248 U.S. 593 (1918).

26 *Fairchild* v. *United States,* 265 Fed. 584 (8th Cir. 1920).

27 *Report of the Attorney General, 1921*, p. 702. See *United States* v. *Sugarman*, 245 Fed. 604 (1917); and *Sugarman* v. *United States,* 249 U.S. 182 (1919).

28 "United States *v.* Hicks," 1743 C.D. 6, United States District Court, Oklahoma City. Unreported case.

29 *Report of the Attorney General, 1919*, p. 518.

30 *Enfield* v. *United States,* 261 Fed. 141 (8th Cir. 1919).

31 *Bryant et al.* v. *United States,* 257 Fed. 378 (5th Cir. 1919).

32 *New York Times,* August 5, 1917.

33 *Ibid.,* July 13.

34 C. Vann Woodward, *Tom Watson, Agrarian Rebel* (New York, 1938), p. 457.

35 *Cong. Rec.,* 65 Cong., 2 Sess., May 2, 1918, p. 5941.

36 This account has been taken from the excellent study of Charles C. Bush, "The Green Corn Rebellion" (Master's thesis, University of Oklahoma, 1932), pp. 18–68.

37 *Report of the Attorney General, 1918*, p. 22.

38 *Cong. Rec.,* 65 Cong., 1 Sess., September 7, 1917, p. 6742.

Chapter v

1 George Creel, *The War, the World, and Wilson* (New York, 1920), p. 145.

2 *Milwaukee Leader,* August 13, 1917.

3   *United States* v. *Krafft,* 249 Fed. 919 (3rd Cir. 1918).

4   State Executive Committee [of the Socialist Party], *Being a True Record of the Case of Frederick Krafft* (Newark, n.d.), pp. 3–8. See also *Report of the Attorney General, 1918,* p. 48.

5   Baker, *Wilson: Life and Letters,* VII, 210.

6   *Ibid.,* p. 313.

7   *United States* ex rel *Milwaukee Social Democratic Publishing Co.* v. *Burleson,* 258 Fed. 282 (1919). See also Chafee, *Freedom of Speech,* pp. 315–17.

8   *Cong. Rec.,* 66 Cong., 1 Sess., November 10, 1919, p. 8228.

9   William Hard, "Burleson and the Call," *New Republic,* XXI (January 7, 1920), 158.

10 Quoted in Hough, *The Web,* p. 74.

11 *Minneapolis Journal,* September 26, 1917.

12 Norman Thomas, *The Conscientious Objector in America* (New York, 1923), p. 85. See also the St. Louis *Post-Dispatch,* March 11, 1918.

13 See Louis Levine, "The Development of Syndicalism in America," *Political Science Quarterly,* XXVIII (September, 1913), 451–79; Paul F. Brissenden, *The I.W.W.: A Study of American Syndicalism* (New York, 1920), p. 341.

14 Quoted in Brissenden, *I.W.W.,* p. 351.

15 Carleton H. Parker, *The Casual Laborer, and Other Essays* (New York, 1920), p. 102.

16 Undated statement of Lincoln Steffens to Colonel Edward M. House, Wilson Papers.

17 W.B. Wilson to Newton D. Baker, June 22, 1917, *ibid.* See also *New York Times,* July 12, 1917.

18 *Cong. Rec.,* 65 Cong., 1 Sess., June 25, 1917, Appendix, p. 594.

19 *Ibid.,* August 23, p. 6264.

20 E. Foster Dowell, *A History of Criminal Syndicalism Legislation in the United States* (Baltimore, 1939), p. 51. Idaho's law was one of the most severe. See pp. 150–51.

21 See the *Minneapolis Journal,* April 14, 30; May 8; June 27, 1917.

22 Edward Delaney and M. T. Rice, *The Bloodstained Trail* (Seattle, 1927), p. 102.

23 *New York Evening Call,* June 4, 1918. See also Haywood, *Bill Haywood's Book,* pp. 299 f.

24 President's Mediation Commission, *Report on the Bisbee Deportations* (Washington, 1918), p. 5. Author's italics.

25 *New York Times,* July 14, 1917. For articles on the Bisbee situation see Robert W. Bruere, "Copper Camp Patriotism," *Nation,* CVI (February 21, 1918), 202–3; "The I.W.W. Raids and Others," *New Republic,* XII (September 15, 1917), 175–77; "The Bisbee Deportations," *Survey,* XXXVIII (July 21, 1917), 353; "The President's Commission at Bisbee," *New Republic,* XIII (December 8, 1917), 140–41. See also Selig Perlman and Philip Taft, *History of Labour in the United States* (New York, 1935), pp. 398–401.

26 Tumulty to Wilson, July 12, 1917, Wilson Papers.

27 Quoted in the *New York Times,* July 14, 1917.

28 Baker, *Wilson: Life and Letters,* VII, 208–9.

29 *Seattle Union-Record,* December 3, 1918. For a list of those arrested for the deportation see the *New York Tribune,* May 15, 1918.

30 *Report on the Bisbee Deportations,* p. 5.

31 *New York Call,* August 23, 1917.

32 *New York Times,* July 22, 1917.

33 Delaney and Rice, *The Bloodstained Trail,* p. 104. See also the *New York Herald,* August 2, 1917.

34 Harrison George, *Is Freedom Dead?* (n.p., n.d.), p. 11.

35 Elting E. Morison, ed., *The Letters of Theodore Roosevelt* (Cambridge, 1954), VIII, 1264.

36 Quoted in *Cong. Rec.,* 71 Cong., 2 Sess., May 12, 1930, p. 8717.

37 Bruere, "Copper Camp Patriotism," pp. 202–3.

38 *Report on the Bisbee Deportations,* p. 6.

39 David Karsner, *The I.W.W. Case* (n.p., n.d.), p. 71.

40 Delaney and Rice, *The Bloodstained Trail,* p. 110.

41 Haywood, *Bill Haywood's Book,* p. 301.

42 Delaney and Rice, *The Bloodstained Trail,* p. 111.

43 Harrison George, *I.W.W. Trial* (n.p., n.d.), p. 20.

44 *New York Times,* August 2, 1917.

45 Delaney and Rice, *The Bloodstained Trail,* p. 111. See also Haywood, *Bill Haywood's Book,* p. 301.

46 Quoted in George, *I.W.W. Trial,* pp. 18–21.

47 Quoted in "Lynch-Law and Treason," *Literary Digest,* LV (August 18, 1917), 13.

48 *Cong. Rec.,* 65 Cong., 1 Sess., August 7, 1917, pp. 5896 ff.

49 Quoted in "Lynch-Law and Treason," p. 13.

Chapter VI

1 *Cong. Rec.,* 65 Cong., 1 Sess., August 11, 1917, p. 5949.

2 George, *Is Freedom Dead?* p. 11.

3 W. W. Folwell, *A History of Minnesota* (St. Paul, 1926, 4 vols.), III, 568.

4 Haywood, *Bill Haywood's Book,* p. 299.

5 Cummings and McFarland, *Federal Justice,* p. 421. For President Wilson's letter to Secretary Baker on investigation of the I.W.W. and other organizations, see Baker, *Wilson: Life and Letters,* VII, 242–43. See also the report of Dr. A. B. Shirer recommending suppression of the I.W.W., Council of National Defense files, September 1, 1917.

6 Hough, *The Web,* p. 133.

7 Ralph Chaplin, *Wobbly* (Chicago, 1948), p. 214.

8 *Ibid.,* p. 224.

9 Memorandum concerning interference with the I.W.W. defense, American Civil Liberties Union files, LXXXVI, 8.

10 Chaplin, *Wobbly,* pp. 222–28.

11 For a sampling of headlines and editorial comment critical of the I.W.W. see Dowell, *Criminal Syndicalism*, pp. 40–43.

12 *San Jose* (California) *Messenger*, September 19, 1917.

13 George, *Is Freedom Dead?* p. 8.

14 Quoted by an unidentified Little Rock, Arkansas, newspaper, September 26, 1917, American Civil Liberties Union files, XXIX, 50.

15 Robert L. Morlan, *Political Prairie Fire: The Nonpartisan League, 1915–1922* (Minneapolis, 1955). For studies of the Nonpartisan League see Theodore Saloutos, "The Rise of the Nonpartisan League in North Dakota, 1915–1917," and "The Expansion and Decline of the Nonpartisan League in the Western Middle West, 1917–1921," *Agricultural History*, XX (January, 1946), 43–61, and (October, 1946), 235–52. See also Charles Edward Russell, *The Story of the Nonpartisan League* (New York, 1920); Herbert E. Gaston, *The Nonpartisan League* (New York, 1920); Andrew A. Bruce, *Non-partisan League* (New York, 1921).

16 "The Farmer and the War," *New Republic*, XIII (November 3, 1917), 8–9.

17 Creel, *Rebel at Large*, p. 200.

18 *Trelease* v. *United States*, 266 Fed. 886 (8th Cir. 1920).

19 Also see Gaston, *The Nonpartisan League*, p. 191.

20 *State* v. *Gilbert*, 141 Minn. 263, 169 N.W. 790 (1918); the Supreme Court of the United States affirmed the decision of the Minnesota Supreme Court in *Gilbert* v. *State of Minnesota*, 254 U.S. 325 (1920).

21 *State* v. *Martin*, 142 Minn. 484, 169 N.W. 792 (1918); in 1919 Martin was granted a new trial. See 173 N.W. 648 (1919).

22 Gaston, *Nonpartisan League*, pp. 197 ff.

23 *Cong. Rec.*, 65 Cong., 1 Sess., August 11, 1917, pp. 5956–57.

24 *New York Times*, August 24, 1917.

25 Quoted in Frank E. Hays, *Senate Election Cases from 1913 to 1940* (Washington, 1941), pp. 52 ff.

26 For La Follette's version of his speech see the *New York Times*, October 12, 1917.

27 *Ibid.*, September 22, 1917.

28 "The Menace of Sedition," *Literary Digest*, LV (September 1, 1917), 11.

29 Quoted in "La Follette as a Foe of Democracy," *Literary Digest*, LV (October 6, 1917), 15–16.

30 *Ibid.*, p. 15.

31 Wilson to Tumulty, October 9, 1917, Wilson Papers.

32 "La Follette as a Foe of Democracy," p. 16.

33 *New York Times*, October 19, 1917.

34 Belle Case La Follette and Fola La Follette, *Robert M. La Follette* (New York, 1953, 2 vols.), II, 930. For a full discussion of the attempt to censure La Follette see pp. 761–931.

35 *New York Tribune*, May 28, 1918.

36 Gaston, *Nonpartisan League*, pp. 208–10.

37 Folwell, *A History of Minnesota*, III, 567.

38 *New York Times*, October 5, 1917.

Chapter VII

1 Tumulty to Wilson, June 18, 1917, Wilson Papers.
2 *Selections From the Correspondence of Theodore Roosevelt and Henry Cabot Lodge, 1884–1918* (New York, 1925, 2 vols.), II, 494.
3 *New York Herald*, July 8, 1917.
4 *New York Times*, August 10, 1917.
5 Wilmington *Evening Journal*, August 13, 1917.
6 Sinclair to Wilson, October 22, 1917, Wilson Papers.
7 "The Menace of Sedition," *Literary Digest*, LV (September 1, 1917), 11.
8 Creel to Lionel B. Moses, August 22, 1917, Committee on Public Information files.
9 *New York Times*, August 29, 1917.
10 "The Pacifist Pilgrims," *Literary Digest*, LV (September 15, 1917), 16.
11 *New York Times*, September 2, 1917.
12 Quoted in Tulsa *Daily World*, September 3, 1917.
13 *New York Times*, September 1, 1917.
14 *Minneapolis Journal*, October 20, 1917.
15 Quoted in "The Pacifist Pilgrims," p. 17.

Chapter VIII

1 Theodore Roosevelt, *The Foes of Our Own Household* (New York, 1926), p. xxv.
2 Theodore Roosevelt, *Roosevelt in the Kansas City Star* (Boston, 1921), p. 177.
3 Roosevelt, *The Foes of Our Own Household*, p. 33.
4 Addams, *Peace and Bread*, p. 113.
5 *New York Herald*, July 15, 1917.
6 American Civil Liberties Union files, XIV, 75.
7 *Ibid.*, p. 79; and LXXVI, 153, 155. See also New York *Evening Post*, February 25, 1918.
8 American Civil Liberties Union files, LXXVIII, 37.
9 *Minneapolis Journal*, July 15, 1917.
10 *Schumann* v. *United States*, 258 Fed. 233 (8th Cir. 1919). Schumann's remarks were made in November, 1917.
11 *Fontana* v. *United States*, 262 Fed. 283 (8th Cir. 1919).
12 Quotation taken from American Civil Liberties Union files, LIX, 25.
13 *Report of the Attorney General, 1919*, p. 509. See also National Civil Liberties Bureau, *Wartime Prosecutions and Mob Violence*, p. 22.
14 *Ibid.*, p. 518.
15 *Balbas* v. *United States et al.*, 257 Fed. 17 (1st Cir. 1919). See also *Report of the Attorney General, 1918*, p. 49.

16 Cummings and McFarland, *Federal Justice,* pp. 418, 427. See also Carl Swisher, "Civil Liberties in Wartime," *Political Science Quarterly,* LV (September, 1940), 335 ff.

17 *Report of the Attorney General, 1918,* p. 36.

18 Baker, *Wilson: Life and Letters,* VII, 29.

19 "East St. Louis Riots," House Doc. No. 1231, 65 Cong., 2 Sess. (1918), p. 4.

20 *Ibid.,* p. 5.

21 See *ibid.,* p. 23. For further data on the East St. Louis riots, see *Riot at East St. Louis, Illinois, Hearings Before the House Committee on Rules,* 65 Cong., 1 Sess. (1917).

22 "Our Tyranny over the Negro," *Literary Digest,* LV (September 22, 1917), 34; for other contemporary accounts of the East St. Louis riot see "What Some Americans Think of East St. Louis," *Outlook,* CXVI (July 18, 1917), 435–36; "East St. Louis Race Riots," *Literary Digest,* LV (July 14, 1917), 10–11; Roger Baldwin, "East St. Louis—Why?" *Survey,* XXXVIII (August 18, 1917), 447–48.

23 See the *New York Times,* July 25, 26, 28, 1917.

24 William E. Walling to Wilson, July 3, 1917, Wilson Papers.

25 Statement in Wilson Papers, July 4, 1917.

26 Wilson to Tumulty, August 1, 1917, Wilson Papers.

27 Forum of Los Angeles to Wilson, July 8, 1917, Wilson Papers.

28 Wilson note attached to *ibid.,* August 1, 1917, Wilson Papers.

29 Quoted in *Cong. Rec.,* 65 Cong., 1 Sess., September 12, 1917, pp. 6990–93.

30 Report on the Houston Riot written by Newton D. Baker to President Wilson, August 22, 1918, Wilson Papers.

31 *Ibid.*

32 *Ibid.*

33 *Bouldin* v. *United States,* 261 Fed. 674 (5th Cir. 1919). The Attorney General reported in Bouldin's case that "it was admitted that the evidence indicating his knowledge of the article prior to its being printed was circumstantial." *Report of the Attorney General, 1921,* p. 662.

34 J. H. Ellis to President Wilson, November 30, 1917, American Civil Liberties Union files, XXIX, 110.

35 *Ibid.*

36 J. H. Ellis to Roger Baldwin, undated (probably February, 1918), in *ibid.,* p. 130.

Chapter ix

1 See James R. Mock, *Censorship, 1917* (Princeton, 1941), pp. 131–52; Thomas F. Carroll, "Freedom of Speech and of the Press in Wartime: The Espionage Act," *Michigan Law Review,* XVII (June, 1919), 622–29; Lindsay Rogers, "Freedom of the Press in the United States," *Living Age,*

CCXCVIII (September 28, 1918), 769–74; and especially Zechariah Chafee, *Free Speech in the United States* (Cambridge, 1941); and O. A. Hilton, "Freedom of the Press in Wartime 1917–1919," *Southwestern Social Science Quarterly*, XXVIII (March, 1948), 346–61.

2 Quoted in Mock, *Censorship, 1917*, p. 176.

3 *United States* v. *Motion Picture Film "The Spirit of '76,"* 252 Fed. 946 (S.D. Cal. 1917).

4 *Ibid*. For Goldstein's appeal see *Goldstein* v. *United States*, 258 Fed. 908 (9th Cir. 1919).

5 Creel to Wilson, November 28, 1917, Wilson Papers.

6 Lindsay Rogers, "Freedom of the Press in the United States," *Living Age*, CCXCVIII (September 28, 1918), 771.

7 John K. Winkler, *W. R. Hearst, An American Phenomenon* (New York, 1928), p. 82.

8 See "Newspapers in Wartime," *Public*, XXI (March 16, 1918), 334–37.

9 See the *New York Times*, May 28, 1917.

10 Carroll, "Freedom of Speech and of the Press in Wartime," p. 628 n.

11 William C. Bullitt to editor of the Philadelphia *Public Ledger*, Committee on Public Information files.

12 See Rogers, "Freedom of the Press in the United States," pp. 769–74; also "Mr. Burleson to Rule the Press," *Literary Digest*, LV (October 6, 1917), 12; and William Hard, "Mr. Burleson, Section 481 1–2B," *New Republic*, XIX (May 17, 1919), 76–77.

13 "Mr. Burleson to Rule the Press," p. 12.

14 Rogers, "Freedom of the Press in the United States," p. 770.

15 Quoted in Mock, *Censorship, 1917*, p. 145.

16 Quoted in Walter Nelles, *A Liberal in Wartime* (New York, 1940), pp. 114 ff.

17 *Ibid.*, p. 116. See also *Masses Pub. Co.* v. *Patten*, 244 Fed. 535 (S.D. New York, 1917). Chafee discusses the *Masses* case in *Free Speech in the United States*, pp. 42–51.

18 *Masses Pub. Co.* v. *Patten*, 244 Fed. 535 (S.D. New York, 1917).

19 Chafee, *Freedom of Speech*, p. 107.

20 *Masses Pub. Co.* v. *Patten*, 246 Fed. 24 (2nd Cir. 1917).

21 Chafee, *Freedom of Speech*, p. 55.

22 Quoted in Baker, *Wilson: Life and Letters*, VII, 178–79.

23 *Ibid.*, p. 165.

24 Rogers, "Freedom of the Press in the United States," p. 772.

25 Quoted in Mock, *Censorship, 1917*, p. 141.

26 Carl F. Wittke, *German-Americans and the World War* (Columbus, Ohio, 1936), p. 129.

27 Chafee, *Freedom of Speech*, p. 95.

28 See *Schaefer* v. *United States*, 251 U.S. 466 (1920). Peter Schaefer was president of the Philadelphia *Tageblatt* Corporation.

29 Wittke, *German-Americans and the World War*, p. 175.

30 *Jeffersonian Pub. Co.* v. *West*, 245 Fed. 585 (S.D. Ga. 1917).

31 Chafee, *Freedom of Speech*, pp. 107–8.

32 *New York Tribune,* July 30, 1918.
33 William Hard, "Mr. Burleson, Section 481 1–2B," pp. 76–78.
34 " 'The Nation' and the Post Office," *Nation,* CVII (September 28, 1918), 336–37. See also Oswald Garrison Villard, *Fighting Years* (New York, 1939), pp. 354–57.
35 *Cong. Rec.,* 65 Cong., 3 Sess., February 8, 1919, p. 2936.
36 Sinclair to Wilson, October 22, 1917, Wilson Papers. Published in the *New York Times,* November 1, 1917.
37 Wilson to Wiley, July 23, 1917, Wilson Papers.
38 Baker, *Wilson: Life and Letters,* VII, 330.
39 Wilson to Tumulty, November 1, 1917, Wilson Papers.
40 Baker, *Wilson: Life and Letters,* VII, 273.

Chapter x

1 Howard K. Beale, *Are American Teachers Free?* (New York, 1936), p. 22.
2 Alexander Trachtenberg, ed., *American Labor Year Book* (New York, 1920), III, 86.
3 Beale, *Are American Teachers Free?* p. 23.
4 *New York Times,* October 2, 1917. See also "Columbia's Dismissed Professors," *Literary Digest,* LV (October 20, 1917), 24.
5 Quoted in the *New York Times,* October 9, 1917.
6 *Ibid.*
7 "A Statement by Charles A. Beard," *New Republic,* XIII (December 29, 1917), 249–50.
8 Committee on Public Information files.
9 *Morning Oregonian* (Portland), July 13, 1917. See also "Trial of the Nebraska Professors, A Reflection," *Educational Review,* LVI (December, 1918), 415–23.
10 Walter Nelles, *Espionage Act Cases* (New York, 1918), pp. 55–56.
11 American Civil Liberties Union files, CIX, 166 f. See also New York *American,* April 2, 1918.
12 See Leon Whipple [Letter to the Editor], *Nation,* CV (December 20, 1917), 690–91. For the case of W. E. Zeuch, a professor at the University of Indiana, see Indianapolis *News,* November 13, 1917.
13 Carter Glass to Edwin A. Alderman, quoted in the *News* (Lynchburg, Va.), November 23, 1917.
14 Wilson to W. W. Guth, May 6, 1918, Wilson Papers.
15 *New York Tribune,* April 30, 1918. See also *Minneapolis Journal,* May 1, 1918.
16 Student Council of Defense of the University of Wisconsin to the National Security League, April 26, 1918. Copy in Elihu Root Papers. Many of the cadets became ill with colds and flu as a result of this episode.
17 Quoted by Charles Van Hise to John G. Hibben, April 29, 1918, in *ibid.*

For an account of the McElroy incident see *National Security League, Hearings before a Special Committee of the House of Representatives*, 65 Cong., 3 Sess., December, 1918, pp. 520–31.

18 Creel to Dodd, September 23, 1918, Committee on Public Information files.
19 *New York Times*, December 9, 1917. See also "The Professors in Battle Array," *Nation*, CVI (March 7, 1918), 255. The *Nation* said, "We hold that [a university] exists for the discovery and proclamation of the truth, not for propaganda purposes, no matter how righteous the propaganda. The university method is freedom to discuss, freedom to differ, freedom to be in a minority."
20 Quoted in Bessie Louise Pierce, *Public Opinion and the Teaching of History in the United States* (New York, 1926), pp. 116–20. See also "The Trial of New York City Teachers," *School and Society*, VI (December 8, 1917), 674–75.
21 Quoted in "New York School House Cleaning," *Literary Digest*, LVI (January 5, 1918), 26.
22 Beale, *Are American Teachers Free?* p. 29.
23 Pierce, *Public Opinion and the Teaching of History*, pp. 114–15.
24 Trachtenberg, *American Labor Year Book*, III, 88.
25 *Milwaukee Leader*, April 14, 1918.
26 *Kammann v. United States*, 259 Fed. 192 (7th Cir. 1919)
27 Beale, *Are American Teachers Free?* p. 36.
28 *Ibid.*
29 *North American* (Philadelphia), December 18, 1917.
30 Beale, *Are American Teachers Free?* p. 27.
31 *Ibid.*, p. 28.
32 *Ibid.*, p. 37.

Chapter XI

1 For an excellent account of the attitude of churches and the clergy during World War I see Ray H. Abrams, *Preachers Present Arms* (New York, 1933).
2 *Ibid.*, pp. 96 ff. A letter to the editor of the *New Republic* entitled "Our Modern Heretic Burners" criticized Hillis "and other of our spiritual shepherds" for their "wild and whirling words." Waldo R. Browne [Letter to the Editor], *New Republic*, XIII (December 1, 1917), 127. Another writer declared that Hillis "has probably done more to preach the doctrine of bitterness and hate than any other minister in America since we got into the war, unless it be the Rev. Dr. Charles A. Eaton." "The Ministry of Hate," *Nation*, CVII (August 10, 1918), 140.
3 Creel to McElroy, November 16, 1917, Committee on Public Information files.
4 Quoted in Abrams, *Preachers Present Arms*, p. 79.

5 *Atlanta Constitution,* December 21, 1917. See also *New York Times,* December 21, 1917.
6 *Ibid.* See also Samuel M. Castleton to Walter Nelles, January 14, 1918, American Civil Liberty Union files, XXI, 231. Castleton wrote that there was no provocation on the part of the interrupter.
7 Abrams, *Preachers Present Arms,* pp. 145–57.
8 *New York Evening Call,* December 21, 1917.
9 *New York Times,* April 22, 1918.
10 *Ibid.,* April 23.
11 Quoted in Abrams, *Preachers Present Arms,* p. 194.
12 *New York Times,* January 17, 1918.
13 See Abrams, *Preachers Present Arms,* p. 205.
14 Quoted in National Civil Liberties Bureau, *The Case of the Christian Pacifists at Los Angeles, California* (New York, 1918), p. 5. Also quoted in Abrams, *Preachers Present Arms,* p. 217. See also *A Brief Account of the Conference of Christian Pacifists in California,* issued by the Christian Pacifist Defense Fund, American Civil Liberties Union files.
15 *The Case of the Christian Pacifists at Los Angeles,* p. 7.
16 *New York Call,* October 4, 1917.
17 William Emmett, "Mania in Los Angeles," *Nation,* CVI (January 17, 1918), 59.
18 *Ibid.*
19 Walter Nelles, *Espionage Act Cases* (New York, 1918), p. 55.
20 *Ibid.*
21 Emmett, "Mania in Los Angeles," p. 59.
22 *Ibid.,* p. 58.
23 Quoted in Abrams, *Preachers Present Arms,* p. 215.
24 "When Conscience and War Join Issue," *Survey,* XXXIX (February 16, 1918), 551–52.
25 Quoted in a letter of John Lord O'Brian to Senator Lee S. Overman, April 26, 1918, in *Cong. Rec.,* 65 Cong., 2 Sess., May 4, 1918, p. 6051.
26 *Report of the Attorney General, 1918,* p. 50; and *1919,* p. 509.
27 Herbert H. Stroup, *The Jehovah's Witnesses* (New York, 1945), pp. 11, 13, 16.
28 Quoted in *Stephens v. United States,* 261 Fed. 590 (9th Cir. 1919). See also *Report of the Attorney General, 1919,* p. 50.
29 Quoted in *Rutherford et al. v. United States,* 258 Fed. 864 (2nd Cir. 1919).
30 *New York Times,* June 21, 1918. For cases involving those who distributed *The Finished Mystery* see *Shaffer v. United States,* 255 Fed. 886 (9th Cir. 1919); *Stephens v. United States,* 261 Fed. 590 (9th Cir. 1919); *Hamm v. United States,* 261 Fed. 907 (9th Cir. 1920); and *Sonnenberg v. United States,* 264 Fed. 327 (9th Cir. 1920).
31 *Rutherford et al. v. United States,* 258 Fed. 863 (2nd Cir. 1919). It was not until 1943 that the Supreme Court ruled that members of this organization could not be constitutionally coerced into saluting the flag if it violated their religious principles. This was a reversal of *Minersville School District, Board of Education of Minersville School District et al. v. Gobitis*

et al. decided in 1940. In the Barnette case the court said: "If there is any fixed star in our constitutional constellation, it is that no official, high or petty, can prescribe what shall be orthodox in politics, nationalism, religion, or other matters of opinion." *West Virginia State Board of Education et al.* v. *Barnette et al.,* 319 U.S. 624 (1943).

32 Herbert Croly to Woodrow Wilson, October 19, 1917, Wilson Papers.

Chapter XII

1 *Cong. Rec.,* 65 Cong., 1 Sess., August 7, 1917, p. 5899.
2 Edward Gibbon, *The History of the Decline and Fall of the Roman Empire* (New York, 1850, 6 vols.), II, 61–62.
3 Quoted in Jane Addams, *Peace and Bread,* p. 124.
4 Secretary of War, *Statement Concerning the Treatment of Conscientious Objectors in the Army* (Washington, 1919), p. 15. This report was prepared by E. P. Keppel, third assistant Secretary of War. It contains a large number of documents which dealt with the policies and problems of handling conscientious objectors. See also "A Defect in the Draft Law," *Nation,* CV (August 23, 1917), 192–93.
5 Providence *Daily Journal,* December 18, 1917. See also American Civil Liberties Union files, XXVI, 132.
6 *Coldwell* v. *United States,* 256 Fed. 805 (1st Cir. 1919). See also U.S. Department of Justice, *Interpretation of War Statutes,* Bulletin No. 158. Refer to *Report of the Attorney General, 1922,* p. 411.
7 Baldwin's full statement of his position and Judge Mayer's reply can be found in *Interpretation of War Statutes,* Bulletin No. 173. See also "Conscience at the Bar," *Survey,* XLI (November 9, 1918), 153–54.
8 *Statement Concerning the Treatment of Conscientious Objectors,* p. 16.
9 *Fraina et al.* v. *United States,* 255 Fed. 28 (2nd Cir. 1918).
10 For a discussion of these orders see *Statement Concerning the Treatment of Conscientious Objectors,* pp. 17–19.
11 National Civil Liberties Bureau, *The Facts about Conscientious Objectors in the United States* (New York, 1918), pp. 14–16.
12 Quoted in *Cong. Rec.,* 66 Cong., 1 Sess., July 23, 1919, p. 3065.
13 *Statement Concerning the Treatment of Conscientious Objectors,* p. 24.
14 See National Civil Liberties Bureau, *The Facts about Conscientious Objectors,* p. 17; and Norman Thomas, *The Conscientious Objector in America* (New York, 1923), pp. 135–36.
15 Sheldon W. Smith to W. Perry Kissick, April 6, 1919, American Civil Liberties Union files, CXI, 174.
16 Quoted in *ibid.,* LXXI, 51.
17 Memorandum dated August 2, 1918, American Civil Liberties Union files, LXXI, 172.
18 Thomas, *Conscientious Objector,* p. 157.

19 Data in the American Civil Liberties Union files, LXXIX, 12, 14.

20 Quoted by Thomas, *Conscientious Objector,* p. 160.

21 *Ibid.,* p. 161.

22 Major General Leonard Wood to Jacob Greenberg, October 21, 1918, American Civil Liberties Union files, XCVI, 17 ff.

23 Greenberg to Wood, October 23, 1918, in *ibid.*

24 *Detroit Sunday News,* February 17, 1918.

25 Statement signed by 18 conscientious objectors and sent to Anna L. Curtiss, October 10, 1918, American Civil Liberties Union files, XCIX, 11 ff.

26 *Statement Concerning the Treatment of Conscientious Objectors,* p. 19.

27 Walter G. Kellogg, *The Conscientious Objector* (New York, 1919), p. 25.

28 *Ibid.,* pp. 29–30.

29 Undated letter from Ernest Meyer to his wife, American Civil Liberties Union files, XLVII, 48, 52.

30 National Civil Liberties Bureau, *Facts about Conscientious Objectors,* p. 17.

31 *Statement Concerning the Treatment of Conscientious Objectors,* pp. 8, 9, 51.

32 *Cong. Rec.,* 65 Cong., 3 Sess., March 4, 1919, p. 5066.

33 W.G.S. to R. C. McCrea, October 23, 1918, American Civil Liberties Union files, LXXVII, 176.

34 Hess to W. L. Ustick, October 20, 1919, *ibid.,* CXI, 107.

35 Thomas, *Conscientious Objector,* p. 242.

36 Record of the court-martial of Charles Carlton Rodolph, June 27, 1918, American Civil Liberties Union files, LXXXII, 124 ff. For the quotation see *ibid.,* XII, 149.

37 Quoted in *ibid.,* L, 141.

38 Quoted by Walter Nelles in a letter to Woodrow Wilson, April 16, 1918, American Civil Liberties Union files, LXXI, 87.

39 Kellogg, *The Conscientious Objector,* p. 45.

40 Thomas, *Conscientious Objector,* p. 168.

41 *New York Times,* June 11, 1918.

42 Addams, *Peace and Bread,* pp. 125–26.

43 Quoted in *Cong. Rec.,* 65 Cong., 3 Sess., February 12, 1919, p. 3240.

44 Quoted in *ibid.,* p. 3235.

45 Quoted in *ibid.,* p. 3237.

46 Ray Abrams, *Preachers Present Arms,* pp. 136–37. See Abrams' discussion on pp. 134–42.

47 A. B. Hart and Herbert R. Ferleger, eds., *Theodore Roosevelt Cyclopedia* (New York, 1941), pp. 100–101.

48 Frederick Palmer, *Newton D. Baker* (New York, 1931, 2 vols.), I, 343–44.

49 Quoted in *Cong. Rec.,* 65 Cong., 3 Sess., February 12, 1919, p. 3237.

50 Wilson to Benedict Crowell, September 13, 1918, Wilson Papers.

51 Tracy D. Mygott to Editor of the *Brooklyn Daily Eagle,* quoted in the San Jose *Herald,* August 2, 1917.

52 Kellogg, *The Conscientious Objector,* p. v.

53 Walter Nelles, *A Liberal in Wartime,* pp. 121, 148 ff.

54 William H. Edward to National Civil Liberties Bureau, September 15, 1919, American Civil Liberties Union files, LXXVIII, 254 ff.

Chapter XIII

1 39 *U.S. Stat.* 919.

2 See the *Minneapolis Journal,* April 3, 1917.

3 *Ibid.*

4 *United States* v. *Stickrath,* 242 Fed. 151 (S.D. Ohio 1917).

5 *Cong. Rec.,* 65 Cong., 1 Sess., April 4, 1917, p. 223.

6 *Kirchner* v. *United States,* 255 Fed. 301 (4th Cir. 1918). See also United States Department of Justice, *Interpretation of War Statutes,* Bulletin No. 69.

7 *Anderson* v. *United States,* 264 Fed. 75 (8th Cir. 1920).

8 *Report of the Attorney General, 1922,* p. 410.

9 For other typical cases see *Hickson* v. *United States,* 258 Fed. 867 (4th Cir. 1919); *Doe* v. *United States,* 253 Fed. 903 (8th Cir. 1918); *United States* v. *Stobo,* 251 Fed. 689 (D. Del. 1918); and *Ragansky* v. *United States,* 253 Fed. 643 (7th Cir. 1918).

10 *Clark* v. *United States,* 250 Fed. 449 (5th Cir. 1918).

11 United States Department of Justice, *Interpretation of War Statutes,* Bulletin No. 101, p. 4.

12 *Ibid.,* p. 2.

13 See *Ragansky* v. *United States,* 253 Fed. 643 (7th Cir. 1918).

14 Nelles, *Espionage Act Cases,* p. 81.

15 See United States Department of Justice, *Interpretation of War Statutes,* Bulletin No. 169, p. 5. See also Bulletin No. 176, p. 4.

16 Report of December 10, 1917, on the activities of the state Councils of Defense in the second Liberty Loan campaign, Council of National Defense files.

17 Charles D. Stewart, "Prussianizing Wisconsin," *Atlantic Monthly,* CXXIII (January, 1919), 99–105.

18 Seattle *Post-Intelligencer,* October 5, 1918.

19 George Creel, *Rebel at Large,* p. 198.

20 Nathaniel R. Whitney, *The Sale of War Bonds in Iowa* (Iowa City, 1923). See Chap. V, especially pp. 126, 136.

21 *Minneapolis Journal,* July 5, 1918.

22 American Civil Liberties Union files, LXX, 28.

23 American Economic Foundation, *What Happens to Civil Liberties,* p. 8. For other examples see Hershberger, *War, Peace, and Nonresistance,* p. 123.

24 United States Department of Justice, *Interpretation of War Statutes,* Bulletin No. 134, p. 2.

25 Quoted in *Balcom* v. *United States,* 259 Fed. 779 (1st Cir. 1919).

26 *Daily Oklahoman* (Oklahoma City, Oklahoma), August 2, 1940.
27 The *Oklahoma Daily* (Norman, Oklahoma), July 16, 1942.
28 *Gerdes* v. *State*, 104 Neb. 35, 175 N.W. 606 (1919).
29 *United States* v. *Pape*, 253 Fed. 270 (S.D. Ill. 1918).
30 *Cong. Rec.*, 65 Cong., 2 Sess., May 3, 1918, p. 5986.
31 Hough, *The Web*, p. 183.
32 *Buffalo Express* (Buffalo, New York), June 10, 11, 1918.
33 Quoted in *United States* v. *Nagler*, 252 Fed. 217 (W.D. Wis. 1918).
34 *Ibid.*
35 United States Department of Justice, *Interpretation of War Statutes*, Bulletin No. 168, p. 7.
36 *Ibid.*, Bulletin No. 166, p. 2.
37 *State* v. *Ludemann*, 143 Minn. 126, 172 N.W. 887 (1919).

Chapter XIV

1 "The Menace of Sedition," *Literary Digest*, LV (September 1, 1917), 11.
2 Quoted in *Cong. Rec.*, 65 Cong., 1 Sess., October 6, 1917, p. 7880. See also *Minneapolis Journal*, October 9, 1917.
3 *Minneapolis Journal*, October 2, 1917.
4 *New York Times*, November 21, 1917.
5 *Ibid.*, November 22, 1917.
6 Quoted in Henry Van Dyke [Letter to the Editor], *New Republic*, XIII (December 22, 1917), 214.
7 Baker, Notebook, December 13, 1917, Wilson Papers.
8 Harry Sullivan to Walter Nelles, January 26, 1918, American Civil Liberties Union files, XXXII, 169.
9 Baker, *Wilson: Life and Letters*, VII, 492.
10 *New York Times*, November 13, 1917.
11 Report from Missouri, December, 1917, Council of National Defense files.
12 See the reports from Montana and New Mexico, April, 1918, in *ibid.*
13 Report from Kansas, February, 1918, *ibid.*
14 *Buffalo Express*, June 11, 1918.
15 Quoted in *Cong. Rec.*, 65 Cong., 1 Sess., October 6, 1917, p. 7878.
16 *Ibid.*
17 National Civil Liberties Bureau, *Wartime Prosecutions and Mob Violence* (New York, 1919), p. 5. See also *New York Tribune*, January 7, 1918.
18 *New York Times*, November 23, 1917.
19 For these and other incidents see *ibid.*, March 26, 1918.
20 *Rhuberg* v. *United States*, 255 Fed. 865 (9th Cir. 1919). In the case of Karl Shilter, who was convicted of attempting to cause insubordination and disloyalty in the armed forces, the appeal court reversed the decision on the basis that the indictment was too vague. *Shilter* v. *United States*, 257 Fed. 724 (9th Cir. 1919).

21 *Deason* v. *United States*, 254 Fed. 259 (5th Cir. 1918).
22 *Wessels* v. *United States*, 262 Fed. 389 (5th Cir. 1919).
23 *Report of the Attorney General, 1921*, p. 683.
24 *Howenstine et al.* v. *United States*, 263 Fed. 1 (9th Cir. 1920).
25 See *Report of the Attorney General, 1921;* for Kennedy, p. 670; for Howenstine, p. 695.
26 Memoranda submitted to the President, American Civil Liberties Union files, XCVIII, 64. See also *Sacramento Bee*, October 18, 1917.
27 *New York Times*, April 5, 1918.
28 Quoted in Nelles, *Espionage Act Cases*, p. 48.
29 *Ibid.* See also *Report of the Attorney General, 1921*, p. 706. See also *ibid., 1922*, p. 411.
30 *The Nonpartisan Leader*, V (October 18, 1917), 4.
31 National Civil Liberties Bureau, *Wartime Prosecutions and Mob Violence*, p. 12.
32 Davis Douthit, *Nobody Owns Us* (Chicago, 1948), pp. 117–25.
33 *Ibid.*, pp. 127–28.
34 *The Nonpartisan Leader*, VI (March 18, 1918), 10.

Chapter xv

1 Quoted in *Cong. Rec.*, 66 Cong., 1 Sess., November 10, 1919, p. 8238.
2 Quoted in the *Sacramento Bee*, February 11, 1918.
3 See the *New York Herald*, October 15, 1917.
4 *New York Times*, November 1, 1917.
5 *Ibid.*, November 2, 1917.
6 Anna Blachly to National Civil Liberties Bureau, undated, American Civil Liberties Union files, CIX, 142–46.
7 Lily M. Iverson to American Civil Liberties Bureau, May 28, 1918, American Civil Liberties Union files, VI, 73–75.
8 *New York Call*, January 29, 1918.
9 Quoted in *Shidler* v. *United States*, 257 Fed. 620 (9th Cir. 1919).
10 For quotation see National Civil Liberties Bureau, *Wartime Prosecutions and Mob Violence*, p. 29. See also the *Seattle Times*, January 12, 1918.
11 *Report of the Attorney General, 1918*, p. 49.
12 "United States v. Louise Olivereau," United States District Court, Western District of Washington, Northern Division, May, 1917. Unreported case.
13 Quoted in American Civil Liberties Union files, LXII, 81.
14 *New York Call*, December 14, 1917.
15 *Cong. Rec.*, 66 Cong., 1 Sess., November 10, 1919, p. 8240.
16 *Report of the Attorney General, 1918*, p. 53.
17 *Milwaukee Leader*, October 3, 1917.
18 *Ibid.*, October 6, 1917. It was not until after the war that Berger said, "Mr. Wilson has coined more democratic phrases than all the Presidents of the

United States combined, and he has taken away more of our liberties than all the Presidents of the United States combined." Quoted in *Cong. Rec.*, 66 Cong., 1 Sess., November 10, 1919, p. 8225. For excerpts from Berger's editorials and statements see *ibid.*, pp. 8241–47.

19 *Cong. Rec.*, 66 Cong., 1 Sess., November 10, 1919, p. 8238.
20 Chafee, *Freedom of Speech*, p. 316.
21 See the *Milwaukee Leader*, December 21, 1917, and March 29, 1918.
22 *Milwaukee Leader*, March 4, 1918.
23 *Ibid.*
24 Quoted in *Cong. Rec.*, 65 Cong., 2 Sess., April 23, 1918, p. 5492.
25 Quoted in Baker, *Wilson: Life and Letters*, VIII, 30.
26 *Cong. Rec.*, 65 Cong., 2 Sess., April 23, 1918, p. 5493.
27 *Ibid.*
28 *New York Times*, March 10, 1918.
29 Quoted in the *New York Call*, April 3, 1918.
30 *Cong. Rec.*, 65 Cong., 2 Sess., April 23, 1918, p. 5490.
31 Adolph Germer, J. Louis Engdahl, William E. Kruse, and Irwin St. John Tucker were the other Socialists involved in the case.
32 Chafee, *Freedom of Speech*, p. 318.
33 See Victor S. Yarros, "The Chicago Socialist Trial," *Nation*, CVIII (January 25, 1919), 116–18.
34 Quoted in *Seattle Union-Record*, March 5, 1919.
35 *New York Call*, February 27, 1919.
36 *Berger et al.* v. *United States*, 275 Fed. 1021 (7th Cir. 1921).
37 Quoted in Bates, *This Land of Liberty*, p. 118. For the Berger case see Chafee, *Freedom of Speech*, pp. 318–21. See also O. G. Villard, "The Berger Victory," *Nation*, CIX (December 27, 1919), 820–21; "The Berger Decision," *New Republic*, XXV (February 23, 1921), 360–61; and "Victor Berger Escapes Punishment," *Outlook*, CXXVII (February 16, 1921), 245–46.

Chapter xvi

1 *New York Times*, February 25, 1918.
2 *Ibid.*, February 28.
3 Lewis Allen Browne, "Bolshevism in America," *Forum*, LIX (June, 1918), 703–17.
4 "Ill Weeds Grow Apace," *Living Age*, CCXCV (November 24, 1917), 492–93.
5 George, *Is Freedom Dead?* p. 10.
6 E. Foster Dowell, "A History of the Enactment of Criminal Syndicalism Legislation in the United States" (Doctoral dissertation, Johns Hopkins University, Baltimore, 1936), p. 78. This is not to be confused with the published abbreviated study of a similar title cited earlier. See also American Civil Liberties Union files, LXIV, 252.

7 George, *Is Freedom Dead?* pp. 10–11.

8 *Reno Evening Gazette,* March 7, 1918.

9 Seattle *Post-Intelligencer,* February 16, 1918.

10 *Ibid.,* January 6, 1918. See also the *New York Evening Call,* January 29, 1918. About this time in England Bertrand Russell was sentenced to six months in jail. He had said that he was not certain about the effectiveness of American soldiers in battle but that they "will no doubt be capable of intimidating strikers, an occupation to which the American army is accustomed at home." See the *New York Times,* February 10, 1918.

11 Dowell, "Criminal Syndicalism," p. 78. See also American Civil Liberties Union files, LXIV, 252.

12 Dowell, "Criminal Syndicalism," p. 79. For later raids see the *Boston Transcript,* March 19, 1918.

13 See American Civil Liberties Union files, XXVI, 132.

14 Affidavit of Jalmar Wintturi, February 18, 1918, sworn before N. E. Foster, Notary Public, Seattle, Washington, American Civil Liberties Union files, XXXIV, 72–76.

15 Affidavit of John U. Heliste, dated January 25, 1918, sworn before H. A. Tyvand, Notary Public, Butte, Montana, American Civil Liberties Union files, XXXIV, 66–68.

16 *New York Tribune,* March 30, 1918.

17 Dowell, "Criminal Syndicalism," p. 442.

18 *New York Evening Call,* December 20, 1917.

19 *Collins* v. *United States,* 253 Fed. 609 (9th Cir. 1918).

20 *Foster et al.* v. *United States,* 253 Fed. 481 (9th Cir. 1918).

21 Report of John B. Meserve on "I.W.W. and pro-German activities in Tulsa," Council of National Defense files, dated January 26, 1918.

22 *Seattle Call,* October 2, 1917.

23 Tulsa *Daily World,* November 9 and 10, 1917. See also National Civil Liberties Bureau, *The Knights of Liberty Mob* (New York, 1918), p. 14. For the judge's statement see "Mob Violence in the United States," *Survey,* XL (April 27, 1918), 102.

24 Tulsa *Daily World,* November 9, 1917.

25 Quoted in National Civil Liberties Bureau, *The Knights of Liberty Mob,* pp. 6–7.

26 Tulsa *Daily World,* November 10, 1917.

27 *Ibid.*

28 Patrick S. Nagle to Roger N. Baldwin, November 24, 1917, American Civil Liberties Union files, XXXVI, 1.

29 Tulsa *Daily World,* December 10, 1917.

30 Delaney and Rice, *The Bloodstained Trail,* p. 106. See also Dowell, "Criminal Syndicalism," pp. 516–18.

31 Dowell, "Criminal Syndicalism," pp. 331–32.

32 *Sacramento Bee,* December 18, 1917.

33 Lubin to Woodrow Wilson, March 29, 1918, Wilson Papers.

34 *Ibid.*

35 Dowell, "Criminal Syndicalism," pp. 332–33. See also *New York Times,* February 9, 1918.

36 See the *Sacramento Bee*, December 26, 1917; also Dowell, "Criminal Syndicalism," p. 333.
37 Author's italics.
38 National Civil Liberties Bureau, *Attack on Right of Defense and of Defense Workers in Trial of I.W.W. at Sacramento, California* (n.p., n.d.), p. 2.
39 Quoted in Harvey Duff, *Silent Defenders*, p. 18. See also "Ol' Rags an' Bottles," *Nation*, CVIII (January 25, 1919), 114–16.
40 National Civil Liberties Bureau, *Attack on Right of Defense*, p. 14.
41 Wilson to Simon Lubin, April 12, 1918, Wilson Papers.
42 Wilson to Gregory, April 3, 1918, *ibid.*

Chapter XVII

1 Arthur Garfield Hays, *City Lawyer* (New York, 1942), p. 79.
2 *Cong. Rec.*, 67 Cong., 4 Sess., December 11, 1922, p. 486. See also Chafee, *Freedom of Speech*, pp. 79–80.
3 In this Montana case the county attorney had kept certain information from the jury and he was upheld by the judge. Albert Brooks, an I.W.W., was denied additional peremptory challenges, despite the attempt of his attorney to challenge for cause. The higher court said that the court erred in overruling the "challenge for cause" of a juror who was clearly prejudiced. See *State* v. *Brooks*, 57 Mont. 480, 188 Pac. 942 (1920). See also *Caughman* v. *United States*, 258 Fed. 434 (4th Cir. 1919). In the Caughman case the appeal court said that the defendant had been denied the right to present evidence which would prove his loyalty. This, the court said, was "erroneous and prejudicial."
4 *Berger et al.* v. *United States*, 255 U.S. 22 (1921).
5 Bruce Rogers to National Civil Liberties Bureau, July 29, 1919, American Civil Liberties Union files, XC, 1.
6 Perker H. Sercombe to Major Pullman, Police Department, Washington, D.C., American Civil Liberties Union files, XC, 280. Copy.
7 Quoted in Thomas W. Gregory, "Suggestions of Attorney-General Gregory . . . in Relation to the Department of Justice," *American Bar Association Journal*, IV (July, 1918), 312.
8 *Cong. Rec.*, 65 Cong., 2 Sess., April 8, 1918, p. 4771.
9 See the *New York Tribune*, May 13, 1918; and New York *Evening Post*, March 5, 1918.
10 See *Holzmacher* v. *United States*, 266 Fed. 979 (7th Cir. 1920). Holzmacher's conviction for criticizing members of the military was reversed by the appeal court.
11 See *State* v. *Kahn*, 56 Mont. 108, 182 Pac. 107 (1919). See also *Rietz* v. *United States*, 257 Fed. 731 (8th Cir. 1919). Rietz was supposed to have said that the country had no business in the war and that it was a rich man's fight. He was given five years in Leavenworth. In considering the case in

1920 the attorney general stated that Rietz's offense was not "a flagrant one," and that his remarks were due "more to his anxiety over his son's being compelled to join the army and to his opposition to the war than to any real disloyalty." *Report of the Attorney General, 1920,* p. 759; and *ibid., 1921,* p. 676.

12 *White* v. *United States,* 263 Fed. 17 (6th Cir. 1920).

13 *United States* v. *Schulze,* 253 Fed. 377 (S.D. Cal. 1918).

14 *Mead* v. *United States,* 257 Fed. 639 (9th Cir. 1919).

15 *Report of the Attorney General, 1921,* p. 693.

16 *United States* v. *Boutin,* 251 Fed. 313 (N.D. N.Y. 1918).

17 *Bentall* v. *United States,* 254 Fed. 294 (8th Cir. 1918).

18 *Report of the Attorney General, 1918,* p. 52.

19 *United States* v. *Peterson* (D.C. 4th Div. Minn. 1918). Unreported case, Docket 388.

20 See the *New York Herald,* March 13, 1918.

21 Quoted in *United States* v. *Nearing et al.,* 252 Fed. 223 (S.D. N.Y. 1918); *American Socialist Soc.* v. *United States,* 266 Fed. 212 (2nd Cir. 1920). See also *The Trial of Scott Nearing and the American Socialist Society* (New York, 1919); and *United States* v. *American Socialist Soc. et al.,* 260 Fed. 885 (S.D. N.Y. 1919).

22 *United States* v. *Nearing et al.,* 252 Fed. 223 (S.D. N.Y. 1918).

23 *Herman* v. *United States,* 257 Fed. 601 (9th Cir. 1919). See also *Report of the Attorney General, 1918,* p. 50.

24 *Partan et al.* v. *United States,* 261 Fed. 515 (9th Cir. 1919). A. J. Partan was involved in distributing antiwar literature. In one pamphlet, *War for What,* it was stated that patriotism "is bait laid for fools, rot fed to mules by every tyrant, king, czar, and president at the head of governments— used by the industrial ruling class."

25 *Stokes* v. *United States,* 264 Fed. 18 (8th Cir. 1920). On March 9, 1920, the Circuit Court of Appeals granted Stokes a new trial. The Court said that side issues had entered into the case and that "patriotic zeal" of the Court had placed "too heavy a burden upon the defendant" in an attempt to answer evidence against her.

26 *Milwaukee Leader,* May 24, 1918.

27 Wilson to Gregory, June 24, 1918, Wilson Papers.

28 "Ten Years of Criticism," *Literary Digest,* LVII (June 15, 1918), 13.

29 *The Nonpartisan Leader,* VI (April 29, 1918), 4.

30 *Ibid.,* pp. 3–4. For an account of the Nonpartisan League in Oklahoma see Gilbert C. Fite, "The Nonpartisan League in Oklahoma," *Chronicles of Oklahoma,* XXIV (Summer, 1946), 146–57.

31 *The Nonpartisan Leader,* VI (May 6, 1918), 13.

32 *Ibid.* (June 24, 1918), p. 9. For a fuller account of the widespread campaign against the League see Herbert E. Gaston, *The Nonpartisan League* (New York, 1920), pp. 217–36. See also Morlan, *Political Prairie Fire,* pp. 173–80.

33 W. Harry King to C. N. Day, May 18, 1918, Norbeck Papers.

34 King to Olaf Eidem, May 8, 1918, *ibid.*

35 Norbeck to King, May 2, 1918, *ibid.*
36 Gilbert C. Fite, "Peter Norbeck and the Defeat of the Nonpartisan League in South Dakota," *Mississippi Valley Historical Review,* XXXIII (September, 1946), 229.
37 Quoted in *The Nonpartisan Leader,* VI (May 13, 1918), 3.
38 For the Nonpartisan League in the 1918 campaign in South Dakota see Fite, "Peter Norbeck and the Defeat of the Nonpartisan League," pp. 217–36. For an account of the Nonpartisan League in South Dakota see Carl J. Hofland, "The Nonpartisan League in South Dakota" (unpublished Master's thesis, University of South Dakota, Vermillion, 1940).
39 *The Nonpartisan Leader,* VI (April 8, 1918), 7.
40 Davis Douthit, *Nobody Owns Us: The Story of Joe Gilbert, Midwestern Rebel* (Chicago, 1948), pp. 137–43. See also Gaston, *The Nonpartisan League,* pp. 233–34.
41 See the *Minnesota Leader* (St. Paul), February 23, March 2, 9, 16, 1918. See also Morlan, *Political Prairie Fire,* pp. 187–201, for comment on the 1918 gubernatorial election in Minnesota.
42 Gaston, *The Nonpartisan League,* p. 232.
43 Charles A. Lindbergh, Sr., *Your Country at War* (Philadelphia, 1934), p. 9. See also Walter E. Quigley, "Like Father, Like Son," *Saturday Evening Post,* CCXIII (June 21, 1941), 36.
44 Lindbergh, *Your Country at War,* pp. 8–9.
45 Morlan, *Political Prairie Fire,* pp. 187–201. See also "Lawlessness in Minnesota," *Public,* XXI (July 13, 1918), 876–78.
46 Quoted in *The Nonpartisan Leader,* VI (May 6, 1918), 5.
47 Quoted in Lynn and Dora B. Haines, *The Lindberghs* (New York, 1931), p. 28.
48 *Cong. Rec.,* 65 Cong., 2 Sess., June 8, 1918, p. 7542.
49 *New York Times,* June 8, 1918.
50 *Memorial to the Congress of the United States Concerning Conditions in Minnesota* (St. Paul, 1918).
51 *New York Times,* May 2, 1918.
52 Quoted in Douthit, *Nobody Owns Us,* pp. 155–56. See also "The Nonpartisan League and the Loyalty Issue," *New Republic,* XVI (September 14, 1918), 188.
53 Wilson to Gregory, June 12, 1918, Wilson Papers.
54 Morlan, *Political Prairie Fire,* p. 200.
55 Quoted in *State* v. *Townley et al.,* 140 Minn. 413, 168 N.W. 591 (1918).
56 *Ibid.*
57 *Ibid.*
58 Quoted in Charles Edward Russell, *The Story of the Nonpartisan League* (New York, 1920), p. 246. See also Creel to Woodrow Wilson, April 2, 1918, Wilson Papers.
59 *State* v. *Gilbert,* 141 Minn. 263, 169 N.W. 790 (1918).
60 *State* v. *Townley et al.,* 149 Minn. 5, 182 N.W. 773 (1921).
61 *Townley et al.* v. *State of Minnesota,* 257 U.S. 643 (1921).

62 *State* v. *Townley et al.*, 149 Minn. 5, 182 N.W. 773 (1921).
63 "Lawlessness in Minnesota," pp. 876–78.

Chapter xviii

1 A quotation from the magazine, *Merchant Plumber and Fitter,* undated, Committee on Public Information files.
2 See the *Minneapolis Journal,* April 20 and 21, 1918. Judge James D. Elliott spoke of the "stonewall at sunrise." See April 21. See also Seattle *Post-Intelligencer,* March 10, 1918.
3 Richmond (Virginia) *Journal,* quoted in "Boloism in this Country," *Literary Digest,* LVI (March 2, 1918), 15.
4 "Mob Violence and War Psychology," *New Republic,* XVI (August 3, 1918), 6.
5 *Atlanta Constitution,* April 19, 1918.
6 Richard L. Metcalfe to E. D. Smith, February 6, 1918, Council of National Defense files.
7 *Minneapolis Journal,* April 22, 1918.
8 *Milwaukee Leader,* April 20, 1918, quoting the Tampa *Daily Times.*
9 *Roosevelt in the Kansas City Star,* p. 110.
10 *New York Tribune,* December 29, 1917.
11 See the Seattle *Post-Intelligencer,* April 4, 1918.
12 Quoted in "American Students Boycotting German," *Literary Digest,* LVI (March 30, 1918), 29.
13 *New York Times,* December 2, 1918. Such sentiments, however, were not unanimous. The editor of the *New York Globe* condemned the anti-German language campaign as narrow-minded and childish. "Ignorance of the language and customs of our enemies harms us, not them," he wrote. Quoted in "American Students Boycotting German," p. 29.
14 Seattle *Post-Intelligencer,* June 9, 1918.
15 Tulsa *Daily World,* August 10, 1917.
16 "American Students Boycotting German," p. 30. This issue of the *Literary Digest* carried a very extensive report by states. See pp. 44, 46–50, 52, 54–55, 58, 61–64, 66, 70, 72–74.
17 New York *Evening World,* March 28, 1918.
18 Tulsa *Daily World,* July 3, 1918.
19 *Spartanburg* (South Carolina) *Herald,* September 12, 1918.
20 *Chicago Herald,* April 13, 1918.
21 Little Rock *Arkansas Gazette,* December 20, 1917. Arkansas had other instances of flag-kissings later. See the *Gazette* for April 2, 1918, and the *Memphis Press* for April 30, 1918. Beatings and tarring and featherings often accompanied the flag-kissings.
22 *New York Herald,* March 1, 1918. See also the Seattle *Post-Intelligencer,* March 1, 1918.

23 Seattle *Post-Intelligencer,* March 1, 1918.

24 New York *Evening Post,* March 4, 1918.

25 Camden (New Jersey) *Evening Courier,* May 1, 1918.

26 *Ex parte Starr,* 263 Fed. 145 (D. Mont. 1920).

27 *Ibid.* For other cases of flag-kissings see the *New York Tribune* for March 7 and 9, 1918; the Williamsport (Pa.) *Gazette and Bulletin,* July 3, 1918; Seattle *Post-Intelligencer,* March 22, 1918; Tulsa *Daily World,* March 26, 1918; *Pittsburgh Chronicle Telegraph,* March 14, 1918.

28 *Pittsburgh Post,* October 29, 1917.

29 Louis P. Goldberg and Eleanore Levenson, *Lawless Judges* (New York, 1935), p. 169.

30 See the *American* (New York), April 2, 1918.

31 *Milwaukee Journal,* April 14, 1918.

32 *Milwaukee Leader,* May 2, 1918. See also April 19.

33 Seattle *Post-Intelligencer,* March 19, 1918.

34 *San Rafael Chronicle,* May 7, 1918.

35 Unidentified newspaper clipping from Salt Lake City, April 11, 1918, American Civil Liberties Union files, LXX, 274.

36 Baltimore *Evening Sun,* April 8, 1918.

37 New York *American,* April 2, 1918. See the American Civil Liberties Union files for many other such incidents, especially LXX, 213. See also the *New York Times* index under "sedition."

38 *Sykes et al.* v. *United States,* 264 Fed. 945 (9th Cir. 1920). See also National Civil Liberties Bureau, *Wartime Prosecutions,* p. 8.

39 *Philadelphia Enquirer,* March 20, 1918.

40 *New York Evening Journal,* April 7, 1918. The New York *Evening Post* of May 22, 1918, tells of his restoration.

41 *Denver Post,* April 20, 1918.

42 *New York Tribune,* April 13, 1918.

43 Unidentified newspaper clipping, American Civil Liberties Union files, LXX, 9.

44 *San Francisco Examiner,* May 13, 1918.

45 See the *New York Evening Call,* March 7, 1918; Little Rock *Arkansas Gazette,* March 29, 1918; *New York Tribune,* March 29, 1918; *Butte* (Montana) *Post,* May 25, 1918.

46 *St. Paul Dispatch,* May 23, 1918.

47 *New York Times,* March 21, 1918. See also the *New York Tribune,* April 9, 1918.

48 Clipping from unidentified newspaper reproduced in *Survey,* XL (April 27, 1918), 101.

49 New York *American,* April 2, 1918.

50 *Fort Worth Record,* March 20, 1918.

51 *Washington* (D.C.) *Post,* April 28, 1918.

52 *New York Evening Call,* April 26, 1918.

53 Quoted in "Lynch-Law as Treason," *Literary Digest,* LVIII (August 10, 1918), 13.

54 New York *World,* April 16, 1918.

55 Seattle *Post-Intelligencer,* April 23, 1918.
56 *Boston Daily Advertiser,* May 7, 1918.
57 See the *Atlanta Constitution,* July 1, 1918. See also May 23 and 24.
58 *Springfield* (Missouri) *Daily News,* March 25, 1918.
59 Tulsa *Daily World,* March 24, 1918.
60 *Ibid.,* March 26, 1918.
61 See the American Civil Liberties Union files, LXX, 172.
62 See *ibid.*
63 St. Louis *Post-Dispatch,* March 23, 1918.
64 *New York Tribune,* March 26, 1918. See the *New York Times* for the same date.
65 See the letter from Edith M. Short to Roger N. Baldwin, July 28, 1918, American Civil Liberties Union files, XX, 122–27.
66 *Collinsville* (Illinois) *Herald,* May 18 and 22, and June 21, 1918.
67 *New York Times,* April 5, 1918.
68 St. *Louis Republic,* April 5, 1918. See also the *New York Call,* April 6, 1918.
69 *Chicago Daily News,* April 17, 1918.
70 From an undated *New York Tribune* clipping in the American Civil Liberties Union files, LXX, 1.
71 *Collinsville* (Illinois) *Herald,* April 5, 1918. See also "Mob Violence in the United States," *Survey,* XL (April 27, 1918), 101–2.
72 Quoted in *Cong. Rec.,* 65 Cong., 2 Sess., May 9, 1918, p. 6233.
73 *Ibid.,* April 8, 1918, p. 4769.
74 *Chicago Daily Tribune,* April 9, 1918.
75 *New York Times,* April 6, 1918.
76 See "The First War-Lynching," *Literary Digest,* LVII (April 20, 1918), 16–17.
77 *Collinsville* (Illinois) *Herald,* June 7, 1918. For an account of the Prager affair, including the trial, see the *New York Times* for April 5, 6, 8, 9, 11, 12; May 14, 27, 29; June 2, 3.
78 *New York Tribune,* May 17, 1918.
79 *Ibid.,* June 1, 1918. For a later account of the trial see Marguerite Edith Jenison, *The War-Time Organization of Illinois* (Volume V of Illinois in the World War; Springfield, 1923), p. 7. It was said that because it was dark when Prager was hanged, identity of the leaders could not be certain. Thus, the verdict of "not guilty."
80 Quoted in *New York Tribune,* June 15, 1918. Shortly after Prager was hanged S. J. Walker was shot and killed by an army officer in Hawaii for allegedly "condemning the course of the United States in entering the War," New York *Evening Post,* May 1, 1918.
81 For other instances of mob actions see *Sacramento Bee,* May 2 and 3, 1918; Tulsa *Daily World,* April 14, 1918; *Minneapolis Journal,* April 24, 1918; and *Collinsville* (Oklahoma) *Star,* April 27, 1917. For a sample taken from different parts of the country see the *New York Times* index under "sedition."
82 Baker, *Wilson: Life and Letters,* VIII, 78.

83 See the *New York Times,* April 12 and June 13, 1918.

84 John Lord O'Brian, Memorandum for the Attorney General, April 18, 1918, Wilson Papers.

85 Wilson to Mrs. Anita McCormick Blaine, April 22, 1918, in Baker, *Wilson: Life and Letters,* VIII, 102–3.

86 Council of National Defense, Bulletin No. 99, June 11, 1918. Statement was signed by W. S. Gifford.

87 Wilson to Creel, July 21, 1918, in Baker, *Wilson: Life and Letters,* VIII, 289.

88 Lawrence Todd to Roger Baldwin, July 30, 1918, American Civil Liberties Union files, VIII, 1.

89 *New York Times,* July 27, 1918.

90 "Mob Violence and War Psychology," *New Republic,* XVI (August 3, 1918), 5–6.

91 *New York Times,* July 27, 1918.

Chapter xix

1 *New York Times,* March 3, 1918.

2 *Minneapolis Journal,* April 5, 1918.

3 *Christian Science Monitor,* April 1, 1918.

4 *New York Times,* December 2, 1917.

5 *Cong. Rec.,* 65 Cong., 2 Sess., March 28, 1918, p. 4199.

6 *Ibid.,* April 5, p. 4645.

7 *Ibid.,* April 4, p. 4570.

8 *Cong. Rec.,* 65 Cong., 2 Sess., June 21, 1918, pp. 8113–16. The Robbins list of sabotage incidents by enemy agents was gleaned from the *New York Times* index.

9 *New York Herald,* April 6, 1918.

10 See Gregory's speech to the American Bar Association in *Cong. Rec.,* 65 Cong., 2 Sess., May 9, 1918, p. 6233.

11 Cummings and McFarland, *Federal Justice,* p. 425.

12 *United States* v. *Hall,* 248 Fed. 150 (D. Mont. 1918).

13 *Cong. Rec.,* 65 Cong., 2 Sess., April 4, 1918, p. 4559.

14 *New York Times,* April 6, 1918.

15 *Christian Science Monitor,* April 16, 1918.

16 *Cong. Rec.,* 65 Cong., 2 Sess., April 5, 1918, p. 4645.

17 *New York Times,* March 22, 1918.

18 *New York Herald,* April 6, 1918.

19 Quoted in Marguerite Edith Jenison, *War Documents and Addresses* (Vol. VI of Illinois in the World War; Springfield, 1923), pp. 351–52.

20 *New York Herald,* April 2, 1918.

21 *Collinsville* (Illinois) *Herald,* April 5, 1918.

22 See "The First War-Lynching," *Literary Digest,* LVII (April 20, 1918),

16–17; and "Stronger Curb on Enemies at Home," *ibid.* (May 4, 1918), p. 19.

23 See Senator King's comments in *New York Times*, March 22, 1918.

24 *Cong. Rec.*, 65 Cong., 2 Sess., April 5, 1918, p. 4638.

25 See part of law quoted in *ibid.*, April 4, p. 4561.

26 See the Los Angeles *Times*, May 4, 1918.

27 *New York Times*, April 19, 1918.

28 *Milwaukee Journal*, April 14, 1918.

29 *Christian Science Monitor*, April 4, 1918.

30 *Vernon's Annotated Penal Code of the State of Texas* (Kansas City, Mo., 1938), I, Art. 153.

31 *Cong. Rec.*, 65 Cong., 2 Sess., February 26, 1918, p. 2672.

32 *Cong. Rec.*, 65 Cong., 2 Sess., March 4, 1918, pp. 3003–4.

33 *Ibid.*

34 *Ibid.*

35 *Ibid.*, April 3, p. 4526.

36 *Ibid.*, April 4, p. 4562.

37 40 *U.S. Stat.* 553–54.

38 *Cong. Rec.*, 65 Cong., 2 Sess., May 7, 1918, Appendix, p. 355.

39 *Ibid.*, April 5, p. 4645.

40 *Ibid.*, p. 4652.

41 "Patrioteering and Hysteria," *Public*, XXI (April 27, 1918), 527.

42 Quoted in *Cong. Rec.*, 65 Cong., 2 Sess., May 9, 1918, p. 6234.

43 See Frederic L. Paxson, *America at War: 1917–1918* (Boston, 1939), p. 290.

44 Roger N. Baldwin to Lawrence Todd, April 20, 1918, American Civil Liberties Union files, VIII, 160.

45 Todd to Baldwin, April 3, 1918. In *ibid.*, p. 5.

46 "M" to Baldwin, April 17, 1918. In *ibid.*, p. 6.

47 *Cong. Rec.*, 65 Cong., 2 Sess., April 4, 1918, p. 4562.

48 *Roosevelt in the Kansas City Star*, pp. 131–32.

49 Hardwick's statements are found in *Cong. Rec.*, 65 Cong., 2 Sess., May 2, 1918, pp. 5938–39, and April 5, p. 4639.

50 *Ibid.*, April 4, pp. 4566–67.

51 *Ibid.*, April 24, p. 5544.

52 *Ibid.*, May 4, pp. 6036–37.

53 *Ibid.*, April 5, p. 4631.

54 *Ibid.*, April 6, p. 4712.

55 *Ibid.*, April 9, pp. 4835–38.

56 *Ibid.*, April 24, p. 5541.

57 For O'Brian's letter to Webb see *ibid.*, April 24, p. 5542; and to Overman, *ibid.*, May 4, pp. 6051–52.

58 *Ibid.*, April 24, p. 5544.

59 *Ibid.*, May 2, p. 5937.

60 *Ibid.*, p. 5947.

61 *Ibid.*, April 4, p. 4562.

62 *Ibid.*, April 5, p. 4645.

63 *Cong. Rec.*, 65 Cong., 2 Sess., April 4, p. 4568. Watson was referring in the Senate debate to articles written by George Creel in 1911.
64 *Ibid.*, April 5, p. 4631.
65 *Ibid.*, p. 4636.
66 *Ibid.*, p. 4637.
67 *Ibid.*, May 4, p. 6057.
68 *Ibid.*, May 7, pp. 6186–87.
69 *Atlanta Constitution*, May 7, 1918.
70 *Milwaukee Leader*, May 23, 1918.

Chapter xx

1 Clipping in the American Civil Liberties Union files, LXIV, 25. About the same time a play was produced in New York entitled "Watch Your Neighbor." See the *New York Times*, September 3, 1918.
2 *Atlanta Constitution*, June 5, 1918.
3 Robert Ferrari, "The Trial of Political Criminals Here and Abroad," *Dial*, LXVI (June 28, 1919), 648. One writer said in a letter to the *Nation* that "a lawyer cannot accept regular employment from the I.W.W. and remain respectable." W. L. [Letter to the Editor], *Nation*, CX (February 14, 1920), 202.
4 Samuel M. Castleton to Walter Nelles, July 31, 1918, American Civil Liberties Union files, XXIX, 19.
5 Cummings and McFarland, *Federal Justice*, p. 426.
6 *United States* v. *Jasick*, 252 Fed. 931 (E.D. Mich. 1918).
7 *Dierkes* v. *United States*, 274 Fed. 75 (6th Cir. 1921). See also *Report of the Attorney General, 1922*, p. 415.
8 *United States* v. *William Powell*, Indictment No. 6218, July 3, 1918 (E.D. Mich. 1918). Photostatic copy of the indictment is in the author's possession. See also *Report of the Attorney General, 1919*, p. 518. Powell's sentence was commuted to two years.
9 William Powell to American Civil Liberties Union, March 1, 1919, American Civil Liberties Union files, LXXVIII, 79.
10 Francis H. Warren to Oswald Garrison Villard, August 7, 1918, in *ibid.*, p. 74. See also the *Detroit Free Press*, July 27, 1918.
11 *Wimmer* v. *United States*, 264 Fed. 11 (6th Cir. 1920).
12 *Shoborg* v. *United States*, 264 Fed. 1 (6th Cir. 1920).
13 *Report of the Attorney General, 1921*, p. 741.
14 *Ibid.*
15 *Shoborg* v. *United States*, 264 Fed. 1 (6th Cir. 1920). In June, 1921, the sentences of Shoborg and Kruse were commuted to expire at once, and that of Feltman, too, if he paid a $10,000 fine. *Report of the Attorney General, 1921*, p. 741.
16 *Lockhart* v. *United States*, 264 Fed. 14 (6th Cir. 1920).

17 *Ibid.*

18 *Albers* v. *United States,* 263 Fed. 27 (9th Cir. 1920).

19 *Ibid.*

20 *United States* v. *Binder,* 253 Fed. 978 (E.D. N.Y. 1918).

21 *Ibid.* See also the *New York Evening Call,* July 9, 1918. For two other interesting cases of opponents of war see *Buessel* v. *United States,* 258 Fed. 811 (2nd Cir. 1919); and *Bold* v. *United States,* 265 Fed. 581 (9th Cir. 1920).

22 See Mamaux's account in the American Civil Liberties Union files, CIV, 11; see also pp. 6–9.

23 *Mamaux* v. *United States,* 264 Fed. 816 (6th Cir. 1920).

24 For a more detailed account of the Abrams case see Chafee, *Freedom of Speech,* pp. 120–60.

25 Chafee quotes two of the leaflets in full, pp. 120–23. See also quotations from the leaflets in *Abrams et al.* v. *United States,* 250 U.S. 616 (1919).

26 Chafee, *Freedom of Speech,* p. 122.

27 American Civil Liberties Union files, XCI, 230.

28 Chafee, *Freedom of Speech,* p. 145.

29 American Civil Liberties Union files, XCI, 229–31.

30 Quoted by Chafee, *Freedom of Speech,* p. 134.

31 *Ibid.,* p. 137.

32 *Ibid.,* p. 148.

33 *New York Times,* October 28, 1918.

34 *Abrams et al.* v. *United States,* 250 U.S. 616 (1919). In 1921 the defendants were released provided they would return to Russia. See *Report of the Attorney General, 1921,* p. 717.

35 *New York Times,* July 12, 1918.

36 *Ibid.,* July 14. See also Emerson Hough's somewhat exaggerated account in *The Web,* pp. 143–44.

37 *New York Times,* August 16, 1918.

38 Tulsa *Daily World,* August 18, 1918.

39 Hough, *The Web,* p. 144.

40 See the *New York Times,* July 8, 1918; also the *Atlanta Constitution,* June 10; and Tulsa *Daily World,* July 15, 1918.

41 *Cong. Rec.,* 65 Cong., 2 Sess., September 6, 1918, p. 10067.

42 *Ibid.,* September 5, 1918, p. 9977.

43 *New York Times,* September 4, 1918.

44 Quoting Attorney General Gregory in *ibid.,* September 12, 1918.

45 Reprinted in *Cong. Rec.,* 65 Cong., 2 Sess., September 5, 1918, p. 9976.

46 Frank Cobb to Joseph P. Tumulty, September 5, 1918, Wilson Papers.

47 *New York Times,* September 6, 1918.

48 *Cong. Rec.,* 65 Cong., 2 Sess., September 5, 1918, p. 9979.

49 *Ibid.*

50 *Ibid.,* September 6, 1918, p. 10070.

51 *Ibid.,* p. 10066.

52 *Ibid.,* p. 10067.

53 *Ibid.,* September 5, 1918, p. 9977.

54 *Cong. Rec.,* 65 Cong., 2 Sess., September 6, 1918, p. 10063. See also "The Slacker and the Careless Man," *Outlook,* CXX (September 11, 1918), 82.

55 Gregory's letter to Wilson was printed in the *New York Times,* September 12, 1918.

56 *Ladysmith News-Budget* (Ladysmith, Wisconsin), September 20, 1918.

57 *New York Times,* February 19, 1920; see also *ibid.,* February 20.

58 See the *Final Report of the Provost Marshal to the Secretary of War on the Operations of the Selective Service System to July 15, 1919* (Washington, 1920), pp. 52–53.

Chapter xxi

1. *New York Times,* May 2, 1918.

2. Seattle *Post-Intelligencer,* June 17 and 19, 1918.

3 *Sacramento Bee,* June 3, 1918.

4 *State* v. *Griffith,* 56 Mont. 241, 184 Pac. 219 (1919). The Attorney General admitted that if Griffith had not used vulgar language there would have been no case against him. The use of such language was no crime, said the appellate court.

5 See the *Memorandum Showing Interference by Federal Agents with the Operations of the General Defense Committee of the Industrial Workers of the World,* American Civil Liberties Union files, LXXXVI, 9.

6 T. Everett Harré, *The I.W.W.: An Auxiliary of the German Espionage System* (n.p., 1918), pp. 12–13.

7 *Ibid.,* p. 64.

8 *Memorandum Showing Interference by Federal Agents . . . ,* American Civil Liberties Union files, LXXXVI, 8–9.

9 *Cong. Rec.,* 65 Cong., 2 Sess., May 2, 1918, p. 5948.

10 See the *Christian Science Monitor,* April 1, 1918.

11 See *Haywood et al.* v. *United States,* 268 Fed. 795 (7th Cir. 1920).

12 For data on the trial see the daily press releases. See especially the *New York Times* for April 1, 2, 3, 7, 16; May 11, 14, 18, 19, 22, 25, 31; July 2, 3, 7; and August 4, 10, 12, 18, 31. See also Victor S. Yarros, "The Story of the I.W.W. Trial," *Survey,* XL (August 31, September 7, and September 14, 1918), 603–4, 630–32, 660–63. Harrison George, *The I.W.W. Trial* (Chicago, n.d.); *Evidence and Cross-Examination of William D. Haywood in the Case of the U.S.A. vs. William D. Haywood et al.* (n.p., n.d.); *Bill Haywood's Book,* pp. 313–26; *Brief and Arguments for Plaintiffs in Error,* United States Court of Appeals, Seventh Circuit, October, 1919.

13 *Brief and Arguments for Plaintiffs in Error,* pp. 309, 312.

14 *Ibid.,* pp. 45–46.

15 *Ibid.,* p. 218.

16 For examples, see *ibid.,* pp. 289, 340.

17 *Ibid.,* pp. 212–14.

18 *Ibid.*, pp. 177–78. See also *Haywood et al.* v. *United States,* 268 Fed. 795 (7th Cir. 1920).

19 See Yarros, "The Story of the I.W.W. Trial," pp. 660–63. This deals with an account of the defense.

20 *Report of the Attorney General, 1918,* pp. 53–54.

21 United States Department of Justice, *Interpretation of War Statutes,* Bulletin No. 175, pp. 1–17.

22 For a list of the defendants and their sentences see *Brief and Arguments for Plaintiffs in Error,* pp. 15–16.

23 See the *Christian Science Monitor, Boston Herald,* and *New York Times* for August 31, 1918. See also Yarros, "The Story of the I.W.W. Trial," p. 663.

24 Quoted in "Branding the I.W.W.," *Literary Digest,* LVIII (August 31, 1918), 14–16. Haywood later claimed the result was just what he had expected. See *Bill Haywood's Book,* p. 315.

25 This summary is taken from *ibid.*

26 *Ibid.*, p. 16.

27 *Report of the Attorney General, 1918,* pp. 53–54.

28 *Ibid.*, *1922,* p. 410.

29 *Ibid.*, p. 452.

30 Paul F. Brissenden, *Justice and the I.W.W.* (Chicago, n.d.). A pamphlet.

31 *Haywood et al.* v. *United States,* 268 Fed. 795 (7th Cir. 1920).

32 *Brief and Arguments for Plaintiffs in Error,* pp. 15–16.

33 For accounts of this trial see Dowell, "A History of the Enactment of Criminal Syndicalism Legislation in the United States," pp. 347–54; Harvey Duff, *Silent Defenders* (Chicago, n.d.), pp. 17–63; and *New Solidarity,* December 21, 1918. See footnote 44 for comments on *Solidarity* and *New Solidarity.*

34 Dowell, "A History of the Enactment of Criminal Syndicalism Legislation in the United States," p. 344; and Duff, *Silent Defenders,* p. 26.

35 *Anderson et al.* v. *United States,* 269 Fed. 65 (9th Cir. 1920).

36 *Ibid.*

37 Dowell, "A History of the Enactment of Criminal Syndicalism Legislation in the United States," p. 344. On interference with I.W.W. mail see Vincent St. John to Roger N. Baldwin, May 27, 1918, American Civil Liberties Union files, XXVII, 98–99.

38 Duff, *Silent Defenders,* pp. 29–30.

39 *Ibid.*, p. 30.

40 See *Anderson et al.* v. *United States,* 269 Fed. 65 (9th Cir. 1921).

41 G. S. Arnold to Woodrow Wilson, September 26, 1918, Wilson Papers.

42 William Kent to Wilson, October 3, 1918, Wilson Papers.

43 Wilson to George M. LaMonte, October 26, 1918, Wilson Papers.

44 See especially articles in *Solidarity* for May 12 and July 28, 1917. *Solidarity* and *New Solidarity* are not the same paper. *Solidarity* ceased publication October 17, 1917; *New Solidarity* started publication on November 16, 1918. Between November, 1917, and November 9, 1918, the I.W.W. published the *Defense News Bulletin.*

45 See "Ol' Rags an' Bottles," *Nation*, CVIII (January 25, 1919), 114–16. The writer for the *Nation* said: "The mere spectator . . . would at first have laughed with the defendants over the futility and absurdity of the whole attempt, over the absolute impossibility that anyone should take this [trial] seriously. But as the days wore on and the faces of the jury grew more and more set, till it seemed that the shadow of conviction creeping over their eyes had obscured the light, then a chill would have crept up the spectator's spine" (p. 115).

46 *Ibid.*, pp. 115–16.

47 Unsigned statement in the American Civil Liberties Union files, LXXXVI, 194. Frederick Esmond was reported in an insane asylum in 1923. The writer of the above statement said of Esmond, "He has, we fear, lost his mind."

48 *Anderson et al.* v. *United States*, 269 Fed. 65 (9th Cir. 1921).

49 *New York Times,* June 8, 1918.

50 *Ibid.,* June 13.

51 *Ibid.,* May 31.

52 See American Civil Liberties Bureau, *The Truth About the I.W.W. Prisoners* (New York, 1922), pp. 21–24.

53 *New York Times,* December 19, 1919. This account incorrectly gave 27 rather than 26 men as being convicted.

54 *Anderson et al.* v. *United States*, 273 Fed. 20 (8th Cir. 1921). This case is not to be confused with the California case of the same name. The California Anderson was Elmer; the Kansas Anderson was C. W.

55 *New York Times,* December 2, 1919.

Chapter XXII

1 For biographies of Debs see McAlister Coleman, *Eugene V. Debs* (New York, 1930); and Ray Ginger, *The Bending Cross: A Biography of Eugene Victor Debs* (New Brunswick, 1949).

2 Ginger, *The Bending Cross,* p. 331.

3 *Ibid.,* p. 347.

4 *Ibid.,* p. 354.

5 *Ibid.,* p. 350; see also Coleman, *Eugene V. Debs,* pp. 283–84.

6 For the Debs Canton speech see A. M. Schlesinger, Jr., *Writings and Speeches of Eugene V. Debs* (New York, 1948), pp. 417–33. See also *Transcript of Record* in the case of *Debs* v. *United States*, 249 U.S. 211 (No. 714, October Term, 1918), pp. 2–15.

7 See Coleman, *Eugene V. Debs,* p. 287.

8 *Debs* v. *United States*, 249 U.S. 211 (1919).

9 For a critical account of the trial see Max Eastman, *The Trial of Eugene V. Debs* (New York, n.d.). For the best account of the trial see Ginger, *The Bending Cross,* pp. 360–76. See also Coleman, *Eugene V. Debs,* pp. 290–93.

10 Quoted in Ginger, *The Bending Cross,* p. 365.

11 *Ibid.,* pp. 367–68.

12 Coleman, *Eugene V. Debs,* p. 290.

13 *Ibid.;* see also Ginger, *The Bending Cross,* p. 365; and the *New York Times,* September 11, 1918.

14 Eastman, *The Trial of Eugene V. Debs,* p. 16.

15 For a somewhat abridged account of Debs' speech to the jury, see Schlesinger, *Writings and Speeches of Eugene V. Debs,* pp. 433–37.

16 *Ibid.,* p. 436.

17 See *Transcript of Record* in the case of *Debs* v. *United States,* 249 U.S. 211 (No. 714, October Term, 1918), pp. 248–64.

18 See Debs' "Statement to the Court," in Schlesinger, *Writings and Speeches of Eugene V. Debs,* pp. 437–39.

19 Brief of Gilbert E. Roe, as *Amicus Curiae,* in the case of *Debs* v. *United States,* 249 U.S. 211 (No. 714, October Term, 1918).

20 *Debs* v. *United States,* 249 U.S. 211 (1919).

21 "The Higher Law," *Nation,* CVIII (April 19, 1919), 596.

22 *New York Times,* March 12, 1919.

23 "The Trial of Eugene V. Debs," *Survey,* XL (September 21, 1918), 695–96.

Chapter XXIII

1 Quoted in Lillian Symes and Travers Clement, *Rebel America* (New York and London, 1934), pp. 307–8.

2 Baker to Woodrow Wilson, July 22, 1918, Wilson Papers.

3 Kate Richards O'Hare, *In Prison* (New York, 1923), pp. 101–2. This book is not to be confused with the pamphlet of the same title published in St. Louis in 1920.

4 O'Hare, *In Prison* (St. Louis, 1920), p. 29.

5 O'Hare, *In Prison* (New York, 1923), pp. 104–6.

6 Quoted in the *Public,* XXII (June 21, 1919), 644.

7 Quoted by an unnamed correspondent to the *New York Call* in American Civil Liberties Union files, XXVI, 130–31. See also Earl M. Humphreys to Newton D. Baker, August 12, 1919, in *ibid.,* CXI, 196, for conditions at Fort Leavenworth and a mention of restrictions on mail. Winthrop D. Lane did a series of articles on prison and jail conditions for *Survey.* See "Military Prisons and the C.O.," *Survey,* XLII (May 17, 1919), 276–77; "Solitary," XLII (May 31, 1919), 350–58; "Fort Leavenworth," XLII (July 5, 1919), 531–36, 557; "Alcatraz," XLIV (July 3, 1920), 470–72.

8 Ginger, *The Bending Cross.* For Debs' prison experiences see pp. 390–93, 398–99.

9 See Chapter XXI.

10 Winthrop D. Lane, "Uncle Sam: Jailer," *Survey,* XLII (September 6, 1919), 806–12, 834.

11 *Ibid.*

12 See Chapter XII.

13 Judah L. Magnes, Memorandum to Secretary Newton D. Baker on visit to Fort Jay, Governor's Island, August 20, 1918. The Memorandum was dated August 27. American Civil Liberties Union files, XCIII, 152 f. For the basic study on conscientious objectors see Norman Thomas, *The Conscientious Objector in America* (New York, 1923). Thomas quotes the Magnes Memorandum on pp. 184–85.

14 Colonel Sedgwick Rice to Mrs. W. E. Thomas, November 22, 1918, American Civil Liberties Union files, LXXIX, 195. For Secretary Baker's order abolishing manacling see Thomas, *Conscientious Objector*, pp. 195–96.

15 Evan Thomas, "Disciplinary Barracks," *Survey*, XLI (February 1, 1919), 625–29.

16 *New York Times*, January 27, 1919.

17 Clark H. Getts to Mrs. Anna N. Davis, November 14, 1918, American Civil Liberties Union files, LXXI, 215.

18 Guy F. Hershberger, *War, Peace, and Nonresistance* (Stockdale, Pa., 1946), p. 122.

19 *Ibid.* See also Thomas, *Conscientious Objector*, pp. 197–200.

20 Paul Michenen to W. Lee Ustick, December 18, 1919, American Civil Liberties Union files, CXI, 71.

21 Hershberger, *War, Peace, and Nonresistance*, p. 121. For a list of conscientious objectors who died in prison see American Civil Liberties Union files, LXXI, 67.

22 William Dill to Walter Nelles, January 23, 1919, American Civil Liberties Union files, LXXVIII, 204.

23 *Ibid.* See also Thomas, *Conscientious Objector*, pp. 247–48.

24 "The Release," *Survey*, XLV (December 4, 1920), 349.

25 William Dill to Nelles, January 23, 1919, American Civil Liberties Union files, LXXVIII, 204.

26 Hershberger, *War, Peace, and Nonresistance*, pp. 121–22.

27 Thomas, *Conscientious Objector*, p. 199.

28 *Ibid.*, pp. 237–40.

29 *Ibid.*, p. 233 n.

30 Letter from "Van" to "Comrade," April 13, 1919, American Civil Liberties Union files, XCIV, p. 311.

31 Thomas, *Conscientious Objector*, p. 199.

32 *Ibid.*, p. 238.

33 *Ibid.*, p. 134.

Chapter xxiv

1 Quoted in "Free Speech and Jailed Speakers," *Literary Digest*, LXXVII (June 16, 1923), 11.

2 Louis F. Post Manuscript, pp. 398–99.

3 *New York Times,* December 1, 1918.

4 Quoted in *Cong. Rec.,* 65 Cong., 3 Sess., March 4, 1919, p. 5066. For Roe's entire speech see pp. 5066–68. Someone suggested that George Bernard Shaw visit the United States. Shaw reportedly answered that if he should go to the United States he would have "to put up at your best prisons." He added that the country's "choicest spirits," men and women like Debs and O'Hare, were in prison. If he traveled to the United States, Shaw continued, he would say the same things that Debs and others had said and he feared the result would be the same. See the *New York Call,* March 13, 1920.

5 John N. Sayre, "Political Prisoners in America" [Letter to the Editor], *Dial,* LXV (December 28, 1918), 623–24.

6 Washington *Evening Star,* December 25, 1918.

7 Committee on Public Information, *Official Bulletin,* III (January 23, 1919), 1. For accounts of conscientious objectors in military confinement see the New York *World,* January 13 and 22, 1919. For a fuller study of the problem see Norman Thomas, *The Conscientious Objector in America* (New York, 1923).

8 New York *World,* May 10, 1919.

9 *New York Times,* March 2, 1919.

10 *Ibid.,* April 18, 1919.

11 *Ibid.,* June 11, 1919.

12 "Release Political Prisoners," *Dial,* LXVI (January 11, 1919), 5–6.

13 "To What End, Mr. Baker?" *New Republic,* XIX (June 7, 1919), 171–72.

14 On the problem of Army courts-martial see Charles Johnson Post, "Court-Martial Bureaucracy," *Public,* XXII (March 29, 1919), 321–23. See also "The Injustice of Army Justice," *Literary Digest,* LXI (April 12, 1919), 13; and *Cong. Rec.,* 65 Cong., 3 Sess., February 19, 1919, pp. 3809–10; and March 4, 1919, pp. 5032–33.

15 Quoted by Loula D. Lasker, "America and Her Political Prisoners," *Survey,* XLIV (August 2, 1920), 578.

16 Quoted in *Cong. Rec.,* 67 Cong., 2 Sess., June 7, 1922, p. 8352.

17 Gregory to Wilson, March 1, 1919, Wilson Papers. See also the *New York Times,* March 3, 1919.

18 See American Civil Liberties Union files, CVI, 64.

19 *New York Times,* July 2, 1919.

20 *Ibid.,* July 3.

21 See the *New York Times,* September 14 and 15, 1919; also the *Seattle Union-Record,* September 15, 1919. For an interesting but not a very accurate account of the meeting see Louis Adamic, "The 'Assassin' of Wilson," *American Mercury,* XXI (October, 1930), 138–46.

22 Palmer, Memorandum for the President, July 30, 1919, Wilson Papers.

23 *Ibid.*

24 *Ibid.*

25 Wilson to Palmer, August 1, 1919, in *ibid.*

26 *Report of the Attorney General, 1922,* p. 415. When an appeal was later made to release the Anarchist Ricardo Magon, Daugherty was quoted as

saying, "He in no manner evinces any evidence of repentance." Quoted in *Cong. Rec.*, 67 Cong., 4 Sess., December 14, 1922, p. 488.

27 David Karsner, *Debs, His Authorized Life and Letters from Woodstock Prison to Atlanta* (New York, 1919), p. 3.

28 Woodrow Wilson to W. B. Wilson, November 9, 1920, Wilson Papers.

29 Villard to Lansing, November 5, 1919, Lansing Papers.

30 Quoted in *United States* v. *Steene et al.*, 263 Fed. 130 (N.D. N.Y. 1920).

31 *Ibid.*

32 See the *New York Times*, November 24, 25, and 26, 1919.

33 *Ibid.*, January 19, 1920.

34 *Ibid.*, February 27, 1920.

35 "Forgiving War-Offenders," *Literary Digest*, LXVII (October 2, 1920), 18–19. See also the *New York Times*, May 30, 1920.

36 *New York Times*, July 25, 1920.

37 *Ibid.*, October 8, 1920.

38 "Forgiving War-Offenders," p. 18.

39 *Ibid.*, pp. 18–19. John Spargo, one of the Socialists who had supported the war, wrote that Debs' sentence had been too harsh, as were the sentences of others. Writing in September, 1920, Spargo said it was time to speak out against the "brutal and czaristic spirit which those in authority have manifested since the cessation of hostilities." See John Spargo, "Democracy Must Not Be Vindictive," *Independent*, CIII (September 11, 1920), 303.

40 "War-Time Offenders Out of Jail," *Literary Digest*, LXVII (December 11, 1920), 20.

41 Palmer to Wilson, October 1, 1920; and Wilson to Palmer, October 4, 1920, Wilson Papers.

42 *New York Times*, November 16, 1921.

43 Gompers to Wilson, December 15, 1920, Wilson Papers.

44 *New York Times*, November 7, 1920. See also "War-Time Offenders Out of Jail," p. 20.

45 *New York Times*, November 8, 1920.

46 F. W. Galbraith to Woodrow Wilson, November 9, 1920, Wilson Papers. See also the *New York Times*, November 10, 1920.

47 Joseph P. Tumulty, *Woodrow Wilson As I Knew Him* (New York, 1921), p. 505. Norman Hapgood wrote to Wilson that he did not know of any case which "compares with the Debs case in the intensity of war psychology." Then he added, "It and other cases have separated some of my best and most influential friends from the Administration." Hapgood to Wilson, November 9, 1920, Wilson Papers.

48 Ray Ginger, *The Bending Cross*, p. 405.

49 Quoted in C. Vann Woodward, *Tom Watson, Agrarian Rebel* (New York, 1938), p. 476.

50 *Cong. Rec.*, 67 Cong., 1 Sess., November 22, 1921, p. 8143. For sample of earlier petitions see *ibid.*, 65 Cong., 3 Sess., February 24, 1919, p. 4200.

51 *New York Times*, April 5, 1921.

52 *Ibid.*, April 6, 1921.

53 *Ibid.,* November 16, 1921.
54 *Ibid.,* December 14, 1921.
55 Sen. Exec. Doc. No. 113, 67 Cong., 2 Sess. (1922), Ser. 7987.
56 *New York Times,* December 24, 1921.
57 Samuel Hopkins Adams, *Incredible Era* (Boston, 1939), p. 256.
58 See the *New York Call,* March 17, 1922.
59 *New York Times,* April 28, 1922.
60 *Ibid.,* April 30, 1922.
61 Quoted in *Cong. Rec.,* 67 Cong., 2 Sess., June 7, 1922, p. 8353.
62 *Ibid.,* May 16, 1922, pp. 7078–79.
63 *Ibid.,* June 7, 1922, p. 8353.
64 *Ibid.*
65 *Magon et al.* v. *United States,* 260 Fed. 811 (9th Cir. 1919).
66 See *Cong. Rec.,* 67 Cong., 4 Sess., December 11, 1922, p. 298.
67 Quoted in *ibid.,* December 14, 1922, p. 488.
68 *Ibid.,* December 11, 1922, p. 299.
69 *Ibid.,* December 14, 1922, pp. 485–86.
70 *Ibid.,* p. 489.
71 See "Free Speech and Jailed Speakers," *Literary Digest,* LXXVII (June 16, 1923), 10.
72 *Ibid.,* p. 11.
73 St. Louis *Post-Dispatch,* June 27, 1923. This report said that ten men refused the offer. See also "The Political Prisoners' Reply," *New Republic,* XXXVI (August 29, 1923), 21. The number of men who refused clemency was given as eleven in this account.
74 "U.S. Press in Amnesty Plea," *Illinois Miner,* III (November 17, 1923), 1.
75 Quoted in New York *Advance,* November 16, 1923.
76 *New York Times,* November 29, 1923.
77 *Ibid.*
78 *Ibid.,* December 16, 1923.
79 *Ibid.*
80 *Ibid.,* December 17, 1923.
81 *Ibid.,* December 18, 1923.

Chapter xxv

1 Jane Addams, *The Second Twenty Years at Hull-House* (New York, 1930), p. 174.
2 It is not the purpose of the authors to retell the story of the Red Scare here. This has been done by numerous writers. One of the best older accounts is that of Frederick Lewis Allen in *Only Yesterday,* Chap. III. The present writers, however, have relied most heavily on the new, lively and authentic account by Robert K. Murray entitled *Red Scare: A Study in National Hysteria, 1919–1920* (Minneapolis, 1955).

3 Murray, *Red Scare*, pp. 34–36, 46–47.
4 Quoted in *New Solidarity*, November 30, 1918. Gregory's letter was dated November 21, 1918.
5 Murray, *Red Scare*, pp. 58–66.
6 *Ibid.*, pp. 68–72.
7 *Ibid.*, pp. 80–81.
8 *Cong. Rec.*, 65 Cong., 3 Sess., February 8, 1919, p. 2937.
9 *Ibid.*, p. 2942.
10 *Ibid.*, p. 2943.
11 *Ibid.*, p. 2949.
12 *Ibid.*, February 17, 1919, p. 3542.
13 See E. Foster Dowell, "Criminal Syndicalism," pp. 1257–58.
14 For a list of the states see the *Cong. Rec.*, 66 Cong., 2 Sess., February 6, 1920, pp. 2577–78.
15 "Compulsory Military Training," *Literary Digest*, LXIV (February 14, 1920), 19–20. See also Paul Russell Anderson, ed., "Universal Military Training and National Security," *The Annals of the American Academy of Political and Social Science*, CCXLI (September, 1945), 13–14. There was widespread discussion of universal military training in 1919 and 1920. See the list of articles in *Readers' Guide to Periodical Literature*. Consult also the *New York Times* Index for 1919 and early 1920.
16 See Murray, *Red Scare*, pp. 166–89.
17 For the Cincinnati incident see the *New York Call*, November 20, 1919; the situation in Philadelphia is described in the same paper on November 29.
18 *New York Times*, November 18, 1919. See also the *New York Tribune*, November 18, 1919.
19 Murray, *Red Scare*, pp. 122–34.
20 *Ibid.*, pp. 196–97. See also a discussion of the Lusk Committee in New York in Lawrence H. Chamberlain, *Loyalty and Legislative Action: A Survey of Activity by the New York State Legislature, 1919–1949* (Ithaca, New York, 1951), pp. 9–52.
21 Murray, *Red Scare*, pp. 182–84. See also *New York Times*, November 12 and 13, 1918.
22 *Cong. Rec.*, 66 Cong., 1 Sess., October 27, 1919, p. 7543. For a copy of the bill see *ibid.*, November 3, p. 7881.
23 *Ibid.*, November 17, 1919, p. 8697.
24 *Ibid.*, Extension of remarks, pp. 9155–56.
25 *Ibid.*, 66 Cong., 2 Sess., December 2, 1919, p. 30.
26 Chafee, *Freedom of Speech*, p. 197. See also Murray, *Red Scare*, p. 230; and "Alien and Sedition Bills of 1920," *Literary Digest*, LXIV (February 7, 1920), 11–13.
27 *Cong. Rec.*, 66 Cong., 1 Sess., November 3, 1919, p. 7881. The bill also contained a red flag provision.
28 Murray, *Red Scare*, pp. 213–22. For a contemporary account see *New York Times*, January 3, 1920. See also *Colyer et al.* v. *Skeffington*, 265 Fed. 17 (D.C.D. Mass. 1920).

29 *Cong. Rec.*, 66 Cong., 2 Sess., January 10, 1920, p. 1338. See also "Drastic Sedition Laws," *Literary Digest*, LXIV (January 24, 1920), 18.

30 *Cong. Rec.*, 66 Cong., 2 Sess., January 10, 1920, p. 1334.

31 For a discussion of these factors see Murray, *Red Scare*, pp. 239–62.

32 Creel to Wilson, November 8, 1918, Wilson Papers.

33 Murray, *Red Scare*, p. 240.

34 Hughes to Speaker T. C. Sweet. Quoted in the *New York Times*, January 10, 1920.

35 *Ibid.*, January 21, 1920.

36 In "Albany's Ousted Socialists," *Literary Digest*, LXIV (January 24, 1920), 19–20.

37 For Borah statement see the *New York Times*, January 11, 1920; for Harding, January 9, 1920.

38 *Ibid.*, January 8, 1920.

39 *Ibid.* See also January 9. See further Murray, *Red Scare*, pp. 242–44.

40 Quoted in Ernest S. Bates, *This Land of Liberty*, p. 127.

41 Quoted in Nelles, *Liberal in Wartime*, pp. 198–99.

42 *Cong. Rec.*, 66 Cong., 2 Sess., April 14, 1920, p. 5671.

43 Murray, *Red Scare*, pp. 248–49.

44 *Ibid.*, p. 251.

45 See copy of Palmer's letter to chairman of the House Rules Committee dated January 21, 1920, and a copy of the sedition bill favored by Palmer in *Cong. Rec.*, 66 Cong., 2 Sess., April 14, 1920, p. 5670.

46 See "What Is Attorney General Palmer Doing?" *Nation*, CX (February 14, 1920), 190–91. For a facsimile of material which Palmer's office furnished the press see *ibid.* (March 6, 1920), p. 299.

47 *Cong. Rec.*, 66 Cong., 2 Sess., April 14, 1920, pp. 5671–72.

48 Quoted in "Alien and Sedition Bills of 1920," *Literary Digest*, LXIV (February 7, 1920), 11–13. The following newspapers still favored a peacetime sedition law, according to the *Literary Digest: Indianapolis News, Philadelphia Enquirer, Providence Journal, Miami Herald, Des Moines Capital, Minneapolis Journal, Portland Oregonian, San Diego Union, Pittsburgh Gazette-Times,* and *Washington Post.*

49 Frank I. Cobb, *The Press and Public Opinion* (n.p., n.d.). This was an address delivered before the Women's City Club of New York, December 11, 1919.

Chapter xxvi

1 Hiram Johnson to Theodore Roosevelt, August 20, 1914, Roosevelt Papers.

2 See Robert E. Cushman, "American Civil Liberties in Mid-Twentieth Century," in Robert K. Carr, ed., "Civil Rights in America," *The Annals of the American Academy of Political and Social Science*, CCLXXV (May, 1951), 8.

3 On this point see Zechariah Chafee, Jr., compiler and editor, *Documents on Fundamental Human Rights* (Cambridge, 1951), pp. 587–628.

4 Significant books dealing with problems of Civil Liberties include: Clair Wilcox, ed., *Civil Liberties Under Attack* (Philadelphia, 1951); Robert K. Carr, ed., "Civil Rights in America," *The Annals of the American Academy of Political and Social Science*, CCLXXV (May, 1951); Alison Reppy, *Civil Rights in the United States* (New York, 1951); Harold D. Lasswell, *National Security and Individual Freedom* (New York, 1950); Thomas I. Emerson and David Harber, *Political and Civil Rights in the United States* (Buffalo, 1952); Zechariah Chafee, Jr., compiler and editor, *Documents on Fundamental Human Rights* (Cambridge, 1951); Osmond K. Fraenkel, *Our Civil Liberties* (New York, 1944); Lawrence H. Chamberlain, *Loyalty and Legislative Action: A Survey of Activity by the New York State Legislature, 1919–1949* (Ithaca, New York, 1951); Alan Barth, *The Loyalty of Free Men* (New York, 1951); Francis Biddle, *The Fear of Freedom* (Garden City, New York, 1951); Henry Steele Commager, *Freedom, Loyalty, Dissent* (New York, 1954).

5 54 *U.S. Stat.* 670 (1940). For a discussion of the Alien Registration Act see Zechariah Chafee, *Free Speech in the United States* (Cambridge, 1941), pp. 440–90.

6 Emerson and Harber, *Political and Civil Rights in the United States,* p. 463.

7 64 *U.S. Stat.* 987 (1950).

8 Henry Steele Commager, "The Pragmatic Necessity of Freedom," in Clair Wilcox, ed., *Civil Liberties Under Attack,* p. 10.

9 Alan Barth, *The Loyalty of Free Men,* p. 236.

10 Chafee, *Free Speech in the United States,* p. 79. Author's italics.

11 4 Wall. U.S. 2, *ex parte Milligan.*

12 *Schaefer* v. *United States,* 251 U.S. 495 (1920).

13 Quoted in Francis Biddle, *The Fear of Freedom,* p. 255.

14 Quoted in the *Nashville Tennessean,* August 3, 1955.

The research for this book has been done in a wide variety of sources. The most important bodies of manuscript materials used were the American Civil Liberties Union files and the records of the Committee on Public Information. The materials preserved by the American Civil Liberties Union are very voluminous and include letters sent and received by the Union, memoranda, newspaper clippings, and other data. The fact that the materials are in bound volumes permits exact page references. There is, however, no particular organization of the materials included in each volume. The American Civil Liberties Union files are especially valuable as a source for the treatment of opponents of war in 1917 and 1918. Long letters written by individuals to officers of the Union reveal the many harsh and sometimes cruel indignities suffered by opponents of war. These files are now located at Princeton University, and the New York Public library has a microfilm copy of them. The records are officially known as the American Civil Liberties Union Archives.

The records of the Committee on Public Information are to be found in the General Records Division of the National Archives in Washington, D.C. These materials include general correspondence, printed matter, and other data which refer to the work of this Committee. Most of these files cover the period from April, 1917, to August, 1919.

The records of the Council of National Defense were also used. They are located in the War Record Office of the National Archives. Most of the material relates to the period, 1917–18. Among the files are correspondence of the various officers, minutes of meetings, memoranda, news releases, and newspaper clippings.

The papers of Woodrow Wilson were a rich source of information on many points relating to the opponents of war. These were examined in order to make possible a more accurate evaluation of the President's attitude on opponents of war and the issues relating to them and their activities. The Wilson Collection is large and contains many letters written by or for the President, as well as letters received by him, on matters relating to war opponents. The Wilson Papers are in the Library of Congress and can be used with permission. Other manuscript collections which were examined on some points include those of William Jennings Bryan, Robert Lansing, Theodore Roosevelt, Elihu Root, and

Louis F. Post. These are all located in the Library of Congress. As the footnotes indicate, these papers had much less to offer than those of President Wilson. The Louis F. Post Collection is a very small one but contains the unpublished manuscript of Mr. Post's autobiography.

In addition to manuscripts, newspapers were relied upon heavily. For the entire period of World War I the following newspapers were completely covered: *New York Times,* Oklahoma City *Daily Oklahoman,* Tulsa *Daily World, Minneapolis Tribune, Atlanta Constitution,* Seattle *Post-Intelligencer, Sacramento Bee,* and Los Angeles *Times.* As the footnotes reveal, hundreds of other newspapers were examined on special events and issues. In addition, the clippings in the American Civil Liberties Union files proved exceedingly helpful.

Besides the manuscripts and newspapers, a voluminous amount of material was found in court records. Hundreds of cases were studied which involved opponents of war. Government documents, including hearings, reports, and the *Congressional Record,* were also consulted. Additional material was taken from the periodicals which carried scores of articles on some phases of this subject between 1917 and 1919. The standard books in the field, of which a great many had something of value, including both biography and autobiography, were examined.

Despite years of study and research over a wide range of materials, no pretense is made of having exhausted the sources. It would be impossible in one lifetime personally to examine or study all of the materials relating to the subject under consideration. It is hoped that this presentation will encourage others to pursue some of the problems and aspects of the subject which have been left untouched, or of which space has forbidden a fuller treatment.

Unpublished Manuscripts and Theses

Bush, Charles C. "The Greencorn Rebellion." Master's thesis, University of Oklahoma, 1932.

Dowell, E. Foster. "A History of the Enactment of Criminal Syndicalism Legislation in the United States." Doctoral dissertation, Johns Hopkins University, 1936. This was published in abbreviated form. See Dowell under books.

Hofland, Carl J. "The Nonpartisan League in South Dakota." Master's thesis, University of South Dakota, Vermillion, 1940.

Milham, Chester R. "A History of National Espionage Legislation and its Operation in the United States During the World War." Doctoral dissertation, University of Southern California, 1938.

Post, Louis F. "Living a Long Life." Unpublished manuscript. Library of Congress, Washington, D.C.

Wilkins, Robert P. "North Dakota and the European War, 1914–1917: A Study in Public Opinion." Doctoral dissertation, University of West Virginia, 1954.

Government Publications

Amnesty and Pardon for Political Prisoners, Hearings before a Subcommittee of the Committee on the Judiciary on S. J. Res. 171, 66 Cong., 3 Sess. (1921).

The Annotated Code of the Public General Laws of Maryland, George P. Bagby ed., Vol. II (Baltimore, 1924).

Attorneys General Annual Reports, 1917–22.

Congressional Record. 65, 66, and 67 Congresses.

Department of Justice. *Interpretation of War Statutes.* Bulletin Nos. 1–200 (Washington, 1918).

"East St. Louis Riots," H. Doc. No. 1231, 65 Cong., 2 Sess. (1918), Ser. 7444.

Final Report of the Provost Marshal to the Secretary of War on the Operations of the Selective Service System to July 15, 1919 (Washington, 1920).

National Security League, Hearings before a Special Committee of the House of Representatives, 65 Cong., 3 Sess. (Washington, 1919).

Report on the Bisbee Deportations Made by the President's Commission to the President of the United States, November 6, 1917 (Washington, 1918).

Riot at East St. Louis, Illinois, Hearings before the House Committee on Rules on H. J. Res. 118, 65 Cong., 1 Sess. (1917).

Secretary of War. *Statement Concerning the Treatment of Conscientious Objectors* (Washington, 1919).

Sen. Exec. Doc. No. 153, 66 Cong., 1 Sess. (1919), Ser. 7607.

Sen. Exec. Doc. No. 113, 67 Cong., 2 Sess. (1922), Ser. 7987.

United States Statutes at Large, Vols. XXXIX, XL, XLI, LIV, LXIV.

Vernon's Annotated Penal Code of the State of Texas, Vol. I (Kansas City, Mo., 1938).

Law Cases

Abrams et al. v. *United States,* 250 U.S. 616 (1919).

Albers v. *United States,* 263 Fed. 27 (9th Cir. 1920).

American Socialist Society v. *United States,* 266 Fed. 212 (2nd Cir. 1920).

Anderson v. *United States,* 253 U.S. 495 (1920).

Anderson et al. v. *United States,* 273 Fed. 20 (8th Cir. 1921).

Anderson et al. v. *United States,* 269 Fed. 65 (9th Cir. 1921).

Arver v. *United States,* 245 U.S. 366 (1918).

Balbas v. *United States et al.,* 257 Fed. 17 (1st Cir. 1919).

Balcom v. *United States,* 259 Fed. 779 (1st Cir. 1919).

Becker v. *United States,* 268 Fed. 195 (7th Cir. 1920).

Bentall v. *United States,* 254 Fed. 294 (8th Cir. 1918).

Berger et al. v. *United States,* 275 Fed. 1021 (7th Cir. 1921).

Berger et al. v. *United States,* 255 U.S. 22 (1921).

Billings v. *Truesdell,* 321 U.S. 542 (1944).

Boehner v. *United States,* 267 Fed. 562 (8th Cir. 1920).

Bold v. *United States,* 265 Fed. 581 (9th Cir. 1920).

Bouldin v. *United States,* 261 Fed. 674 (5th Cir. 1919).

Brief of Gilbert E. Roe, as *Amicus curiae,* in the case of *Debs* v. *United States,* 249 U.S. 211 (No. 714, October Term, 1918).

Bryant et al. v. *United States,* 257 Fed. 378 (5th Cir. 1919).

Buessel v. *United States,* 258 Fed. 811 (2nd Cir. 1919).

Caughman v. *United States,* 258 Fed. 434 (4th Cir. 1919).

Clark v. *United States,* 250 Fed. 449 (5th Cir. 1918).

Coldwell v. *United States,* 256 Fed. 805 (1st Cir. 1919).

Collins v. *United States,* 253 Fed. 609 (9th Cir. 1918).

Colyer et al. v. *Skeffington,* 265 Fed. 17 (D.C.D. Mass. 1920).

Deason v. *United States,* 254 Fed. 259 (5th Cir. 1918).

Debs v. *United States,* 249 U.S. 211 (1919).

Dierkes v. *United States,* 274 Fed. 75 (6th Cir. 1921).

Doe v. *United States,* 253 Fed. 903 (8th Cir. 1918).

Enfield v. *United States,* 261 Fed. 141 (8th Cir. 1919).

Equi v. *United States,* 251 U.S. 560 (1920).

Ex parte Milligan, 4 Wallace 2 (1866).

Ex parte Starr, 263 Fed. 145 (D. Mont. 1920).

Fairchild v. *United States,* 265 Fed. 584 (8th Cir. 1920).

Firth et al. v. *United States,* 253 Fed. 36 (4th Cir. 1918).

Fontana v. *United States,* 262 Fed. 283 (8th Cir. 1919).

Foster et al. v. *United States,* 253 Fed. 481 (9th Cir. 1918).

Fraina et al. v. *United States,* 255 Fed. 28 (2nd Cir. 1918).

Gerdes v. *State,* 104 Neb. 35, 175 N.W. 606 (1919).

Gilbert v. *State of Minnesota,* 254 U.S. 325 (1920).

Goldman et al. v. *United States,* 245 U.S. 474 (1918).

Goldstein v. *United States,* 258 Fed. 908 (9th Cir. 1919).

Hamm v. *United States,* 261 Fed. 907 (9th Cir. 1920).

Hammerschmidt et al. v. *United States,* 287 Fed. 817 (6th Cir. 1923).

Haywood et al. v. *United States,* 268 Fed. 795 (7th Cir. 1920).

Haywood et al. v. *United States, Brief and Arguments for Plaintiffs in Error,* U.S. Court of Appeals, 7th Cir., October, 1919.

Head v. *United States,* 248 U.S. 593 (1918).

Herman v. *United States,* 257 Fed. 601 (9th Cir. 1919).

Heynacher v. *United States,* 257 Fed. 61 (8th Cir. 1919).

Hickson v. *United States,* 258 Fed. 867 (4th Cir. 1919).

Holzmacher v. *United States,* 266 Fed. 979 (7th Cir. 1920).

Howenstine et al. v. *United States,* 263 Fed. 1 (9th Cir. 1920).

In re Margolis, 269 Pa. 206, 112 Atl. 478 (1921).

Jeffersonian Publishing Co. v. *West,* 245 Fed. 585 (S.D. Ga. 1917).

Kammann v. *United States,* 259 Fed. 192 (7th Cir. 1919).

Kirchner v. *United States,* 255 Fed. 301 (4th Cir. 1918).

Kramer et al. v. *United States,* 245 U.S. 478 (1918).

Lockhart v. *United States,* 264 Fed. 14 (6th Cir. 1920).

Magon et al. v. *United States,* 260 Fed. 811 (9th Cir. 1919).

Mamaux v. *United States,* 264 Fed. 816 (6th Cir. 1920).

Masses Publication Co. v. *Patten,* 246 Fed. 24 (2nd Cir. 1917).

Masses Publication Co. v. *Patten,* 244 Fed. 535 (S.D. N.Y. 1917).

Mead v. *United States,* 257 Fed. 639 (9th Cir. 1919).

O'Connell et al. v. *United States,* 253 U.S. 142 (1920).

O'Hare v. *United States,* 253 Fed. 538 (8th Cir. 1918).

Partan et al. v. *United States,* 261 Fed. 515 (9th Cir. 1919).

Pierce et al. v. *United States,* 252 U.S. 239 (1920).

Ragansky v. *United States,* 253 Fed. 643 (7th Cir. 1918).

Rhuberg v. *United States,* 255 Fed. 865 (9th Cir. 1919).

Rietz v. *United States,* 257 Fed. 731 (8th Cir. 1919).

Ruthenberg et al. v. *United States,* 245 U.S. 480 (1918).

Rutherford et al. v. *United States,* 258 Fed. 864 (2nd Cir. 1919).

Schaefer v. *United States,* 251 U.S. 466 (1920).

Schenck v. *United States,* 249 U.S. 47 (1919).

Schumann v. *United States,* 258 Fed. 233 (8th Cir. 1919).

Shaffer v. *United States,* 255 Fed. 886 (9th Cir. 1919).

Shidler v. *United States,* 257 Fed. 620 (9th Cir. 1919).

Shilter v. *United States,* 257 Fed. 724 (9th Cir. 1919).

Shoborg v. *United States,* 264 Fed. 1 (6th Cir. 1920).

Sonnenberg v. *United States,* 264 Fed. 327 (9th Cir. 1920)

State v. *Brooks,* 57 Mont. 480, 188 Pac. 942 (1920).

State v. *Gilbert,* 141 Minn. 263, 169 N.W. 790 (1918).

State v. *Griffith,* 56 Mont. 241, 184 Pac. 219 (1919).

State v. *Kahn,* 56 Mont. 108, 182 Pac. 107 (1919).

State v. *Ludemann,* 143 Minn. 126, 172 N.W. 887 (1919).

State v. *Martin,* 142 Minn. 484, 169 N.W. 792 (1918).

State v. *Townley et al.,* 140 Minn. 413, 168 N.W. 591 (1918).

State v. *Townley et al.,* 149 Minn. 5, 182 N.W. 773 (1921).

Steene et al. v. *United States,* 255 U.S. 580 (1920).

Stephens v. *United States,* 261 Fed. 590 (9th Cir. 1919).

Stilson v. *United States,* 250 U.S. 583 (1919).

Stokes v. *United States,* 264 Fed. 18 (8th Cir. 1920).

Sugarman v. *United States,* 249 U.S. 182 (1919).

Sykes et al. v. *United States,* 264 Fed. 945 (9th Cir. 1920).

Townley et al. v. *State of Minnesota,* 257 U.S. 643 (1921).

Transcript of Record in the case of *Debs* v. *United States,* 249 U.S. 211 (No. 714, October Term, 1918).

Trelease v. *United States,* 266 Fed. 886 (8th Cir. 1920).

Uhl v. *United States,* 263 Fed. 79 (5th Cir. 1920).

United States v. *American Socialist Society,* 260 Fed. 885 (S.D. N.Y. 1919).

United States v. *Baker et al.,* 247 Fed. 124 (D. Md. 1917).

United States v. *Binder,* 253 Fed. 978 (E.D. N.Y. 1918).

United States v. *Boutin,* 251 Fed. 313 (N.D. N.Y. 1918).

United States v. *Bryant et al.,* 245 Fed. 682 (N.D. Tex. 1917).

United States v. *Debs,* 73 Fed. 1021 (N.D. Ohio 1918).

United States v. *Hall,* 248 Fed. 150 (D. Mont. 1918).

"United States v. Hicks," 1743 C. D. 6, United States District Court, Oklahoma City. Unreported case.

United States v. *Jasick,* 252 Fed. 931 (E.D. Mich. 1918).

United States v. *Krafft,* 249 Fed. 919 (3rd Cir. 1918).

"United States v. Louise Olivereau," United States District Court, Western District of Washington, Northern Division, May, 1917. Unreported case.

United States v. *Motion Picture Film "The Spirit of '76,"* 252 Fed. 946 (S.D. Cal. 1917).

United States v. *Nagler,* 252 Fed. 217 (W.D. Wis. 1918).

United States v. *Nearing et al.,* 252 Fed. 223 (S.D. N.Y. 1918).

United States v. *Pape,* 253 Fed. 270 (S.D. Ill. 1918).

United States v. *Pass,* 256 Fed. 731 (9th Cir. 1919).

United States v. *Peterson* (D.C. 4th Div. Minn. 1918). Unreported case.

United States v. *Pierce et al.*, 245 Fed. 878 (N.D. N.Y. 1917).

United States v. *William Powell*, Indictment No. 6218, July 3, 1918 (E.D. Mich. 1918). Unreported case.

United States v. *Schenck et al.*, 253 Fed. 212 (1918).

United States v. *Schulze*, 253 Fed. 377 (S.D. Cal. 1918).

United States v. *Steene et al.*, 263 Fed. 130 (N.D. N.Y. 1920).

United States v. *Stickrath*, 242 Fed. 151 (S.D. Ohio 1917).

United States v. *Stobo*, 251 Fed. 689 (D. Del. 1918).

United States v. *Sugar et al.*, 252 Fed. 79 (6th Cir. 1918).

United States v. *Sugarman*, 245 Fed. 604 (1917).

United States v. *Wangerin*, 245 U.S. 355 (1918).

United States ex rel. Milwaukee Social Democratic Publishing Co. v. *Burleson*, 258 Fed. 282 (1919).

Wells et al. v. *United States*, 257 Fed. 605 (9th Cir. 1919).

Wessels v. *United States*, 262 Fed. 389 (5th Cir. 1919).

West Virginia State Board of Education et al. v. *Barnette et al.*, 319 U.S. 624 (1943).

White v. *United States*, 263 Fed. 17 (6th Cir. 1920).

Wimmer v. *United States*, 264 Fed. 11 (6th Cir. 1920).

Articles

Adamic, Louis. "The 'Assassin' of Wilson," *American Mercury*, XXI (October, 1930), 138–46.

"Albany's Ousted Socialists," *Literary Digest*, LXIV (January 24, 1920), 19–20.

"Alien and Sedition Bills of 1920," *Literary Digest*, LXIV (February 7, 1920), 11–13.

Allen, Frederick Lewis. "The Forty-Eight Defenders: A Study of the Work of the State Councils of Defense," *Century*, XCV (December, 1917), 261–66.

"American by Decree," *New Republic*, XXII (April 28, 1920), 262–63.

"American Students Boycotting German," *Literary Digest*, LVI (March 30, 1918), 29–31, 44, 46–50, 52, 54–55, 58, 61–64, 66, 70, 72–74.

"America's Shame," *Independent*, XCVIII (May 24, 1919), 277.

"The Anarchist Deportations," *New Republic*, XXI (December 24, 1919), 96–98.

"Another 'Man Without a Country,'" *Nation*, CX (March 6, 1920), 289.

Ascher, Charles S., and James M. Wolf, editors-in-charge. "Criminal

Syndicalism," *Columbia Law Review,* XX (February, 1920), 232–35.

Baldwin, Roger. "East St. Louis—Why?" *Survey,* XXXVIII (August 18, 1917), 447–48.

Barkley, F. R. "Jailing Radicals in Detroit," *Nation,* CX (January 31, 1920), 136–37.

Beard, Charles A. "A Statement by Charles A. Beard," *New Republic,* XIII (December 29, 1917), 249–51.

"The Berger Decision," *New Republic,* XXV (February 23, 1921), 360–61.

Bevis, Howard L. "The Deportation of Aliens," *University of Pennsylvania Law Review,* LXVIII (January, 1920), 97–119.

"The Bisbee Deportations," *Survey,* XXXVIII (July 21, 1917), 353.

"The Bisbee Deportations Illegal," *Survey,* XXXIX (December 8, 1917), 291–92.

"Boloism in this Country," *Literary Digest,* LVI (March 2, 1918), 14–15.

Bourquin, Judge George M. (opinions of). "A Federal Judge Speaks Up," *New Republic,* XXII (March 31, 1920), 135.

"Branding the I.W.W.," *Literary Digest,* LVIII (August 31, 1918), 14–16.

"Bringing the Constitution into Disrepute," *New Republic,* XXI (February 18, 1920), 330–31.

Browne, Lewis Allen. "Bolshevism in America," *Forum,* LIX (June, 1918), 703–17.

Browne, Waldo R. Letter to the Editor, "Our Modern Heretic Burners," *New Republic,* XIII (December 1, 1917), 127.

Bruere, Robert W. "Copper Camp Patriotism," *Nation,* CVI (February 21, 1918), 202–3.

"The Call to Toleration," *New Republic,* XX (November 26, 1919), 360–62.

Carr, Robert K., ed. "Civil Rights in America," *The Annals of the American Academy of Political and Social Science,* CCLXXV (May, 1951), 1–161.

Carroll, Thomas F. "Freedom of Speech and of the Press in Wartime: The Espionage Act," *Michigan Law Review,* XVII (June, 1919), 621–65.

"Centralia," *New Republic,* XXII (April 14, 1920), 217–20. Signed E.M.

Chafee, Zechariah, Jr. "Freedom of Speech in War Time," *Harvard Law Review,* XXXII (June, 1919), 932–73.

———. "Legislation Against Anarchy," *New Republic,* XIX (July 23, 1919), 379–85.

———. "Sedition," *Encyclopedia of the Social Sciences,* XIII, 638.

Claghorn, Kate H. "Aliens and Sedition in the New Year," *Survey,* XLIII (January 17, 1920), 422–23.

Cobb, Frank I. "The Press and Public Opinion," *New Republic,* XXI (December 31, 1919), 144–47.

Colcord, Lincoln. "Martens and Our Foreign Policy," *Nation,* CX (March 13, 1920), 324–27.

"Columbia's Dismissed Professors," *Literary Digest,* LV (October 20, 1917), 24.

"Compulsory Military Training," *Literary Digest,* LXIV (February 14, 1920), 19–20.

"Congressional Queries," *Independent,* XCVII (January 18, 1919), 81.

"Conscience at the Bar," *Survey,* XLI (November 9, 1918), 153–54.

Corwin, E. S. "Freedom of Speech and Press under the First Amendment: A Résumé," *Yale Law Journal,* XXX (November, 1920), 48–55.

Creel, George. "Our Aliens—Were They Loyal or Disloyal?" *Everybody's Magazine,* XL (March, 1919), 36–38, 70–73.

"Criminal Syndicalism," *Encyclopedia of the Social Sciences,* IV, 582.

Cushman, R. E. "National Police Power under the Postal Clause of the Constitution," *Minnesota Law Review,* IV (May, 1920), 402–40.

"A Defect in the Draft Law," *Nation,* CV (August 23, 1917), 192–93.

"Deporting a Political Party," *New Republic,* XXI (January 14, 1920), 186.

Dillard, J. H. "History and Free Speech," *Public,* XXII (March 8, 1919), 236–37.

"Drastic Sedition Laws," *Literary Digest,* LXIV (January 24, 1920), 18.

"East St. Louis Race Riots," *Literary Digest,* LV (July 14, 1917), 10–11.

Emmett, William. "Mania in Los Angeles," *Nation,* CVI (January 17, 1918), 58–59.

"The Espionage Act Interpreted," *New Republic,* XX (November 26, 1919), 377–83.

"The Espionage Cases," *Harvard Law Review,* XXXII (February, 1919), 417–20.

"The Farmer and the War," *New Republic,* XIII (November 3, 1917), 8–9.

"A Federal Campaign Against Mob Violence," *Survey,* XL (May 25, 1918), 225–26.

"Federal Sedition Bills: Speech Restriction in Theory and Practice," *Columbia Law Review,* XXXV (June, 1935), 917–27.

Ferrari, Robert. "The Trial of Political Criminals Here and Abroad," *Dial,* LXVI (June 28, 1919), 647–49.

"The First War-Lynching," *Literary Digest,* LVII (April 20, 1918), 16–17.

Fite, Gilbert C. "The Nonpartisan League in Oklahoma," *Chronicles of Oklahoma,* XXIV (Summer, 1946), 146–57.

————. "Peter Norbeck and the Defeat of the Nonpartisan League in South Dakota," *Mississippi Valley Historical Review,* XXXIII (September, 1946), 217–36.

"Forgiving War-Offenders," *Literary Digest,* LXVII (October 2, 1920), 18–19.

"Free Speech and Jailed Speakers," *Literary Digest,* LXXVII (June 16, 1923), 10–12.

"Free Speech in Time of Peace," *Yale Law Journal,* XXIX (January, 1920), 337–44. Signed K.N.L.

Freund, Ernst. "Burning Heretics," *New Republic,* XXI (January 28, 1920), 266–67.

————. "The Debs Case and Freedom of Speech," *New Republic,* XIX (May 3, 1919), 13–15.

Gannett, Lewis S. "The Socialists' Trial at Albany: A Summary," *Nation,* CX (March 20, 1920), 361–63.

Garrett, G. P. "Free Speech and the Espionage Act," *Journal of the American Institute of Criminal Law and Criminology,* X (May, 1919), 71–75.

Graham, Robert A. "Universal Military Training in Modern History," *Annals of the American Academy of Political and Social Science,* CCXLI (September, 1945), 13–14.

Gregory, Thomas W. (statements of). "Suggestions of Attorney-General Gregory . . . in Relation to the Department of Justice," *American Bar Association Journal,* IV (July, 1918), 305–16.

Hale, Swinburne. Letter to the Editor, "Criminal Anarchy," *New Republic,* XXI (January 28, 1920), 270.

Hall, Covington. Letter to the Editor, *New Republic,* XIII (December 1, 1917), 126–27.

[Hard, William.] "Burleson and the Call," *New Republic,* XXI (January 7, 1920), 157–58.

————. "Mr. Burleson, Espionagent," *New Republic,* XIX (May 10, 1919), 42–45.

————. "Mr. Burleson, Section 481 1–2B," *New Republic,* XIX (May 17, 1919), 76–78.

————. "Perhaps the Turn of the Tide," *New Republic,* XXI (February 11, 1920), 313–16.

Henderson, Gerard C. "What Is Left of Free Speech," *New Republic,* XXI (December 10, 1919), 50–52.

"The Higher Law," *Nation,* CVIII (April 19, 1919), 596.

"Hillquit on the Socialist Programme," *Review,* II (February 28, 1920), 193–94.

Hilton, O. A. "Freedom of the Press in Wartime 1917–1919," *Southwestern Social Science Quarterly,* XXVIII (March, 1948), 346–61.

————. "The Minnesota Public Safety Commission in World War I, 1917–1919," Oklahoma Agricultural and Mechanical College, Arts and Sciences Studies *Bulletin,* XLVII (Stillwater, Oklahoma, May 15, 1951), 1–44.

Hough, Charles M. "Law in War Time—1917," *Harvard Law Review,* XXXI (March, 1918), 692–701.

Howard, Sidney. "The Colyer Trial Opens," *Survey,* XLIV (April 17, 1920), 105.

Hutchinson, William T. "The American Historian in Wartime," *Mississippi Valley Historical Review,* XXIX (September, 1942), 163–86.

"Ill Weeds Grow Apace," *Living Age,* CCXCV (November 24, 1917), 492–93.

"An 'Imperial Wizard' and His 'Klan,'" *Literary Digest,* LXVIII (February 5, 1921), 42, 45–46.

"The Injustice of Army Justice," *Literary Digest,* LXI (April 12, 1919), 13.

"The Issues in the Fight at Albany," *Review,* II (February 7, 1920), 121–23.

"The I.W.W. Raids and Others," *New Republic,* XII (September 15, 1917), 175–77.

Johnson, C. R. "The Conviction of Townley," *New Republic,* XX (August 6, 1919), 18–20.

"Judiciary," *Time,* XLI (June 21, 1943), 16.

"The Kaiser's Secret Army Here," *Literary Digest,* LV (December 1, 1917), 15–16.

King, Judson. "The Prosecution of Mr. Townley," *Nation,* CIX (August 2, 1919), 143–44.

L., W. Letter to the Editor, *Nation,* CX (February 14, 1920), 202.

"La Follette as a Foe of Democracy," *Literary Digest,* LV (October 6, 1917), 15–16.

"La Follette Condemned at Home," *Literary Digest,* LVI (March 23, 1918), 17–18.

Lane, Winthrop D. "Alcatraz," *Survey*, XLIV (July 3, 1920), 470–72.

———. "The Buford Widows," *Survey*, XLIII (January 10, 1920), 391–92.

———. "Fort Leavenworth: The Interplay of Military and Penal Discipline in the Regeneration of Men," *Survey*, XLII (July 5, 1919), 531–36, 557.

———. "Military Prisons and the C. O.," *Survey*, XLII (May 17, 1919), 276–77.

———. "Solitary," *Survey*, XLII (May 31, 1919), 350–58.

———. "The Strike at Fort Leavenworth," *Survey*, XLI (February 15, 1919), 687–93.

———. "Uncle Sam: Jailer," *Survey*, XLII (September 6, 1919), 806–12, 834.

Lasker, Loula D. "America and Her Political Prisoners," *Survey*, XLIV (August 2, 1920), 578–82.

———. "Back in the Districts: What New York Assemblymen's Constituents Are Thinking," *Survey*, XLIII (March 20, 1920), 767–69.

"Lawlessness in Minnesota," *Public*, XXI (July 13, 1918), 876–78.

Levine, Louis. "The Development of Syndicalism in America," *Political Science Quarterly*, XXVIII (September, 1913), 451–79.

"Lynch-Law and Treason," *Literary Digest*, LV (August 18, 1917), 12–13.

"Lynch-Law as Treason," *Literary Digest*, LVIII (August 10, 1918), 13.

"The Menace of Sedition," *Literary Digest*, LV (September 1, 1917), 9–11.

"The Ministry of Hate," *Nation*, CVII (August 10, 1918), 140.

"Minority Rights at Albany," *Nation*, CX (March 6, 1920), 288.

"The Mob in High Places," *New Republic*, XXI (February 4, 1920), 279–81.

"Mob Violence and War Psychology," *New Republic*, XVI (August 3, 1918), 5–7.

"Mob Violence in the United States," *Survey*, XL (April 27, 1918), 101–2.

" 'The Most Brainiest Man,' " *Nation*, CX (April 17, 1920), 510–11. Signed L.S.G.

"Mr. Burleson to Rule the Press," *Literary Digest*, LV (October 6, 1917), 12.

" 'The Nation' and the Post Office," *Nation*, CVII (September 28, 1918), 336–37.

"A New Alien and Sedition Law," *New Republic*, XX (November 26, 1919), 366.

"Newspapers in Wartime," *Public,* XXI (March 16, 1918), 334–37.

"New York School House Cleaning," *Literary Digest,* LVI (January 5, 1918), 26.

"The Nonpartisan League and the Loyalty Issue," *New Republic,* XVI (September 14, 1918), 187–90.

"Ol' Rags an' Bottles," *Nation,* CVIII (January 25, 1919), 114–16.

"Old Soldier," *Time,* XLII (November 15, 1943), 55–56, 58, 60.

"On Behalf of Louis F. Post," *New Republic,* XXII (April 28, 1920), 264–66.

Oneal, James. "The Socialists in the War," *American Mercury,* X (April, 1927), 418–26.

"Our Tyranny Over the Negro," *Literary Digest,* LV (September 22, 1917), 34.

"The Pacifist Pilgrims," *Literary Digest,* LV (September 15, 1917), 16–17.

Parker, Carleton H. "The I.W.W.," *Atlantic Monthly,* CXX (November, 1917), 651–62.

"Patrioteering and Hysteria," *Public,* XXI (April 27, 1918), 527.

Perry, Ralph Barton. "Americanism" (a review of *My Four Years in Germany,* by James W. Gerard, and *Foes of Our Own Household,* by Theodore Roosevelt), *Yale Review,* VII (April, 1918), 663–72.

"The Political Prisoners' Reply," *New Republic,* XXXVI (August 29, 1923), 21.

Post, Charles Johnson. "Court-Martial Bureaucracy," *Public,* XXII (March 29, 1919), 321–23.

"The President and Tom Mooney," *Literary Digest,* LVII (April 13, 1918), 14.

"The President's Commission at Bisbee," *New Republic,* XIII (December 8, 1917), 140–41.

"The President's Hand in the Primaries," *Literary Digest,* LVIII (August 24, 1918), 10–11.

"The Professors in Battle Array," *Nation,* CVI (March 7, 1918), 255.

Quigley, Walter Eli. "Like Father, Like Son," *Saturday Evening Post,* CCXIII (June 21, 1941), 27, 34, 36, 39–40, 42.

"The Raid on the Reds," *Review,* II (January 10, 1920), 22–23.

"The Red Hysteria," *New Republic,* XXI (January 28, 1920), 249–52.

"The Release," *Survey,* XLV (December 4, 1920), 349.

"Release Political Prisoners," *Dial,* LXVI (January 11, 1919), 5–6.

Rogers, Lindsay. "Freedom of the Press in the United States," *Living Age,* CCXCVIII (September 28, 1918), 769–74.

Ruhl, Arthur. "The North Dakota Idea," *Atlantic Monthly*, CXXIII (May, 1919), 686–96.

Ryan, John A. "Freedom of Speech in War Time," *Catholic World*, CVI (February, 1918), 577–88.

Saloutos, Theodore. "The Expansion and Decline of the Nonpartisan League in the Western Middle West, 1917–1921," *Agricultural History*, XX (October, 1946), 235–52.

————. "The Rise of the Nonpartisan League in North Dakota, 1915–1917," *Agricultural History*, XX (January, 1946), 43–61.

Sayre, John N. "Political Prisoners in America" (Letter to the Editor), *Dial*, LXV (December 28, 1918), 623–24.

"Sedition," *Encyclopaedia Britannica* (14th ed.), XX, 271.

"The Slacker and the Careless Man," *Outlook*, CXX (September 11, 1918), 82.

"Socialism on Trial at Albany," *Literary Digest*, LXIV (February 7, 1920), 14–15.

"The Socialist as Patriot," *Literary Digest*, LIV (June 16, 1917), 1836–37.

Spargo, John. "Democracy Must Not Be Vindictive," *Independent*, CIII (September 11, 1920), 303–4.

"Speaker Sweet Does His Bit," *New Republic*, XXI (January 21, 1920), 210–12.

Stewart, Charles D. "Prussianizing Wisconsin," *Atlantic Monthly*, CXXIII (January, 1919), 99–105.

Strong, Anna Louise. "Centralia: An Unfinished Story," *Nation*, CX (April 17, 1920), 508–10.

————. "A Newspaper Confiscated—and Returned," *Nation*, CIX (December 13, 1919), 738–40.

"Stronger Curb on Enemies at Home," *Literary Digest*, LVII (May 4, 1918), 19.

"The Supreme Court vs. the Supreme Court," *New Republic*, XXII (April 21, 1920), 235–38.

Swisher, Carl B. "Civil Liberties in Wartime," *Political Science Quarterly*, LV (September, 1940), 321–47.

"Ten Years of Criticism," *Literary Digest*, LVII (June 15, 1918), 13.

Thomas, Evan. "Disciplinary Barracks," *Survey*, XLI (February 1, 1919), 625–29.

"To What End, Mr. Baker?" *New Republic*, XIX (June 7, 1919), 171–72.

"The Trial of Eugene V. Debs," *Survey*, XL (September 21, 1918), 695–96.

"Trial of the Nebraska Professors, A Reflection," *Educational Review*, LVI (December, 1918), 415–23. Signed Jurisconsultus.

"The Trial of New York City Teachers," *School and Society*, VI (December 8, 1917), 674–75.

Tyler, Robert L. "Violence at Centralia, 1919," *Pacific Northwest Quarterly*, XLV (October, 1954), 116–24.

"Up to the Voters," *New Republic*, XXII (April 14, 1920), 200–202.

Vance, W. R. "Freedom of Speech and of the Press," *Minnesota Law Review*, II (March, 1918), 239–60.

Van Dyke, Henry. Letter to the Editor, *New Republic*, XIII (December 22, 1917), 213–14.

"Victor Berger Escapes Punishment," *Outlook*, CXXVII (February 16, 1921), 245–46.

Villard, O. G. "The Berger Victory," *Nation*, CIX (December 27, 1919), 820–21.

Warren, Charles. "What Is Giving Aid and Comfort to the Enemy?" *Yale Law Journal*, XXVII (January, 1918), 331–47.

"War-Time Offenders Out of Jail," *Literary Digest*, LXVII (December 11, 1920), 20.

"What Is Attorney General Palmer Doing?" *Nation*, CX (February 14, 1920), 190–91.

"What Some Americans Think of East St. Louis," *Outlook*, CXVI (July 18, 1917), 435–36.

"When Conscience and War Join Issue," *Survey*, XXXIX (February 16, 1918), 551–52.

"Where Civil Liberties Stand Today," *New Republic*, LXXXIII (June 26, 1935), 187–92.

"Whose Home Will Be Safe?" *New Republic*, XIX (July 9, 1919), 303–5.

Whipple, Leon. Letter to the Editor, *Nation*, CV (December 20, 1917), 690–91.

Wigmore, John H. "Abrams *v.* U.S.: Freedom of Speech and Freedom of Thuggery in War-time and Peace-time," *Illinois Law Review*, XIV (March, 1920), 537–61.

Yarros, Victor S. "The Chicago Socialist Trial," *Nation*, CVIII (January 25, 1919), 116–18.

————. "The Story of the I.W.W. Trial," *Survey*, XL (August 31, September 7, and September 14, 1918), 603–4, 630–32, 660–63.

Books and Pamphlets

Abrams, Ray H. *Preachers Present Arms*. New York, 1933.

Adamic, Louis. *Dynamite: The Story of Class Violence in America*. New York, 1935.

Adams, Samuel Hopkins. *Incredible Era*. Boston, 1939.

Addams, Jane. *Peace and Bread in Time of War.* New York, 1922.

———. *The Second Twenty Years at Hull-House.* New York, 1930.

American Civil Liberties Union. *The Truth about the I.W.W. Prisoners.* New York, 1922.

American Economic Foundation. *What Happens to Civil Liberties During Times of War?* Cleveland, 1942. A pamphlet.

Anarchism on Trial: Speeches of Alexander Berkman and Emma Goldman before the United States District Court in the City of New York, 1917. Ed. B. L. Reitman. New York, 1918.

Bailey, Thomas A. *Woodrow Wilson and the Lost Peace.* New York, 1944.

Baker, Ray Stannard. *Woodrow Wilson: Life and Letters.* Vols. VII, VIII. New York, 1939.

——— and William E. Dodd. *The Public Papers of Woodrow Wilson: War and Peace.* 6 vols. New York, 1925–27.

Barth, Alan. *The Loyalty of Free Men.* New York, 1951.

Bates, Ernest S. *This Land of Liberty.* New York, 1930.

Beale, Howard K. *Are American Teachers Free?* New York, 1936.

Beman, Lamar T. *Selected Articles on Censorship of Speech and the Press.* New York, 1930.

Bernhard, Edgar, *et al.*, eds. *Pursuit of Freedom: A History of Civil Liberty in Illinois, 1787–1942.* Chicago, 1942.

Biddle, Francis B. *The Fear of Freedom.* Garden City, N.Y., 1951.

A Brief Account of the Conference of Christian Pacifists in California. Issued by the Christian Pacifist Defense Fund. American Civil Liberties Union files.

Brissenden, Paul Frederick. *The I.W.W.: A Study of American Syndicalism.* New York, 1920.

———. *Justice and the I.W.W.* Chicago, n.d.

Brooks, John Graham. *American Syndicalism: The I.W.W.* New York, 1913.

Bruce, Andrew Alexander. *Non-partisan League.* New York, 1921.

Chafee, Zechariah, Jr., comp. and ed. *Documents on Fundamental Human Rights.* Cambridge, 1951.

———. *Freedom of Speech.* New York, 1920.

———. *Free Speech in the United States.* Cambridge, 1941.

———. *The Inquiring Mind.* New York, 1928.

Chamberlain, Lawrence H. *Loyalty and Legislative Action: A Survey of Activity by the New York State Legislature, 1919–1949.* Ithaca, New York, 1951.

Chaplin, Ralph. *Wobbly*. Chicago, 1948.

Clark, Jane Perry. *Deportation of Aliens from the United States to Europe*. New York, 1931.

Cobb, Frank I. *The Press and Public Opinion*. N.p., n.d. A pamphlet.

Coleman, McAlister. *Eugene V. Debs*. New York, 1930.

Commager, Henry Steele. *Freedom, Loyalty, Dissent*. New York, 1954.

————. *Majority Rule and Minority Rights*. London, 1943.

Costrell, Edwin. *How Maine Viewed the War, 1914–1917*. Orono, Maine, 1940.

Creel, George. *Rebel at Large: Recollections of Fifty Crowded Years*. New York, 1947.

————. *The War, the World, and Wilson*. New York, 1920.

Crighton, John C. *Missouri and the World War, 1914–1917: A Study in Public Opinion*. Columbia, Mo., 1947.

Cummings, Homer, and Carl McFarland. *Federal Justice: Chapters in the History of Justice and the Federal Executive*. New York, 1937.

Cummins, Cedric C. *Indiana Public Opinion and the World War, 1914–1917*. Indianapolis, 1945.

Curti, Merle. *Bryan and World Peace*. Smith College Studies in History, XVI. Northampton, Mass., 1931.

————. *Peace or War: The American Struggle, 1636–1936*. New York, 1936.

Delaney, Edward, and M. T. Rice. *The Bloodstained Trail*. Seattle, 1927.

Douthit, Davis. *Nobody Owns Us: The Story of Joe Gilbert, Midwestern Rebel*. Chicago, 1948.

Dowell, E. Foster. *A History of Criminal Syndicalism Legislation in the United States*. Baltimore, 1939. A fuller version of Dowell's study is cited under unpublished manuscripts.

Duff, Harvey. *The Silent Defenders: Courts and Capitalism in California*. Chicago, n.d.

Eastman, Max. *The Trial of Eugene V. Debs*. New York, n.d. A pamphlet.

Emerson, Thomas I., and David Harber. *Political and Civil Rights in the United States*. Buffalo, 1952.

Evidence and Cross-examination of William D. Haywood in the Case of the U.S.A. vs. William D. Haywood et al. N.p., n.d.

Folwell, W. W. *A History of Minnesota*. 4 vols. St. Paul, 1926.

Fraenkel, Osmond K. *Our Civil Liberties*. New York, 1944.

————. *The Supreme Court and Civil Liberties*. New York, 1937.

Frankfurter, Felix. *Mr. Justice Holmes and the Supreme Court*. Cambridge, Mass., 1938.

Gabriel, Ralph Henry. *The Course of American Democratic Thought: An Intellectual History Since 1815.* New York, 1940.

Gambs, John S. *The Decline of the I.W.W.* New York, 1932.

Gaston, Herbert E. *The Nonpartisan League.* New York, 1920.

George, Harrison. *Is Freedom Dead?* N.p., n.d.

————. *The I.W.W. Trial.* Chicago, n.d.

Gibbon, Edward. *The History of the Decline and Fall of the Roman Empire.* 6 vols. New York, 1850.

Ginger, Ray. *The Bending Cross: A Biography of Eugene Victor Debs.* New Brunswick, 1949.

Goldberg, Louis P., and Eleanore Levenson. *Lawless Judges.* New York, 1935.

Goldman, Emma. *Living My Life.* 2 vols. New York, 1931.

Greene, Laurence. *The Era of Wonderful Nonsense: A Casebook of the 'Twenties.* Indianapolis, 1939.

Haines, Lynn, and Dora B. Haines. *The Lindberghs.* New York, 1931.

Hale, William G., and Ivan Benson. *The Law of the Press.* St. Paul, 1933.

Hapgood, Norman, ed. *Professional Patriots.* New York, 1927.

Harnack, Adolf. *Militia Christi, Die Christliche Religion und der Soldatenstand in den ersten drei Jahrhunderten.* Tübingen, 1905.

Harré, T. Everett. *The I.W.W.: An Auxiliary of the German Espionage System.* N.p., 1918.

Hart, Albert Bushnell, and Herbert Ronald Ferleger, eds. *Theodore Roosevelt Cyclopedia.* New York, 1941.

Hayes, Carlton J. H. *Essays on Nationalism.* New York, 1937.

Hays, Arthur Garfield. *City Lawyer.* New York, 1942.

————. *Let Freedom Ring.* New York, 1928.

Hays, Frank E. *Senate Election Cases from 1913 to 1940.* Washington, 1941.

Haywood, William D. *Bill Haywood's Book.* New York, 1929.

Heaton, John L. *Cobb of "The World."* New York, 1924.

Hershberger, Guy Franklin. *War, Peace, and Nonresistance.* Scottdale, Pa., 1946.

Hibben, Paxton. *The Peerless Leader, William Jennings Bryan.* New York, 1929.

Hopkins, Ernest Jerome. *Our Lawless Police.* New York, 1931.

Hough, Emerson. *The Web.* Chicago, 1919.

Hugh-Jones, E. M. *Woodrow Wilson and American Liberalism.* London, 1947.

Huxley, Aldous. *Grey Eminence: A Study in Religion and Politics.* New York, 1941.

Jenison, Marguerite Edith. *War Documents and Addresses.* Vol. VI of Illinois in the World War. Springfield, 1923.

————. *The War-time Organization of Illinois.* Vol. V of Illinois in the World War. Springfield, 1923.

Jones, Richard Seelye. *A History of the American Legion.* Indianapolis, 1946.

Jordan, David Starr. *The Days of a Man.* 2 vols. New York, 1922.

Joughin, G. Louis, and Edmund M. Morgan. *The Legacy of Sacco and Vanzetti.* New York, 1948.

Karsner, David. *Debs, His Authorized Life and Letters from Woodstock Prison to Atlanta.* New York, 1919.

————. *The I.W.W. Case.* N.p., n.d.

Kellogg, Walter Guest. *The Conscientious Objector.* New York, 1919.

La Follette, Belle Case, and Fola La Follette. *Robert M. La Follette.* 2 vols. New York, 1953.

Laidler, Harry W. *Socialism in Thought and Action.* New York, 1920.

Laski, H. J. *Liberty in the Modern State.* London and New York, 1930.

Lasswell, Harold D. *National Security and Individual Freedom.* New York, 1950.

Leland, Waldo G., and Newton D. Mereness. *Introduction to the American Official Sources for the Economic and Social History of the World War.* New Haven, 1926.

Lindbergh, Charles A. *Your Country at War.* Philadelphia, 1934.

Lippman, Walter. *Liberty and the News.* New York, 1920.

Manahan, James. *Trials of a Lawyer.* St. Paul, 1934.

Mock, James R. *Censorship, 1917.* Princeton, 1941.

Morison, Elting E., ed. *The Letters of Theodore Roosevelt.* Vol. VIII. Cambridge, 1954.

Morlan, Robert L. *Political Prairie Fire: The Nonpartisan League, 1915–1922.* Minneapolis, 1955.

Murray, Robert K. *Red Scare: A Study in National Hysteria, 1919–1920.* Minneapolis, 1955.

National Civil Liberties Bureau. *Attack on Right of Defense and of Defense Workers in Trial of I.W.W. at Sacramento, California.* N.p., n.d.

————. *The Case of the Christian Pacifists at Los Angeles, California.* New York, 1918. A pamphlet.

————. *The Facts About Conscientious Objectors in the United States.* New York, 1918.

————. *The Knights of Liberty Mob and the I.W.W. Prisoners at Tulsa, Oklahoma, November 9, 1917.* New York, 1918.

National Civil Liberties Bureau. *Wartime Prosecutions and Mob Violence.* New York, 1919.

Nearing, Scott. *Europe and the Next War.* New York, 1920.

――. *The Great Madness: A Victory for the American Plutocracy.* New York, 1917.

Nelles, Walter. *Espionage Act Cases, with Certain Others on Related Points.* New York, 1918.

――. *A Liberal in Wartime.* New York, 1940.

――. *Seeing Red: Civil Liberty and Law in the Period Following the War.* New York, 1920.

Nevins, Allan. *John D. Rockefeller: The Heroic Age of American Enterprise.* Vol. II. New York, 1940.

Nonpartisan League. *Memorial to the Congress of the United States Concerning Conditions in Minnesota.* St. Paul, 1918.

O'Hare, Kate Richards. *In Prison.* New York, 1923.

――. *In Prison.* St. Louis, 1920. A pamphlet.

Painter, Floy Ruth. *That Man Debs and His Life Work.* Bloomington, 1929.

Palmer, Frederick. *Newton D. Baker.* 2 vols. New York, 1931.

Parker, Carleton H. *The Casual Laborer, and Other Essays.* New York, 1920.

Patterson, Giles J. *Free Speech and a Free Press.* Boston, 1939.

Paxson, Frederic L. *America at War: 1917–1918.* Boston, 1939.

Perlman, Selig, and Philip Taft. *History of Labour in the United States.* New York, 1935.

Pfeiler, W. K. *War and the German Mind.* New York, 1941.

Pierce, Bessie Louise. *Public Opinion and the Teaching of History in the United States.* New York, 1926.

Post, Louis Freeland. *The Deportations Delirium of Nineteen-Twenty.* Chicago, 1923.

Report of the Minnesota Commission of Public Safety. Minneapolis, 1919.

Reppy, Alison. *Civil Rights in the United States.* New York, 1951.

Roosevelt, Theodore. *The Foes of Our Own Household.* New York, 1926.

――. *Roosevelt in the Kansas City Star.* Boston, 1921.

Roseboom, E. H., and F. P. Weisenburger. *A History of Ohio.* New York, 1934.

Rudin, Harry R. *Armistice, 1918.* New Haven, 1944.

Russell, Charles Edward. *The Story of the Nonpartisan League.* New York, 1920.

Schlesinger, Arthur, Jr., ed. *Writings and Speeches of Eugene V. Debs.* New York, 1948.

Schroeder, Theodore. *Free Speech Bibliography.* New York, 1922.

————. *Free Speech for Radicals.* New York, 1916.

Secretary of War. *Statement Concerning the Treatment of Conscientious Objectors in the Army.* Washington, 1919.

Seldes, George. *Witch Hunt: The Technique and Profits of Redbaiting.* New York, 1940.

Selections from the Correspondence of Theodore Roosevelt and Henry Cabot Lodge, 1884–1918. 2 vols. New York, 1925.

State Executive Committee [of the Socialist Party]. *Being a True Record of the Case of Frederic Krafft.* Newark, New Jersey, n.d.

Stroup, Herbert H. *The Jehovah's Witnesses.* New York, 1945.

Symes, Lillian, and Travers Clement. *Rebel America.* New York and London, 1934.

Thomas, Norman. *The Conscientious Objector in America.* New York, 1923.

Trachtenberg, Alexander, ed. *The American Labor Year Book, 1919–1920.* Vol. III. New York, 1920.

The Trial of Scott Nearing and the American Socialist Society. New York, 1919.

Tumulty, Joseph P. *Woodrow Wilson as I Knew Him.* New York, 1921.

Veblen, Thorstein. *The Higher Learning in America.* New York, 1918.

Villard, Oswald Garrison. *Fighting Years.* New York, 1939.

Walling, William English, ed. *The Socialists and the War.* New York, 1915.

Whipple, Leon. *The Story of Civil Liberty in the United States.* New York, 1927.

White, Walter. *Rope and Faggot.* New York, 1929.

Whitney, Nathaniel R. *The Sale of War Bonds in Iowa.* Iowa City, 1923.

Wilcox, Clair, ed. *Civil Liberties Under Attack.* Philadelphia, 1951.

Winkler, John K. *W. R. Hearst, An American Phenomenon.* New York, 1928.

Wittke, Carl F. *German-Americans and the World War.* Columbus, Ohio, 1936.

Woods, Arthur. *Policeman and Public.* New Haven, 1919.

Woodward, C. Vann. *Tom Watson, Agrarian Rebel.* New York, 1938.

INDEX

Abbott, Leonard D.: quoted on conscription, 25

Aberdeen, South Dakota: I.W.W. beaten in, 55

Abilene, Texas: man arrested for anti-conscription activities, 24

Abrams, Jacob: published radical leaflets, 227; arrested, 228; sentenced, 229; importance of case, 230

Addams, Jane: on popular approval of war, 6; defended foreigners, 27–28

Agrarian radicals, 157

Agrarian reformers, 154

Agricultural Workers Industrial Union, 55

Albers, Henry: sentenced for pro-German remarks, 226; importance of, 230

Alcatraz: conditions at, 262–64

Alien and Sedition Acts of 1798, 219, 280

Alien Registration Act of 1940, 299

Aliens: little sympathy for, 81–86 *passim;* numbers arrested, 86

All-Allied Anti-German League, 18

Alsop, Stewart: quoted, 305–6

American Anti-Anarchy Association, 18

American Association of University Professors: condemned action in Cattell case, 109

American Bankers Association: speech by Butler to, 69

American Civil Liberties Union: best data on conscientious objectors, 127; purpose of, 138; reports on I.W.W.'s in Washington to, 168; on prison conditions, 257; active for amnesty, 268

American Defense Society: active against sedition, 18; backed teachers' oath drive, 109; and war propaganda, 120; against German language teaching, 195; in southern Illinois, 201; active in 1918, 223; on amnesty, 282; anti-Red campaign of, 287

American Federation of Labor: Wilson speech to, 151; resolution on free speech and press, 269; amnesty committee of, 273

American Legion: criticism of amnesty, 267; on release of political prisoners, 275, 283, 284; on Debs, 276; in anti-Red campaign, 287; in mob action, 289; and parade in Centralia, 290

American Newspaper Publishers: petitioned Congress, 16

American Patriots Association: document on conscription law issued by, 33

American Protective League: 18; description of, 19; broke up meetings in Michigan, 48; in attack on I.W.W., 62; and Red Cross funds, 145; and slacker raids, 231, 234; postwar activity of, 286

American Revolution: in *Spirit of '76,* 92; economic motives of, cause for dismissal of professor, 105

American Rights League, 18

Camp Lewis: remarks about, 171; stickers for amnesty appeared at, 267

Camp Merritt: soldiers court-martialed at, 154

Camp Travis: Negroes hanged near, 90

Camp Upton: conscientious objector punished at, 127; court-martial at, 132

Canton, Ohio: Debs' speech at, 249–51

Capitalism: 43–45; and I.W.W., 49; Debs on, 251

Capitalists. *See* Capitalism

Carillo, Vicente: antiregistration speech of in Los Angeles, 24

Carnegie Endowment for International Peace: Butler once prominent in, 103

Carnegie Hall: meeting at to celebrate Russian Revolution, 3

Cattell, Professor James M.: fired by Columbia for fomenting disloyalty, 103

Censorship: of press in Espionage Bill, 16; opposition to in Espionage Bill, 16; of movies, 92–93; of press, 93–101; board for newspapers established, 95; not completely successful, 222

Centralia, Washington: massacre in, 290

Central Labor Union: paraded in Boston, 46

Chamberlain, Senator George Earle: introduced drastic bill, 14–15; urged shooting German agents, 210; on spies and traitors, 216; on slacker raids, 233

Chester, Pennsylvania: race riot in, 88

Chicago, Illinois: meeting of People's Council in, 75; difficulties of People's Council meeting in, 77; teachers dismissed in, 110–11; slacker raids in, 231; I.W.W. trial at, 235–42

Chovenson, Samuel H., student at Rutgers: forced to parade, 199

Christadelphians, 133

Christensen, Parley P.: on amnesty, 274

Christian Pacifists: organized, 115; meetings of, 116–17

Cincinnati, Ohio: People's Council meeting in broken up, 78

Cincinnati, University of: faculty member dismissed, 108

Citizens' Amnesty Committee, 268

Citizens Protective League: meeting of at Bisbee, 53; member of killed in Bisbee, 54

Civilization, banned movie, 92

Civil liberty: overridden by clear and sudden danger, 13

Clark, Champ: against conscription, 21–22

Clayton, Judge Henry D.: assigned to Abrams case, 228–29

"Clear and present danger": theory in Espionage Act, 17; in Schenck case, 32

Cleary, William B., attorney in Bisbee deportation, 53

Cobb, Frank Irving, editor of New York *World:* Wilson to on tolerance, 11; on slacker raids, 232

Cochise County (Arizona): and Bisbee deportation, 54; cheered vigilantes for deportation, 55

Coldwell, Joseph: objected to treatment of political conscientious objectors, 122–23

Cole, Judge R. S.: presided at trial of Krieger in Tulsa, 176

Collins, William M.: sentenced for remarks about Camp Lewis, 170–71

Collinsville (Illinois) Council of Defense: advocated loyalty pledges, 202

Columbia University: student expelled, 103; professors dismissed, 103–4